RESEARCH ON STUDENT CIVIC OUTCOMES IN
SERVICE LEARNING

IUPUI Series on Service Learning Research

Series Editors
Robert G. Bringle and Julie A. Hatcher

RESEARCH ON STUDENT CIVIC OUTCOMES IN SERVICE LEARNING

Conceptual Frameworks and Methods

EDITED BY

*Julie A. Hatcher, Robert G. Bringle,
and Thomas W. Hahn*

VOL. 3: IUPUI Series on Service Learning Research

1996–2016 20TH ANNIVERSARY

Stylus
PUBLISHING, LLC.

STERLING, VIRGINIA

Published by Stylus Publishing, LLC
22883 Quicksilver Drive
Sterling, Virginia 20166-2102

Library of Congress Cataloging-in-Publication Data
Library of Congress Cataloging-in-Publication
Data Names: Hatcher, Julie A., 1953- editor. |
Bringle, Robert G., editor. | Hahn, Thomas W., 1966- editor.
Title: Research on student civic outcomes in service learning :
conceptual frameworks and methods /
edited by Julie A. Hatcher, Robert G. Bringle, and
Thomas W. Hahn.
Description: First edition. |
Sterling, Virginia : Stylus Publishing, LLC, 2016. |
Series: IUPUI series on service learning research ; v. 3 |
Includes bibliographical references and index.
Identifiers: LCCN 2016016628 (print) |
LCCN 2016029463 (ebook) |
ISBN 9781579223427 (cloth : alk. paper) |
ISBN 9781579223434 (pbk. : alk. paper) |
ISBN 9781579223441 (library networkable e-edition) |
ISBN 9781579223458 (consumer e-edition) |
Subjects: LCSH: Service learning. |
Service learning--Research--Methodology.
Classification: LCC LC220.5 .R478 2016 (print) |
LCC LC220.5 (ebook) | DDC 361.3/70973--dc23
LC record available at https://lccn.loc.gov/2016016628

13-digit ISBN: 978-1-57922-342-7 (cloth)
13-digit ISBN: 978-1-57922-343-4 (paperback)
13-digit ISBN: 978-1-57922-344-1 (library networkable e-edition)
13-digit ISBN: 978-1-57922-345-8 (consumer e-edition)

Bulk Purchases

Quantity discounts are available for use in workshops and for
staff development.
Call 1-800-232-0223

First Edition, 2017

10   9   8   7   6   5   4   3   2   1

CONTENTS

Change does not come easily to higher education, but service learning has demonstrated its capacity to have an influence on dimensions of the academy that are among the most difficult to change: curriculum, faculty work, organizational infrastructure, budget allocations, promotion and tenure, assessment of student learning, and campus-community partnerships. These changes have manifested themselves across institutional types and with a tenacity that suggests that they are not mere fads but enduring trends. Over 1,100 institutions are now members of Campus Compact, which reports increasing numbers of students, faculty, and community partners involved in service learning (Campus Compact, 2014). Stimulated by the model of service learning, institutions of higher education have examined how civic engagement more broadly can change the nature of faculty work, enhance student learning, advance institutional missions, provide a basis for public accountability, and improve quality of life in communities (e.g., Beaumont & Stephens, 2003; Boyer, 1994, 1996; Bringle, Games, & Malloy, 1999; Calleson, Jordan, & Seifer, 2005; Colby, Ehrlich, Edgerton, 1994; Harkavy & Puckett, 1994; O'Meara & Rice, 2005; Percy, Zimpher, & Brukardt, 2006; Rice, 1996; Saltmarsh & Hartley, 2011).

However, when the degree and nature of the changes associated with service learning, and civic engagement more broadly, are assessed for their quality, breadth, and depth, interpretations vary. Saltmarsh, Giles, O'Meara, Sandmann, Ward, and Bringle (2009) analyzed portfolios for the Carnegie Community Engagement Classification and found uneven evidence of institutional change; change had occurred in all classified institutions, but there was also evidence of resistance to change (e.g., in the arena of promotion and tenure), and there were consistent shortcomings (e.g., with respect to community campus reciprocity and community impact). Butin's (2005) edited volume presented multiple perspectives that raised issues about the degree to which the assumptions, values, and operations of service learning are incompatible with the ingrained culture of higher education— constraining the capacity of the pedagogy to generate transformational institutional change. Saltmarsh, Hartley, and Clayton (2009) questioned the

Portions of this preface are from Bringle, Hatcher, and Jones (2010) and Clayton, Bringle, and Hatcher (2012).

degree to which the changes associated with civic engagement more generally have been fundamental and systemic.

Regardless of how full or how empty the glass is thought to be, service learning has produced and is aligned with changes not only in the curriculum but also more broadly, and this is not a trivial outcome. In the absence of a consensual goal, either among civic engagement practitioners or leaders in higher education in general, to produce systemic transformation, the amount of change service learning and civic engagement have produced in higher education can be viewed as an extraordinary accomplishment. Many of the criticisms that change has been slow, small, incomplete, or otherwise fallen short of ideals underacknowledge and perhaps undervalue the significant changes that have occurred. Furthermore, the very existence of these interpretations, analyses, and critiques indicates that (a) scholars have some progress to review; (b) they care enough about the impact of service learning to invest their resources in studying it; and (c) there are aspirations and standards against which incomplete, though significant, accomplishments can be evaluated. Ongoing reflection on the extent and nature of change within and across institutions can inform future development of service learning and civic engagement. This series contributes to the progress by highlighting research-grounded perspectives on the processes and outcomes of service learning to this national and international conversation.

The growth of service learning learning and civic engagement on the Indiana University-Purdue University Indianapolis (IUPUI) campus mirrors national developments. Starting with opening an IUPUI Office of Service Learning in 1993 (now incorporated into the IUPUI Center for Service and Learning), service learning has been purposefully nurtured on a campus of more than 30,000 students with strong traditions of community involvement among its many professional schools. Through strategic decisions by executive leadership (Bringle & Hatcher, 2004; Bringle, Hatcher, & Holland, 2007; Plater, 2004), significant commitments to infrastructure were made to support the growth of service learning. That growth has been guided by a Comprehensive Action Plan for Service Learning (CAPSL) that identified 10 key tasks—planning, increasing awareness, identifying a prototype of good practice, gathering resources, expanding programs, providing recognition, monitoring, evaluating, conducting research, and institutionalization—and four key stakeholders—institution, faculty, students, and community (Bringle & Hatcher, 1996). There is evidence of institutional progress across all areas of CAPSL at IUPUI (Bringle & Hatcher, 2004; Bringle, Hatcher, & Clayton, 2006; Bringle, Hatcher, Hamilton, & Young, 2001; Bringle, Hatcher, & Holland, 2007; Bringle, Hatcher, Jones, & Plater, 2006; Bringle, Officer, Grim, & Hatcher, 2009; Bringle, Studer, Wilson, Clayton, &

Steinberg, 2011; Hatcher, Bringle, Brown, & Fleischhacker, 2006; Officer, Grim, Medina, Foreman, & Bringle, 2013; Plater, 2004).

In addition, independent external reviews support the assessment of significant institutional progress at IUPUI around service learning and civic engagement. For example, IUPUI's service learning program has been recognized every year since 2003 as one of the top programs in the country by *U.S. News and World Report.* In 2006, IUPUI was recognized in the Saviors of Our Cities national report by the New England Board of Higher Education as one of 25 urban colleges and universities that have dramatically strengthened the economy and quality of life of neighboring communities; IUPUI was the highest ranked public university receiving this distinction and was again recognized in 2009. Most noteworthy, in 2006, the inaugural year for the award, IUPUI was selected by the Corporation for National and Community Service as one of three universities in the country (out of 510 campuses that applied) to receive the Presidential Award for exceptional accomplishments in General Student Community Service activities. In 2006 IUPUI was a member of the first group of colleges and universities to receive the Carnegie Community Engagement Classification, in the two categories of Curricular Engagement and Outreach and Partnerships. The classification for community engagement was reaffirmed in 2014.

With the intention to build on these accomplishments and to continue its field-building leadership, the IUPUI Center for Service and Learning (CSL) applied for and received an internal designation in 2007 as an IUPUI Signature Center and established the CSL Research Collaborative. The mission of the CSL Research Collaborative is to do the following:

- Increase the capacity of faculty to engage in research on service learning practice
- Convene service learning scholars to develop new conceptual frameworks and methodological tools to improve the quality of service learning research
- Disseminate high-quality scholarship through books, research briefs, monographs, a web site that provides information on resources (e.g., grant opportunities, tools for research), presentations at scholarly conferences, and publications in peer-reviewed journals

The CSL Research Collaborative has provided the basis for launching several new initiatives for advancing scholarship on campus, nationally, and internationally, including the IUPUI Series on Service Learning Research.

This series was designed by identifying themes around which scholarship would advance the field and meet strategic goals of IUPUI. The theme for the first volume in the series, *International Service Learning: Conceptual Frameworks and Research* (Bringle, Hatcher, & Jones, 2011), grew out of a collaboration between CSL and the IUPUI Office of International Affairs and emphasized service learning as a distinctive aspect of the development of study abroad and strategic international partnerships. That collaboration included partnering with the International Partnership for Service-Learning and Leadership and Indiana Campus Compact to host two conferences at IUPUI focused on international service learning and two symposia at IUPUI at which authors and discussants shaped the chapters for the first volume.

The second volume, *Research on Service Learning: Conceptual Frameworks and Assessment, Vol. 2A* and *Vol. 2B* (Clayton, Bringle, & Hatcher, 2013a, 2013b), grew out of CSL's long-standing commitment to advance service learning research through improved assessment (Bringle, Phillips, & Hudson, 2004), theory (Bringle, 2003; Bringle & Hatcher, 2005), and rigorous research design (Bringle & Hatcher, 2000; Steinberg, Bringle, & Williams, 2010). Assessment, as used here, encompasses measurement and is not limited to gauging student performance in a course for the sake of giving a grade. Measurement is relevant to qualities of process and to outcomes and, in the case of service learning, includes but transcends a focus on students. Furthermore, assessment and measurement are not isolated endeavors. Implicit or explicit in any measurement procedure, whether quantitative or qualitative, is a conceptual understanding of the construct that is being measured. Each construct that is part of systematic research is, or should be, embedded in a theoretical context that explains the manifestations of the construct and the relationships between it and other constructs. In addition, how the measurement is being taken (i.e., research design) and its implications for practice are both critical to its meaningfulness. Although elsewhere we have emphasized the importance of quantitative measurement (e.g., Bringle & Hatcher, 2000; Bringle et al., 2004), here measurement is construed more broadly as any procedure that is used to systematically collect evidence, data, or indicators of a construct.

We have taken seriously the challenge to produce edited volumes that have coherence, while at the same time allowing contributors latitude to make distinctive contributions. To achieve the former, we convened authors to discuss the overall vision for a book and the contents of individual chapters. Authors were asked to take on a task that was expansive and forward looking: Develop a research agenda and recommendations for practice within a particular topic area, draw upon theory from cognate areas, critique extant research, and identify methods and tools for assessment that will improve research. This was an intellectual challenge, and all authors are to be commended for their work in producing chapters that will shape future research on service learning. As a result, we expect each volume to advance the field by enhancing the understanding of, investigation of, and implementation of service learning in innovative and meaningful ways.

Dean Uday Sukhatme, past executive vice chancellor and dean of the faculties at IUPUI, provided the years of support for the CSL Research Collaborative through the Signature Center initiative. A special note of appreciation is extended to Dean William M. Plater, who served as executive vice chancellor and dean of the faculties at IUPUI from 1987 to 2006 and then as the director of the Office of International Community Development. Dean Plater was the architect for advancing much of IUPUI's work on civic engagement and service learning as well as providing persistent and pervasive support to CSL and the work associated with the CSL Research Collaborative.

Robert G. Bringle
March 2016

References

Boyer, E. L. (1994, March 9). Creating the new American college. *Chronicle of Higher Education, 40*(27), A48.

Boyer, E. L. (1996). The scholarship of engagement. *Journal of Public Service and Outreach, 1*(1), 11–20.

Bringle, R. G. (2003). Enhancing theory-based research on service-learning. In S. H. Billig & J. Eyler (Eds.), *Deconstructing service-learning: Research exploring context, participation, and impacts* (pp. 3–21). Greenwich, CT: Information Age Publishing.

Bringle, R. G., Games, R., & Malloy, E. A. (1999). Colleges and universities as citizens: Issues and perspectives. In R. G. Bringle, R. Games, & E. A. Malloy (Eds.), *Colleges and universities as citizens* (pp. 1–16). Needham Heights, MA: Allyn & Bacon.

Bringle, R. G., & Hatcher, J. A. (1996). Implementing service learning in higher education. *Journal of Higher Education, 67*, 221–239.

Bringle, R. G., & Hatcher, J. A. (2000). Meaningful measurement of theory-based service-learning outcomes: Making the case with quantitative research. *Michigan Journal of Community Service Learning*, Fall, 68–75.

Bringle, R. G., & Hatcher, J. A. (2004). Advancing civic engagement through service-learning. In M. Langseth & W. M. Plater (Eds.), *Public work and the academy: An academic administrator's guide to civic engagement and service-learning.* Boston, MA: Anker Press.

Bringle, R. G., & Hatcher, J. A. (2005). Service learning as scholarship: Why theory-based research is critical to service learning. *Acta Academica Supplementum, 3*, 24–44.

Bringle, R. G., Hatcher, J. A., & Clayton, P. H. (2006). The scholarship of civic engagement: Defining, documenting, and evaluating faculty work. *To Improve the Academy, 25*, 257–279.

Bringle, R. G., Hatcher, J. A., Hamilton, S., & Young, P. (2001). Planning and assessing campus/community engagement. *Metropolitan Universities, 12*(3), 89–99.

Bringle, R. G., Hatcher, J. A., & Holland, B. (2007). Conceptualizing civic engagement: Orchestrating change at a metropolitan university. *Metropolitan Universities, 18*(3), 57–74.

Bringle, R. G., Hatcher, J. A., & Jones, S. G. (Eds.). (2011). *International service learning: Conceptual frameworks and research.* Sterling, VA: Stylus.

Bringle, R. G., Hatcher, J. A., Jones, S., & Plater, W. M. (2006). Sustaining civic engagement: Faculty development, roles, and rewards. *Metropolitan Universities, 17*(1), 62–74.

Bringle, R. G., Officer, S., Grim, J., & Hatcher, J. A. (2009). George Washington Community High School: Analysis of a partnership network. In I. Harkavy & M. Hartley (Eds.), *New directions in youth development* (pp. 41–60). San Francisco, CA: Jossey-Bass.

Bringle, R. G., Phillips, M. A., & Hudson, M. (2004). *The measure of service learning: Research scales to assess student experiences.* Washington, DC: American Psychological Association.

Bringle, R. G., Studer, M. H., Wilson, J., Clayton, P. H., & Steinberg, K. (2011). Designing programs with a purpose: To promote civic engagement for life. *Journal of Academic Ethics, 9*(2), 149–164.

Butin, D. W. (Ed.). (2005). *Service-learning in higher education: Critical issues and directions.* New York: Palgrave.

Calleson, D. C., Jordan, C., & Seifer, S. D. (2005). Community-engaged scholarship: Is faculty work in communities a true academic enterprise? *Academic Medicine, 80*(4), 317–321.

Campus Compact. (2014). *Three decades of institutionalizing change: 2014 annual member survey.* Boston, MA. Retrieved from http://compact.org/initiatives/membership-survey/

Clayton, P. H., Bringle, R. G., & Hatcher, J. A. (Eds.). (2013a). *Research on service learning: Conceptual frameworks and assessment (Vol 2A).* Sterling, VA: Stylus.

Clayton, P. H., Bringle, R. G., & Hatcher, J. A. (Eds.). (2013b). *Research on service learning: Conceptual frameworks and assessment (Vol. 2B).* Sterling, VA: Stylus.

Colby, A., Ehrlich, T., Beaumont, E., & Stephens, J. (2003). *Educating citizens: Preparing America's undergraduates for lives of moral and civic responsibility.* San Francisco, CA: Jossey-Bass.

Edgerton, R. (1994). The engaged campus: Organizing to serve society's needs. *AAHE Bulletin, 47,* 2–3.

Harkavy, I., & Puckett, J. L. (1994). Lessons from Hull House for the contemporary urban university. *Social Science Review, 68,* 299–321.

Hatcher, J. A., Bringle, R. G., Brown, L. A., & Fleischhacker, D. A. (2006). Indiana University-Purdue University Indianapolis: Supporting student involvement through service-based scholarships. In E. Zlotkowski, N. Longo, & J. Williams (Eds.), *Students as colleagues: Expanding the circle of service-learning leadership* (pp. 35–48). Providence, RI: Campus Compact.

Officer, S., Grim, J., Medina, M., Foreman, A., & Bringle, R. G. (2013). Strengthening community schools through university partnerships. *Peabody Journal of Education, 88*, 564–577.

O'Meara, K., & Rice, R. E. (Eds.). (2005). *Faculty priorities reconsidered: Rewarding multiple forms of scholarship.* San Francisco, CA: Jossey-Bass.

Percy, S. L., Zimpher, N., & Brukardt, M. (Eds.). (2006). *Creating a new kind of university.* Bolton, MA: Anker Press.

Plater, W. M. (2004). Civic engagement, service-learning, and intentional leadership. In M. Langseth & W. M. Plater (Eds.), *Public work and the academy: An academic administrator's guide to civic engagement and service-learning* (pp. 1–22). Bolton, MA: Anker Press.

Rice, R. E. (1996, January). *Making a place for the new American scholar.* Paper presented at the AAHE Conference on Faculty Roles and Rewards, Atlanta, GA.

Saltmarsh, J., Giles, D. E., Jr., O'Meara, K. A., Sandmann, L., Ward, E., & Buglione, S. M. (2009). The institutional home for faculty engagement: An investigation of reward policies at engaged campuses. In B. E. Moely, S. H. Billig, & B. A. Holland (Eds.), *Creating our identities in service-learning and community engagement. Advances in service-learning research* (pp. 3–30). Denver, CO: RMC Research Corp.

Saltmarsh, J., & Hartley, M. (Eds.). (2011). *"To serve a larger purpose": Engagement for democracy and the transformation of higher education.* Philadelphia, PA: Temple University Press.

Saltmarsh, J., Hartley, M., & Clayton, P. H. (2009). *Democratic engagement white paper.* Boston, MA: New England Resource Center for Higher Education.

Steinberg, K. S., Bringle, R. G., & Williams, M. J. (2010). *Service learning research primer.* Scotts Valley, CA: National Service-Learning Clearinghouse.

Nearly 25 years ago, a six-member campus team from Indiana University Purdue University Indianapolis (IUPUI) led by Executive Vice Chancellor William Plater was invited to attend the Campus Compact summer institute on Integrating Service Into Academic Study. At this weeklong institute in Boulder, Colorado, we were supported by the leadership of Campus Compact; energized by service experiences within the community; and inspired by the urgency of Ira Harkavy, currently associate vice president of University of Pennsylvania, to take seriously the public purposes of higher education. We made a number of decisions that week that established the trajectory for establishing the IUPUI Office of Service Learning (e.g., it would be led by a faculty director, it would be funded with campus-based funding, it would report up through academic affairs). Since that time, the Center for Service and Learning (CSL) was established to support both curricular and cocurricular programming through strategic partnerships, both in the community and across the campus. Leadership and campus resources have been leveraged and dedicated to support the development of service learning courses as one of the most important strategies to enact the campus mission of civic engagement.

As a metropolitan university located in the capital city, IUPUI comprises more than 30,000 students enrolled in 18 different schools, each with traditions of community involvement, particularly among the professional schools. The campus has established a pervasive and well-integrated culture for community engagement and has received national recognition for its commitment to and excellence in service learning (e.g., Association of Public and Land-grant Universities W.K. Kellogg Foundation Engagement Award, 2010; Carnegie Foundation Elective Classification for Community Engagement, 2006, 2015; President's Higher Education Community Service Honor Roll, 2006–2014; *U.S. News & World Report* "America's Best Colleges for Service-Learning," 2002–2015). Currently, under the leadership of Chancellor Nasser Paydar, the IUPUI Strategic Plan, *Our Commitment to Indiana and Beyond,* states that "Deepening Our Commitment to Community Engagement" (strategicplan.iupui.edu) is a key campus strategy that is "crucial to the success of our students, the institution, our city, and our state" (IUPUI, 2014, p. 7).

Development of Service Learning

Through a number of early and strategic decisions by executive leadership (Bringle & Hatcher, 2004; Bringle, Hatcher, & Clayton, 2006; Bringle, Hatcher, & Holland, 2007; Plater, 2004), significant commitments to infrastructure were made to support the development and growth of service learning courses. One of the key strategic decisions to support service learning and community engagement more broadly was designating campus scholarship funds to recognize "service" as a form of merit for scholarships. The Sam H. Jones Community Service Scholarship program, now in its 22nd year, began with two scholars in 1994 and has grown to more than 200 service-scholars annually in eight distinct programs (Bringle, Studer, Wilson, Clayton, & Steinberg, 2011; Hatcher, Bringle, Brown, & Fleischhacker, 2006). As an innovative practice in civic engagement (Bringle & Hatcher, 2009), service is valued as a form of merit for these campus designated scholarship funds, in a similar way as merit is often awarded for academic achievement or athletic ability. In 2014–2015, CSL awarded $220,000 in funding of student scholarships to support faculty/staff and to advance civically engaged teaching, innovation, research, scholarship, and creative activity. Service learning assistants help faculty and staff implement service learning courses, conduct research or scholarship on service learning and community engagement, or serve as a liaison between community organizations and the campus.

The development of service learning at IUPUI mirrors many national developments in the fields of higher education and community engagement. From the beginning, we have valued service learning as the best indicator of the level of institutional commitment to civic engagement (Bringle & Hatcher, 1996, 2004). Starting in 2008, IUPUI reconfirmed the importance of service learning as a high-impact teaching practice (Finley, 2011) by elevating it as a core aspiration in the undergraduate curriculum through the RISE to the IUPUI Challenge Initiative, which emphasizes the importance of undergraduate research (R), international study abroad (I), service learning (S), and experiential (E) learning courses. The RISE Initiative is significant for many reasons as it contributes to marketing the strengths of the campus to students, highlights community engagement as a component of the mission, focuses faculty and curricular development initiatives, and creates norms and expectations for undergraduate student learning. In addition, it resulted in extending the use of systematic tagging of service learning courses through the Service Learning Course Inventory to capture data (e.g., student participation, hours of service, community partners) and gaining additional funding allocations for curriculum development grants to support faculty innovation. Information on service learning courses is annually gathered, tracked, and reported to campus and community stakeholders.

Although important, the RISE Initiative and the increase in the number of service learning courses across the years is not enough. In accordance with significant national conversations and initiatives over the past decade that have elevated the importance of civic learning in higher education (chapters 1.1, 1.2, and 1.3), since 2008 we have worked within CSL to determine how we can best design educationally meaningful service experiences through service learning and all cocurricular programming. This has resulted in exploring the concepts of civic-minded professional (CMP) (Hatcher, 2008) and civic-minded graduate (CMG) (Bringle & Steinberg, 2010; Steinberg, Hatcher, & Bringle, 2011). A *CMP* is defined as "one who is skillfully trained through formal education with the ethical disposition as a social trustee of knowledge, and the capacity to work with others in a democratic way to achieve public goods" (Hatcher, 2008, p. 21), and this represents the integration of ones' (a) identity; (b) work, career, and profession; and (c) civic attitudes, civic action, and public purpose. In a similar way, a *CMG* is defined as

> a person who has completed a course of study (e.g., bachelor's degree), and has the capacity and desire to work with others to achieve the common good. "Civic-Mindedness" refers to a person's inclination or disposition to be knowledgeable of and involved in the community, and to have a commitment to act upon a sense of responsibility as a member of that community. (Bringle & Steinberg, 2010, p. 429)

The attributes of a CMG emanate from the intersection of a student's (a) identity, (b) educational experiences, and (c) civic experiences. The work on conceptualizing the CMG and developing and evaluating measures (i.e., CMG Scale, CMG Narrative Prompt, CMG Rubric, CMG Interview Protocol) is one basis for assessment and research on civic outcomes of service learning (Steinberg et al., 2011). As such, it provides a model for approaching civic development at different levels of analysis (individual, course, major, program, institution) and across time (Bringle & Steinberg, 2010; Bringle et al., 2011; Steinberg et al., 2011). We posit that service learning is the best way for higher education to develop CMGs and CMPs.

Scholarship and Research

For many years, under the leadership of Robert Bringle, the executive director of the IUPUI CSL from 1994 to 2012, significant work has been dedicated to scholarship and research on service learning and civic engagement in higher education. My involvement and professional development, first as the associate director, and currently as executive director, have benefitted from Bringle's ongoing mentorship to do the work in a "scholarly way" and as scholarship (Glassick, Huber, & Maeroff, 1997). This approach enacts Boyer's (1996) vision for the scholarship of engagement by systematically gathering information and conducting research so that others can learn from, critique, and build on the successes and challenges that we have encountered along the way. In 2007, we applied for and secured campus designation as a "Signature Center" to support research on service learning through a number of new initiatives. The CSL Research Collaborative received campus funding for three years. However, more important, this was an important impetus to enhance our focus on research and scholarship as a defining attribute of CSL. The mission of the CSL Research Collaborative was to do the following:

- Increase the capacity of faculty to engage in research on service learning practice
- Convene service learning scholars to develop new conceptual frameworks and methodological tools to improve the quality of service learning research
- Disseminate high-quality scholarship through books, research briefs, annual monographs, a web site that provides information on resources (e.g., grant opportunities, scales for research), presentations at scholarly conferences, and publications in peer-reviewed journals

The CSL Research Collaborative provided the basis for launching many new research activities for advancing scholarship on campus and nationally, including the IUPUI Series on Service Learning Research (Bringle, Hatcher, & Jones, 2011; Clayton, Bringle, & Hatcher, 2013) of which this volume is the third in the series. We, along with our colleagues in CSL and other faculty from across campus, have conducted research, written numerous articles and book chapters, convened various faculty learning communities, presented at national and international conferences, hosted a variety of workshops and conferences, and published Research Briefs through a digital scholarship repository (scholarworks.iupui.edu/handle/1805/2613). Each of these mechanisms is designed to support the development of IUPUI scholars and those at other institutions and improve the understanding of service learning and civic engagement through knowledge generation and sharing.

This volume, which focuses on student civic outcomes, was initially conceived after we hosted the IUPUI Symposium on Assessing Civic Outcomes in May 2009. In collaboration with the American Association for State Colleges and Universities (AASCU), the CSL invited two dozen scholars to campus for a two-day symposium on civic learning outcomes. Representatives from AASCU's American Democracy Project, Bonner Foundation, Higher Education Research Institute, and National Survey of Student Engagement

(NSEE) joined invited scholars from across the country and colleagues from campus to present current research and assessment strategies of civic outcomes. The symposium focused on definitional issues and participants shared assessment tools that could be used to explore student civic outcomes (Keen, 2009).

To further our commitment to research on service learning and civic engagement, after the symposium we hosted the 10th Annual Conference for the International Association for Research on Service Learning and Community Engagement (Hatcher & Bringle, 2012) and sponsored the first IUPUI Research Academy. Now in its eighth year, the Research Academy annually hosts approximately 30 scholars from 20 institutions across the country and from international institutions each May for a two-and-a-half-day institute to support scholarship and research on service learning (csl.iupui.edu/about/conferences/academy.shtml). Through plenary sessions and various workshops, participants are introduced to research methods and designs and topics relevant to working with faculty and institutional partners to advance research on service learning. Some authors in this current volume have joined us as faculty and facilitators at the Research Academy, sharing their expertise with graduate students, faculty, and campus administrators in attendance. Using a faculty learning community model (Bringle, Games, Ludlum, Osgood, & Osborne, 2000; Cox, 2004; Furco & Moely, 2012) guided by two facilitators, groups of seven to eight participants provide each other with feedback on their research question and approach, discuss and debate ideas, and leave the Research Academy with a plan for action that supports their goals for scholarship and research.

Service Learning and Student Civic Outcomes

This third volume is focused, in particular, on stimulating research on student civic outcomes resulting from participation in service learning courses. There are a number of intended purposes that shaped the design of this volume and guided the invitations extended to chapter authors. We were most pleased with the enthusiastic response from a number of experts in the fields of service learning, civic learning, and research in higher education who agreed to contribute to this volume. Additionally, many authors have partnered with graduate students as coauthors, and this approach bodes well for developing a future cadre of scholars on community engagement. Although the chapters have implications for assessment, program evaluation, and course design, our primary goal is to improve research on service learning and civic outcomes in higher education. The intended audience for the book is broad and includes service learning and civic engagement researchers, doctoral students, institutional researchers, scholars and teachers, program evaluators, and assessment practitioners. The chapters in this volume can lead to new insights into service learning research and provide ideas about how service learning can provide *in vivo* ways to evaluate and elaborate cognate theories.

In May 2015, as with other volumes in the IUPUI Series on Service Learning Research, we convened chapter authors on campus for one-and-a-half days to strengthen our common understanding of research on civic outcomes through service learning, terminology, and the purpose of the volume and individual chapters. Each set of authors prepared a working outline and presented a draft of their approach to writing a chapter. Feedback and questions emerged amid friendly dialogue and debate, and we generated consensus on the distinctive contribution of each chapter. Most importantly, the face-to-face interaction (including Skype calls both during and after the gathering from those who could not attend) built coherence across chapters and generated a shared enthusiasm for completing the task in a timely manner. The authors devoted significant time and attention to forging new areas of work associated with civic outcomes and service learning that clearly goes beyond past work by themselves and others in innovative ways. In doing so, they have demonstrated persistence and dedication to all of the activities that were associated with the production of this volume, including their willingness to discuss, review, listen, and use their own professional judgment as a means for improving all of the chapters.

The contents of this volume have confirmed that there is great potential for the development of service learning in higher education and that there is a great need for scholarly analysis, assessment, and research to understand its relationship to civic outcomes.

I am indebted to the strong collaboration among the editorial team. Robert Bringle, who now serves as a senior scholar with the CSL, has been the lead editor on this entire series, and his work on this volume has provided further evidence of his dedication to scholarly excellence. He has been through this process a number of times, yet his enthusiasm for this particular book was evident from the start as he provided thorough and thoughtful feedback on each chapter. Tom Hahn, director of research and program evaluation, joined CSL three years ago to further support research and scholarship. His attentiveness to shepherding this process, communicating with authors and publishers, and editing each chapter to comply with style guidelines was most appreciated. This has been a fun process and a rewarding culmination of our collective work to date. I sincerely hope that this volume contributes to improving quality in service learning course design and ultimately supports the development of civic-minded graduates and professionals.

Julie A. Hatcher
March 2016

References

Boyer, E. L. (1996). The scholarship of engagement. *Journal of Public Service and Outreach, 1,* 11–20.

Bringle, R. G., Games, R., Ludlum, C., Osgood, R., & Osborne, R. (2000). Faculty Fellows Program: Enhancing integrated professional development through community service. *American Behavioral Scientist, 43,* 882–894.

Bringle, R. G., & Hatcher, J. A. (1996). Implementing service learning in higher education. *Journal of Higher Education, 67,* 221–239.

Bringle, R. G., & Hatcher, J. A. (2004). Advancing civic engagement through service-learning. In M. Langseth & W. M. Plater (Eds.), *Public work and the academy: An academic administrator's guide to civic engagement and service-learning* (pp. 125–145). Boston, MA: Anker Press.

Bringle, R. G., & Hatcher, J. A. (2009). Innovative practices in service-learning and curricular engagement. In L. R. Sandmann, C. H. Thornton, & A. J. Jaeger (Eds.), *Institutionalizing community engagement in higher education: The first wave of Carnegie classified institutions. New Directions for Higher Education* (pp. 37–46). San Francisco, CA: Jossey-Bass/Wiley.

Bringle, R. G., Hatcher, J. A., & Clayton, P. H. (2006). The scholarship of civic engagement: Defining, documenting, and evaluating faculty work. *To Improve the Academy, 25,* 257–279.

Bringle, R. G., Hatcher, J. A., & Holland, B. (2007). Conceptualizing civic engagement: Orchestrating change at a metropolitan university. *Metropolitan Universities, 18*(3), 57–74.

Bringle, R. G., Hatcher, J. A., & Jones, S. G. (Eds.). (2011). *International service learning: Conceptual frameworks and research.* Sterling, VA: Stylus.

Bringle, R. G., & Steinberg, K. (2010). Educating for informed community involvement. *American Journal of Community Psychology, 46,* 428–441.

Bringle, R. G., Studer, M. H., Wilson, J., Clayton, P. H., & Steinberg, K. (2011). Designing programs with a purpose: To promote civic engagement for life. *Journal of Academic Ethics, 9*(2), 149–164.

Clayton, P. H., Bringle, R. G., & Hatcher, J. A. (Eds.). (2013). *Research on service learning: Conceptual frameworks and assessment.* Sterling, VA: Stylus.

Cox, M. D. (2004). Introduction to faculty learning communities. *New Directions for Teaching and Learning, 97,* 5–23.

Finley, A. (2011). *Civic learning and democratic engagements: A review of the literature on civic engagement in postsecondary education.* Paper prepared for the U. S. Department of Education as part of Contract: ED-OPE-10_C-0078. Retrieved from www.civiclearning.org/SupportDocs/LiteratureReview_CivicEngagement_Finley_Jul2011.pdf

Furco, A., & Moely, B. E. (2012). Using learning communities to build faculty support for pedagogical innovation: A multi-campus study. *The Journal of Higher Education, 83*(1), 128–153.

Glassick, C. E., Huber, M. T., & Maeroff, G. I. (1997). *Scholarship assessed: Evaluation of the professoriate.* San Francisco, CA: Jossey-Bass.

Hatcher, J. A. (2008). *The public role of professionals: Developing and evaluating the civic-minded professional scale* (Doctoral dissertation). Retrieved from https://scholarworks.iupui.edu/handle/1805/1703

Hatcher, J. A., & Bringle, R. G. (Eds.) (2012). *Understanding service-learning and community engagement: Crossing boundaries through research*, a volume in *Advances in Service-Learning Research*. Charlotte, NC: Information Age.

Hatcher, J. A., Bringle, R. G., Brown, L. A., & Fleischhacker, D. A. (2006). Indiana University-Purdue University Indianapolis: Supporting student involvement through service-based scholarships. In E. Zlotkowski, N. V. Longo, & J. R. Williams (Eds.), *Students as colleagues: Expanding the circle of service-learning leadership* (pp. 35–48). Providence, RI: Campus Compact.

Indiana University-Purdue University, Indianapolis (2014). *Our commitment to Indiana and beyond: IUPUI Strategic Plan.* Retrieved from http://strategicplan.iupui.edu

Keen, C. (2009). New efforts to assess civic outcomes. *Journal of College and Character, 10*(7), 1–6.

Plater, W. M. (2004). Civic engagement, service-learning, and intentional leadership. In M. Langseth & W. M. Plater (Eds.), *Public work and the academy: An academic administrator's guide to civic engagement and service-learning* (pp. 1–22). Bolton, MA: Anker Press.

Steinberg, K., Hatcher, J. A., & Bringle, R. G. (2011). A north star: Civic-minded graduate. *Michigan Journal of Community Service Learning, 18*(1), 19–33.

PART ONE

SERVICE LEARNING AND STUDENT CIVIC OUTCOMES

INTRODUCTION TO RESEARCH ON SERVICE LEARNING AND STUDENT CIVIC OUTCOMES

Robert G. Bringle, Julie A. Hatcher, and Thomas W. Hahn

The current context for community engagement in American higher education places an emphasis on civic outcomes for college students (e.g., National Task Force on Civic Learning and Democratic Engagement, 2012). There is a consistent call for a renewed commitment of colleges and universities to create campus cultures that support and challenge student understanding of and commitment to civic participation. This call has come from national associations and membership organizations, foundations, and government entities and is coupled with academic leadership at colleges and universities across the country, indeed the globe. This call has contributed to a sustained movement in higher education over the past two decades to support the civic development of college students and graduates. Indeed, a recent survey of 141,189 first-year college and university students from around the United States found that political and civic engagement is at its highest level in 50 years (UCLA Higher Education Research Institute, 2016).

In terms of national associations, the Association of American Colleges & Universities (AAC&U) has provided significant leadership for initiatives (e.g., Civic Engagement VALUE rubric, annual conferences) and publications (e.g., *Liberal Education, Diversity & Democracy*). Since 2002, the Bringing Theory to Practice project, funded through foundations and private gifts, has functioned in close collaboration with AAC&U to support various initiatives that link liberal learning with civic engagement practices and the well-being of college students (e.g., grants to more than 300 institutions; conferences; The Civic Series, composed of five monographs on civic learning). In 2012, the AAC&U, the Bringing Theory to Practice project, and others were convened by the U.S. Department of Education to form the National Task Force on Civic Learning and Democratic Engagement. The resulting report, *A Crucible Moment: College Learning & Democracy's Future,* highlights the importance of civic learning as a fundamental aspect of liberal education and recommends that public policy endorse "civic learning for democratic engagement as an expected component of program integrity and quality standards at all levels of education," including all types of postsecondary education (National Task Force on Civic Learning and Democratic Engagement, 2012, p. 34). The AAC&U tracks the ongoing use and impact of *A Crucible Moment,* and to date more than 48,000 copies of the report have been downloaded and viewed through the AAC&U website (www.aacu .org/sites/default/files/files/crucible/CrucibleUpdate2016.pdf).

Similar initiatives have been sponsored by other national associations. Since 2003, the American Association of State Colleges and Universities (AASCU) has supported the American Democracy Project, an ongoing project that involves more than 250 colleges and universities that support the civic development of college students. In collaboration with AASCU, in 2009, our Center for Service and Learning hosted the IUPUI Symposium on Assessing Student Civic Outcomes, and this initial gathering of scholars laid an important foundation for this current volume (Keen, 2009). AASCU is also a lead collaborator on The Democracy Commitment, an initiative among community colleges to advance and study the impact of community college experiences on student civic outcomes. Additionally, the NASPA Student Affairs Administrators in Higher Education, beginning in 2012, has sponsored the Lead Initiative to advance a Civic Learning and Democratic Engagement constituent group within cocurricular programming. Each year professionals from more than 100 campuses share good practice through structured collaboration, peer mentoring, and national conferences. Thus, within the domains of both curricular and cocurricular initiatives, there is a strong emphasis on civic learning.

Membership organizations that support civic engagement have also seen a steady growth over the past two decades. Campus Compact, this year celebrating its 30th anniversary, represents more than 1,100 colleges and universities and is composed of a network of 34 state and regional compacts throughout the United States. Other membership organizations (e.g., Anchor Institution Task Force, Community-Campus Partnerships in Health, Imagining America, International Association for Research on Service-Learning and Community Engagement, Research University Civic

Engagement Network) convene academics with specific disciplinary interests and approaches to community engagement and public scholarship. Journals within the field of civic engagement (e.g., *Journal of Public Service and Out-reach, Michigan Journal of Community Service Learning, Public: A Journal of Imagining America, The International Journal of Research on Service-Learning and Community Engagement*) and special awards and designations (e.g., Thomas Ehrlich Civic Engagement Faculty Award, Ernest A. Lynton Award for Scholarship of Engagement, William M. Plater Award for Leadership in Civic Engagement, Academy of Community Engagement Scholarship) reinforce the level of commitment to the public purposes of higher education. In addition, there are parallel international initiatives focused on service learning and civic engagement across the globe (e.g., Talloires Network, Campus Engage, Service Learning Asia Network, Centro Latinoamericano de Aprendizaje y Servicio Solidario, Ma'an Arab University Alliance for Civic Engagement, South African Higher Education Community Engagement Forum, Engagement Australia, Europe Engage).

The call for civic renewal in higher education is also supported by foundation programs and private funding to support program implementation (e.g., Carnegie Foundation, Charles Engelhard Foundation, Christian A. Johnson Endeavor Foundation, Kettering Foundation, Lumina Foundation) as well as research on student civic outcomes (e.g., Spencer Foundation, Teagle Foundation, Templeton Foundation). Of these foundation initiatives, one of the most important catalysts for change in American higher education has been the Carnegie Community Engagement Classification. To date, a total of 361 colleges and universities have received this elective classification by completing an extensive application portfolio of evidence demonstrating institutionalized and effective community engagement. Although this elective classification covers a broad spectrum of institutional factors, attention is also given to assessment of student learning and civic outcomes resulting from service learning courses and other forms of community engagement.

IUPUI Series on Service Learning Research

This third volume, as well as the entire IUPUI Series on Service Learning Research, is one response to the call for renewed emphasis on civic engagement in higher education. The overarching goal of the series is to stimulate more and better research on service learning. This volume is focused on providing an analysis of student civic outcomes and contributing to research strategies for enhancing an understanding of the means to prepare students for civic participation through their personal and professional lives. In the second volume, *Research on Service Learning: Conceptual Frameworks and Assessment, Vol. 2A* and *Vol. 2B* (Clayton, Bringle, & Hatcher, 2013a, 2013b), research was conceptualized as incorporating theory, measurement, design, and practice (see Figure 1.1.1). Authors of chapters in those volumes were specifically asked

> to introduce theories and measurement approaches from cognate areas, to use those theories to critique extant research studies (including designs and analyses), and to integrate those theoretical lenses with what has and has not been undertaken and learned in work to date in order to generate recommendations for practice and an agenda for future research. (p. 17)

This general framework for understanding research also shaped the guidance that authors were given in the present volume.

   With the goal of advancing research on student civic outcomes, we have requested chapters for this volume that conceptualize civic outcomes and the nature of service learning's contributions to civic outcomes, present theoretical frameworks, and suggest research methodologies. Part One provides an overview

Figure 1.1.1. Research situated within the context of theory, measurement, design, and practice.

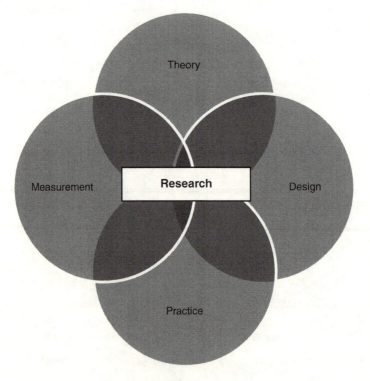

of civic learning outcomes and then lays a foundation for the importance of service learning course design and implementation to reach civic outcomes. In Part Two, authors identify key relevant cognate theories from various disciplinary or theoretical perspectives on civic outcomes, provide a critical evaluation of past research on service learning from that perspective, identify a research agenda for future research based on the theoretical perspectives and what has not been studied in past research, and identify implications for good practice for service learning based on the analysis. In Part Three, authors describe specific research methods and designs (e.g., quantitative, qualitative, cross-institutional research, longitudinal research, gathering authentic data, using local and national data sets) to improve research, provide a review and critique of past research using a particular methodological perspective, and make recommendations for future research to advance understanding of the relationship between service learning and civic outcomes. Each chapter provides useful information to both practitioners and researchers and clarifies the rationale for practice recommendations emanating from both cognate theories and past research approaches.

There are a number of intended purposes that shaped the design of this volume, as well as the invitations extended to chapter authors. Although the chapters have implications for assessment, program evaluation, and course design, our primary goal is to improve research on service learning and student civic outcomes in higher education. We asked authors not only to review the literature to date but also to provide a forward-thinking perspective on where research should be focused to improve understanding of student civic outcomes through service learning. Many authors have identified key questions that can shape the research agenda going forward and they illustrate how cognate theories generate new or refined questions related to designing service learning courses and their connections to student civic outcomes. The authors have identified theories from cognate domains (e.g., education, critical theories, philanthropic studies, political science, psychology, well-being) to generate a new set of questions and recommendations to deepen understanding of service learning. Although gaps exist in terms of theoretical perspectives that are not well represented in this volume, other disciplinary sources are available (e.g., sociology, see Follman, 2015; religious studies, see Devine, Favazza, & McLain, 2002; economics, see McGoldrick, Battle, & Gallagher, 2000; Zlotkowski, 2000) to support scholarship and practice. The chapters in this volume extend past analyses and provide new insights to service learning researchers and provide other researchers with ideas about how service learning can provide in vivo ways to evaluate and refine the relevance of cognate theories for student civic outcomes.

Although the primary focus is to provide resources to researchers, the intended audience for the book is intentionally broader and includes graduate students, institutional researchers, scholars and teachers, program evaluators, assessment practitioners, and scholars of teaching and learning. We view scholarship as a broader category of inquiry, analysis, and synthesis than research. Both the scholarship on teaching and learning and rigorous research strategies can enhance the understanding of the broad range of civic outcomes that can be achieved through service learning, including the long-term commitments of college graduates to be actively engaged in their communities after graduation as citizens and civic-minded professionals.

Although our focus is on American higher education, research within K–12 education has been brought to bear on analyses, and there are implications from each chapter for scholars focused on civic development among youth and high school students as well as for those designing cocurricular programs and activities to develop civic outcomes (Bringle, Studer, Wilson, Clayton, & Steinberg, 2011; Weinberg, 2005). Similarly, we appreciate contextual issues associated with situating this volume primarily within the American context (e.g., Hatcher & Bringle, 2012). Going forward, we aspire to a subsequent volume on framing civic outcomes from various cross-cultural perspectives and exploring the similarities and differences in concepts such as the civic-minded graduate (Hatcher, McIlrath, McMillan, & McTighe-Musil, 2014). We would expect, however, that this volume will provide inspiration, advice, and resources for international researchers who study service learning and civic outcomes of their students.

Civic Engagement and Service Learning

Civic Engagement

Within the field of community engagement, definitional issues often arise (Holland, 2000; Torney-Purta, Cabrera, Roohr, Liu, & Rios, 2015). Figure 1.1.2 takes the traditional faculty activities within universities (i.e., teaching, research, service) and illustrates that each has implications for both faculty and students and that each can occur in communities as well as on campuses (Bringle, Games, & Malloy, 1999). Courses can be delivered at off-campus sites in communities, researchers can collect data in communities, and faculty can share professional expertise in communities. In addition, Figure 1.1.2 illustrates that these three areas can overlap; although not shown in this diagram, the intersection of teaching and research can occur both on campus and in communities. Community involvement, then, is teaching, research, and/or service (and their intersections) that takes place in communities. Community involvement activities are defined by place; they can occur in all sectors of society (e.g., nonprofit, government, business) and in local or international contexts (Bringle, Hatcher, & Clayton, 2006).

Figure 1.1.2. Civic engagement as faculty, staff, and student activities "in and with" communities.

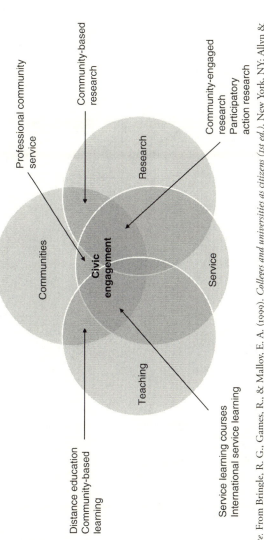

Professional community service

Community-based research

Community-engaged research
Participatory action research

Research

Communities

Civic engagement

Service

Distance education
Community-based learning

Teaching

Service learning courses
International service learning

Note. From Bringle, R. G., Games, R., & Malloy, E. A. (1999). *Colleges and universities as citizens (1st ed.).* New York, NY: Allyn & Bacon. Reprinted by permission of Pearson Education, Inc. New York, New York.

The term *civic engagement*, however, not only indicates where community–campus interactions occur but also specifies qualities of process (i.e., how it occurs). Bringle and colleagues (2006) differentiate between community involvement and civic engagement in the following way:

> Civic engagement is a subset of community involvement and is defined by both location as well as process (it occurs not only in but also with the community). According to this distinction, civic engagement develops partnerships that possess integrity and that emphasize participatory, collaborative, and democratic processes (e.g., design, implementation, assessment) that provide benefits to all constituencies. (p. 258)

This differentiation between activities done only in communities and activities done *in* and *with* communities (Jameson, Clayton, & Jaeger, 2011; Kirby, 2010; Saltmarsh, Hartley, & Clayton, 2009) illustrates that the public purposes of civic engagement "go beyond outcomes benefiting either the academy (i.e., students, faculty, institutions) or the community (i.e., organizations, residents) to include collective capacity building, collective transformation (i.e., growth), and the mutual empowerment of all participants as democratic agents" (Bringle & Clayton, 2012, p. 104). One implication of this characterization of civic engagement is that civic learning outcomes can be designed within and emanate from various civic engagement activities (e.g., civically engaged teaching, research, service). An additional implication is that civic learning outcomes are not limited to students but can also occur for faculty, campus staff and administrators, community partners in community-based organizations, and community residents.

Service Learning

Because there are a number of definitions of *service learning* (Jacoby, 2015) and there is a lack of clarity about service learning as a high-impact teaching strategy (Finley, 2011; Giles & Eyler, 2013), for the analysis and examination of research on service learning in this volume, we have asked authors to use a common definition. We define *service learning* as

> a course or competency-based, credit-bearing educational experience in which students (a) participate in mutually identified service activities that benefit the community, and (b) reflect on the service activity in such a way as to gain further understanding of course content, a broader appreciation of the discipline, and an enhanced sense of personal values and civic responsibility. (Bringle & Clayton, 2012, p. 105; adapted from Bringle & Hatcher, 1996)

A number of characteristics embedded within this definition are further described in the following subsections.

Civic Outcomes

The definition "personal values and civic responsibility" acknowledges a unique contribution that *service learning* provides to broadening and deepening the specific and general learning outcomes in higher education: civic learning outcomes. Figure 1.1.3 illustrates three domains of learning objectives: academic learning, civic learning, and personal growth. There is accumulating evidence that each of these domains can be enhanced through service learning (e.g., Bowman, 2011; Celio, Durlak, & Dymnicki, 2011; Novak, Markey, & Allen, 2007; Warren, 2012; Yorio & Ye, 2012). Figure 1.1.3 also illustrates that the civic outcome domain can be an integral part of the academic content of the service learning course (area 4) or students' personal development (area 6) as well as an area of growth and learning that independently but intentionally occurs (area 2). Jameson, Clayton, and Ash (2013) provide an analysis of research that has been conducted across disciplines on academic learning, examining both research that measured changes across time and research that compared service learning to traditional pedagogies. The

Figure 1.1.3. Learning domains that community service can enhance.

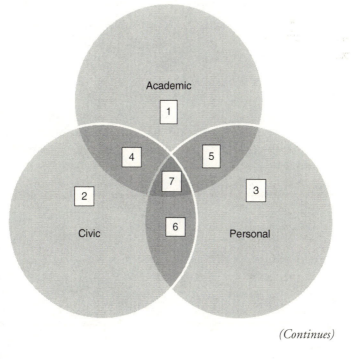

(Continues)

Figure 1.1.3. *(Continued)*

1. Community service illustrates or informs a deeper understanding of an academic concept, theory, or research finding (e.g., students learn to differentiate the use of positive reinforcement, negative reinforcement, and punishment while they reflect on their observations of an elementary teacher's interaction with children in the classroom).

2. Community service contributes to civic growth in ways that are not necessarily related to the course content (e.g., students increase their knowledge of the nonprofit sector or better understand the dynamics of power and privilege, but these are not topics in the psychology course).

3. Community service contributes to personal growth in ways that are not necessarily related to the course content (e.g., students clarify personal values or career plans, but these are not topics in the psychology course).

4. Community service connects academic content to civic learning (e.g., the course content covers intergroup contact theory and students learn better approaches for interacting with diverse groups in the community based on the theory and research presented on the intergroup contact theory as well as better learning the material on intergroup contact hypothesis).

5. Community service connects academic content to personal growth (e.g., the course presents information on nonverbal communication and students analyze nonverbal cues at the site and become more aware of their nonverbal cues that they are displaying at the service site).

6. Community service contributes to civic learning and personal growth in ways that are not necessarily related to the course content (e.g., students become more knowledgeable about a community issue and more empathetic toward those persons associated with the community issue, but the community issue is not a specific topic in the psychology course).

7. Community service connects academic content to civic learning and personal growth (e.g., the course content on stigma influences how students conduct their service activities, the power of stigma in their interactions and the interactions of others, their awareness of their own attitudes and prejudices, and their understanding of the course material on stigma).

Note. From Bringle, Reeb, Brown, & Ruiz, 2015.

purpose of this volume is to examine how research on service learning can contribute to civic outcomes, including civic outcomes that might be a part of course content or related to personal growth. Civic outcomes are complex (Hatcher, 2011); they vary across disciplines (Battistoni, 2002); and they typically are described as a combination of knowledge, skills, attitudes, and behaviors (chapters 1.2 and 1.3).

Type of Community Activities

The definition of *service learning* includes service activities within community settings that are mutually selected or developed by instructors and community partners in a way that meets learning objectives for the course and that benefit communities. Service learning courses can include at least four types of community activities by students (e.g., Bringle, Reeb, Brown, & Ruiz, 2015; Florida Department of Education, 2009): (a) direct service learning, (b) indirect service learning, (c) research service learning, and (d) advocacy service learning. These categories are not mutually exclusive, and community-based activities might involve one or more of them. The type of community-based activity that is most appropriate for a service learning course will be the result of considering learning objectives and discussions with community partners.

Reflection

The definition of *service learning* also identifies reflection as a central component of service learning. Well-designed reflection activities should (a) intentionally link the service experience to course-based learning objectives, (b) be structured, (c) occur regularly, (d) allow feedback and assessment, and (e) include the clarification of values (Bringle & Hatcher, 1999; Hatcher & Bringle, 1997; Hatcher, Bringle, & Muthiah, 2004). Good reflection can occur before, during, and after the community service (Eyler, 2002). Structured reflection has been found to support academic learning (Jameson et al., 2013); yet informal reflection has also been found to have an additive value to the likelihood that students report civic outcomes after the college years (Richard, Keen, Pease, & Hatcher, 2016).

Relationships

The definition of *service learning* highlights the importance of particular types of relationships and partnerships between the campus and communities in order to reach civic outcomes (Bringle & Clayton, 2013). Consistent with Dewey's (1916) analysis, building democratic capacities is contingent on face-to-face interactions in the public sphere, and "society must have a type of education which gives individuals a personal interest in social relationships" (p. 99). Levine's (2013) research found that simply involving students in community service activities was insufficient for developing civic learning and civic skills; deliberate collaboration was more effective for developing civic outcomes. Bowman's (2011) meta-analysis found that face-to-face interactions with diverse groups resulted in favorable and significant effects on civic attitudes, behavioral intentions, and behaviors, compared to classroom-based educational experiences and cocurricular activities. Students must also be involved in collaborative relationships in the civic realm. Partnerships between students and community members that contain democratic qualities (e.g., fair, inclusive, participatory; Saltmarsh et al., 2009) are critical to developing civic outcomes. Bringle, Clayton, and Bringle (2015), using psychological theory and research, explore how the democratic nature of partnerships can be related to the development of civic identity of students. Engaging in democratic partnerships can also enhance civic skills and civic identity of faculty, staff at community organizations, administrative staff and leaders on campus, community leaders, and residents, although this is largely unexplored in empirical research.

SOFAR

Although the focus of this book is primarily on students, there are many stakeholders in and contributors to the service learning endeavor. Some of the primary stakeholders are identified in the SOFAR model (Clayton, Bringle, Senor, Huq, & Morrison, 2010), which identifies the various relationships that are formed in a service learning course among students (S), staff at community organizations (O), faculty (F), administrators (A), and community residents (R) or clients. Although this volume is focused on the process of producing civic outcomes for students, the process can also be analyzed for other constituencies. Accordingly, we have asked authors to identify implications for the other constituencies when relevant.

IUPUI Taxonomy for Service Learning Courses

With heightened interest in high-impact teaching strategies (Finley, 2011; Kuh, 2008) comes heightened institutional accountability to gather data related to the efficacy of service learning courses. Researchers, in turn, need to attend to the course design, implementation of the course, and the students' experiences in the course as part of the research process (Giles & Eyler, 2013). Very few studies assess the quality of the service learning course from the perspective of course design, the instructor, the students, or community partners (e.g., Gelmon, Holland, Driscoll, Spring, & Kerrigan, 2001). This focus of inquiry can broaden a more extensive agenda of types of evidence about service learning course quality; sources of evidence about course quality; and their relationships to outcomes, particularly civic outcomes (Terry, Smith, & McQuillan, 2014).

In order to assess student learning and improve the quality of course design on our campus, the IUPUI executive vice chancellor asked that each unit (e.g., Center for Service and Learning, Office of International Affairs) with responsibility for a high-impact teaching practice (e.g., internship, service learning, study abroad, undergraduate research) develop a framework (i.e., taxonomy) for course design. This initial step is part of a comprehensive campus assessment strategy managed through the Office of Institutional Research and Decision Support. Influenced in large part by the California State University's analysis of high-impact practices (e.g., learning communities, summer bridge, undergraduate research), this assessment approach has been adapted by our campus to support faculty development and gather data on course design. In the Center for Service and Learning, we recognize that this institutional assessment task is an important way to support both good practice and future research. After conducting an extensive literature review on service learning research and best practices, including Jacoby's (2015) recent work, we identified six essential attributes of service learning courses. Next, we articulated a range of characteristics for each attribute (from level one to level three) based on research findings. We then obtained feedback from colleagues and content experts, presented a draft of the taxonomy through a webinar series sponsored by the International Association for Research on Service Learning and Community Engagement (Hahn & Hatcher, 2015), and made subsequent revisions. The IUPUI Taxonomy for Service Learning Courses (see Table 1.1.1) can contribute to the campus and to research on service learning because the taxonomy accomplishes the following:

1. Creates a common approach in working with instructors to support the fidelity and quality of high-impact teaching practices, including service learning courses
2. Supports institutional assessment and research on high-impact practices by asking instructors to report on selected course attributes (dimensions of the course design that may vary) and then explore the relationship between these course variables and student outcomes
3. Informs and advances a research agenda for service learning by identifying those course attributes (i.e., variables) that may relate to student outcomes (e.g., civic learning, academic learning, personal growth), as well as other outcomes (e.g., faculty development, community impact, community partner collaboration and satisfaction)
4. Supports institutional and multi-campus research on service learning courses through the use of a common taxonomy that describes variations in course attributes
5. Provides a framework and approach for other institutions to either adapt or adopt the taxonomy, depending upon how service learning is conceptualized within various institutional missions and contexts

TABLE 1.1.1
IUPUI Taxonomy for Service Learning Courses—Course Design Centric for Institutional Assessment and Research

Service Learning Course Attributes	Level One	Level Two	Level Three
1. Reciprocal partnerships and processes shape the community activities and course design.	The instructor contacts a community organization to host students and provides a brief overview of the course (e.g., learning outcomes, syllabus) and the purposes of the community activities.	The instructor meets with the community partner(s) to discuss the course (e.g., preparation/orientation of students, learning outcomes, syllabus) and to identify how the community activities can enrich student learning and benefit the organization.	The instructor collaborates with and learns from the community partner(s) as coeducators in various aspects of course planning and design (e.g., learning outcomes, readings, preparation/orientation of students, reflection, assessment), and together they identify how the community activities can enrich student learning and add to the capacity of the organization.
2. Community activities enhance academic content, course design, and assignments.	The instructor includes community activities as added components of the course, but they are not integrated with academic content or assignments. The syllabus does not address the purposes of the community activities.	The instructor utilizes the community activities as a "text" to provide additional insight into student understanding of academic content and ability to complete assignments. The syllabus describes the relationship of the community activities to learning outcomes.	The instructor integrates the community activities and relevant social issue(s) as critical dimensions for student understanding of academic content and ability to complete assignments. The syllabus provides a strong rationale for the relationship of the community activities to learning outcomes.

3. Civic competencies (i.e., knowledge, skills, disposition, behavior) are well integrated into student learning.	The instructor focuses on discipline-based content with little attention/priority given to civic learning or development of civic competencies.	The instructor focuses on discipline-based content and connects to civic learning and civic competencies when relevant to the community activities.	The instructor focuses on the integration of discipline-based content with civic learning and civic competencies and emphasizes the relevance of the community activities to the public purposes of the discipline in society.
4. Diversity of interactions and dialogue with others across difference occurs regularly in the course.	The instructor, the course, and community activities offer students limited opportunities for interaction and dialogue with others across difference.	The instructor, the course, and community activities engage students in periodic interactions and dialogue with others across a range of experiences and diverse perspectives.	The instructor and community partner(s) engage students in frequent interactions and dialogue with peers and community members across a range of experiences and diverse perspectives.
5. Critical reflection is well integrated into student learning.	The instructor asks students, on a limited basis, to create reflective products about the community activities, usually only at the end of the semester.	The instructor structures reflection activities and products about the community activities that connect the experience to academic content, require moderate analysis, lead to new action, and provide ongoing feedback to the student throughout the semester.	The instructor builds student capacity to critically reflect and develop products that explore the relevance of the experience to academic content, use critical thinking to analyze social issues, recognize systems of power, lead to new action. The instructor provides ongoing feedback to the students throughout the semester.
6. Assessment is used for course improvement.	The instructor articulates student learning outcomes, but no measurement tool is in place for assessing the service learning component of the course.	The instructor articulates student learning outcomes and uses a measurement tool to assess the service learning component of the course.	The instructor and community partner(s) articulate student learning outcomes, and use measurement tools to assess the service learning component of the course and influence on community outcomes.

Within the taxonomy are variables in course design that relate to civic outcomes, including opportunities for reflection, orientation of community activities, dialogue across difference, and student interaction with community members. For example, Conway, Amel, and Gerwien's (2009) meta-analysis of service learning's association with academic, personal, social, and citizenship outcomes found that programs with structured reflection were associated with greater changes in these outcome measures than those that did not. Moely and Ilustre's (2014) study also showed that opportunities for reflection were positively associated with learning about the community and mastering academic content. Regarding orientation of community activities, Moely, Furco, and Reed's (2008) multicampus study found that students who indicated a preference for charity or social change orientations to community activities, or both, had better learning outcomes and changes in attitude when there was a fit between service preference and actual community activities than when they experienced a lack of fit. Bowman's (2011) meta-analysis of college diversity and civic engagement indicated that diversity experiences were related to increases in civic attitudes, behavioral intentions, and behaviors. Also, the magnitude of this association was higher for interpersonal interactions with racial diversity than for curricular and cocurricular diversity experiences. Likewise, Nelson Laird's (2005) research indicated that college students with increased exposure to diversity, especially participation in diversity courses and positive experiences with diverse fellow students, were more likely to have higher scores on social agency, critical thinking disposition, and academic self-confidence. The six course design attributes identified are only a sample of potential variables that could be used to measure course quality and that might influence student outcomes.

The meaningfulness of the taxonomy as an adequate sample of important course components warrants empirical evaluation. We acknowledge and have identified "gray areas" (see Figure 1.1.4) that include additional variables that are not part of the taxonomy. Some of these additional variables are explored more fully within this volume; for example, consider campus mission and culture (chapters 1.2 and 3.3), the instructor's teaching philosophy and epistemology (chapters 1.3 and 2.7), and prior learning experiences or motivation of students (chapters 2.1 and 2.4). The six course attributes as well as the variables within the "gray area" are dimensions of service learning course design that may vary in *intensity,* and each may have a particular link to student civic outcomes that future research should investigate.

We acknowledge that identifying the various component parts of a service learning course poses significant challenges for research, and clarity about the "it" under study is fundamental (Finley, 2011; Giles & Eyler, 2013). This is a complex task, and we acknowledge that there are other attributes that may be critically

Figure 1.1.4. Service learning course attributes.

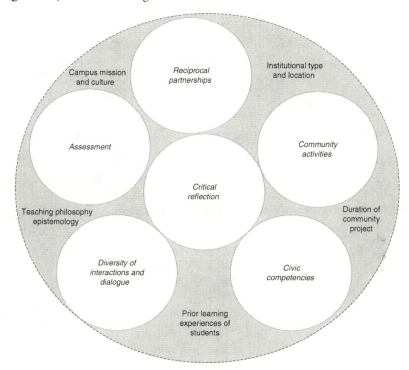

important to the design and implementation of a service learning course (e.g., chapter 2.2). To that end, exploring the practices and attributes embodied in the definition of *service learning* (Bringle & Clayton, 1996; Bringle & Clayton, 2013) as well as the six course attributes described in the IUPUI Taxonomy for Service Learning Courses should contribute to improved research and research that will more clearly enhance understanding for how particular qualities of a service learning course contribute to civic learning outcomes.

Finally, the initial use of the taxonomy for campus-level assessment, as currently presented, is based on a self-assessment of the course attributes by the instructor. At the end of the semester, instructors of high-impact practices will be asked to report on three course attributes, and this campus census will be used to understand the relationship between course attributes and student self-reported learning across service learning courses and other high-impact teaching practices. The taxonomy, and its use, should be modified and expanded so that it can solicit similar assessments from students as well as community partners. The taxonomy represents further clarity for researchers to address "the vague specification of the experiences students actually have in their service learning classes" (Giles & Eyler, 2013, p. 55) and provides a tool to assess course quality and to relate course quality to variations in course outcomes. This would allow an evaluation of the similarities and differences among different perspectives (e.g., faculty, student, community partner) on the quality of the service learning course and empirical evaluation of the relative importance of different perspectives on civic outcomes.

Conclusion

We initiated the concept for this book a number of years ago and are pleased to see it through to completion. In 2009, our Center for Service and Learning hosted the IUPUI Symposium on Assessing Student Civic Outcomes, an invited gathering of 22 scholars in collaboration with the American Association for State Colleges and Universities (AASCU). That gathering was one of the first of its kind to bring together scholars across higher education with a common interest in student civic outcomes (Keen, 2009). George Mehaffy, then vice president for academic leadership and change at AASCU, noted:

> While the conclusions demonstrate that there is much work to be done, this initial conference provides a great beginning of a substantive national dialogue, cross institutional collaboration, further study, and the development of improved assessment processes and instruments to gauge progress in the civic engagement field. If we are entering an era when learning outcomes assume more importance, then those of us in the civic engagement field must make sure that among learning outcomes, civic outcomes occupy a prominent position. (Mehaffy, 2009, p. 1)

Since that time, there have been various initiatives and subsequent gatherings of scholars, including the Civic Learning and National Service Summit at the Jonathan M. Tisch College of Citizenship and Public Service at Tufts University and the Bringing Theory to Practice National Initiative on Well-Being in Washington, DC, in 2014. Through each of these events, as well as professional relationships established with scholars at national conferences, we have been honored and inspired to identify and work with dedicated scholars who are advancing research on service learning and student development in important ways. As evidenced by our chapter contributors, the number of graduate students and young scholars who are establishing their scholarly trajectory within this line of inquiry is gratifying.

The chapters in this volume were designed to support this type of scholarly path. Theories are identified, new questions are posed, complexities are presented, and methodologies are recommended to deepen the inquiry and improve the research on the relationship between service learning and civic outcomes. Indeed, the field has grown over the past two decades, and the questions that have emerged within this volume alone demonstrate that there remains significant work ahead. Given our common aim to enact the public purposes of higher education, we trust that this volume will contribute to and deepen understanding of how to best develop civic-minded graduates (Steinberg, Hatcher, & Bringle, 2011), civic-minded professionals (Hatcher, 2008), and civic-minded institutions (National Task Force on Civic Learning and Democratic Engagement, 2012) through a renewed commitment to service learning and civic engagement. Education is a public good that sustains democracy and civil society, and service learning is a pedagogy that is well positioned to contribute to this goal. We posit that participation in well-designed service learning courses is one of the best pedagogies, if not the best pedaogy, for generating civic outcomes among college students. The extent to which this claim holds true in American higher education and across various cultural contexts will inform the longevity and adaptability of this approach to teaching and learning.

References

Battistoni, R. (2002). *Civic engagement across the curriculum: A resource book for service-learning faculty in all disciplines.* Providence, RI: Campus Compact.

Bowman, N. A. (2011). Promoting participation in a diverse democracy: A meta-analysis of college diversity experiences and civic engagement. *Review of Educational Research, 81*(1), 29–68.

Bringle, R. G., & Clayton, P. H. (2012). Civic education through service-learning: What, how, and why? In L. McIlrath, A. Lyons, & R. Munck (Eds.), *Higher education and civic engagement: Comparative perspectives* (pp. 101–124). New York, NY: Palgrave.

Bringle, R. G., & Clayton, P. H. (2013). Conceptual framework for partnerships in service learning. In P. H. Clayton, R. G. Bringle, & J. A. Hatcher (Eds.), *Research on service learning: Conceptual frameworks and assessment* (Vol. 2B, pp. 539–571). Sterling, VA: Stylus.

Bringle, R. G., Clayton, P., & Bringle, K. E. (2015). From teaching democratic thinking to developing democratic civic identity. *Partnerships: A Journal of Service-Learning and Civic Engagement, 6*(1), 51–76.

Bringle, R. G., Games, R., & Malloy, E. A. (1999). *Colleges and universities as citizens.* Needham Heights, MA: Allyn and Bacon.

Bringle, R. G., & Hatcher, J. A. (1996). Implementing service learning in higher education. *The Journal of Higher Education, 67,* 221–239.

Bringle, R. G., & Hatcher, J. A. (1999). Reflection in service learning: Making meaning of experience. *Educational Horizons, 77*(4), 179–185.

Bringle, R. G., Hatcher, J. A., & Clayton, P. H. (2006). The scholarship of civic engagement: Defining, documenting, and evaluating faculty work. *To Improve the Academy, 25*, 257–279.

Bringle, R. G., Reeb, R., Brown, M. A., & Ruiz, A. (2015). *Service learning in psychology: Enhancing undergraduate education for the public good.* Washington, DC: American Psychological Association.

Bringle, R. G., Studer, M. H., Wilson, J., Clayton, P. H., & Steinberg, K. (2011). Designing programs with a purpose: To promote civic engagement for life. *Journal of Academic Ethics, 9*(2), 149–164.

Celio, C. I., Durlak, J., & Dymnicki, A. (2011). A meta-analysis of the impact of service-learning on students. *Journal of Experiential Education, 34*, 164–181.

Clayton, P. H., Bringle, R. G., & Hatcher, J. A. (Eds.). (2013a). *Research on service learning: Conceptual frameworks and assessment (Vol 2A).* Sterling, VA: Stylus.

Clayton, P. H., Bringle, R. G., & Hatcher, J. A. (Eds.). (2013b). *Research on service learning: Conceptual frameworks and assessment (Vol. 2B).* Sterling, VA: Stylus.

Clayton, P. H., Bringle, R. G., Senor, B., Huq, J., & Morrison, M. (2010). Differentiating and assessing relationships in service-learning and civic engagement: Exploitative, transactional, or transformational. *Michigan Journal of Community Service Learning, 16*(2), 5–21.

Conway, J. M., Amel, E. L., & Gerwien, D. P. (2009). Teaching and learning in the social context: A meta-analysis of service learning's effects on academic, personal, social, and citizenship outcomes. *Teaching of Psychology, 36*, 233–245.

Devine, R., Favazza, J. A., & McLain, F. M. (Eds.). (2002). *From cloister to commons: Concepts and models for service learning in religious studies.* Sterling, VA: Stylus.

Dewey, J. (1916). *Education and democracy: An introduction to the philosophy of education.* New York: Macmillan.

Eyler, J. S. (2002). Reflection: Linking service and learning—Linking students and communities. *Journal of Social Issues, 58*, 517–534.

Finley, A. (2011). *Civic learning and democratic engagements: A review of the literature on civic engagement in postsecondary education.* Paper prepared for the U. S. Department of Education as part of Contract: ED-OPE-10_C-0078. Retrieved from www.civiclearning.org/SupportDocs/LiteratureReview_CivicEngagement_Finley_Jul2011.pdf

Florida Department of Education. (2009). *Standards for service-learning in Florida: A guide for creating and sustaining quality practice.* Tallahassee, FL: Florida Learn & Serve.

Follman, J. (2015). An overlooked lens: Applying structuration theory, actor-network theory, and theories of space to service-learning. *The International Journal of Research on Service-Learning and Community Engagement, 3*(1). Retrieved from http://journals.sfu.ca/iarslce/index.php/journal/article/view/119/93

Gelmon, S. B., Holland, B. A., Driscoll, A., Spring, A., & Kerrigan, S. (2001). *Assessing service-learning and civic engagement: Principles and techniques.* Boston, MA: Campus Compact.

Giles, Jr., D. E., & Eyler, J. (2013). Review essay: The endless quest for scholarly respectability in service-learning research. *Michigan Journal of Community Service Learning, 20*(1), 53–64.

Hahn, T. W., & Hatcher, J. A. (2015, September 30). *What about service-learning matters? Using a taxonomy to identify variables to improve research and practice* [Webinar]. In *IARSLCE Webinar Series*. Retrieved from https://www.youtube.com/watch?v=O3W27s3-XTw

Hatcher, J. A. (2008). *The public role of professionals: Developing and evaluating the civic-minded professional scale* (Doctoral dissertation). Retrieved from https://scholarworks.iupui.edu/handle/1805/1703

Hatcher, J. A. (2011). Civic knowledge and engagement. In J. Penn (Ed.), *Measuring complex general education learning outcomes. Jossey-Bass Quarterly Sourcebooks* (pp. 81–92). San Francisco, CA: Jossey-Bass.

Hatcher, J. A., & Bringle, R. G. (1997). Reflections: Bridging the gap between service and learning. *Journal of College Teaching, 45*, 153–158.

Hatcher, J. A., & Bringle, R. G. (2012). Exploring similarities and differences through cross-cultural comparative research. In J. A. Hatcher & R. G. Bringle (Eds.), *Understanding service-learning and community engagement: Crossing boundaries through research* (pp. ix–xxii). Charlotte, NC: Information Age.

Hatcher, J. A., Bringle, R. G., & Muthiah, R. (2004). Designing effective reflection: What matters to service-learning? *Michigan Journal of Community Service Learning, 11*(1), 38–46.

Hatcher, J. A., McIlrath, L, McMillan, J., & McTighe-Musil, C. (2014, December). *Developing civic-minded graduates: Cross-cultural perspectives*. Paper presented at Talloires Network international conference, Stellenbosch, South Africa.

Holland, B. A. (2000). Institutional impacts and organizational issues related to service-learning. *Michigan Journal of Community Service Learning, 4*(1), 30–41.

Jacoby, B. (2015). *Service-learning essentials: Questions, answers, and lessons learned.* San Francisco, CA: Jossey-Bass.

Jameson, J. K., Clayton, P. H., & Ash, S. L. (2013). Conceptualizing, assessing, and investigating academic learning in service learning. In P. H. Clayton, R. G. Bringle, & J. A. Hatcher (Eds.), *Research on service learning: Conceptual frameworks and assessment* (Vol. 2A, pp. 85–110). Sterling, VA: Stylus.

Jameson, J. K., Clayton, P. H., & Jaeger, A. J. (2011). Community-engaged scholarship through mutually transformative partnerships. In L. M. Harter, J. Hamel-Lambert, & J. L. Millesen (Eds.), *Participatory partnerships for social action and research* (pp. 259–278). Dubuque, IA: Kendall Hunt.

Keen, C. (2009). New efforts to assess civic outcomes. *Journal of College and Character, 10*(7), 1–6.

Kirby, C. (2010). Community investment—a strategic approach. *Keeping Good Companies, 62*, 438–440.

Kuh, G. D. (2008). *High-impact educational practices: What they are, who has access to them, and why they matter.* Washington, DC: Association of American Colleges & Universities.

Levine, P. (2013). *We are the ones we have been waiting for: The promise of civic renewal in America.* New York, NY: Oxford University Press.

McGoldrick, K., Battle, A., & Gallagher, S. (2000). Service-learning and the economics course: Theory and practice. *The American Economist, 44*(1), 43–52.

Mehaffy, G. (2009, May). *Report on the Symposium on Assessing Students' Civic Outcomes. AASCU.* Briefing paper presented at the Symposium on Assessing Students' Civic Outcomes, Indianapolis, IN.

Moely, B. E., Furco, A., & Reed, J. (2008). Charity and social change: The impact of individual preferences on service-learning outcomes. *Michigan Journal of Community Service Learning, 15*(1), 37–48.

Moely, B. E., & Ilustre, V. (2014). The impact of service-learning course characteristics on university students' learning outcomes. *Michigan Journal of Community Service Learning, 21*(1), 5–16.

National Task Force on Civic Learning and Democratic Engagement. (2012). *A crucible moment: College learning & democracy's future.* Washington, DC: Association of American Colleges & Universities.

Nelson Laird, T. F. (2005). College students' experiences with diversity and their effects on academic self-confidence, social agency, and disposition toward critical thinking. *Research in Higher Education, 46,* 365–387.

Novak, J. M., Markey, V., & Allen, M. (2007). Evaluating cognitive outcomes of service learning in higher education: A meta-analysis. *Communication Research Reports, 24*(2), 149–157.

Richard, D., Keen, C., Hatcher, J. A., & Pease, H. (2016). Pathways to adult civic engagement: Benefits of reflection and dialogue across difference in college service-learning programs. *Michigan Journal of Community Service Learning.*

Saltmarsh, J., Hartley, M., & Clayton, P. H. (2009). *Democratic engagement white paper.* Boston, MA: New England Resource Center for Higher Education.

Steinberg, K., Hatcher, J. A., & Bringle, R. G. (2011). A north star: Civic-minded graduate. *Michigan Journal of Community Service Learning, 18*(1), 19–33.

Terry, J. D., Smith, B. H., & McQuillan, J. D. (2014). Teaching evidence-based practice in service-learning: A model for education and service. *Journal on Excellence in College Teaching, 25*(1), 55–69.

Torney-Purta, J., Cabrera, J. C., Roohr, K. C., Liu, O. L., & Rios, J. A. (2015). Assessing civic competency and engagement in higher education: Research background, frameworks, and directions for next-generation assessment. *ETS Research Report Series, 2015*(2), 1–48.

UCLA Higher Education Research Institute. (2016). *College students' commitment to activism, political and civic engagement reach all-time highs.* Retrieved from http://newsroom.ucla.edu/releases/college-students-commitment-to-activism-political-and-civic-engagement-reach-all-time-highs

Warren, J. L. (2012). Does service-learning increase student learning? A meta-analysis. *Michigan Journal of Community Service Learning, 18*(2), 56–61.

Weinberg, A. S. (2005). Residential education for democracy. *Learning for Democracy, 1*(2), 29–45.

Yorio, P. L., & Ye, F. (2012). A meta-analysis on the effects of service-learning on the social, personal, and cognitive outcomes of learning. *Academy of Management, 11*(1), 9–27.

Zlotkowski, E. (2000). Service-learning in the disciplines. *Michigan Journal of Community Service Learning, Special Issue,* 61–67.

STUDENT CIVIC OUTCOMES IN HIGHER EDUCATION

Kevin M. Hemer and Robert D. Reason

This chapter provides an overview of civic outcomes for college students in American higher education. After an extensive review of literature, Finley (2012b) concluded that much of what we know about civic engagement and civic outcomes in higher education comes from research in service learning courses. Service learning is a pedagogical intervention that leads to many civic outcomes in higher education. In this chapter, we focus broadly on student civic outcomes that result from both curricular and cocurricular experiences within the collegiate context. We take this broader approach to provide a wider lens on civic outcomes through which the subsequent chapters, which focus more directly on service learning as a catalyst for civic outcomes, can be understood.

We begin this chapter with a discussion of conceptual issues related to civic outcomes, focusing specifically on how higher education professionals define and study these essential outcomes. We then summarize our current understanding of civic outcomes from higher education derived from Ehrlich's (2000) definition of *civic engagement*. According to Ehrlich, civic engagement is

> working to make a difference in the civic life of our communities and developing the combination of knowledge, skills, values, and motivations to make that difference. It means promoting the quality of life in a community through both political and nonpolitical processes. (p. vi)

Torney-Purta, Cabrera, Roohr, Liu, and Rios's (2015) assessment framework of civic learning also influences discussions of civic outcomes in terms of both civic competencies (i.e., civic knowledge, skills) and engagement (i.e., motivation, values, participation). As stated previously, our approach is informed primarily by Ehrlich's (2000) definition of *civic engagement*, which was designed with considerations for assessment and research of civic learning—a goal consistent with this book.

Conceptual Issues in the Study of Civic Outcomes

In 2012 the National Task Force on Civic Learning and Democratic Engagement, in cooperation with the Association of American Colleges & Universities (AAC&U) and the U.S. Department of Education, published *A Crucible Moment: College Learning & Democracy's Future,* calling for more investment in higher education's capacity to build and renew the nation's civic and democratic capital (National Task Force, 2012). *A Crucible Moment* is just one of the latest publications in a growing corpus of scholarship focusing on the civic purposes of higher education and highlights a movement to reassert the civic purposes of colleges and universities, which began in the 1980s and grew throughout the 1990s in response to the growing civic and political disaffection among America's youth (Saltmarsh & Hartley, 2011). Before administrators and researchers, in cooperation with community partners, can begin to reassert the civic mission of higher education, we first must understand the multiple ways to define or operationalize civic outcomes and the various methodological and research design decisions associated with the research of civic outcomes of college.

Definitional Issues Around Civic Outcomes

Research into the development of civic outcomes, along with the emphasis of civic purposes of higher education, suggest to some a field of study that has "come of age" (Sherrod, Torney-Purta, & Flanagan, 2010, p. 1). The study of civic outcomes, however, is not a high consensus field; rather, it is informed by multiple academic disciplines and theoretical perspectives, some of which are presented in subsequent chapters. Although this diversity of perspective is a strength as we generate ideas and emerging research, the lack of a shared definition of *civic outcomes* can be a challenge to developing a broadly shared understanding of the outcomes under investigation and encouraging development of these outcomes (Finley, 2012a; Hatcher, 2011; Jacoby, 2009; Torney-Purta et al., 2015).

Nearly all definitions understand civic outcomes to be multidimensional (Finley, 2012a; Reason & Hemer, 2015; Torney-Purta et al., 2015). We use Ehrlich's (2000) definition of *civic engagement* to guide our understanding of civic outcomes for three primary reasons: it can be broadly applied across multiple contexts within higher education, it includes both political and apolitical perspectives, and it is commonly cited in the civic engagement literature (AAC&U, 2009; Hatcher, 2011; National Task Force, 2012). Although *civic outcomes* can be narrowly understood, especially in some disciplinary traditions, Ehrlich's broad conceptualization including knowledge, skills, values, and motivations allows for a robust examination of outcomes. For this chapter, we adapt Ehrlich's understanding by adding civic attitudes along with civic values, an approach that is congruent with Torney-Purta and colleagues' (2015) definition; therefore, we identify and discuss four categories of civic outcomes: (a) knowledge, (b) skills, (c) attitudes and values, and (d) behaviors. Beyond these four, we pay attention to different conceptualizations of civic identity, as it is a broader outcome inclusive of the four we address (Bringle, Clayton, & Bringle, 2015). We also restrict our focus to civic outcomes attributable to college attendance and participation. Although we acknowledge differences exist in civic outcomes between those who attend college and those who do not (Flanagan, Levine, & Settersten, 2009; Syvertsen, Wray-Lake, Flanagan, Osgood, & Briddell, 2011; Trostel, 2015), a complete exploration of those differences is beyond the scope of this chapter.

Measurement Issues in Civic Outcomes Research

The most direct challenge associated with a lack of shared definition of what constitutes *civic outcomes* is a difficulty in measuring these outcomes. Reason and Hemer (2015) undertook a review of assessment instruments widely used within higher education that purported to assess one or more of the constituent parts of civic outcomes: knowledge, skills, attitudes and values, and behaviors. This review concluded that few available instruments had civic outcomes as a primary focus and no instrument assessed civic outcomes comprehensively. Often these widely used assessment instruments in higher education investigated a variety of important college campus outcomes, including civic outcomes as only one of many foci.

Currently the primary assessment instruments in higher education that measure civic outcomes rely almost exclusively on student self-report data (Reason & Hemer, 2015). Where direct measures exist, the measures tend to count hours of service or voting behaviors (as discussed later in this chapter), proxies that researchers often use in place of direct measures of civic learning. The development of direct measures of civic outcomes to replace the overreliance on students' self-reported gains will strengthen understanding of what interventions truly affect the development of civic outcomes among college students (Bowman, 2011).

Although it is easy to think of the lack of shared definition and resulting multitude of assessment instruments as solely a challenge, it has benefits.

Because some of the most widely used instruments include items related to civic outcomes (e.g., National Survey of Student Engagement [NSSE], Cooperative Institutional Research Program [CIRP], Personal and Social Responsibility Inventory [PSRI]), a great deal of data is collected each year. Furthermore, civic outcomes research can emerge from a range of disciplinary traditions. Political science and sociology traditionally have been at the forefront of teaching and studying civic learning (Torney-Purta et al., 2015). Over the last two decades, psychology, human development, history, and many humanities departments have increased their focus on civic outcomes related to both student learning and academic research (Torney-Purta et al., 2015).

Methodological Approaches to Civic Outcomes

The emphasis on assessment instruments described in the previous section indicates some tendency toward a survey-based, quantitative research approach to the study of civic outcomes. Our review (Reason & Hemer, 2015) did find that the vast majority of researchers' inquiries into civic outcomes used quantitative methods, often based on student self-report instruments and cross-sectional designs. The emergence of civic identity as a civic outcome, as well as the call to explore interactions between and among the various civic outcomes, reinforces a need to expand beyond quantitative methods to include more qualitative methods and mixed methods.

Finley (2012a) and Kirlin (2003) called for expanded use of longitudinal research designs to improve research on civic outcomes in college students. Hill, Pasquesi, Bowman, and Brandenberger (chapter 3.4) echo this call and begin to expand upon the issues associated with longitudinal study of the effects of service learning on civic outcomes. All of these calls (e.g., chapters 2.3, 2.5) highlight the need for engagement with college students over a period of years in order to determine the developmental trajectory of civic outcomes and the importance of repeated engagement with intentional learning opportunities in the development of civic outcomes.

In addition to quantitative methods, qualitative approaches to studying civic outcomes can provide unique insights to address different questions and provide more depth into the process of civic learning. These approaches offer lenses to investigate questions related to "how" or "why" in the process of civic learning in service learning courses. Jones and Foste (chapter 3.2) argue that qualitative approaches to the study of civic outcomes allow for a more holistic understanding of the interactions between experiences and civic outcomes that might be missed in solely quantitative research approaches. Bringle, Clayton, and Bringle (2015) suggest that the nuanced interactions between the components of civic outcomes constitute the development of a civic identity. Civic identity, an outcome we discuss later in this chapter, might be particularly appropriate for qualitative investigation (e.g., Malin, Ballard, & Damon, 2015).

Current Understandings of Civic Outcomes

We turn now to review the current empirical literature of civic outcomes. We acknowledge that presenting these outcomes as distinct domains is artificial, as these outcomes are likely overlapping and interrelated. However, we treat them as distinct for ease of presentation and analysis. We encourage readers to consider how development in one domain likely encourages development in the others, even when existing research does not fully uncover those inter-actions. Civic identity is a notable exception to presenting these domains as distinct; it is superordinate and represents the intersection of many of these other outcomes (Bringle et al., 2015).

Civic Knowledge

The acquisition of knowledge, of which civic knowledge is one component, is a primary outcome of higher education. Knowledge is developed through formal curriculum experiences as well as cocurricular college experiences (e.g., involvement in campus organizations; volunteering in the community; informal interactions with peers, instructors, and staff). The historical con-ceptualization of civics as an area of study is best understood as the acquisi-tion of civic knowledge. For example, civic knowledge includes how well students understand the structures of government and basic history, topics related to the study of civics. In *A Crucible Moment*, the National Task Force (2012) suggested that citizens need to know the cultural and global contexts in which their communities exist, understand the historical and sociological relevance of important social movements, be exposed to multiple cultural and religious traditions, and understand how their political systems function (National Task Force, 2012). Engberg (2013) found that service learning was associated with increases in students' cognitive processes and requisite knowl-edge vital to being a global citizen compared to college students who did not participate in these experiences. Bringle and colleagues (2015) described how employing service learning promotes greater civic knowledge through action and application, noting, "action-based experiences uniquely improve cognitive skills in ways that can be applied in subsequent situations and in ways that may not be possible through didactic and other forms of non-experiential teaching and learning" (p. 6).

Situating the acquisition of civic knowledge as the traditional study of civics limits the scope of understanding for how college students develop civic knowledge. Civic knowledge in higher education is often discipline specific and perceived by some to be academic learning. Civic knowledge includes the unique perspectives disciplines bring to understanding democratic societies and emphasizes different areas of knowledge (Battistoni, 2002, 2013). Civic knowledge deals with "actionable" information, related to a discipline, which can allow individuals to come together and make positive change (Hatcher, 2011, p. 84). Civic knowledge, understood as academic learning, can often be achieved through well-structured service learning and critical reflection (Jameson, Clayton, & Ash, 2013).

Political knowledge, including both foundational knowledge (political theories, institutions, and organizations) and knowledge of current issues (political and economic events relevant at the local, state, national, and global level), is an explicit form of civic knowledge (Colby, Beaumont, Ehrlich, & Corngold, 2005). Foundational knowledge is most often associated with disciplinary knowledge from political science (chapter 2.2). Political awareness, one aspect of political knowledge, is highest among those with bachelor's and advanced degrees (Trostel, 2015). Individuals with some college and associate degrees also exhibit higher levels of political awareness than individuals who have not attended any college (Trostel, 2015).

Although evidence suggests that attending college is associated with higher levels of civic knowledge, civic knowledge is not evenly distributed across the population; groups such as women, students from low-income backgrounds, and Black and Latino students show lower levels of political knowledge (Colby et al., 2005; Pascarella & Terenzini, 2005). These between-group differences may appear for a variety of reasons. One possibility is that a researcher's conceptual framing of civic knowledge might privilege the cultural norms of a particular group over others. However, it is also possible that meaningful between-group differences in students' civic knowledge exist and might be an area for further study, especially in the context of service learning courses.

Civic Skills

Broad skill development is another outcome commonly associated with attending an institution of higher education. Civic skills include and go beyond skills for political practice (Colby, Ehrlich, Beaumont, & Stephens, 2003). *A Crucible Moment* (National Task Force, 2012) identifies a number of important, specific skills for civic participation: (a) critical inquiry, analysis, and reasoning; (b) quantitative reasoning; (c) gathering and evaluating multiple sources of evidence; (d) seeking, engaging, and being informed by multiple perspectives; (e) written, oral, and multimedia communication; (f) deliberation and bridge building across differences; (g) collaborative decision-making; and (h) an ability to communicate in multiple languages. This range of skills is analytical as well as participatory or involvement based (Torney-Purta et al., 2015).

Service learning has been widely investigated as a pedagogical practice to improve college students' civic skills. Service learning is related to a wide array of civic skills, including cognitive, interpersonal, analytical, leadership, and communication skills (Astin & Sax, 1998; Barnhardt, Sheets, & Pasquesi, 2015; Bowman, 2011; Colby et al., 2005; Moely, Mercer, Ilustre, Miron, & McFarland, 2002). Developing civic skills has been tied to a number of other campus-related experiences and environments. The development of civic skills was positively associated with diversity experiences in college (Bowman, 2011; Bowman, Park, & Denson, 2015), and there is evidence that engaging in social-change behaviors has some positive influence on perspective-taking skills (Johnson, 2014). After controlling for students' demographic and experiential characteristics, perceptions of a campus climate that advocates for students to be responsible citizens supported the growth of skills to effectively change society for the better (Barnhardt et al., 2015). Finally, peer-to-peer discussion about contributing to the larger community has been found to support the development of civic skills (Barnhardt et al., 2015). This last piece is important because utilizing peer-to-peer reflection with college students can occur across an array of experiences including service learning.

Civic Attitudes and Values

Civic attitudes and values are sometimes treated as discrete but related outcomes (Torney-Purta et al., 2015) and sometimes treated as a single domain of outcomes (Bowman et al., 2015; Finley, 2012a; Keen, 2009; Reason & Hemer, 2015). Because of the overlapping nature of attitudes and values, we have chosen to group them within one domain in our examination of civic outcomes. Civic attitudes include an interest in being informed and attentive to civic and political information, a willingness to practice the civic skills previously discussed, and a sense of efficacy or agency related to civic issues (Torney-Purta et al., 2015). The term *civic values* refers to the belief in principles of a diverse inclusive democratic society (Torney-Purta et al., 2015), including dispositions such as respect for freedom and dignity, empathy, open-mindedness, tolerance, justice, promoting equality, integrity, and responsibility to a larger good (National Task Force, 2012). Civic values may be related to the public sphere locally, nationally, and globally (National Task Force, 2012; Torney-Purta et al., 2015). Other conceptualizations of values have included being involved in programs to clean up the environment, having an interest in influencing the political structure, and developing a philosophy of life (Lott & Eagan, 2011; Malin et al., 2015). The assessment of civic attitudes and values is challenging to measure and relies primarily on student self-reported data (Finley, 2012a; Keen, 2009).

Utilizing longitudinal survey data from alumni of colleges and universities, Pascarella, Ethington, and Smart (1988) determined students' college experiences were directly related to the broad development of civic values (e.g., developing a meaningful philosophy of life, participating in community action, being informed in politics). A number of college experiences were positively related to civic values including social leadership involvement (Lott, 2013; Pascarella et al., 1988), interacting with faculty and staff (Pascarella et al., 1988), studying abroad (Lott, 2013), coursework related to ethnic or women's studies (Lott, 2013), and volunteering (Lott, 2013). Mayhew and Engberg (2011) found infusing service learning into first-year seminars could improve students' sense of charitable responsibility (helping those less fortunate and increased likelihood of volunteering in the future). Diversity experiences are also related to increases in civic attitudes (Bowman, 2011). According to Bowman, this relationship exists for both curricular and cocurricular diversity experiences and is most strongly related to interpersonal interactions with racial diversity. Student participation in racial/ethnic student organizations is positively correlated with improved civic attitudes (keeping up to date on politics and efficacy to change society) six years after graduation (Bowman et al., 2015). Service learning and peer-to-peer discussion around contributing to the larger community is positively associated with students' commitments to contribute to the larger community, an attitudinal outcome (Barnhardt et al., 2015).

In addition to broad assessments of civic attitudes and values, several assessment scales investigate specific civic attitudes and values. The Pluralistic Orientation Scale (five items) represents a measurement of a person's ability to work effectively with others of diverse backgrounds, openness to new ideas and perspectives, and being empathic to others' perspectives (Hurtado, Engberg, Ponjuan, & Landrewman, 2002). The Pluralistic Orientation Scale emphasizes an openness to having one's views challenged and tolerance for different beliefs, which are crucial attitudes in supporting a diverse democratic society. Engberg and Hurtado (2011) concluded that students' interactions across racial differences were significantly related to pluralistic orientation, with positive interactions resulting in higher pluralistic orientation and negative cross-racial interactions related to lower pluralistic orientation. Engberg (2007) found that some general education coursework has been shown to influence pluralistic orientation, particularly diversity courses for students in hard science majors.

The Openness to Diversity And Challenge (ODC) Scale also assesses civic attitudes and values. ODC was developed as part of the National Study of Student Learning (Pascarella, Edison, Nora, Hagedorn, & Terenzini, 1996; Whitt, Edison, Pascarella, Terenzini, & Nora, 2001). The eight-item scale (reduced to seven in later studies) assesses students' attitudes toward interacting with people from different backgrounds, an important civic outcome. The study was longitudinal in design allowing for stronger causal claims than typical correlational research. Pascarella and colleagues (1996), concerned with the future demographic shifts in the United States, first investigated students' openness to diversity and challenge in the first year of college. After controlling for precollege ODC, student perceptions of a nondiscriminatory racial environment on campus positively affected ODC. The number of hours that students spend studying was also positively related to ODC. Campus residency, participation in a racial/cultural workshop, hours working at a job per week, and interactions with peers (Acquaintances Scale, Topics of Conversation Scale, and Information in Conversations Scale) were found to have positive net effects, whereas joining a fraternity or sorority had a negative effect for White students and a positive correlation for non-White students.

Beyond the first year of college, other predictors consistently supported development of ODC in all three years of college: biological sex (with women scoring higher), age (with older students scoring higher), the degree to which students perceived a nondiscriminatory racial environment, the diversity of students' acquaintances, and conversations with others in which different ways of thinking were emphasized (Whitt et al., 2001). Conversations with others in which different ways of thinking were emphasized is a particularly notable finding, as it is pedagogically consistent with service learning.

Based on research by Pascarella and colleagues (1996) and Whitt and colleagues (2001), Cabrera, Nora, Crissman, Terenzini, Bernal, and Pascarella (2002) examined the role of collaborative learning pedagogy on multiple outcome scales, including ODC, for second-year students. Cooperative learning practices, a five-item scale measuring the frequency with which students engaged in group projects, class discussions, and study groups, had the largest significant effect on ODC. Ryder, Reason, Mitchell, Gillon, and Hemer (2015) also examined classroom-based experiences of students and found that a climate for learning—students' perceptions of instructors' valuing a wide range of ideas and perspectives and instructors' advocacy for the respect of diverse ideas and points of view—was also related to higher levels of ODC. These findings illustrate that both pedagogical and environmental characteristics of the classroom may be leveraged to improve ODC. Instructors who employ a service-learning pedagogy often incorporate cooperative learning practices, and those hoping to support a climate for learning that considers diverse perspectives should note service learning may have beneficial outcomes for ODC as well as other stated course outcomes.

The Socially Responsible Leadership (SRLS) Scale, associated with the social change model of leadership, includes aspects of leadership focused on social responsibility—a civic value (Dugan, 2006; Dugan & Komives, 2010). This is exemplified by the citizenship subscale of leadership, which assesses "the process whereby an individual and the collaborative group become responsibly connected to the community and society through leadership development" (Dugan & Komives, 2010, p. 526). The authors suggest the 14-item citizenship subscale was the lowest-scoring scale among undergraduate students, relative to other subscales, leading to their conclusion that the community aspect of students' leadership is the least developed during the college years, relative to others (Dugan, 2006; Dugan, Komives, & Segar, 2008). This finding was accompanied by the recommendation that colleges intentionally focus on developing this outcome (Dugan et al., 2008). Students' scores on the citizenship subscale were positively related to involvement in community service, positional leadership roles in organizations, participation in student organizations, and formal leadership programs (Dugan, 2006). Parker and Pascarella (2013) found that diversity experiences in college, such as exchanges or conversations with diverse peers, also positively improved students' socially responsible leadership. Service learning involves service and often positions students for diversity experiences, indicating research on the relationship between service learning and socially responsible leaders may be fruitful.

Civic Behaviors and Participation

Civic behaviors can range from volunteering to voting, from dialogue between individuals around difference to addressing public problems with diverse partners. Keen (2009) reviewed civic outcomes assessment methods and concluded that many standardized approaches to assessing civic engagement measure behaviors and participation. Assessments typically utilize self-reported data but some direct measurement does occur. Assessing behaviors can involve assessing skills or abilities in action—often measured as energy expended, time spent, or frequency of certain behaviors. Assessing civic behaviors often includes measuring activity during students' undergraduate years, measuring the kinds of behaviors in which they are likely to participate, or measuring behaviors after graduation.

Civic behaviors are typically treated as an outcome of higher education. However, some research suggests it may be appropriate to reconsider civic behaviors as more than outcomes. Using the Activism Orientation Scale (Corning & Myers, 2002), a measure of students' engagement in civic and political behaviors, Klar and Kasser (2009) found higher levels of activism were related to psychological well-being, suggesting that activism can be conceptualized as both an outcome of college and a mediator for other outcomes (chapter 2.5). Bringle and colleagues (2015) also provide evidence that behaviors and behavioral change influence both attitudes and cognition.

A variety of collegiate campus engagement practices has been connected to civic behaviors as outcomes. Social change behaviors were positively associated with student organizational involvement (Bowman et al., 2015; Johnson, 2014). This was the case for involvement in service-based organizations, assuming positions of student leadership, engaging in discussions of social issues with peers, and participating in racial/ethnic student organizations (Bowman et al., 2015; Johnson, 2014). Participating in racial/ethnic student organizations was positively associated with civic behaviors (e.g., community leadership, volunteer work, donating money to nonprofit organizations and political causes, frequency of accessing news sources) six years after graduation (Bowman et al., 2015). Interpersonal interactions with racial diversity during college also resulted in more frequent participation in civic engagement behaviors (Bowman, 2011).

Volunteering and voting are likely the two most commonly studied civic behaviors. College student volunteering has increased for recent cohorts, while voting is trending downward, even after accounting for greater youth participation in the 2008 presidential election (Syvertsen et al., 2011). A positive relationship between levels of education and voting behaviors is firmly established in the literature (Pascarella & Terenzini, 2005; Syvertsen et al., 2011). According to reports by the Center for Information and Research on Civic Learning and Engagement (CIRCLE) following the 2012 presidential election, college-educated youth between the ages of 18 and 29 were overrepresented among voters compared to their representation among the population as a whole (CIRCLE, 2012). At that time, approximately 60% of all U.S. citizens in that age group had attended postsecondary education, whereas over 70% of voters in that same age group had attended postsecondary education. The gap appears to widen as education level increases; 20% of U.S. citizens between the ages of 18 and 29 held a bachelor's degree in 2012, but 37% of voters in that age group had earned bachelor's degrees.

Although the link between education and voting is well established, the mechanisms present in higher education that encourage greater voter participation are less well understood (Niemi & Hanmer, 2010). In a study of 1,200 students at 285 colleges and universities, Niemi and Hanmer found that demographic characteristics normally predicting voter participation in the general population (e.g., socioeconomic status, race) were not statistically significant among college-educated voters, indicating that participating in higher education may remove some barriers that affect participation among students. Recent research does suggest that service learning is a possible mechanism to encourage voting and greater social responsibility (Kilgo, Pasquesi, Ezell Sheets, & Pascarella, 2014).

Access to information about the voting process, information about specific candidates, and a campus climate that conveys the importance of political participation are likely mechanisms that allow students to overcome traditional barriers and reinforce the importance of voting (Glynn, Huge, & Lunney, 2009; Niemi & Hanmer, 2010; Shulman & Levine, 2012). College students are an easily identifiable and accessible population for political parties and activists to target with information campaigns. Although students who move away from home for college are less likely to vote (Niemi & Hanmer, 2010; O'Loughlin & Unangst, 2006), students reporting that they had been contacted by political parties either by mail or in person were 10% to 15% more likely to vote than were students who had not been contacted, regardless of where they attended college (Niemi & Hanmer, 2010). Information provided by political parties or student groups representing political parties mitigates obstacles encountered when students move away from home and provides students with specific information about candidates.

College students may also be influenced by campus climates and norms that reinforce the importance of political participation (Glynn et al., 2009; Shulman & Levine, 2012). Although neither study directly addresses actual voting behavior, Glynn and colleagues' and Shulman and Levine's studies suggest that colleges and universities can send messages through their support of political activities (e.g., speakers, student groups) that influence general political engagement (Shulman & Levine, 2012) and intention to vote (Glynn et al., 2009).

The research related to how specific educational interventions affect voting behavior of college students is even more sparse. Recent emphasis on reinvigorating civic learning and democratic engagement in college has translated into greater exploration of how college affects civic learning (as noted in other sections of the chapter and other chapters in this volume), but not yet into greater exploration of how college interventions affect voting behavior. Higher education researchers and administrators seem satisfied in understanding that college education is positively related to voting behavior, but seem less interested in moving beyond that descriptive understanding to ask "why." The ongoing work of the National Study of Learning, Voting, and Engagement out of Tufts University holds promise as one of the first, and certainly the most comprehensive, explorations of the relationships between college experiences and voting (Tufts University, n.d.).

Civic Identity

Researchers have begun to explore civic identity as an outcome of college; it is assumed to combine many of the outcomes we have discussed previously in this chapter resulting in a holistic understanding of self (Bringle et al., 2015; chapters 2.1, 2.3; Knefelkamp, 2008; Youniss, McLellan, & Yates, 1997). Bringle and colleagues (2015) define a *democratic civic identity* as the integration of democratic thinking, democratic action, democratic critical reflection, and democratic partnerships. Similarly, Knefelkamp (2008) and McIntosh and Youniss (2010) posit that civic identity results from a holistic practice connecting civic practices, performed in partnership with others, with intellectual and ethical development until democratic engagement is a "deliberately chosen and repeatedly enacted aspect of the self" (Knefelkamp, 2008, p. 3).

We highlight two approaches to understanding civic identity development as a civic outcome of college (see Malin et al., 2015, for an analysis of development of civic purpose in pre-college adolescents). First, the Civic-Minded Graduate (CMG) conceptual model integrates educational and civic domains with identity to understand civic-mindedness as an outcome of college experiences (Steinberg, Hatcher, & Bringle, 2011). Civic mindedness is a person's inclination to be knowledgeable of and involved in the community and have a commitment to act upon that inclination (Bringle & Steinberg, 2010). The conceptual understanding of the CMG "is indicative of the degree to which the student's identity is well-integrated with their educational pursuits and civic attitudes and actions" (Steinberg et al., 2011, p. 21). This model integrates students' knowledge (volunteer opportunities, academic knowledge, and knowledge about social issues), skills (communication and listening, diversity, and consensus-building), dispositions (valuing community engagement, self-efficacy, and serving as a social trustee of knowledge), and behavioral intentions (Steinberg et al., 2011). This conceptual model has been supported using three measurement procedures (interview protocols and rubrics, narrative prompts, and a scale administered using surveys). CMGs are knowledgeable of and involved in the community. CMGs also have a commitment to and sense of responsibility to use the knowledge they have gained in college to address social and community issues (Steinberg et al., 2011). Developing CMGs is recognized as a public purpose of higher education and is an overarching goal of higher education institutions.

Second, students' engagement can also be understood as an expression of their civic identity. Weerts, Cabrera, and Pérez Mejías (2014) utilized a person-oriented latent class analysis to identify groups based on college student engagement in eight civically related categories. They identified four typologies of student engagement: super engagers (highly engaged in all eight civic behaviors), social-cultural engagers (highly engaged in social and cultural activities), apolitical engagers (highly engaged in professional, service, social, and community related activities but not engaged in political activities), and non-engagers (students who were unlikely to engage in any of the eight behaviors assessed).

In a separate study, Weerts and Cabrera (2015) suggested that a "college major may be the most important collegiate factor that predicts or reinforces certain forms of civic action" (p. 34). Apolitical engagers, civically engaged students who did not engage in political activities, were more likely to be female and less likely to have studied a social sciences or humanities discipline (Weerts & Cabrera, 2015). High school leadership experiences were predictive of civic involvement during college, a strong reminder that civic identity development begins prior to college (Weerts & Cabrera, 2015). Cohort-based experiences with peers in college also supports civic identity development (Mitchell, Battistoni, Keene, & Reiff, 2013). Although civic identity begins to develop before college (Bringle et al., 2015; Malin et al., 2015; Youniss et al., 1997) and continues well beyond graduation (Bowman et al., 2015; Mitchell et al., 2013), many of the participatory experiences offered by colleges are important in civic identity development (Youniss et al., 1997). Bringle and his colleagues (2015) argue persuasively for a connection between the development of democratic civic identity and service learning activities, especially service learning activities that intentionally require students to integrate cognitive, affective, and behavioral aspects of a group experience.

Conclusion

Although the study of civic outcomes of college seems to be invigorated by recent attention (National Task Force, 2012), additional research can contribute to a clearer understanding of how collegiate courses and experiences result in civic growth. In addition, the influences of family background and responsibilities, the role of community partners, and engagement of non-college students need further exploration (Keen, 2009). Finely (2012a) argues effectively for more research about distinct student populations (students of color, first generation, transfer, and low income). Investigation into special populations for which civic outcomes may manifest themselves differently from traditional undergraduate students, such as veterans and nontraditional age students, is needed (Reason & Hemer, 2015). Finally, although the connection between more education and increased civic outcomes is well established, more research on the specific mechanisms in college that influence civic outcomes is needed.

This book is designed to improve research on these civic outcomes, specifically as researchers explore the connection between service learning and civic outcomes. This chapter provides a foundation for subsequent chapters as we explore the broader connections between college attendance and experiences (not limited to service learning) and civic outcomes. We conclude that there is still work to be done in measuring, researching, and understanding how civic outcomes are shaped and developed during college and that service learning courses are a particularly fruitful area for study and development of civic outcomes. Research on the connection between service learning and civic outcomes offers opportunities to investigate a structured, established, pedagogical practice with an array of civic outcomes associated with higher education.

As education is a field of practice, researching and promoting civic outcomes should be a collective activity. This work can best be done by tenure-track and non-tenure-track instructors across many disciplines, in collaboration with student affairs professionals in a variety of professional roles senior administrators in their guidance of institutions, and through leveraging relationships with community partners who are vital to service learning. Finally, we cannot forget that students themselves play an important role in shaping environments and exerting developmental influence on their peers. Students, in service learning courses and other campus experiences, are one of the most influential forces for student learning and development. Campus resources, classroom curricula, and institutional policies can and should be intentionally designed to meet civic outcomes. This requires many campus constituencies working together to create opportunities and environments that foster civic outcomes.

References

American Association of College and Universities (AAC&U). (2009). *VALUE Rubrics, VALUE: Valid Assessment of Learning in Undergraduate Education.* Retrieved from https://www.aacu.org/civic-engagement-value-rubric

Astin, A. W., & Sax, L. J. (1998). How undergraduates are affected by service participation. *Journal of College Student Development, 39,* 123–133.

Barnhardt, C. L., Sheets, J. E., & Pasquesi, K. (2015). You expect *what?* Students' perceptions as resources in acquiring commitments and capacities for civic engagement. *Research in Higher Education* Advance online publication.

Battistoni, R. M. (2002). *Civic engagement across the curriculum: A resource book for faculty in all disciplines.* Providence, RI: Campus Compact.

Battistoni, R. M. (2013). Civic learning through service learning: Conceptual frameworks and research. In P. H. Clayton, R. G. Bringle, & J. A. Hatcher (Eds.),

Research on service learning: Conceptual frameworks and assessment (Vol. 2A) (pp. 111–132). Sterling, VA: Stylus.

Bowman, N. A. (2011). Promoting participation in a diverse democracy: A meta-analysis of college diversity experiences and civic engagement. *Review of Educational Research, 81*(1), 29–68.

Bowman, N. A., Park, J. J., & Denson, N. (2015). Student involvement in ethnic student organizations: Examining civic outcomes 6 years after graduation. *Research in Higher Education, 56*, 127–145.

Bringle, R. G., Clayton, P. H., & Bringle, K. E. (2015). From teaching democratic thinking to developing democratic civic identity. *Partnerships: A Journal of Service Learning & Civic Engagement, 6*(1), 1–26.

Bringle, R. G., & Steinberg, K. S. (2010). Educating for informed community involvement. *American Journal of Community Psychology, 46*, 428–441.

Cabrera, A. F., Nora, A., Crissman, J. L., Terenzini, P. T., Bernal, E. M., & Pascarella, E. T. (2002). Collaborative learning: Its impact on college students' development and diversity. *Journal of College Student Development, 43*, 20–34.

Center for Information and Research on Civic Learning and Engagement (CIRCLE). (2012, November). *Young voters in the 2012 presidential election: The educational gap remains.* Retrieved from http://www.civicyouth.org/wp-content/uploads/2012/11/2012-Exit-Poll-by-Ed-Attainment-Final.pdf

Colby, A., Beaumont, E., Ehrlich, T., & Corngold, J. (2005). *Educating for democracy: Preparing undergraduates for responsible political engagement.* San Francisco, CA: Jossey-Bass.

Colby, A., Ehrlich, T., Beaumont, E., & Stephens, J. (2003). *Educating citizens: preparing America's undergraduates for lives of moral and civic responsibility.* San Francisco, CA: Jossey-Bass.

Corning, A. F., & Myers, D. J. (2002). Individual orientation toward engagement in social action. *Political Psychology, 23*, 703–729.

Dugan, J. P. (2006). Involvement and leadership: A descriptive analysis of socially responsible leadership. *Journal of College Student Development, 47*, 335–343.

Dugan, J. P., & Komives, S. R. (2010). Influences on college students' capacities for socially responsible leadership. *Journal of College Student Development, 51*, 525–549.

Dugan, J. P., Komives, S. R., & Segar, T. C. (2008). College student capacity for socially responsible leadership: Understanding norms and influences of race, gender, and sexual orientation. *NASPA Journal, 45*, 475–500.

Ehrlich, T. (2000). *Civic responsibility and higher education.* Phoenix, AZ: Oryx.

Engberg, M. E. (2007). Educating the workforce for the 21st century: A cross-disciplinary analysis of the impact of the undergraduate experience on students' development of a pluralistic orientation. *Research in Higher Education, 48*, 283–317.

Engberg, M. E. (2013). The influence of study away experiences on global perspective-taking. *Journal of College Student Development, 15*, 466–480.

Engberg, M. E., & Hurtado, S. (2011). Developing pluralistic skills and dispositions in college: Examining racial/ethnic group differences. *The Journal of Higher Education, 82*, 416–443.

Finley, A. (2012a). *A brief review on the evidence of civic learning in higher education.* For distribution at the Association of American Colleges & Universities annual meeting in conjunction with the release of *A Crucible Moment: College Learning & Democracy's Future.* Retrieved from http://www.aacu.org/civic_learning/crucible/documents/CivicOutcomesBrief.pdf

Finley, A. (2012b). Civic perspective narrative. In D. W. Harward (Ed.), *Civic provocations* (pp. xvi–xvii). Washington, DC: Bringing Theory to Practice.

Flanagan, C., Levine, P., & Settersten, R. (2009). *Civic engagement and the changing transition to adulthood.* CIRCLE. Retrieved from http://www.womenscolleges.org/files/pdfs/Civic_Engagement_Changing_Transition.pdf

Glynn, C. J., Huge, M. E., & Lunney, C. A. (2009). The influence of perceived social norms on college students' intention to vote. *Political Communication, 26*(1), 48–64.

Hatcher, J. (2011). Assessing civic knowledge and engagement. *New Directions for Institutional Research, 149,* 81–92.

Hurtado, S., Engberg, M. E., Ponjuan, L., & Landrewman, L. (2002). Students' precollege preparation for participation in a diverse democracy. *Research in Higher Education, 42,* 163–186.

Jacoby, B. (2009). *Civic engagement in higher education.* San Francisco, CA: Jossey-Bass.

Jameson, J. K., Clayton, P. H., & Ash, S. L. (2013). Conceptualizing, assessing, and investigating academic learning in service learning. In P. H. Clayton, R. G. Bringle, & J. A. Hatcher (Eds.), *Research on service learning: Conceptual frameworks and assessment* (Vol. 2A, pp. 85–110). Sterling, VA: Stylus.

Johnson, M. (2014). Predictors of college students engaging in social change behaviors. *Journal of College and Character, 15*(3), 149–163.

Keen, C. (2009). New efforts to assess civic outcomes. *Journal of College and Character, 10*(7), 1–6.

Kilgo, C. A., Pasquesi, K., Ezell Sheets, J. K., & Pascarella, E. T. (2014). The estimated effects of participation in service-learning on liberal arts outcomes. *International Journal of Research on Service-Learning and Community Engagement, 2,* 18–31.

Kirlin, M. (2003). *The role of civic skills in fostering civic engagement.* CIRCLE Working Paper 6. Center for Information and Research on Civic Learning and Engagement, University of Maryland. Retrieved from http://www.civicyouth.org/PopUps/WorkingPapers/WP06Kirlin.pdf

Klar, M., & Kasser, T. (2009). Some benefits of being an activist: Measuring activism and its role in psychological well-being. *Political Psychology, 30,* 755–776.

Knefelkamp, L. L. (2008). Civic identity: Locating self in community. *Diversity and Democracy, 11*(2), 1–3.

Lott, J. L. (2013). Predictors of civic values: Understanding student-level and institutional-level effects. *Journal of College Student Development, 54,* 1–16.

Lott, J. L., & Eagan, M. K. (2011). Assessing the psychometric properties of civic values. *Journal of Student Affairs Research and Practice, 48,* 333–347.

Malin, H., Ballard, P. J., & Damon, W. (2015). Civic purpose: An integrated construct for understanding civic development in adolescence. *Human Development, 58*, 103–130.

Mayhew, M. J., & Engberg, M. E. (2011). Promoting the development of civic responsibility: Infusing service-learning practices in first-year "success" courses. *Journal of College Student Development, 52*, 20–38.

McIntosh H., & Youniss J. (2010). Toward a political theory of political socialization of youth. In L. R. Sherrod , J. Torney-Purta, & C. A. Flanagan (Eds.), *Handbook of research on civic engagement in youth* (pp. 23–41). Hoboken, NJ: Wiley.

Mitchell, T. D., Battistoni, R. M., Keene, A. S., & Reiff, J., (2013). Programs that build civic identity: A study of alumni. *Diversity and Democracy, 16*(3), 22–23.

Moely, B. E., Mercer, S., Ilustre, V., Miron, D., & McFarland, M. (2002). Psychometric properties and correlates of the Civic Attitudes and Skills Questionnaire (CASQ): A measure of students' attitudes related to service-learning. *Michigan Journal of Community Service Learning, 8*(2), 15–26.

National Task Force on Civic Learning and Democratic Engagement. (2012). *A crucible moment: College learning & democracy's future.* Washington DC: Association of American Colleges & Universities.

Niemi, R. G., & Hanmer, M. J. (2010). Voter turnout among college students: New data and a rethinking of traditional theories. *Social Science Quarterly, 91*, 301–323.

O'Loughlin, M., & Unangst, C. (2006). *Democracy and college student voting* (3rd ed.). Salisbury, MD: The Institute for Public Affairs and Civic Engagement.

Parker, E. T., III, & Pascarella, E. T. (2013). Effects of diversity experiences on socially responsible leadership over four years of college. *Journal of Diversity in Higher Education, 6*, 219–230.

Pascarella, E. T., Edison, M., Nora, A., Hagedorn, L. S., & Terenzini, P. T. (1996). Influences on students' openness to diversity and challenges in the first year of college. *Journal of Higher Education, 67*, 174–195.

Pascarella, E. T., Ethington, C. A., & Smart, J. C. (1988). The influence of college on humanitarian/civic involvement values. *Journal of Higher Education, 59*, 412–437.

Pascarella, E.T., & Terenzini, P.T. (2005). *How college affects students: Vol. 2. A third decade of research.* San Francisco, CA: Jossey-Bass.

Reason, R. D., & Hemer, K. (2015). *Civic learning and engagement: A review of the literature on civic learning, assessment, and instruments.* Washington, DC: Association of American Colleges & Universities, Degree Qualifications Profile, Civic Learning Task Force. Retrieved from http://www.aacu.org/sites/default/files/files/qc/CivicLearningLiteratureReviewRev1-26-15.pdf

Ryder, A. J., Reason, R. D., Mitchell, J. J., Gillon, K., & Hemer, K. M. (2015). Climate for learning and students' openness to diversity and challenge: A critical role for faculty. *Journal of Diversity in Higher Education.* Advance online publication.

Saltmarsh, J., & Hartley, M. (Eds.). (2011). *To serve a larger purpose: engagement for democracy and the transformation of higher education.* Philadelphia, PA: Temple University Press.

Sherrod, L. R., Torney-Purta, J., & Flanagan, C. A. (Eds.). (2010). *Handbook of research on civic engagement* in youth. Hoboken, NJ: Wiley.

Shulman, H. C., & Levine, T. R. (2012). Exploring social norms as a group-level phenomenon: Do political participation norms exist and influence participation on college campuses? *Journal of Communication, 62,* 532–552.

Steinberg, K. S., Hatcher, J. A., & Bringle, R. G. (2011). Civic-minded graduate: A north star. *Michigan Journal of Community Service Learning, 18*(1), 19–33.

Syvertsen, A. K., Wray-Lake, L., Flanagan, C. A., Osgood, D. W., & Briddell, L. (2011). Thirty-year trends in U.S. adolescents' civic engagement: A story of changing participation and educational differences. *Journal of Research on Adolescence, 21,* 586–594.

Torney-Purta, J., Cabrera, J. C., Roohr, K. C., Liu, O. L., & Rios, J. A. (2015). Assessing civic competency and engagement in higher education: Research background, frameworks, and directions for next-generation assessment. *ETS Research Report Series, 2015*(2), 1–48.

Trostel, P. (2015). *It's not just the money: The benefits of college education to individuals and society.* Lumina Issue Papers. Retrieved from https://www.luminafoundation.org/news-and-events/its-not-just-the-money

Tufts University. (n.d.) *The National Study of Learning, Voting, and Engagements* (NSLVE). Retrieved from activecitizen.tufts.edu/research/nslve

Weerts, D. J., & Cabrera, A. F. (2015). Understanding civic identity in college: Profiles of civically engaged. *Journal of College and Character, 16*(1), 22–36.

Weerts, D. J., Cabrera, A. F., & Pérez Mejías, P. P. (2014). Uncovering categories of civically engaged college students: A latent class analysis. *The Review of Higher Education, 37,* 141–168.

Whitt, E. J., Edison, M. I., Pascarella, E. T., Terenzini, P. T., & Nora, A. (2001). Influences on students' openness to diversity and challenge in the second and third years of college. *Journal of Higher Education, 72,* 172–204.

Youniss, J., McLellan, J. A., & Yates, M. (1997). What we know about engendering civic identity. *The American Behavioral Scientist, 40,* 620–631.

STUDENT CIVIC LEARNING THROUGH SERVICE LEARNING

Instructional Design and Research

Stephanie T. Stokamer and Patti H. Clayton

W hat is meant by the term *civic learning* in service learning? What do we know about cultivating it through service learning courses? What do we still need to learn about how the variables of course design influence civic learning? These questions are the focus of this chapter.

Civic as a category of learning goals refers generally to capacities within individuals and communities to envision "a world that is increasingly peaceful, compassionate, just, inclusive, and verdant" (Clayton et al., 2014, p. 6) and to collaborate on change accordingly. Civic learning empowers citizens (referring not to legal status but rather to individuals who engage with their communities, local to global) to be actors rather than spectators in the processes that shape their own and others' lives, now and into the future. Within higher education, service learning can be a powerful mechanism for nurturing civic learning among students, instructors, staff, and community members.

Service learning has been empirically linked with numerous student civic learning outcomes. Yorio and Ye's (2012) meta-analysis of more than 15 years of studies on the student learning outcomes of service learning found that the pedagogy has a statistically significant effect on students' "understanding of social issues," (p. 11) which includes, for example, cultural awareness, working with diverse others, ethical reasoning, and understanding of and commitment to helping others. In her comprehensive review of research, Stokamer (2011) similarly concluded that "the literature strongly indicates the potential of [service learning] to develop civic competence" (p. 67). Despite consensus among scholars that "it is not enough to acknowledge civic competence as a goal—it must be deliberately integrated into educational practices in order to achieve desired civic outcomes," she found "surprisingly little research about . . . design of community based learning courses, and even less about design specific to developing civic competence" (p. 10). Bringle, Clayton, and Hatcher (2013) agree that "little is known about what variables under what conditions lead to desired outcomes or about why documented outcomes are, in fact, achieved" (p. 7).

The purpose of this chapter is to advance clarity in conceptualizing civic learning goals, facilitate intentionality in designing service learning accordingly, and encourage inquiry into the relationships between design and goals. We begin with examples of how we and others define *civic learning* and an overview of what needs to be investigated related to generating it through service learning. We share a conceptual model of three primary domains of design in service learning: (a) service, (b) academic activities (e.g., readings, classroom activities), and (c) critical reflection. Further, we draw on a systems model for instructional design as we consider possibilities for generating civic learning through intentional design within and across these domains. Informed by the potential of reflective, iterative, scholarly instructional design practice and the range of contextual factors that shape how service learning unfolds in any given setting, we call for inquiry into instructional design for civic learning and offer illustrative questions to guide research.

Civic Learning in Service Learning: What Do We Mean?

Service learning is widely understood to include three defining categories of learning: academic learning, civic learning, and personal growth (see Figure 1.3.1). This framework calls attention to the insufficiency of learning framed solely in academic terms and the possibilities for deeper, broader, and more integrated conceptions of learning. As indicated by the Venn diagram, these three categories of learning goals are both distinct and overlapping, producing the following domains of learning that are related to the civic: (a) civic learning, (b) civic learning-academic learning, (c) civic learning-personal growth, and (d) the triple intersection of civic learning-academic learning-personal growth.

Civic learning may function as a distinct category ("a" in Figure 1.3.1) that includes, for example, learning about the principles of democracy, the workings of governments, the history of public policies and social movements, or the processes of community building (in disciplines for which such topics are not academic content). Civic learning is also conceptualized at the intersection of the civic and academic domains ("b" in the Venn diagram).

Figure 1.3.1. Categories of learning in service learning.

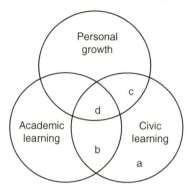

Battistoni (2013) lays out 12 frameworks for defining *citizenship* and associated civic learning goals in various academic disciplines. Saltmarsh (2005) frames civic learning as "illuminat[ing] the socially responsive aspects of disciplinary knowledge" (pp. 52–53) and highlighting the "public purposes and social responsibilities of professional education and practice" (p. 52). Critical thinking, problem-solving, and communication can be simultaneously academic and civic learning goals.

Examples of learning goals at the intersection of civic learning and personal growth ("c" in the Venn diagram) include understanding the assumptions and behavioral tendencies one brings to change-oriented collaboration with diverse others and the meaning one makes of one's own positionality (i.e., gender, ethnicity, class, sexual orientation, abilities) within broader social and cultural systems. These goals may also represent the triple intersection ("d" in the Venn diagram) in some disciplines, such as sociology in its study of critical race theory. In psychology, the triple intersection is illustrated by such learning goals for the major as "interact effectively with others," "exhibit self-efficacy," and "enhance teamwork capacity," all of which apply psychological theory to the self and to collaboration and change (American Psychological Association, 2013). The construct of the civic-minded graduate (CMG; Steinberg, Hatcher, & Bringle, 2011) includes, as two examples of the triple intersection, "sense of responsibility and commitment to use the knowledge gained in higher education to serve others" and "ability to communicate (written and oral) with others, as well as listen to divergent points of view" (p. 22). Other constitutive goals of the CMG that are, in some disciplines, integrative of civic learning, academic learning, and personal growth are related to consensus building, self-efficacy, and working with others.

Civic learning is thus conceptualized in a variety of ways. *Practitioner-scholars*—a term we use to indicate any individuals who partner in service learning with a spirit of inquiry and who connect their learning with that of others so as to advance knowledge and practice—should develop and make explicit their own operational conceptions of civic learning, perhaps informed by these or other frameworks. Doing so grounds their own instructional design and inquiry and may be useful to others conducting related practice, assessment, and research. Further articulating more specific learning outcomes that comprise these broad, and typically vague, learning goals is likewise necessary. Two well-established approaches for expressing otherwise too-general learning goals more precisely are (a) KSA, which stands for knowledge, skills, and attitudes (or values or dispositions) and is sometimes supplemented with behaviors (B) or identity (I) (chapter 1.2), and (b) Bloom's (1956) Taxonomy of the cognitive domain, which helps structure learning objectives developmentally (from lower to higher order reasoning) and lends itself readily to authentic assessment.

In the remainder of this section, we demonstrate such articulation of learning goals and subsequent specification into KSA(B/I) outcomes and Bloom's Taxonomy-based learning objectives in our own work. We find the paradigm of democratic civic engagement (Saltmarsh, Hartley, & Clayton, 2009) particularly relevant to conceptualizing civic learning. In contrast to the technocratic norms of the academy, which frame community-campus collaboration in terms of doing *for* those in need of expertise and resources, democratic engagement calls for being and doing *with* one another through collaboration and inquiry. Democratic engagement insists on "equality of respect for the knowledge and experience that everyone contributes to education and community building" (Saltmarsh, Hartley, & Clayton, 2009, p. 6). It positions everyone involved in service learning, including those otherwise seen as "the served," as cocreators in asking questions; envisioning alternative futures; and designing, implementing, and evaluating collaborative change efforts.

Grounded in this framework, we especially value the following three conceptions of civic learning: (a) *inclusivity*, which has at its core capacities to think beyond the single perspective of one's own worldview and act accordingly; (b) *criticality*, which has at its core capacities to recognize and challenge enshrined structural inequities that limit social justice; and (c) *cocreation*, which has at its core capacities to bring an asset-based orientation to collaboration and to integrate the knowledge, perspectives, and resources of all partners in determining the questions to be addressed, possibilities to be pursued, and strategies for collaborating effectively and with integrity. Table 1.3.1 provides illustrative examples of how we unpack these broad learning goals.

We use this unpacking throughout the chapter to exemplify how clearly articulated civic learning goals can guide the design of service learning courses

TABLE 1.3.1.

Examples of Unpacking Civic Learning Goals

Learning Goal	Sample Unpacking per KSA(B/I)	Sample Unpacking per Bloom's Taxonomy
Inclusivity	Skills: listen attentively to unfamiliar or contrary perspectives Attitudes: hold multiple worldviews in tension rather than immediately privileging one over another; curiosity regarding nondominant perspectives	Analysis: compare and contrast one's own and others' worldviews, what has shaped them, and how they influence particular interactions
Criticality	Knowledge: recognize historical, political, cultural forces that impede equity Attitudes: accept responsibility for how one's choices and actions may reinforce structures that underlie injustice Behaviors: modify one's language so as not to default to using words that assume hierarchy	Analysis: determine the causes and consequences of assumptions (e.g., about knowledge, about power) that underlie various cultural and disciplinary canons Evaluation: critically evaluate levels of equity in access to various sources of power in given contexts
Cocreation	Knowledge: realize the forces within and around us that nurture and hinder cocreation Skills: give and receive constructive critique Identity: see oneself as a cocontributor to the collective shaping of communities through civic action	Application: provide examples of the presence and absence of asset- and deficit-based orientations in a given encounter Evaluation: critically evaluate the influence of concepts from the discipline (e.g., verbal and nonverbal communication) on cocreative dynamics

and provide focus for research. Though we are committed to these learning goals in our own work and also find that they resonate with many colleagues, other practitioner-scholars may or may not find our thinking about civic learning goals relevant to their contexts and commitments. Our intention is to encourage and support instructional design and research that are customized to any particular conceptions of civic learning.

Generating Civic Learning in Service Learning: What Do We Need to Know?

Battistoni (2013) identifies "factors . . . [we] must pay attention to . . . to be successful in achieving desired civic learning outcomes" (p. 122). He highlights: (a) "meaningfulness, duration, and intensity of the service and work students do in the community," (b) "tight connections with a curriculum intentionally designed with civic learning outcomes in mind," (c) "student voice in designing the community projects and making decisions related to the service learning curriculum and programming," (d) "community voice in designing the partnership with educational institutions, implementing the programs, and setting the civic learning outcomes for students," (e) "diversity in the experiences and populations involved," and (f) "critical reflection that generates civic meaning of the community-based experience" (p. 122).

However, with a few exceptions—such as Stokamer's (2011) research confirming the importance of curricular integration and diverse perspectives for civic learning (akin to Battistoni's [2013] [b] and [e])—studies have not typically collected data on the interplay between course design elements and civic learning outcomes. Kiely (2005) points out that although researchers have demonstrated the transformative potential of service learning on students' civic, moral, personal, and intellectual development, they have not explored the specific learning processes that have led to varied results within these domains. This gap limits the utility of the extant body of research for practitioner-scholars who want to design service learning effectively to generate such learning.

Battistoni (2013) suggests that the most significant shortcoming in existing research on civic learning is conceptualizing the independent and dependent variables in such a way as to clarify which specific practices influence civic learning outcomes. Further, most scholarship that does consider instructional design variables has been dominated by single course, self-report descriptions or surveys and use of untriangulated data (Stokamer, 2011). More nuanced research that investigates the relationships between teaching practices (independent variables) and civic learning outcomes (dependent variables) is needed.

Instructional Design in Service Learning: A Systems Approach

Better positioning service learning practitioner-scholars to engage in intentional design for civic learning and associated inquiry into the relationships between design choices and learning outcomes requires focused attention on the constitutive design domains of service learning courses. Figure 1.3.2 provides a conceptual framework for these domains, which integrate selected aspects of Stokamer's (2011) pedagogical elements of service learning with Ash and Clayton's (2009b) components of service learning.

As with the intersections among categories of learning (i.e., civic learning, academic learning, personal growth) explored in Figure 1.3.2, the interplay among these design domains is particularly salient. The paradigm of democratic civic engagement emphasizes connection and interdependence; when applied to course design, it evokes systems thinking. Dick and Carey (1978) developed an instructional design model that frames the relationships among various aspects of teaching and learning as a system. They suggest that it is the *interaction* of such aspects of a course as materials, activities, and learning environments, to name a few, that leads to students achieving desired outcomes. Their model shifts thinking about course design from an additive to an *integrative orientation*, one that highlights dynamic and complex interrelationships. Stokamer (2011) similarly applies this way of thinking about course design as a system to service learning, advocating an interactive model in which pedagogical elements are understood to be and designed to be "mutually reinforcing and equally necessary for civic competence" (p. 67). In this section we highlight key design considerations within each domain (service, academic activities, and critical reflection) and explore the interplay among the domains from a systems perspective.

Figure 1.3.2. Design domains in service learning.

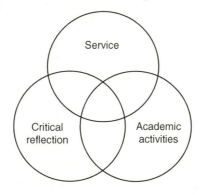

Service

Practitioner-scholars can be guided by their civic learning goals when collaboratively determining service tasks. Although arranging for meaningful
service in service learning courses may be daunting even without considering
specific learning outcomes, this component of the pedagogy is the conceptual linchpin for civic learning in that action is not just the application or
culmination of learning but an integral part of it. When designed to align
with civic (and other) learning goals, service provides an experiential foundation for such learning.

Several studies have concluded that the longer the duration of service the
better, for both community and student outcomes (Astin & Sax, 1998; Smith,
2008). Acknowledging the logistical and relational challenges of short-term
partnerships (as in the case of an academic semester), longer stretches of
time may enable encountering diverse worldviews and the systems of power
and privilege that underlie the public issues in question as well as cocreating
the purposes and processes of service learning activities. Such experiences
confront students (indeed, all partners) with the need for associated learning related to inclusivity, criticality, and cocreation and the opportunity to
achieve such learning through critical reflection focused accordingly.

Although critical reflection can generate learning of a particular concept
through examination of an experience in which the concept is notably absent,
service is generally designed to immerse learners in settings, processes, and
interactions in which the concept in question is present and can be critically
examined. Students may thus be well positioned to compare and contrast
diverse worldviews (inclusivity) through service tasks that enlist their capacity to listen or document, such as through coproducing oral histories with
community members. Community-engaged participatory research is a type
of service that offers a particularly concrete way for all partners to build such
civic skills as giving and receiving constructive feedback and to develop civic
identities as cogenerators of knowledge (cocreation).

A specific example of designing service to provide an experiential seedbed
for civic learning as we define it is a project in southwest Virginia. Siemers,
Harrison, Clayton, and Stanley (2015) describe a partnership among a college, local residents, and a museum in which service involves "organiz[ing]
neglected documents that tell otherwise unknown stories of local African
Americans from slavery through the twentieth century . . . and using [them]
to reveal glimpses of otherwise invisible strands in the history of this place
and these people" (p. 103). Incorporating encounters with silenced voices and
systems of oppression, the service provides a basis for the reflective development of capacities related to criticality (e.g., knowledge of historical, political,
and cultural forces that impede equity). The partners are "re-peopling public

memory and shaping public conversations and local public policy" (p. 103), positioning everyone involved as coeducators, colearners, and cogenerators of knowledge and thereby providing opportunities to examine challenges associated with these counternormative identities. The project also holds learning potential related to inclusivity in that it "surfac[es] perspectives that traditionally may have been silenced or ignored and invit[es] them into conversation with the more visible yet often unquestioned narrative" and thus "requires us to hold rather than dismiss or diminish the inevitable tensions" (p. 103).

Academic Activities

Little guidance exists for service learning practitioner-scholars related to the selection of texts and the design of classroom activities that might be most useful in cultivating civic learning—in general or per any particular conception of civic learning. Both the nature of academic activities and their content can be designed through the lens of civic learning goals.

Axlund, Renner, and Cress's (2009) survey of faculty revealed that although 38% reported discussing civic responsibility or local political issues in class, only 24% assigned readings focused on civic learning goals. Beyond underutilization of civic readings, the selection of texts can easily default to an established and quite possibly nondiverse or noncritical canon. Without careful thought to their selection and use, texts can limit exposure to diverse perspectives, sustain problematic narratives of power, and reinforce rigid and limited conceptions of knowledge, hindering learning related to civic learning goals of inclusivity, criticality, and cocreation unless critical reflection is used with care to make visible and trouble the texts' limitations.

Readings and other "texts" (e.g., films, podcasts, policy briefs, reports, websites) can also, however, introduce students (all partners) to diverse worldviews (inclusivity), examples of institutionalized and grassroots power (criticality), and the various expertise and resources brought to the collaboration by the partners (cocreation) while providing background information as context for service. All partners contributing to the selection of texts most relevant to the learning and service goals and cofacilitating how the texts are interrogated may help ensure a well-designed and well-used set of readings. Non-text-based modalities may be particularly useful in conveying and supporting critical exploration of nondominant perspectives (inclusivity). Use of oral narratives, embodied activities, artistic expressions, music, and photographs or videos can, while sharing bodies of thought and raising key questions, also invite learners to analyze canonic assumptions about knowledge creation and dissemination (criticality).

Academic activities in and beyond the classroom can similarly provide firsthand experience with and opportunities to examine dynamics related to inclusivity, criticality, and cocreation (as examples of civic learning goals). Nontraditional speakers in the classroom and in non-traditional settings, such as in public community spaces and on site at partnering community organizations, can share perspectives that challenge dominant ideologies and thus offer a basis for critical comparison across worldviews (inclusivity). Observation exercises, role playing exercised, and power analysis activities can engage participants in critical examination of the ways in which language can reinforce or challenge hierarchy, including in the classroom setting itself (criticality). Collaborative problem-solving activities, including those designed primarily in support of academic learning, might be framed and reflected upon as instances of cocreation among group members that reveal asset- and deficit-based orientations to one another. Similarly, critical reflection might proceed and follow a structured debate activity to help participants determine and problematize the conditions under which they do and do not tend to listen attentively to unfamiliar or contrary perspectives (inclusivity).

As a specific example of such intentional design of academic activities toward these learning goals, Siemers and colleagues (2015) share a service learning project in Alaska that "brought together students, faculty, and staff from two colleges along with community members and agencies to create a dialogue around climate change, a controversial and pressing issue with direct impact on communities in the state" (p. 102). The focal point of the project was an exhibit of visual art, poems, public presentations, and scientific writing that was "designed to utilize story and creative expression in interchanges that gave equal space to a wide range of perspectives and nurtured interconnectivity among various knowledge and value systems" (pp. 102–103). Texts and activities explicitly incorporated "a wide range of perspectives and nurtured interconnectivity among various knowledge and value systems": "Traditional story . . . talk circles, walking the land, and interacting with elders [who] gave voice to changes in the natural world over time . . . factored alongside technical reports and ocean acidification studies" (p. 103). Such design elements provided a basis for the reflective development of dispositions to hold multiple worldviews in tension rather than immediately privileging one over another (inclusivity) and for analysis of cultural assumptions about knowledge (criticality). "Shared stories of place [to] bridge perceived boundaries and nurture a sense of community through distributing expertise and enabling shared meaning making and the co-generation of knowledge" (p. 103) provided opportunities for learning related to cocreation.

Critical Reflection

Eyler and Giles' (1999) landmark study concluded "we have discovered that the learning in service-learning is in the questions" (p. 207) and thereby firmly established the necessity of intentionally designing questions that guide meaning making through critical reflection in order for learners to achieve and demonstrate learning. More is known about the influence of design variables in critical reflection on student learning outcomes than is the case with the two other design domains we consider here (Stokamer, 2011). We are aware of no studies, however, that comprehensively examined variables related to critical reflection specifically in terms of their role in learners' attainment of well-articulated civic learning goals.

Particularly relevant to civic learning outcomes, including but not limited to our own conceptions (i.e., inclusivity, criticality, cocreation), is the adjective *critical* in reflection, which can be framed from the following different but related intellectual traditions that are both especially salient to civic learning: (a) critical thinking and (b) critical theory. The critical thinking connotation frames critical reflection as "a cognitive and metacognitive activity that both generates learning . . . and builds capacities to think about thinking (which can enhance the quality of reasoning and of how that reasoning manifests in and is informed by action)" (Norris, Siemers, Clayton, Weiss, & Edwards, in press). Using the critical theory sense of the adjective, Brookfield (2009) sets critical reflection in terms of "analyzing commonly held ideas and practices for the extent to which they perpetuate economic inequity, deny compassion, foster a culture of silence and prevent people from realizing a sense of common connectedness" (p. 298). Mitchell (2008) applies critical theory to service learning, distinguishing between traditional and critical approaches to the pedagogy, and urges practitioner-scholars to integrate critical perspectives into their work to enhance social justice outcomes (chapter 2.6). Norris and colleagues bring these two conceptualizations of "critical" into conversation with one another in an attempt to fully harness the power of the adjective in deepening reflective processes and resultant civic learning outcomes in service learning.

Beyond the clear links to the civic learning goal of criticality as we conceptualize it, critical reflection understood in both of these ways can be designed as a space for all learners to engage with their ideas in relation to those of diverse others, advancing learning related to inclusivity and cocreation. Whitney and Clayton (2011) suggest that incorporating critical reflection effectively involves the following levels of intentional design: (a) an overall strategy for its role in a course or project (e.g. frequency, sequence, venues, participants, feedback processes) and (b) the particular mechanisms through which that strategy unfolds (i.e., prompts and assessment criteria that align with learning objectives to guide reflective meaning making in any of a variety of formats). A critical reflection strategy designed such that all partners are, at one time or another, involved—as learners, in developing prompts, in giving and receiving feedback—may provide otherwise missed opportunities for civic learning. This may be especially the case if the experience of such a collaborative approach to reflection is itself critically reflected upon. For example, participants could examine their own tendencies to listen (or not) to unfamiliar or contrary perspectives as they reflect together and give one another feedback (inclusivity), their assumptions about who has knowledge and power in the collaboration (criticality), and the influence of concepts studied in the course on the process of cocreating the strategy (cocreation).

An example structure that can guide the design of critical reflection mechanisms that are tightly aligned with desired civic (and other) learning goals is the DEAL model of critical reflection (see Ash & Clayton, 2009a, 2009b). This customizable, research-grounded model prompts learners to describe their experiences (D), examine them using prompts linked to learning goals (E), and then articulate (A) learning (L) in a way that leads to enhanced future action and learning (specifically, by answering four questions: What did I learn? How did I learn it? Why does this learning matter? What will I do in light of it?). Tools and rubrics affiliated with the DEAL model use Paul and Elder's (2001) standards of critical thinking and Bloom's (1956) Taxonomy to deepen the quality of thinking and practice and support metacognitive development within any category of learning (e.g., civic learning, academic learning, personal growth) through feedback and opportunities to refine thinking.

In terms of our conceptions of civic learning, for example, examine prompts can be written to (a) help learners become more aware of their own and others' worldviews and to analyze similarities and differences between them (inclusivity); (b) facilitate learners recognizing dynamics of power, privilege, oppression, and resistance and focusing their attention on the sources and significance of structural inequities, including the ways in which their own choices contribute to or challenge these structures (criticality); and (c) engage learners in critical evaluation of their own and others' identities and behaviors as cocreators and of the individual, interpersonal, social, and cultural forces that nurture and hinder these roles (cocreation). As a specific example, in a communications course a set of examine prompts that calls attention to the ways various forms of communication can either invite or silence others' voices, build or undermine trust, reinforce or enact alternatives to hierarchical norms, and positively or negatively influence interpersonal interactions might generate learning about cocreation in a way that is linked to academic learning.

Design Domains as a System

Simultaneously enriching and complicating service learning pedagogy and research is the interdependence of these three domains of instructional design. The domains comprise an overlapping, integrated, and interactive framework, building upon and playing off each other in the design of service learning courses. The act of service in well-designed, integrated service learning is inextricably intertwined with academic activities and critical reflection, and critical reflection is the practice that supports examination of service and texts in light of each other. Texts and service can each be used to provide information, perspectives, and questions to supplement the other; integrating critical reflection enables learners to bring elements of these two domains into dialogue with one another.

Activities in one domain can also be designed to compensate for, even put to good use, shortcomings in another. As an example related to our conceptualizations of civic learning, if an assigned reading implicitly or explicitly portrays people in the community as helpless "others" rather than as cocontributors to local solutions and visions, critically reflective conversations with community partners can interrogate its deficit-based orientation and bring to bear alternative perspectives. As illustrated previously with debates and problem-solving exercises, many academic activities function most effectively as learning opportunities when they, too, are framed as experiences upon which to reflect, particularly in light of their relationship with content and service.

As a specific example of a systems approach to designing service learning courses, Hess (in Clayton et al., 2014) designs the first days of his service learning course on natural resource measurements as a microcosm of the interdependent and synergistically interacting domains (service, academic activities, critical reflection) that characterize the course as a whole. Hess and his students partner with local community and governmental organizations around such issues as the preservation of public lands and the use of greenways. The first two days of the course consist of intentionally designed academic activities and critical reflection that introduce course content, frame the service learning project, invite students to think about learning, and establish connections between the discipline and broader public concerns. For example, students are asked to estimate the number of blades of grass in a nearby field, using methods of their choice and documenting their process, their questions, and the limitations of their results. Critical reflection on this process explores assumptions about teaching and learning and about measurement techniques, power dynamics within the academy and society more generally, teamwork, and the relationship between technical decisions and results citizens have reason to trust. This exercise engages students in a highly transparent way with the academic and civic content and processes they will be experiencing as they serve on a multifaceted natural resources project throughout the semester.

The core insight underlying Hess' systems approach is that service learning within the paradigm of democratic civic engagement is, intentionally and in almost every way, a deeply counternormative experience (Clayton & Ash, 2004; Howard, 1998). Many students have been socialized into hierarchy and individualism as characteristics of educational systems and have had little opportunity within the curriculum to develop capacities as responsible cocreators of their work and their world. Leveraging this counternormativity, the systems approach of synergistic design at the triple intersection of service, academic activities, and critical reflection launches the course in ways that have the potential to fundamentally transform students' (and facilitators') orientations to service and to learning. The design of the first two days of class— including its intentional surfacing of frustrations as expectations and default roles are challenged—helps students begin to shift their perspectives, practices, and identities as learners, emerging professionals, and civic actors.

The thorough intertwining of these domains of instructional design is perhaps most visible when the course design process itself is critically examined. The experiential nature of service learning means that practitioner-scholars must carefully design service, academic activities, and critical reflection in order to maximize learning but at the same time be open to and prepared to capitalize on unanticipated learning opportunities. Cultivating civic learning through service learning framed as democratic civic engagement requires intentionally and reflectively integrating both advance design and emergent possibilities that invariably arise in cocreated processes characterized by power sharing. Nimble, adaptable critical reflection may be a key to successfully navigating this tension, though how various partners engage with and facilitate learning from unexpected experiences has not, to our knowledge, been well studied. Indeed, given the complex interactions of service, academic activities, and critical reflection, designing for civic (and other) learning requires more attention than the field has yet paid to the nuances of how all partners as coeducators do, might, and should codesign service learning projects and courses and how they embrace what emerges through their collective experiences in service and in learning.

Inquiry Into Instructional Design: From Reflective Practice to Research

Practitioner-scholars can benefit from guidance in designing within and across these domains and an evidence base with which to explain their choices and on which to build their own scholarship. Developing an iterative, reflective practice (Stokamer, 2011) is a key step in expanding focus on instructional design to incorporate research that both draws on and contributes to what is known about cultivating civic (and other) learning through service learning. Such an orientation provides a helpful framing of the challenging work of cultivating civic learning as it suggests that practitioner-scholars do not have to get everything "right" the first time but are instead engaged in an ongoing learning process. Individual and collaborative reflection on practice, in the moment and as it evolves over time, helps turn difficulties and mishaps into questions and learning opportunities while also honoring successes and progress, thus enabling ongoing improvement. Further, iterative, reflective practice involves assessment of both learning outcomes and course design and establishes a context for scholarship (of teaching and learning, of engagement). It surfaces questions about the service learning process, insists on documenting design choices and rationales, and encourages systematic inquiry into outcomes and the relationship between design and outcomes. When this process is made public for others to critique and build upon—when it becomes scholarship—design and associated inquiry become even more deeply collaborative.

An example of how this iterative, reflective, scholarly practice of inquiry relates to our conceptualization of civic learning is Tilley-Lubbs's (2009) critical examination of her service learning course. Using autoethnography to investigate the challenges of integrating service learning into a course, she studied her design and the consequences of a service activity in which her students delivered clothes to the homes of people she had framed as in need of their help. As a result, she became acutely aware of a misalignment between her learning goals and her design. Contrary to the goals she held for her students' civic learning (akin to the learning goal of *criticality* as we define it) and her own commitment to reciprocity, the service she had designed recreated hegemonic identities of "haves" and "have-nots" among her students, herself, and local community members. Her reflective practice led her to shift the nature of the service in future semesters so that it had significant stakes for everyone involved and was cocreated with community members. This was not an easy transition but was necessary on several levels, including in terms of her students' civic learning and her own ongoing growth as an educator, a partner, and a citizen. Her example demonstrates the value of an iterative, reflective, scholarly approach to design, not just for one's own course but, when disseminated, for other practitioner-scholars seeking to integrate service, academic activities, and critical reflection effectively so as to generate civic learning.

Such an approach can be part of systematic inquiry into practice within and across the design domains discussed previously. Furthermore, research examining influences on processes and outcomes beyond these domains is necessary in order to generate and test theory about the conditions under which particular design choices might contribute to particular civic learning outcomes. Stokamer (2011) identified four categories of contextual factors that shape the practical realities within which service learning courses and projects are designed and implemented and, in turn, affect civic (and other) learning outcomes. The categories are (a) students (e.g., cognitive and moral development), (b) faculty (e.g., position with respect to rank or tenure), (c) higher education institutions (e.g., scheduling restrictions), and (d) community partners (e.g., the extent to which and ways in which they function as coeducators). For example, the number and type of local community organizations is likely to affect the design of service, departmental expectations may shape academic activities, and student development could (and should) guide how critical reflection unfolds. The type of higher education institution, its mission, and its academic focus may affect the entire design system.

Building on iterative, reflective, scholarly practice and with attention to contextual factors, systematic inquiry (i.e., research that integrates practice, measurement, theory, and design; chapter 1.1) on instructional design is needed to establish evidence-based guidance for practitioner-scholars seeking to cultivate specific civic learning outcomes. Such research will help the field move beyond simply tallying hours or categorizing courses as "service learning" or "not service learning" to more in-depth understanding of the significance of design choices in the domains of service, academic activities, and critical reflection with respect to civic outcomes. Moreover, because these domains interact and enhance each other, research that approaches all three as an instructional design system is particularly important. Although investigators have a sizable undertaking focusing on each domain independently, conducting research from a systems perspective and with the precision of definition we advocate holds great potential to enhance design of service learning courses and deepen associated civic learning outcomes.

In Table 1.3.2 we offer illustrative research questions for each of the design domains and for the design system as a whole. We note examples of design choices that can serve as independent variables or sample descriptors that could inform understanding in research focused on generating an evidence base to guide design for civic learning. Although we intentionally leave these research questions generic so as to speak to design related to any conception of civic learning, rather than focusing on our particular civic learning goals, we encourage practitioner-scholars to contextualize research questions in light of their own framings of civic learning.

Beyond specific questions such as these, we suggest four future directions for research on instructional design and civic learning. First, the sampling of research questions in Table 1.3.2 largely positions civic learning as the

TABLE 1.3.2

Inquiry Into Service Learning Course Design Domains for Civic Learning

Sample Research Questions	*Sample Descriptors/Variables*
Course Design Domain: Service	
What factors determine the relative influence of academic and civic learning goals on the design of service?	Conditions: program requirements, professional development, institutional mission, community involvement in course design, faculty interests, discipline
What characteristics of the service experience are most apt to confront learners firsthand with systems of power and privilege?	Types of service: organizational placement (direct service, indirect, or combination), advocacy, participation in public governance, community-engaged participatory research, grassroots organizing
Course Design Domain: Academic Activities	
In what ways do academic activities that involve taking civic action (e.g., writing a letter to a legislator) influence civic learning outcomes differently from those that do not?	Types of activities: action oriented (campus-based, political, advocacy, protest), research (interviews, papers), reflective (dialogue, papers)
What characterizes texts and in-class activities intended to prepare students for service learning, and what is their influence on subsequent civic learning outcomes?	Characteristics of preparation: site (community based, classroom), facilitators (community partner, instructor, both), framing of service ("for"/"with")
Course Design Domain: Critical Reflection	
What specific critical reflection mechanisms are practitioner-scholars using to facilitate examination of such civic issues as power and equity? Which generate authentic evidence of civic learning?	Techniques: equity- or power-specific prompts, intergroup dialogue, open-ended questions, games
Under what conditions does community partner feedback as an element of critical reflection strategies enhance student civic learning? Enhance community partner civic learning?	Feedback style: medium used, focused on content of ideas or on reasoning process or both; taking the form of questions or statements Feedback structure: when given, frequency, use of rubrics

(Continues)

TABLE 1.3.2. *(Continued)*

Sample Research Questions	Sample Descriptors/Variables
Design Domains as a System	
What are the primary challenges all partners face in bringing an intentional civic learning orientation to service, academic activities, and critical reflection? In what ways does a systems approach to design exacerbate or ameliorate these challenges?	Challenge descriptors: personal/work style, structural/institutional, collaboration-related, understanding of *civic*, student related, counternormativity
What sort of scaffolding supports partners in building capacities to integrate service, academic activities, and critical reflection as contributors to their learning?	Supports: use of a critical reflection model (e.g., DEAL), strategic approach, preparatory assignment, feedback, professional development, early and meaningful involvement of community partners in all elements of course design Structure: timing, frequency, duration of partnership over time
How do practitioner-scholars make decisions about one domain in light of the others and respond to changes in one that influence the others?	Characteristics of decision-making processes, degree of flexibility in response to unexpected learning opportunities

dependent variable and calls attention to the range of factors potentially influencing its attainment. Inquiry in the reverse direction—into the influence of conceptions of civic learning on instructional design choices—may be equally meaningful. Because constructions of *civic learning* vary so widely, the underlying framework that contextualizes research related to any particular definition may significantly influence both questions and findings. Positioning conceptions of civic learning as independent variables might also help problematize lack of specificity in articulating these learning goals and encourage increased precision.

Second, in addition to examining the influences of design on civic learning and vice versa, there are also many complexities within various conceptions of civic learning that warrant investigation. Using our learning goal of inclusivity as an example, how might practitioner-scholars hold in creative, synergistic tension the emphasis on thinking beyond the perspective of one's own worldview and other key civic capacities such as developing and using one's own voice? *Inclusivity*, as we define it, explicitly includes not immediately privileging any one lens on the world over others. How might practitioner-scholars best frame this dynamic so that engaging with it in service learning does not result in either diminishment of one's own narrative or uncritical adoption of others' perspectives—especially given the contextual factors that can make nuance difficult to retain?

Third, we see the contextual factors within which instructional design for civic learning operates as emblematic of the constraints that make the most significant social and environmental problems of our time so intractable. Understanding and resolving intransigent issues through processes of democratic civic engagement means working with, through, and around personnel and personalities, institutional structures and cultures, and relationship strengths and foibles. Exploring the ways in which practitioner-scholars embrace the realities of their contexts, engage creatively with the difficulties they face, and reframe challenges as opportunities for growth may be instructive for students (all partners) learning how to engage with a world in which making a difference is likewise complicated by mundane realities and enshrined systems. In our experience, community engagement professionals regularly encounter the influence of contextual factors that sometimes constrain and sometimes advance the work of the full range of partners involved in service learning. They are well positioned to investigate the contextual factors that affect design for civic learning and to develop strategies for engaging with them.

Fourth, and relatedly, we would like to see research linking elements of the system of design variables to the ways in which all participants in service learning understand, navigate, and ultimately leverage challenges to civic action, at all levels (e.g., individual, organizational, cultural). Better understanding how the forces that otherwise silence and shut down agency can, instead, be deliberately used to advance civic learning, and change is key to conceptualizing and designing for the civic learning at the heart of democratic civic engagement in the twenty-first century.

Conclusion

Democracy presents practical challenges and is fraught with tensions—which, if we do not shy away, can be embraced and leveraged to more fully strengthen both civic processes and civic outcomes. So too does instructional design for and research on civic learning confront us with difficulties that can push us toward innovative ways of thinking about teaching and inquiry. In light of significant challenges amid great potential, we encourage practitioner-scholars to build their capacities to design and implement service learning in ways that tap its rich civic learning potential and to be especially wary of practices that undermine civic learning outcomes. Perhaps the greatest opportunity and challenge is engaging all partners in the shared task of designing and investigating civic learning processes and outcomes. Thus understood and undertaken as democratic civic engagement, service learning has significant potential to strengthen citizens, communities, and democracy itself.

References

American Psychological Association. (2013). *APA guidelines for the undergraduate psychology major* (Version 2.0). Washington, DC: Author.

Ash, S. L., & Clayton, P. H. (2009a). Generating, deepening, and documenting learning: The power of critical reflection for applied learning. *Journal of Applied Learning in Higher Education, 1*(1), 25–48.

Ash, S. L., & Clayton, P. H. (2009b). *Learning through critical reflection: A tutorial for students in service-learning* (Instructor version). Raleigh, NC: Authors.

Astin, A. W., & Sax, L. J. (1998). How undergraduates are affected by service participation. *Journal of College Student Development, 39*, 251–263.

Axlund, R., Renner, T., & Cress, C. M. (2009). *Faculty engagement in service-learning and community-based research.* WRCCC Survey Data Summary. Bellingham, WA: Washington Campus Compact.

Battistoni, R. M. (2013). Civic learning through service learning: Conceptual frameworks and research. In P. H. Clayton, R. G. Bringle, & J. A. Hatcher (Eds.), *Research on service learning: Conceptual frameworks and assessment* (Vol. 2A, pp. 111–132). Sterling, VA: Stylus.

Bloom, B. S. (1956). *Taxonomy of educational objectives: Handbook I. Cognitive domain.* New York, NY: David McKay.

Bringle, R. G., Clayton, P. H., & Hatcher, J. A. (2013). Research on service learning: An introduction. In P. H. Clayton, R. G. Bringle, & J. A. Hatcher (Eds.), *Research on service learning: Conceptual frameworks and assessments* (Vol. 2A, pp. 3–25). Sterling, VA: Stylus.

Brookfield, S. (2009). The concept of critical reflection: Promises and contradictions. *European Journal of Social Work, 12*, 293–304.

Clayton, P. H., & Ash, S. L. (2004). Shifts in perspective: Capitalizing on the counter-normative nature of service-learning. *Michigan Journal of Community Service-Learning, 11*(1), 59–70.

Clayton, P. H., Hess, G., Hartman, E., Edwards, K. E., Shackford-Bradley, J., Harrison, B., & McLaughlin, K. (2014). Educating for democracy by walking the talk in experiential learning. *Journal of Applied Learning in Higher Education, 6*, 3–36.

Dick, W., & Carey, L. M. (1978). *The systematic design of instruction.* New York, NY: HarperCollins.

Eyler, J. S., & Giles, Jr., D. E. (1999). *Where's the learning in service-learning?* San Francisco, CA: Jossey-Bass.

Howard, J. P. F. (1998). Academic service learning: A counternormative pedagogy. *New Directions for Teaching and Learning, 73,* 21–29.

Kiely, R. (2005). A transformative learning model for service-learning: A longitudinal case study. *Michigan Journal of Community Service Learning, 12*(1), 5–22.

Mitchell, T. (2008). Traditional vs. critical service-learning: Engaging the literature to differentiate two models. *Michigan Journal of Community Service Learning, 14*(2), 50–65.

Norris, K. E., Siemers, C., Clayton, P. H., Weiss, H. A., & Edwards, K. E. (in press). Critical reflection and civic mindedness: Expanding conceptualizations and practices. In C. Dolgon, T. Eatman, & T. Mitchell (Eds.), *The Cambridge handbook of service-learning and community engagement.* Boston, MA: Cambridge University Press.

Paul, R. P., & Elder, L. (2001). *The miniature guide to critical thinking.* Santa Rosa, CA: Foundation for Critical Thinking (www.criticalthinking.org).

Saltmarsh, J. (2005). The civic promise of service learning. *Liberal Education, 91*(2), 50–55.

Saltmarsh, J., Hartley, M., & Clayton, P. H. (2009). *Democratic engagement white paper.* Boston, MA: New England Resource Center for Higher Education.

Siemers, C., Harrison, B., Clayton, P. H., & Stanley, T. (2015). Engaging place as partner. *Michigan Journal of Community Service Learning, 22*(1), 101–104.

Smith, M. C. (2008). Does service learning promote adult development? Theoretical perspectives and directions for research. *New Directions for Adult and Continuing Education, 118,* 5–15.

Steinberg, K., Hatcher, J. A., & Bringle, R. G. (2011). Civic-minded graduate: A north star. *Michigan Journal of Community Service Learning, 18*(1), 19–33.

Stokamer, S. T. (2011). *Pedagogical catalysts of civic competence: The development of a critical epistemological model for community-based learning* (Doctoral dissertation). Available from ProQuest Dissertations and Theses database. (UMI No. 3468983).

Tilley-Lubbs, G. A. (2009). Good intentions pave the way to hierarchy: A retrospective autoethnographic approach. *Michigan Journal of Community Service Learning, 16*(1), 59–68.

Whitney, B. C., & Clayton, P. H. (2011). Research on the role of reflection in international service learning. In R. G. Bringle, J. A. Hatcher, & S. G. Jones (Eds.), *International service learning: Conceptual frameworks and research* (pp. 145–187). Sterling, VA: Stylus.

Yorio, P. I., & Ye, F. (2012). A meta-analysis on the effects of service-learning on the social, personal, and cognitive outcomes of learning. *Academy of Management Learning & Education, 11*(1), 9–27.

PART TWO

THEORETICAL FRAMEWORKS FOR RESEARCH ON SERVICE LEARNING AND STUDENT CIVIC OUTCOMES

SOCIAL PSYCHOLOGY AND STUDENT CIVIC OUTCOMES

Robert G. Bringle

As a discipline focused on the scientific study of behavior and the mind, psychology has much to offer research on service learning. Analyses have been offered through the lens of the following subdisciplines: developmental psychology (e.g., Brandenberger, 2013), cognitive psychology (Fitch, Steinke, & Hudson, 2013), and community psychology (Reeb & Folger, 2013). Social psychology also provides a rich source for advancing understanding of service learning and its outcomes, including civic outcomes. Social psychology is the scientific study of how people perceive and relate to one another. Topics of research include social perception and cognition, attitudes and persuasion, prejudice and discrimination, friendships and close relationships, group and intergroup behavior, and prosocial and antisocial behavior. Social psychology was pioneered by psychologists seeking answers to real-world questions with action research that came out of their experiences during and after World War II. Kurt Lewin said, "There is nothing so practical as a good theory" (1951, p. 169). This statement was an exhortation to psychologists to undertake theory-driven research that would ultimately effect positive change in the world.

This chapter reviews four theoretical social psychological perspectives that can contribute to future research on service learning and civic outcomes: identity, emotions, motivations, and attitudes. Implications from each of these perspectives for practice are also explored.

Margaret Brown provided input for and feedback on the development of this chapter.

Social Psychological Theories and Perspectives

Because social psychology covers a broad range of topics, familiarity with two guiding tenets (Ross & Nisbett, 2011) brings coherence to seemingly disparate bodies of theory and research. First, situations are powerful determinants of behavior. Awareness of the power of situations can guide service learning instructors to be more intentional when planning and implementing courses, selecting community-based experiences to produce intended outcomes, and designing reflection activities (chapter 1.3). An analysis of situations can also help students become more sensitive to and better informed about how situations influence the behavior of themselves and others in civic contexts. Second, subjective perception of the world is more important in predicting behavior than is objective reality. Awareness of the nature of subjective perceptions provides a basis for studying how reflection and interpretations of service experiences are related to civic outcomes. In addition, an understanding of perceptions can improve students' ability to interact effectively with diverse persons and points of view.

Previously, social psychological analyses of service learning focused on interpersonal relationships (Bringle & Clayton, 2013; Bringle & Hatcher, 2002); attitude, cognition, and behavior (e.g., Bringle, 2005; Bringle, Clayton, & Bringle, 2015); intergroup contact theory (Bringle, 2005; Erickson & O'Connor, 2000); analyses of attributions by those serving and those being served (Bringle & Velo, 1998); and Nadler's theory of intergroup social dominance (Brown, 2011a, 2011b). Summaries of four additional social psychological theories are offered to guide theory-based research into the processes and civic outcomes of service learning.

Self and Civic Identity

The development of one's sense of self begins in infancy and continues throughout one's life. Especially during adolescence and early adulthood, civic identity develops and, most importantly, can change as a product of interactions with others (chapter 2.3; Yates & Youniss, 1998; Youniss & Yates, 1999). In addition, identities are a function of memberships in groups (e.g., Tajfel & Turner, 1986). Recently, the comprehensive cognitive-developmental model of social identity integration (Amiot, de la Sablonniere, Terry, & Smith, 2007; Amiot, de la Sablonniere, Smith, & Smith, 2015) describes how multiple social identities (e.g., civic, political, democratic, moral, activist, volunteer) develop over time and can eventually become integrated.

Bandura's self-efficacy is a function of success experiences, modeling others, and persuasion (Bandura, 1994). People with high self-efficacy are more likely to believe they can master challenging problems, recover from setbacks, and have a sense of well-being (see chapter 2.5). Social situations provide opportunities for social modeling (e.g., service learning experiences) that can increase self-efficacy and a sense of civic agency resulting in civic action (Astin, Vogelgesang, Ikeda, & Yee, 2000; Reeb & Folger, 2013).

Emotions and Moods

Emotions (e.g., sadness, fear, happiness, surprise) and moods (e.g., euphoria, empathy, compassion) can influence civic actions and contribute to civic identities. In particular, research evidence supports empathy's role in developing civic motives and behaviors (Batson, 1991), although motives and behaviors related to empathy may be mediated by the principle of caring (Wilhelm & Bekkers, 2010). Empathy supplies the affective and motivational foundation for moral development (Eisenberg & Eggum, 2009) and promotes helping and prosocial behaviors (Batson, 1991; Eisenberg & Miller, 1987). Empathy can have trait-like qualities (Davis, 1983; Eisenberg & Miller, 1987) and state-like qualities (Batson, Ahmad, & Tsang, 2002). Trait-like aspects can be construed as being a component of identity. Theory and research on trait-like qualities have addressed a stable prosocial and altruistic personality trait (Batson, 1991; Eisenberg et al., 1999) and the virtue of generosity as an enduring attribute (Collette & Morrisey, 2007). State-like empathy, an emotional reaction that occurs in a particular situation, is a function of perceived similarity between the observer and the other person, or it can result from priming instructions to take the other person's point of view (Batson, Turk, Shaw, & Klein, 1995).

Batson and Ahmad (2009) construed empathy as either a cognitive response (e.g., imaging one's self in the other person's circumstances, imaging what the other person's perspective is) or an emotional response (e.g., emotional concern for the other person, experiencing emotions of the other person). Depending on the attribution, empathic distress may be transformed in whole or in part into (a) sympathetic distress when the cause is unknown or beyond the victim's control (e.g., illness, accident, loss); (b) empathy-based guilt when one is the cause, when one's efforts to help have not prevented or alleviated the victim's distress (Batson & Weeks, 1996), or guilt over inaction when one has not tried to help; (c) empathic anger when someone else is the cause, even if the victim is distressed and not angry; or (d) empathy over injustice, when there is a discrepancy between a victim's fate and what is deserved (Hoffman, 2010). Each of these types of manifestations of empathy can provide a basis for understanding civic action.

Motivation

Motivation is presumed to activate behavior. Why are some persons intrinsically motivated for civic involvement, whereas others only become involved when they are asked or there are external inducements, and still others show low levels of civic involvement regardless of incentives? Self-determination theory (Deci & Ryan, 2002) examines extrinsic and intrinsic motivation and has important implications for how service learning experiences can be designed to develop motivation in unmotivated students, how intrinsic motivation for civic involvement can be enhanced, and how erosion of intrinsic motivation among students who possess it can be prevented. According to self-determination theory, people have three psychological needs that contribute to intrinsic motivation: relatedness, competence, and autonomy. However, different strategies can be used by educators for students with different levels of motivation. Unmotivated students can be motivated toward civic engagement by external rewards, inducements with instrumental value, and external requirements. However, the civic involvement will end when the external motivators are removed. The challenge for educators is to promote the growth of autonomous regulation of civic involvement and the integration of civic behaviors into a student's self-concept initially through relatedness and the development of competency (chapter 2.3). Thus, educators face the challenge of nurturing the enhancement of self-determined behavior that is fully integrated with the self and inherently satisfying in students who are motivated by a mix of internal and external forces.

The Volunteer Process Model (Snyder & Omoto, 2008) examines the antecedents, experiences, and consequences of volunteering at the individual, interpersonal, organizational, and societal level. Within this model Clary and colleagues (1998) developed the Volunteer Functions Inventory to asses both self-focused and other-focused motivations for volunteering: (a) values (altruistic concern for others), (b) understanding (opportunities for new learning), (c) social (being with friends), (d) career (clarify vocational choices), (e) protective (avoiding guilt), and (f) enhancement (personal growth, positive feelings). Jiranek, Kals, Humm, Strubel, and Wehner (2013) added a social justice motive. The strength of the motives, the match of motives to outcomes, and the diversity of motives are assumed to support persistence in volunteering. The model posits that different individuals can engage in the same civic action for different motives. Furthermore, motives are dynamic, and what attracts a volunteer to be engaged may not be the same motive that subsequently sustains the volunteering (Snyder & Omoto, 2008). This suggests that engaging students in community service for one reason (e.g., it is required) can be transformed into other motives (e.g., caring about an individual or a social issue).

Batson and colleagues (2002) differentiate four types of motivation for community involvement: egoism, altruism, collectivism, and principlism. Their typology ranges from interest in one's own welfare (egoism); to interest in another individual (altruism); a group of persons including groups of which the person is a member (collectivism); and, broadly, everyone based on moral principles (principlism). They note that each of these types of involvement and motives has strengths and weakness. They suggest ways to design experiences that can overcome weaknesses and build on the strengths of one or more of the motives in order to promote civic engagement.

Attitudes

Attitude is a central concept in social psychology because of the presumption that attitudes are a precursor to behavior—how a person feels toward an issue, entity, object, or person will influence subsequent behavior. Research demonstrates that attitudes guide behavior under particular conditions: when they are specific (e.g., attitudes toward an act versus very general attitudes), stable, consistent, accessible, and based on direct experience and when situational constraints and social norms are relatively weak (Baron, Byrne, & Branscombe, 2007).

Attitude change is a central interest to social psychologists because of the corollary presumption that changing attitudes will result in corresponding behavioral change. Most research has focused on the influence of different types of persuasive communications on attitude change. This is particularly relevant to the educational context because some educators have, as a learning objective, changing students' attitudes (e.g., toward social justice, marginalized groups, climate change) through persuasive communications (e.g., lectures, readings, community experiences). Much of the research on attitude change has been focused on who says what to whom and with what effect (Baron et al., 2007). Communicator variables have included trustworthiness, credibility, and attractiveness. Message variables have included one-sided versus two-sided messages, amount and quality of information presented, and fear approaches versus factual presentations. Recipient variables have included prior attitudes (e.g., strength, accessibility), motivation, personal relevance, and mood.

The elaboration likelihood model posits two different kinds of attitude change processes: peripheral and central (Petty & Cacioppo, 1986). When motivation is low or capacity to process information is low, peripheral processing results from paying attention to surface characteristics like the communicator's attributes (e.g., expertise) or the nature of the communication (e.g., number of arguments presented). When motivation and ability are high, central processing, which is a more deliberate, effortful, and thoughtful cognitive evaluation of the quality of the information presented in the communication, is more likely to occur. Central processing produces attitude change that is more stable and less susceptible to counterarguments. Given this difference, educators would do well to aspire to having students critically examine evidence about civic and social issues through central processing in order to produce enduring changes.

The theory of planned behavior (Ajzen, 1991) details how an attitude is only one component that determines behavioral intentions and the possibility of subsequent behavior. In addition to attitudes, the theory posits that social norms (i.e., the expectations others have for an individual's behavior) and perceived behavioral control (i.e., one's capacity to perform a particular behavior) influence behavioral intentions. Furthermore, the theory states that these components may be differentially weighted. Thus, civic behaviors may be tied to personal attitudes, and/or social influences (e.g., peer influence), and/or perceived self-efficacy. Finally, the theory makes salient the role of cognitive beliefs as a basis for each of the three components. Although this theory is primarily concerned with the manner in which cognitions and attitudes determine behavior, Bringle and colleagues (2015) examined the ways in which behavior and behavioral change can influence civic attitudes and civic cognitions.

Social Psychology in Past Service Learning Research

Social psychological theory and research have had only a limited presence in extant research that has directly focused on service learning. This is in spite of the high relevance of research evaluating social psychological theories that focus on volunteering, reactive and deliberate altruistic behaviors, values, motivations associated with helping others, activism and political involvement, and attitudes toward community involvement.

Self and Civic Identity

Civic identity is posited to be a superordinate educational goal for service learning (see chapter 2.3; Bringle et al., 2015), resulting from democratic community experiences, democratic partnerships, and appropriate reflection (Bringle et al., 2015; chapter 1.3). Metz, McLellan, and Youniss (2003) found that service focused on aiding persons and social issues (versus other types of service or no service) resulted in the development of aspects of civic identity in high school students such as concern for social issues, future unconventional civic intentions, and future intended service. Bringle and Hahn (2015) found that civic-mindedness was associated with civic identity.

Jones and Abes (2004) used qualitative methods to study the effects of service learning on identity development and self-authorship (see chapter 2.3). They found that two to four years after service learning experiences, students reported a more integrated identity in regard to thinking about self and relationships with others, openness to new ideas and experiences, and future civic commitments. Batchelder and Root (1994), when comparing service learning students to a comparison group, found similar results of gains for service learning students on three components of civic identity: prosocial decision making, prosocial reasoning, and identity processing.

Although some consideration has been given to social identities in the service learning literature (e.g., civic identity, moral development, political identity; e.g., Mitchell, Visconti, Keene, & Battistoni, 2011; Scott, 2012), little research has reflected the social psychology research and theories related to identity formation, development, and measurement (see chapter 2.3).

Emotions and Moods

Several studies have investigated empathy as a mediating variable and an outcome variable. Brown (2011b) found that empathy mediated the effects of community service on decreases in social dominance orientation. Lundy (2007) found that service learning was associated with gains in empathy scores across a semester. Similar results have been found for international service learning (Kiely, 2005) and service learning students working with elderly populations (Green, Johnson, & Stewart, 1998; Wilson, 2011). Bringle, Hedgepath, and Stephens (2015) developed an alternative measure of trait empathic anger (i.e., becoming angry rather than sad as a result of observing suffering) and found that those scoring higher on empathic anger were altruistic, not aggressive, oriented toward advocacy rather than charitable service, endorsed a social justice perspective, reported higher levels of civic-mindedness, and were active in communities in ways independent of the campus.

Motivation

According to self-determination theory, people have three basic psychological needs that contribute to the development of intrinsic motivation: relatedness, competence, and autonomy. Pavey, Greitemeyer, and Sparks (2011) found that highlighting relatedness led to higher interest in volunteering, intentions to volunteer, and donating more money to charity. They also found that writing about relatedness experiences promoted feelings of connectedness to others, which predicted greater prosocial intentions. Levesque-Bristol and

Stanek (2009) found that students who perceived the learning environment to support autonomy also reported increases in motivation (e.g., effort). Richards and Levesque-Bristol (2015) reported that community self-efficacy and situational intrinsic motivation predicted community engagement, cultural competence, and ethical leadership. Levesque-Bristol, Knapp, and Fisher (2010) demonstrated that well-designed service learning courses (e.g., involvement, in-class discussion, reflection) resulted in more motivation, better civic skills and problem solving, and higher appreciation for diversity over the course of the semester. Structured reflection (versus non-structured reflection) was associated with personal self-efficacy scores (Sanders, Oss, & McGeary, 2016).

Because of the centrality of choice, control, and autonomy to self-determination theory, research has examined the role of required versus optional community service. Bringle, Hatcher, Muthiah, and McIntosh (2001) analyzed conflicting findings regarding required versus optional service learning and speculated on how different constructs might explain the inconsistent results. Required versus optional participation in service learning is a gross variable that fails to directly measure students' perceived choice and autonomy. Bringle and colleagues noted that required service learning may still have the perception of choice, and optional service learning can have qualities that erode intrinsic motivation (e.g., use of deadlines, threats, and surveillance; Deci, Koestner, & Ryan, 1999; Deci & Ryan, 2002). Bringle and colleagues (2001) reported results that the quality of the learning environment and the degree to which academic content was integrated with the community service were both more important to attitudes of civic responsibility than was required or optional community service. Yorio and Ye's (2012) meta-analysis found that choice (rather than required participation in service learning) was associated with higher cognitive learning outcomes, but not understanding of social issues or personal insight.

Bringle and Hahn (2015) reported that civic-mindedness was significantly correlated with all six motives measured by the volunteer functions inventory (Clary et al., 1998). The strong association between the six motives and civic-mindedness suggests that the civic-minded students will likely have higher persistence and resiliency during community service experiences because of the strength and breadth of motives that support their engagement.

Attitudes

Attitude, and variations thereof, has been the dominant outcome variable in service learning research (e.g., beliefs, values, motives, dispositions) (chapter 1.2; Simons, 2015). In spite of its prevalence as a measured outcome, research on service learning and civic outcomes has failed to incorporate social psychology theories on attitudes (e.g., attitude formation, attitude change, stereotypes, discrimination). Furthermore, the service learning research has not yet reflected theories on the relationships between and among attitudes, cognition, behavioral intentions, motives, and behavior (Bringle et al., 2015).

Implications for Future Research

Social psychology provides a rich theoretical and empirical basis for studying students' civic outcomes from the perspective of the person, the situation, and the interaction of person and situation. Service learning affords students with the opportunity to (a) experience the multiplicity of real-world connections to course content, (b) see disciplinary concepts in connection with social issues and social systems in their communities, (c) consider how relationships with community partners contribute to their development, and (d) reflect on ways to be actively engaged with civic communities and members in social change. All of these perspectives provide opportunities for theory-based research on the processes and civic outcomes of service learning.

Self and Civic Identity

What are the situational factors that can be designed into service learning courses that contribute to the development of civic identity as an enduring attribute? The components posited by Bringle and colleagues (2015) that contribute to civic identity (i.e., democratic experiences, democratic partnerships, appropriate reflection activities) need to be evaluated for their relative contributions for integrating civic attitudes, values, beliefs, self-efficacy, and motives into civic identity, particularly for students with weak or poorly developed civic identities. How do different types of situations such as community placements and activities, various approaches to reflection, and past service experiences contribute to developing self-efficacy and shaping civic identity (chapter 1.3)? Invitations from an adult mentor or older peer were instrumental in developing civic purpose and civic identity in adolescents (Malin, Ballard, & Damon, 2015). Democratic values and the value of social responsibility were also associated with the development of civic purpose.

The relationships between civic identity and other social identities (e.g., moral, political) need to be explored to determine how they might be integrated and what factors contribute to their integration. Amiot and colleagues (2007) suggested that the degree to which crossed-categorization occurs (i.e., degree of overlap between current social identities: moral identify, religious identity, political identity, civic identity) could also determine the strength of civic identity. Based on Amiot and colleagues' (2007) theory of social identity development, inhibiting factors (i.e., feelings of threat, status/power asymmetries) and facilitating factors (i.e., coping and adaptation, social support) could be evaluated for their role in changes in civic identity of service learning students. Because identity is linked to group membership, future research can investigate how civic identity is related to multiple identities (e.g., female, student, Black, poor). Dividio, Gaertner, Ufkes, Saguy, and Pearson (2016) present a strong case that majority and minority students will have very different predilections for unified (e.g., "we are all in this together") versus multiple identities, with minority groups preferring dual identities. This might be further complicated when students come from communities in which they are doing their service (chapter 2.5). Research can examine how the determinants of motives proposed by self-determination theory (Deci & Ryan, 2002) and the volunteer process model (Clary et al., 1998) account for civic behaviors and how relevant they are to the extent to which people endorse a civic identity.

Emotions and Moods

Empathy is a reliable mediator of helping others, but what facilitates the development of state and trait empathy in regard to an individual, groups of individuals, or social issues? Batson (1991) and Hoffman (2010) raise the issue of empathic concern at different levels of analysis (e.g., one's self, a particular individual who is suffering, one's in-group, a group or category of individuals, humankind in general). Research can investigate how different levels of analysis, particularly for others who are similar or different, are related to different types of civic orientations (e.g., charity, social justice). What is the role of cognitive perspective versus emotional reactions for empathic responses? What is the result of developing caring relationships on empathy, and with what long-term consequences? Wilhelm and Bekkers (2010) suggested that empathy may be a powerful predictor of helping close others (e.g., family, friends, in-group members). In contrast, the principle of care is viewed as a more powerful determinant of helping those who are in out-groups or only known in the abstract. Research within the context of service learning courses can investigate the similarities and distinctions between these two motives.

Empathy is typically construed as occurring when an observer experiences sadness and compassion in response to an individual who is suffering (Davis, 1983). Hoffman (2010) recognized the broader social dimensions of empathy and called for expanding empathy to create a moral and just society by going beyond empathy for an individual to empathy for groups. Hoffman emphasized the role of causal attributions in the arousal of empathic responses (sympathy, sadness, anger), but this is unstudied in service learning research. If the observer blames the victim, empathic distress is reduced (Bringle & Velo, 1998). Bringle and colleagues (2015) examined how anger can be an empathic response. Empathic anger was found to be associated with a social justice orientation to community involvement, which research has shown to be not noticably salient among college students (Bringle, Hatcher, & MacIntosh, 2006). In addition to examining empathy that is manifested in sadness and anger, research could also investigate the degree to which empathic responses implicate surprise, disgust, happiness, and fear as a basis for responsiveness and civic engagement.

Motivation

To an unknown extent, service learning research has been biased toward studying students who have positive civic attitudes and motives, at the expense of understanding how to develop those attributes across a broader range of student motives and interests. How can service learning courses be designed to motivate unmotivated students so that extrinsic motivation for civic involvement can be transformed into intrinsic motivation? According to self-determination theory and research, relatedness and a sense of competency move the unmotivated along the motivational continuum, and autonomy is subsequently critical to integrating motivation with the self and achieving intrinsic motivation. Research can clarify the role of each of these constructs, determine the best timing and relative importance they bring to different stages of motivation, identify how community-based activities and relationships with others support them, and provide more detail about how they relate to students' motives for future civic engagement and civic identity. In what ways can service learning course design support transformations from a charity orientation to a social justice orientation (e.g., systemic orientation to social issues, empathic anger, principled altruism)? The fundamental research question is how to design service learning course experiences (types of service activities, reflection, readings, relationships; chapter 1.3) in ways that integrate students' civic knowledge and skills, intrinsic motivation for civic involvement, and self-efficacy into the self-concept.

Attitudes

How do theory and research on the nature of attitude formation and attitude change provide a basis for understanding students' civic outcomes (e.g., beliefs, attitudes, values, behaviors)? The voluminous social psychological literature on attitude change provides significant resources for understanding and conducting research on how attitudes (e.g., civic attitudes, prejudice) can be changed and how they can be moderators and mediators of change for civic outcomes (e.g., stereotypes, knowledge, understanding, attributions, identity, communication skills). Instructors, community members, peers, and residents can fulfill the role of coeducators of students in well-designed service learning courses (chapter 1.3). Research can investigate the dynamics of various persons being persuasive in producing changes in students' civic attitudes. What attributes (e.g., credible, trustworthy, likeable, expertise) are associated with the strength of impact of different persons in various roles on students' civic attitudes? How can reflection assignments before, during, and after community-based activities contribute to or detract from the capacity of persons in these roles to influence students' civic attitudes? Direct experience and central processing have a demonstrated impact on the strength of attitudes (e.g., accessibility, relevance). What kinds of direct experiences and effortful central processing (e.g., detailed analysis of causes and consequences of experiences) produce positive outcomes in the civic domain and why? The cognitive response model of attitude change posits that it is not the communication that produces attitude change but what the recipient says (covertly or overtly) and thinks in response to a message or experience (Baron et al., 2007). How can relationships, community service activities, and reflection activities be structured to produce positive student responses that facilitate desired civic attitude change and resistance to counterarguments? How can reflection activities be structured to produce central processing of information from various sources (e.g., instructor, peer, texts, community partners), increase motivation, and enhance personal relevance?

Implications for Practice

Because of social psychology's emphasis on both the power of the situation and on the importance of perceptions, social psychological theory and research have the potential to guide the design and implementation of successful service learning courses. For example, Bringle, Reeb, Brown, and Ruiz (2016) provide examples for how to develop reflection prompts for specific learning objectives based on the DEAL framework (Ash & Clayton, 2009a, 2009b), including how student perceptions and community situations contribute to their civic learning. Bringle and colleagues (2015) provide analyses of the centrality of democratic thinking, democratic partnerships, and reflection contributing to democratic identity (chapter 1.3). Each of the following recommendations for practice also provides opportunities to develop research questions to evaluate its efficacy and to explore moderator and mediating variables.

Self and Civic Identity

- Identity exploration can use different modalities of student reflection (e.g., written, group discussion, artistic expression). Students high on openness have a preference for exploring breath of identity (e.g., alternative identities), whereas students with low openness prefer exploring depth of identity and commitment. Extraverts, in comparison to introverts, prefer using collaborative processes that allow them to affirm and develop self-defining meaning from their experiences (Lilgendahl, 2015).
- Individuals have unreliable, overly optimistic, and inaccurate estimates of their civic behaviors, indicating a discontinuity between their cognitions and their actions (e.g., Dunning, 2006). Dunning notes that these inaccuracies are not necessarily intentional and that they may occur even when individuals are motivated to provide accurate assessments of self-knowledge and predictions of behavior. One of Dunning's recommendations for correcting the inaccuracies of self-awareness and the discrepancies between beliefs about the self and behavior is through relationships with others who can provide accurate feedback. This emphasizes the importance of having students in community settings that involve them in partnerships with peers and community members who can provide feedback on skills (e.g., communication skills, self-efficacy, democratic skills, listening skills, diversity skills) to improve self-awareness, accuracy, and self-efficacy.
- Damon, Menon, and Bronk (2003) conceptualized purpose as "a dedication to causes greater than the self, show high degrees of religiosity, consolidated identities, and deeper sense of meaning" (p. 126). One of the central developmental tasks facing young adult students in developing purpose is formulating career plans based on accurate self-assessment of abilities, motivation, and work habits. Community-based activities and reflection prompts as well as community-based mentors can provide a basis for students to clarify career goals and develop plans for careers in ways that incorporate civic perspectives.
- Service learning experiences provide opportunities for students to clarify their current and future roles regarding community involvement, social responsibility, and prosocial behaviors. Community service activities and reflections can be designed to emphasize the similarities between the students and those with whom they are working, which is known to increase empathy and future helping. Students can continue their community engagement by being informed about opportunities for other community-based learning experiences after

a service learning course (e.g., volunteer service, practica, internship, participatory action community research).

- Students can examine the role of common identity (i.e., "we-ness") versus multiple identities and how they relate to civic identity and attitudes toward social justice. Multiple identities seem more critical to adaptation by minority students than majority students (Dividio et al., 2016) and, therefore, can be supported through appropriate reflection activities.
- Research (Levy, 1996) demonstrates that focusing attention on positive aspects of one's self (e.g., contributions through service, accomplishments) can enhance self-efficacy. Tailoring community-based tasks to students' skills and to the course's timeframe can contribute to self-efficacy. Reflection activities can be structured to enhance these effects by priming and guiding awareness about one's accomplishments and skills to enhance self-efficacy (Sanders et al., 2016).

Emotions

- Because of the power of empathy, community activities can be selected to enhance cooperative activities, and reflection activities can be focused on developing greater sensitivity to community partners and listening to the stories and experiences of others to enhance empathic responses.
- Because state-like empathy is a function of perceived similarity, relationships with community partners and reflection activities can be structured to focus students' attention on similarities with other persons in communities, including priming instructions to take the other person's point of view (e.g., imaging one's self in the other person's circumstances, imaging what the other person's perspective is) and focus attention on emotional responses (e.g., emotional concern for the other person, experiencing emotions of the other person).
- Reflection activities can focus students' attention on not only the individuals with whom they are interacting but also groups of individuals in similar circumstances and broad civic principles and values as a means for enhancing empathy for distant groups, out-groups, and abstract others.

Motivation

- As Bringle and colleagues (2001) noted, the connections among required service, perceptions of control, and motivation are complex.

Self-determination theory provides a basis for instructors encouraging students to be in educational and service settings that provide support and allow students to engage in activities where they can feel efficacious. Community activities and reflection can be structured to support all of these factors that are known to contribute to intrinsic motivation (relatedness, competency, autonomy) and positive attitudes toward community engagement.

- The design of service learning courses needs to include some of the following factors that are known to increase intrinsic motivation: unanticipated rewards (Bradley & Mannell, 1984); social rewards; feedback that reinforces efficacy and civic values; and requests for students to reflect on their autonomy, choice, and intrinsic motives for engaging in community service.
- Through structured reflection, students can examine the various motives for community activities (Clary et al., 1998) for themselves, fellow students, and community partners.
- Students can be asked to reflect, for themselves and others, on the respective strengths and weaknesses of different levels of analysis (Batson et al., 2002): selfishness (easily evoked but may be solely of instrumental value); altruism (powerful but may be limited to empathy response); collectivism (focus on common good but may be limited to in-group members); principlism (focus on universal good but may be weak).

Attitudes

- Because central, rather than peripheral, processing results in stronger, more accessible attitudes and because responses to messages are important to their impact, research has supported the following ways to stimulate thinking (Baron et al., 2007): use rhetorical questions, present multiple communicators with similar messages, have students assume responsibility for evaluating information, focus attention on message content, provide intriguing examples to illustrate points, and challenge students with difficult problems. These approaches can be incorporated into reflection activities and group discussions on civic aspects of the curriculum and community-based experiences.
- Service activities, relationships, and reflection activities can encourage familiarity with unfamiliar community groups and emphasize the diversity of members of groups in order to examine and reduce stereotypes, prejudice, and discrimination.

- Persistent prejudices and beliefs are difficult to change. One strategy that can be designed into reflection is asking students to analyze why the opposite may be the case (e.g., persons who are experiencing homelessness are not lazy), which can reduce or eliminate belief and attitude perseverance (Anderson & Sechler, 1986).
- Community service, partnerships, and reflection activities can be designed to provide opportunities for students to exhibit respect for members of diverse groups with sensitivity to issues of power, privilege, and discrimination. This might include both focusing on similarities as well as differences between students and community partners (Dovidio et al., 2016).
- Because norms can influence behavior, community-based activities, partnerships, role models, and reflection activities can focus students' attention on others who contribute and volunteer to community activities and social issues.

Conclusion

Social psychology provides intrapersonal and interpersonal perspectives on how students approach community activities in a service learning course, interpret and incorporate those experiences, base subsequent actions on those experiences, and integrate those experiences into their identity. Social psychological theory and research results can move the study of service learning beyond merely description of civic outcomes and provide a basis for understanding the processes by which change occurs. Service learning also provides an excellent opportunity for in vivo research to evaluate the generalizability, refinement, and limitations of social psychological theory in a manner that can improve the pedagogy (e.g., Brown, 2011a, 2011b).

References

Ajzen, I. (1991). The theory of planned behavior. *Organizational Behavior and Human Decision Processes, 50*, 179–211.

Amiot, C. E., de la Sablonniere, R., Smith, L. E., & Smith, J. R. (2015). Capturing changes in social identities over time and how they become part of the self-concept. *Social and Personality Psychology Compass, 9*(4), 171–187.

Amiot, C. E., de la Sablonniere, R., Terry, D. J., & Smith, J. R. (2007). Integration of social identities in the self: Toward a cognitive-developmental model. *Personality and Social Psychology Review, 11*, 364–388.

Anderson, C. A., & Sechler, E. S. (1986). Effects of explanation and counterexplanation on the development and use of social theories. *Journal of Personality and Social Psychology, 50,* 24–34.

Ash, S. L., & Clayton, P. H. (2009a). Generating, deepening, and documenting learning: The power of critical reflection for applied learning. *Journal of Applied Learning in Higher Education, 1,* 25–48.

Ash, S. L., & Clayton, P. H. (2009b). *Learning through critical reflection: A tutorial for students in service-learning* (Instructor version). Raleigh, NC: Authors.

Astin, A. W., Vogelgesang, L. J., Ikeda, E. K., & Yee, J. A. (2000). How service learning affects students. *Higher Education,* 144. Retrieved from http://digital-commons.unomaha.edu/slcehighered/144

Bandura, A. (1994). Self-efficacy. In V. S. Ramachaudran (Ed.), *Encyclopedia of human behavior* (Vol. 4, pp. 71–81). New York, NY: Academic Press.

Baron, R. A., Byrne, D. R., & Branscombe, N. R. (2007). *Mastering social psychology.* New York, NY: Pearson.

Batchelder, T. H., & Root, S. (1994). Effects of an undergraduate program to integrate academic learning and service: Cognitive, prosocial cognitive, and identity outcomes. *Journal of Adolescence, 17,* 341–355.

Batson, C. D. (1991). *The altruism question: Toward a social-psychological answer.* Hillsdale, NJ: Erlbaum.

Batson, C. D., & Ahmad, N. (2009). Using empathy to improve intergroup attitudes and relations. *Social Issues and Policy Review, 3,* 141–177.

Batson, C. D., Ahmad, N., & Tsang, J. (2002). Four motives for community involvement. *Journal of Social Issues, 58,* 429–445.

Batson, C. D., Turk, C. L., Shaw, L. L., & Klein, T. R. (1995). Information function of empathic emotion: Learning that we value the other's welfare. *Journal of Personality and Social Psychology, 68,* 300–313.

Batson, C. D., & Weeks, J. L. (1996). Mood effects of unsuccessful helping: Another test of the empathy-altruism hypothesis. *Personality and Social Psychology Bulletin, 22,* 148–157.

Bradley, W., & Mannell, R. C. (1984). Sensitivity of intrinsic motivation to reward procedure instructions. *Personality and Social Psychology Bulletin, 10,* 426–431.

Brandenberger, J. W. (2013). Investigating personal development outcomes in service learning. In P. H. Clayton, R. G. Bringle, & J. A. Hatcher (Eds.), *Research on service learning: Conceptual frameworks and assessment* (Vol. 2A, pp. 133–156). Sterling, VA: Stylus.

Bringle, R. G. (2005). Designing interventions to promote civic engagement. In A. Omoto (Ed.), *Processes of community change and social action* (pp. 167–187). Mahwah, NJ: Erlbaum.

Bringle, R. G., & Clayton, P. H. (2013). Conceptual frameworks for partnerships in service learning. In P. H. Clayton, R. G. Bringle, & J. A. Hatcher (Eds.), *Research on service learning: Conceptual frameworks and assessment* (Vol. 2B, pp. 539–571). Sterling, VA: Stylus.

Bringle, R. G., Clayton, P. H., & Bringle, K. E. (2015). Teaching democratic thinking is not enough: The case for democratic action. *Partnerships: A Journal of Service Learning & Civic Engagement, 6*(1), 1–26.

Bringle, R. G., & Hahn, T. W. (2015, November). *Civic-minded graduate: Construct validation evidence.* Paper presented at the 15th meeting of the International Association for Research on Service Learning and Community Engagement, Boston, MA.

Bringle, R. G., & Hatcher, J. A. (2002). University-community partnerships: The terms of engagement. *Journal of Social Issues, 58,* 503–516.

Bringle, R. G., Hatcher, J. A., & MacIntosh, R. (2006). Analyzing Morton's typology of service paradigms and integrity. *Michigan Journal of Community Service Learning, 13(1),* 5–15.

Bringle, R. G., Hatcher, J. A., Muthiah, R., & McIntosh, R. (2001, October). *The case for required service in service-learning classes: A multi-campus study of service-learning.* Paper presented at the First Annual International Conference on Service-Learning Research, Berkeley, CA.

Bringle, R. G., Hedgepath, A., & Stephens, D. (2015, February). *"I'm so angry I could . . . Help!" Examining empathic anger as a motive for volunteering.* Paper presented at the Pathways to Achieving Civic Engagement Conference, Elon, NC.

Bringle, R. G., Reeb, R., Brown, M. A., & Ruiz, A. (2016). *Service learning in psychology: Enhancing undergraduate education for the public good.* Washington, DC: American Psychological Association.

Bringle, R. G., & Velo, P. M. (1998). Attributions about misery. In R. G. Bringle & D. K. Duffy (Eds.), *With service in mind: Concepts and models for service-learning in psychology* (pp. 51–67). Washington, DC: American Association for Higher Education.

Brown, M. A. (2011a). The power of generosity to change views on social power. *Journal of Experimental Social Psychology, 47,* 1285–1290.

Brown, M. A. (2011b). Learning from service: The effect of helping on helpers' social dominance orientation. *Journal of Applied Social Psychology, 41,* 850–871.

Clary, E. G., Snyder, M., Ridge, R. D., Copeland, J., Stukas, A. A., Haugen, J., & Meine, P. (1998). Understanding and assessing the motivations of volunteers: A functional approach. *Journal of Personality and Social Psychology, 74,* 1516–1530.

Collette, J. L., & Morrissey, C. A. (2007). *The social psychology of generosity: The state of current interdisciplinary research.* Retrieved from http://generosityresearch.nd.edu/assets/17634/social_psychology_of_generosity_final.pdf

Damon, W., Menon, J., & Bronk, K. C. (2003). The development of purpose in adolescence. *Applied Developmental Science, 7*(3), 119–128.

Davis, M. (1983). Measuring individual differences in empathy: Evidence for a multidimensional approach. *Journal of Personality and Social Psychology 44,* 113–126.

Deci, E. L., Koestner, R., & Ryan, R. M. (1999). A meta-analytic review of experiments examining the effects of extrinsic rewards on intrinsic motivation. *Psychological Bulletin, 125,* 627–668.

Deci, E., & Ryan, R. (Eds.). (2002). *Handbook of self-determination research*. Rochester, NY: University of Rochester Press.

Dovidio, J. F., Gaertner, S. I., Ufkes, E. G., Saguy, T., & Pearson, A. R. (2016). Included but invisible? Subtle bias, common identity, and the darker side of "we." *Social Issues and Policy Review, 10*(1), 6–46.

Dunning, D. (2006). Strangers to ourselves? *The Psychologist, 19*, 600–603.

Eisenberg, N., & Eggum, N. D. (2009). Empathic responding: Sympathy and personal distress. In J. Decety & W. Ickes (Eds.), *The social neuroscience of empathy* (pp. 71–83). Cambridge, MA: MIT Press.

Eisenberg, N., Guthrie, I. K., Murphy, B. C., Shepard, S. A., Cumberland, A., & Carlo, G. (1999). Consistency and development of prosocial dispositions: A longitudinal study. *Child Development, 70*, 1360–1372.

Eisenberg N., & Miller, P. A. (1987). The relation of empathy to prosocial and related behaviors. *Psychological Bulletin, 101*, 91–119.

Erickson, J. A., & O'Connor S. E. (2000). Service-learning: Does it promote or reduce prejudice? In C. R. O'Grady (Ed.), *Integrating service-learning and multicultural education in colleges and universities* (pp. 59–70). Mahwah, NJ: Erlbaum.

Fitch, P., Steinke, P., & Hudson, T. D. (2013). Research and theoretical perspectives on cognitive outcomes of service learning. In P. H. Clayton, R. G. Bringle, & J. A. Hatcher (Eds.), *Research on service learning: Conceptual frameworks and assessment* (Vol. 2A, pp. 57–84). Sterling, VA: Stylus.

Green, D., Johnson, J. R., & Stewart D. (1998). Student perceptions of aging and disability as influenced by service learning. *Physical & Occupational Therapy in Geriatrics, 15*(3), 39–55.

Hoffman, M. L. (2010). Empathy and prosocial behavior. In M. Lewis, J. M. Haviland-Jones, & L. F. Barrett (Eds.), *Handbook of emotions* (3rd ed., pp. 440–455). New York, NY: Guilford Press.

Jiranek, P., Kals, E., Humm, J. S., Strubel, I. T., & Wehner, T. (2013). Volunteering as a means to an equal end? The impact of a social justice function on intention to volunteer. *The Journal of Social Psychology, 153*, 520–541.

Jones, S. R., & Abes, E. S. (2004). Enduring influences of service-learning on college students' identity development. *Journal of College Student Development, 45*, 149–166.

Kiely, R. (2005). A transformative learning model for service-learning: A longitudinal case study. *Michigan Journal of Community Service Learning, 12*(1), 5–22.

Levesque-Bristol, C., Knapp, T. D., & Fisher B. J. (2010). The effectiveness of service-learning: It's not always what you think. *Journal of Experiential Education, 33*, 208–224.

Levesque-Bristol, C., & Stanek, L. R. (2009). Examining self-determination in a service-learning classroom. *Teaching of Psychology, 36*, 1–5.

Levy, B. (1996). Improving memory in old age through implicit self-stereotyping. *Journal of Personality and Social Psychology, 71*, 1092–1107.

Lewin, K. (1951). *Field theory in social science: Selected theoretical papers*. D. Cartwright (Ed.). New York, NY: Harper & Row.

Lilgendahl, J. (2015). The dynamic role of identity processes in personality development: Theories, patterns, and new directions. In K. C. McLean & M. Syed (Eds.), *The Oxford handbook of identity development* (pp. 490–507). Oxford, England: Oxford University Press.

Lundy, B. L. (2007). Service learning in life-span developmental psychology: Higher exam scores and increased empathy. *Teaching of Psychology, 34*, 23–27.

Malin, H., Ballard, P. J., & Damon, W. (2015). Civic purpose: An integrated construct for understanding civic development in adolescence. *Human Development, 58*, 103–130.

Metz, E., McLellan, J., & Youniss, J. (2003). Types of voluntary service and adolescents' civic development. *Journal of Adolescent Research, 18*, 188–203.

Mitchell, T., Visconti, V., Keene, A., & Battistoni, R. (2011). Educating for democratic leadership at Stanford, UMass, and Providence College. In N. V. Longo & C. M. Gibson (Eds.), *From command to community: A new approach to leadership education in colleges and universities* (pp. 115–148). Boston, MA: Tufts University Press.

Pavey, L., Greitemeyer, T., & Sparks, P. (2011). Highlighting relatedness promotes prosocial motives and behavior. *Personality and Social Psychology Bulletin, 37*, 905–917.

Petty, R. E., & Cacioppo, J. T. (1986). The elaboration likelihood model of persuasion. *Advances in Experimental Social Psychology, 19*, 123–205.

Reeb, R. N., & Folger, S. F. (2013). Community outcomes in service learning: Research and practice from a systems perspective. In P. H. Clayton, R. G. Bringle, & J. A. Hatcher (Eds.), *Research on service-learning: Conceptual models and assessment* (pp. 389–418). Sterling, VA: Stylus.

Richards, K. A. R., & Levesque-Bristol, C. (2015, April). *The influence of self-efficacy and self-regulated motivation on civic learning in service-learning courses.* Poster presented at the SHAPE America National Convention, Seattle, WA.

Ross, L., & Nisbett, R. E. (2011). *The person and the situation.* London: Pinter & Martin.

Sanders, M. J., Oss, T. V., & McGeary, S. (2016). Analyzing reflections in service learning to promote personal growth and community self-efficacy. *Journal of Experiential Education, 39*(1), 73–88.

Scott, J. H. (2012). The intersection of service-learning and moral growth. *New Directions for Student Services, 139*, 27–38.

Simons, L. (2015). Measuring service-learning and civic engagement. In R. S. Jhangiani, J. D. Troisi, B. Fleck, A. M. Legg, & H. D. Hussey (Eds.), *A compendium of scales for use in the scholarship of teaching and learning* (pp. 102–122). Retrieved from http://teachpsych.org/ebooks/compscalessotp

Snyder, M., & Omoto, A. M. (2008). Who gets involved and why? The psychology of volunteerism. In E. S. C. Liu, M. J. Holosko, & T. Wing Lo (Eds.), *Youth empowerment and volunteerism: Principles, policies, and practices* (pp. 3–26). Hong Kong, China: City University.

Tajfel, H., & Turner, J. C. (1986). The social identity theory of inter-group behavior. In S. Worchel & L. W. Austin (eds.), *Psychology of intergroup relations* (pp. 7–24). Chicago: Nelson-Hall.

Wilhelm, M. O., & Bekkers, R. (2010). Helping behavior, dispositional empathic concern, and the principle of care. *Social Psychology Quarterly, 73,* 11–32.

Wilson, J. C. (2011). Service-learning and the development of empathy in US college students. *Education and Training, 53,* 207–217.

Yates, M., & Youniss, J. (1998). Community service and political identity development in adolescence. *Journal of Social Issues, 54,* 495–512.

Yorio, P. L., Ye, F. (2012). A meta-analysis on the effects of service-learning on the social, personal, and cognitive outcomes of learning. *Academy of Management, 11*(1), 9–27.

Youniss, J., & Yates, M. (1999). Youth service and moral-civic identity: A case for everyday morality. *Educational Psychology Review, 11,* 361–376.

POLITICAL THEORY AND STUDENT CIVIC OUTCOMES

Steven G. Jones

Amerrican political science has an ambivalent position relative to civic education and civic engagement. On the one hand, the discipline's largest professional organization, the American Political Science Association, accepts and promotes a civic education and civic engagement mission (Schacter, 1998; Snyder, 2001). On the other hand, many political scientists reject that mission as an appropriate goal for political science education (Battistoni, 2013; Flatham, 1996; Macedo et al., 2005). Still, there are political scientists who have embraced the civic education and civic engagement mission of the discipline, and their scholarship—some of which is reviewed in this chapter—reflects their acceptance of that mission.

Furthermore, theories of political science, regardless of the degree to which their adherents actively accept a civic education role, offer implicit and explicit definitions of *citizenship* and other constructs related to civic outcomes from which can be derived measurable civic outcomes in the areas of knowledge, behavior, motivations, identity, attitudes, and values. This chapter will focus on three theoretical traditions within the discipline: liberalism, civic republicanism, and critical theories.

Liberal theories are likely to define *citizenship* in terms of the legal (e.g., legal rights as stated as defined by law and judicial decisions) and procedural aspects of citizenship (e.g., equal application of citizens' legal rights) rather than the normative aspects of citizenship. As such, they fail to address the tensions between citizens' rights and citizens' responsibilities that are important to developing students' understanding of the values and attitudes required of democratic citizens. Thus, this approach toward citizenship reflects the liberal perspective that the only responsibilities that attend to rights are the legal obligations not to infringe upon the rights of others. Another perspective within the liberal framework also emphasizes the procedural aspects of democratic citizenship, but it is also amenable to the notion of responsibilities as well as rights. Although this perspective shares the dominant liberal view that "the good" is a matter of personal selection based on free choice and not imposition, it also recognizes that certain shared norms and political values are needed to preserve the liberal polity that makes choices possible (e.g., Rawls, 1971, 2001). This chapter will explore the arguments of specific liberal theorists in the section that follows.

In contrast to liberalism, civic republican political theorists do not focus on only the rights that attend democratic citizenship; they also identify civic duties and responsibilities. Civic republicans, such as Benjamin Barber (1992) and Michael Sandel (1996), argue that democratic societies are characterized by more than just the political and legal procedures that protect liberty and political equality. Democratic polities are also communities that develop important norms and values that form a collective narrative or tradition. Although these collectively and historically derived norms and values should not be imposed on citizens, they frame the choices citizens make in the exercise of their liberties. As a result, citizens not only have responsibilities to honor their political values and traditions but also have intergenerational obligations to both the past and the future.

An alternative school of thought focuses not on commonalities among members of democratic polities, but on their differences. These theorists argue that the proceduralism lauded by liberals is not equally applied across gender, ethnic, or religious identities and that the democratic narrative, at least in the United States, has been exclusive to dominant groups and consequently does not present a common framework for civic behavior for those who have been excluded or marginalized. Following a review of these different theoretical positions, this chapter outlines sets of civic learning outcomes that can be deduced from these distinct positions. These civic outcomes are presented in measurable terms that will help researchers identify specific hypotheses with respect to how different pedagogical interventions may influence student achievement of the outcomes. These outcomes might be used by institutional researchers to determine which of the theoretical perspectives and the associated outcomes best describe student attitudes and beliefs at their respective institutions. Before addressing these characteristics in detail, a review of previous definitions of *civic learning outcomes* is provided.

Review of Political Science Theories

Battistoni (2001) outlines conceptual frameworks that can be used to articulate civic learning objectives. Battistoni summarizes the frameworks most familiar to political scientists in Table 2.2.1.

TABLE 2.2.1

Battistoni's Summary of Political Science Conceptual Frameworks on Civic Engagement

Conceptual Framework	View of Citizenship	Understanding of Civic Education	Associated Civic Skills	Disciplinary Affinities
Liberalism	Rights-bearing individuals; voter	Learning about government, laws, elections	Political knowledge Critical thinking	Political Science Law Policy Studies
Communitarianism	"Good neighbor" Duty to the common good	Learning about community values and civic responsibilities	Civic judgment Community building	Philosophy Religious Studies Social Work
Participatory Democracy	Active participant in public life	Learning the processes of democratic participation	Communication Collective action Civic imagination	Political Science Education
Public Work	Cocreator of things of public value	Learning the skills, practices, habits, and values of working with others	Public problem solving Coalition building	Political Science Public Administration Professional disciplines
Social Capital	Membership in associations of civic society	Learning about social connections and institutions	Communication Organizational analysis	Sociology Non-profit management

Note. Battistoni (2002). Reprinted with permission of Campus Compact.

The usefulness of Battistoni's approach is that it provides a variety of discipline-based conceptual frameworks from which to frame civic learning outcomes. Although Battistoni identifies general characteristics of citizenship based on those frameworks, he does not explicitly describe specific, demonstrable, and measurable learning outcomes that can be derived from those frameworks. Furthermore, those general characteristics do not identify specific outcomes in terms of knowledge, skills, and dispositions, attitudes, or values.

Harry Boyte (1999) offers three definitions of *citizenship*:

1. *Rights-bearing individuals,* who are members of a political system, choosing their leaders, ideally those of virtue and talent, through elections
2. *Caring and responsible members of a moral community* or of a civil society who share common responsibilities toward each other and deliberate together about the common good
3. *Producers of the commonwealth:* active creators of public goods and undertakers of public tasks . . . expressed in the ideal of citizenship as public work (pp. 260–261)

Although Boyte provided broad definitions, those definitions are not in themselves measurable outcomes, a limitation shared by Battistoni's approach. Furthermore, although Battistoni offered a breadth of conceptual frameworks, his approach lacks depth. Boyte's approach lacks both breadth, in that it fails to consider the strengths and limitations of multiple theoretical definitions of *citizenship*, and depth in that it fails to define specific civic outcomes based on the theories he does describe, except in the case of his preferred approach, in which *civic outcomes* are defined in terms of public work. The review of political science approaches in this chapter will provide service learning researchers with both a breadth of conceptual frameworks as well as depth in terms of specific, measurable civic-learning outcomes.

John Rawls's Liberal Theory of Citizenship

Any concerted effort at civic education will rest on at least an implicit theory of citizenship because one cannot legitimately identify civic outcomes in the absence of such a theory. However, to the extent that there is agreement among practitioners and researchers that service learning is linked to civic education, there does not appear to be any consensus as to what a theory of citizenship should entail. Without a theoretical foundation, the link between service learning and civic education is tenuous at best, and research activities to identify that link are handicapped. The following sections outline theoretical approaches to citizenship developed by American political scientists over the past 30 years.

Prior to John Rawls's (1971) publication of *A Theory of Justice*, most American political science theories of citizenship and democratic society had concerned themselves with commentary on the works of prior scholars. Rather than continuing to offer new answers to fundamental questions like "What is the best kind of society? What is the best kind of political arrangement? What is justice?", they tended to focus on how their predecessors had addressed those questions and whether their answers had any contemporary relevance. Rawls (1971) developed a thoroughly contemporary philosophical analysis to those fundamental questions. In so doing, he spurred other political philosophers to examine his ideas and to refute them or improve them if they could (see Alejandro, 1998; Daniels, 1975; Kukathas & Pettit, 1990; and Mulhall & Swift, 1992).

Rawls's political theory is rich and complex and not easily summarized, but there is universal agreement that Rawls advocates a "liberal" political philosophy because he gives ontological priority to the individual and as a consequence considers justice and civic responsibility to be rights-based rather than based on a conception of "the good" or "the good society." Rawls (1971) developed his theory of justice through a thought experiment, which he calls "the original position" (p. 17). In his thought experiment, Rawls imagines a situation in which individuals are to decide among themselves principles of justice that will constitute the basis for their political, social, and economic relations. He also imagines that the individuals in the original position deliberate from behind a "veil of ignorance" (p. 19) in which individuals have an interest in maximizing individual happiness, but they do not know what their particular advantages are relative to others. Because everyone in the original position is equally uncertain about their status in society, Rawls reasons that they will select principles of justice that are to the advantage of all members. He then deduces from this scenario that the following principles would be chosen:

> First: each person is to have an equal right to the most extensive basic liberty compatible with a similar liberty for others.
>
> Second: social and economic inequalities are to be arranged so that they are both (a) reasonably to be to everyone's advantage, and (b) attached to positions and offices open to all. (Rawls, 1971, p. 60)

Rawls further argues that these principles are hierarchical—the first principle is prior to the second, and principle 2a is prior to principle 2b. That is, attempts to satisfy the second cannot violate the first, and attempts to satisfy principle 2b cannot violate 2a. From these two principles, Rawls derives a "general conception of justice," which states that "All social values—liberty and opportunity, income and wealth, and the bases of self-respect—are to be distributed equally unless an unequal distribution of any, or all, of these values is to everyone's advantage" (p. 62).

Consequently, Rawls is not advocating a system of complete political, social, and economic equality. Rather, he is proposing principles by which the justice or injustice of existing inequalities can be determined. Inequalities are just if the distribution of these inequalities "is to everyone's advantage" (p. 62). Of course, Rawls and other commentators have gone to great lengths to elucidate the practical application of these principles (Davion & Wolf, 2000; Dombrowski, 2001; Freeman, 2003; Pogge, 1989). The aim of this chapter is not to explore their application to the real world, but rather to identify whether they can provide researchers with a theory of citizenship that can serve as the basis for developing civic learning outcomes to which service learning can be applied and tested. I believe his theory does provide an implicit theory of citizenship by asserting what a citizen in a just society looks like.

Based on Rawls's political philosophy, several qualities of citizenship can be deduced. First, a good citizen understands the importance of fundamental political rights and liberties and is committed to the equal application of those rights and liberties to all citizens. Second, such a citizen recognizes that inequalities are a feature of society but also seeks to address inequalities through the application of the principles of justice as described by Rawls. Third, such a citizen is committed to the principle of equality of opportunity. Fourth, a good citizen understands that equality of opportunity defined by merit is inherently unjust. This is one of the fundamental lessons of Rawls's original position and the veil of ignorance—social positions should not be based on the unequal distribution of life's opportunities. Later in this chapter, these qualities are restated as civic education outcomes.

Civic Republican Theory

There are three fundamental civic republican critiques of liberal political theory in general and Rawls's theory in particular. The first critique focuses on liberalism's acceptance of universal rights that exist independent of social traditions, values, and beliefs (see MacIntyre, 1984, pp. 200–205; Walzer, 1983, p. 5). Civic republicans do recognize the importance of political and economic rights, but they do not explain those rights as existing independent of social groupings. Whereas liberals believe that rights are inherent in human beings *qua* human beings, regardless of their particular historical or social setting, civic republicans believe rights are social and moral constructs that develop over time according to particular social traditions, which themselves vary by cultures and subcultures.

The second critique is related to the first. By placing ontological priority on the individual, liberalism creates an image of human beings as disaggregated social atoms, or what Michael Sandel (1984) calls "unencumbered selves" (p. 86). According to many of his civic republican critics, particularly Sandel, Rawls creates an image of the self as someone who defines goals and conceptions of the good life independent of membership in multiple social settings (e.g., family, church, school) (Sandel, 1982).

The third critique follows from the first two. If human beings are endowed with inherent, universal rights, and if human beings are to be viewed as independent (*autonomous* is the preferred term of liberals) of socially or politically compelled definitions of one's aims and values, then individuals have no fundamental duties toward another person other than to respect one another's rights and to follow the principles of justice as understood by liberal theorists. Accordingly, liberalism is seen as contributing to a belief in radical individualism through which social order is undermined by the pursuit of individual gain and personal rights at the expense of civic duties and moral obligations.

What is the civic republicans' theoretical alternative to liberalism? Although there are alternatives, depending on the political theorist, there are some central ideas common to most civic republicans. First, they argue that the social institutions that reinforce shared norms and values within and across social groups should be strengthened (Putnam, 2000). Second, civic republicans claim that citizens should understand their civic duties and responsibilities as well as their liberties and rights (Sandel, 1996). Third, civic republicans contend that citizens should understand the historical narratives that serve as a basis for a common civic identity (MacIntyre, 1984; Walzer, 1983).

From its critiques of liberalism and its own alternative contributions to political theory, one can describe the civic republican view of citizenship. Citizens understand not only their rights but also their responsibilities. Second, this understanding of rights is based on the citizen's understanding of the multiple social groups, including national society, to which members belong. Third, citizens are capable of recognizing the public good and will willingly contribute to the public good, even if that means foregoing individual interests in the short term.

Both the liberal and civic republican theories of citizenship are subject to criticism from critical theorists who associate democratic liberalism in practice with the marginalization of women, minorities, and/or certain social classes (Young, 1990).

Critical Theories

Although civic republicanism places priority on group membership over individualism, many civic republicans tend to focus on the nation as the primary group in terms of defining rights and responsibilities. Not surprisingly, critical theorists, including feminist and critical race theorists (chapters 1.3 and 2.6), are dissatisfied with both the liberal and the civic republican approaches. Many feminist and multicultural political scientists share with civic republicans the view that liberal ideas about rights and the autonomy of the individual are themselves social constructs. However, whereas civic republicans frequently see validity in such constructs, feminist and multicultural theorists often see those constructs as reflecting the dominant interests within the larger society. From the perspective of many critical theorists, the question is whether it is possible to develop an approach to civic education that can take into consideration the diversity of histories, traditions, and social and political values systems of groups and identities that make up the U.S. citizenry.

The challenges to answering the question of whether an approach to civic education can integrate the cultural diversity of U.S. society can be seen by examining competing theories of citizenship that take diversity into account. For example, Gutmann (1999), in the epilogue to the second edition of *Democratic Education*, suggests an approach to multiculturalism based on liberal-democratic theory:

> A democratic education that is consistent with [conceptions of deliberative democracy and political liberalism] calls for two different responses to multiculturalism, but the two responses are united by a single principled aim of treating individuals as civic equals . . . . The first response—in reaction to exclusions of the experiences of entire groups from the curriculum—is publicly recognizing the experiences of oppressed groups. . . . The second response to a relatively different set of practices is similarly inspired by a commitment to mutual respect among citizens. The response is toleration—agreeing to disagree about beliefs and practices that are a matter of basic liberty. (pp. 303–304)

However, Gutmann also argues that public recognition and tolerance are not and should not be synonymous with according special status to groups. As she puts it, "Democratic education supports a 'politics of recognition' based on *respect for individuals and their equal rights as citizens*, not on deference to tradition, proportional representation of groups, or the survival rights of cultures" (p. 306, italics added). Thus, Gutmann's approach to multiculturalism is consistent with the universalizing tendencies of liberal-democratic political theory.

This approach to multiculturalism is not likely to satisfy political theorists who define *citizenship* according to civic republican or conflict theories.

Indeed, taken to an extreme, accommodating the realities of multiculturalism from civic republican and critical positions tends not toward a civic education, but several civic educations. In other words, civic education would involve teaching and learning the skills and attitudes necessary for meaningful political involvement within and across particular cultural or group contexts. To the extent that a particular culture has a history of exclusion and disenfranchisement, civic education becomes a kind of empowerment training.

However, from a more radical position, the liberal-democratic conception of civic education itself can be viewed as an exercise in power by the dominant group. Drawing on Lukes' (1974) theory of power, the political sociologist and activist John Gaventa (1999) argues that the powerful dominate politics by controlling the mechanisms for conflict management and the procedures by which minority grievances are heard. In his view, the dominant group regulates social conflict, "not only by influencing action upon recognized grievances, but through influencing consciousness and awareness of such grievances through such mechanisms as socialization, education, media, secrecy, information control, and the shaping of political beliefs and attitudes" (p. 57). He continues,

> What are the competencies necessary for enabling citizens to challenge this . . . dimension of power? Here the discussion of skills becomes those involving strategies of awareness building, liberating education, promotion of a critical consciousness, overcoming internalized oppressions, developing indigenous or popular knowledge . . . . The building of citizen competence for democracy must also include processes of education for critical consciousness, the recovery and development of people's knowledge as a basis for action, and the modeling and promotion of democratic values in organizational development. (pp. 56, 61)

This view of developing citizen competence among and within historically oppressed groups is consistent with other theories based on what political theorist Iris Marion Young (1990) refers to as "the politics of difference" (p. 11). Reflecting a particularistic definition of *citizenship* and critical of liberal conceptions she argues the following:

> Far from implying one another, the universality of citizenship, in the sense of the inclusion and participation of everyone, stands in tension with the other two meanings of universality embedded in modern political ideas: universality as generality, and universality as equal treatment. First, the ideal that the activities of citizenship express or create a general will that transcends the particular differences of group affiliation, situation, and

interest has in practice excluded groups judged not capable of adopting the general point of view; the ideal of citizenship as expressing a general will has tended to enforce a homogeneity of citizens. To the degree that contemporary proponents of revitalized citizenship retain the ideal of a general will and common life, they implicitly support the same exclusions and homogeneity. Thus, I argue that the inclusion and participation of everyone in public discussion and decision making requires *mechanisms for group representation*. Second, where differences in capacities, culture, values, and behavioral styles exist among groups, but some of these groups are privileged, strict adherence to a principle of equal inclusion and partici-pation of everyone in social and political institutions therefore sometimes requires the articulation of *special rights* that attend to group differences in order to undermine oppression and disadvantage. (1995, pp. 176–177, italics added)

Thus, Young's conception of citizenship in multicultural societies is at odds with the liberal-democratic view. Furthermore, Young advocates the very mechanisms rejected by Gutmann in terms of defining *group rights*. In other words, whereas liberals and some civic republicans are likely to see groups in instrumental terms, feminist and multicultural theorists see groups in intrinsic terms. That is, for liberals, groups provide meaning to free and equal individuals qua individuals. For group theorists, groups have independent standing qua groups. Indeed, to group theorists such as Young, speaking of equality among citizens if there is not equality among groups makes no sense.

What definitions of *citizenship* can we derive from the feminist and multicultural perspectives (chapter 2.6)? In addition to those compe-tencies identified by Gaventa as cited here, citizens take a critical stance toward government. They ask the question, "Who benefits?" and seek to identify the degree to which policies benefit some groups over others. In finding answers to those questions, they also possess the knowledge and skills necessary to redress the unbalanced distribution of benefits provided by government policy. Further, such citizens understand the histories of oppression and resistance of groups to which they themselves may not belong, and seek to find solidarity with their struggles. Consequently, coa-lition building in terms of redressing past oppression or resisting current oppression is an important civic skill from the feminist and multicultural perspectives.

Having reviewed political science theories that can inform definitions of *civic outcomes*, the contributions of political scientists to the literature of civic engagement and service learning are reviewed next.

Political Science Research and Civic Learning

As ubiquitous as the term *civic engagement* has become in higher education, as Berger (2009) points out, the term did not appear in political science literature until 1993, and Battistoni (2002) notes that political scientists did not begin to examine civic education as a desired teaching outcome until the late 1990s. Still, since the late 1990s civic engagement and civic learning have become valid areas for political science research and much of that research has focused on service learning as the principal pedagogy for teaching civic engagement.

Tables 2.2.2 and 2.2.3 are suggestive of the growth in political scientists' interest in civic engagement, civic education, and service learning. A keyword search was conducted in the journal *PS: Political Science and Politics*, which is the American Political Science Association's primary journal for articles related to teaching and the profession, and the *Journal of Political Science*

TABLE 2.2.2

Keyword Search Results by Appearances in Abstracts and Article Titles in *PS: Political Science and Politics:* 1990–1999; 2000–2009; and 2010–2015

Keyword	1990–1999		2000–2009		2010–2015	
	Abstract	Title	Abstract	Title	Abstract	Title
Civic	12	14	39	20	6	3
Civic Education	1	10	18	8	8	5
Civic Engagement	12	0	10	5	14	11
Citizenship	12	5	38	11	22	5
Service Learning	6	3	19	11	4	1

TABLE 2.2.3

Keyword Search Results by Appearances in Abstracts and Titles in the *Journal of Political Science Education:* 2005–2015

Keyword	2005–2015	
	Abstract	Title
Civic	17	30
Civic Education	10	7
Civic Engagement	13	14
Citizenship	0	0
Service Learning	6	8

Education, which was first published in 2005, for the frequency with which keywords "civic," "civic education," "civic engagement," "citizenship," and "service learning" appeared in article abstracts and article titles.

Between 2000 and 2009, there was a relative increase in the appearance of these topics as measured by the keyword searches in *PS: Political Science and Politics* compared to the previous decade. It remains to be seen whether that trend will continue during the 2010 through 2019 decade. Because the *Journal of Political Science Education* is a relatively new journal, a similar comparison could not be made. Still, over the past decade, the journal has published an average of 4.7 articles per year related to the topic "civic"; 1.7 articles per year related to the topic "civic education"; 2.7 articles per year related to the topic "civic engagement"; and 1.4 articles per year related to the topic "service learning." The remainder of this section provides a brief overview of political science research on service learning and civic engagement and some of the limitations of the research so far.

One of the first major works by a political scientist to examine the relationship between civic engagement (although the author uses *citizenship* as the preferred term) and service learning was Benjamin Barber's (1992) *An Aristocracy of Everyone*. Barber argues for a civic republican conception of citizenship and service in which service emerges from individuals' sense of mutual obligation, community, and civic responsibility. Barber also argues that service learning not only is the preferred mechanism for preparing college students for a life of active citizenship, but also should be a required component of college education. However, he never specifies which particular civic education and citizenship outcomes should be pursued through service learning other than general outcomes of "autonomy," "public judgement," "mutual responsibility," and "empowerment" (p. 231).

One of the main contributions of Barber's work is that it is grounded in an explicit theory of civic engagement and therefore gives the researcher the basis for assumptions and hypotheses related to civic learning outcomes. For example, Westheimer and Kahne (2004) applied Barber's and others' theories to construct a typology of three kinds of citizen—the personally responsible citizen, the participatory citizen, and the justice-oriented citizen—and developed operational measures for each citizen type. They then compared two high school–level civic education programs to evaluate the degree to which the respective programs reinforced one citizen type over the others.

Another major contribution by political scientists was the edited volume by Battistoni and Hudson (1997), *Experiencing Citizenship: Concepts and Models for Service-Learning in Political Science*, which was a volume in the service learning in the disciplines series (then published by the American Association for Higher Education, now published by Stylus Publishing) with Edward Zlotkowski as the series editor. Although that volume provided powerful examples of how service learning could be integrated into political science courses, it did not provide for competing models for civic learning outcomes. Furthermore, from a scholarly perspective, the volume offered single-case studies and, as the title of the volume states, models for service learning, but not necessarily models for civic learning or research on civic learning from the perspective of political science.

Also in 1997, the American Political Science Association, under the leadership of Elinor Ostrom, established a Task Force for Civic Education in the 21st Century in response to a perceived crisis of civic and political disengagement (Carter & Elshtain, 1997). The work of the task force established civic engagement and civic education as important and necessary goals for American political scientists and gave impetus to the scholarship of teaching and learning with respect to civic engagement. I summarize some of the results of that impetus in the following section.

The September 2000 issue of *PS: Political Science and Politics* included a special section focusing on the importance of service learning to the civic education mission of the discipline. Authors reported research results on the impact of service learning on students' political knowledge (Delli Carpini & Keeter, 2000; Hepburn, Niemi, & Chapman, 2000), civic values and attitudes (Campbell, 2000; Hildreth, 2000; Hunter & Brisbin, 2000), and political participation (Walker, 2000). As useful as these articles were for highlighting the importance of service learning as civic engagement and civic education, the articles lacked explicit theoretical frameworks and cited only general civic learning outcomes.

Another contribution by political scientists to the civic engagement and service learning literature is Redlawsk and Rice's (2009) *Civic Service: Service-Learning with State and Local Government Partners*. This volume presents case studies of service learning partnerships between universities and state and local government agencies, generally driven by political science instructors and courses. Such partnerships, they argue, "have the potential to engage five constituencies: students in the service learning classes; professors teaching the classes; officials with the government agencies; other individuals and groups of the communities . . . and the citizens served by the government agencies" (p. 5). Furthermore, the result of the interaction among these constituencies leads to "the building of civic assets and the production of tangible benefits [for all constituents]" (p. 7). One of the contributions of this volume is that it focuses on service learning partnerships as the primary unit of analysis with a special emphasis on the impact on community partners and the populations served by those partners. On the other hand, because the volume focuses on partnerships, civic outcomes of students are not considered.

More recently, the American Political Science Association published an edited volume on civic education titled *Teaching Civic Engagement: From Student to Active Citizen* (McCartney, Bennion, & Simpson, 2013). Containing conceptual chapters as well as case studies on civic education within subdisciplines of political science, the volume serves an advocacy role for and is an exemplar of teaching political science for civic engagement. Several of the chapters focus on service learning as a principle pedagogical tool for preparing students for active citizenship. However, few of the volume's 28 chapters offer specific civic learning outcomes appropriate to the discipline. Beaumont's (2013) chapter, "Political Learning and Democratic Capacities: Some Challenges and Evidence of Promising Approaches," comes closest to identifying specific civic learning outcomes in her summary of the survey used in the Carnegie Foundation's Political Engagement Project (PEP). The survey identified four categories of civic and political engagement: political knowledge, political motivation, civic and political skills, and civic and political involvement.

This chapter's review of political science theories and the recent political science literature on civic engagement illuminates two key points. First, political science theories can provide conceptual frameworks from which researchers can identify specific civic learning outcomes. Second, although defining *civic learning outcomes* is possible within these frameworks, political scientists have rarely used the frameworks to differentiate and generate more specific delineations of civic learning outcomes and, when they have, the identified outcomes were too broad or vague to measure. The following sections seek to correct this oversight by specifying specific civic learning outcomes that can be derived from these theories and existing instruments that can be applied to the measurement and evaluation of those outcomes.

Civic Learning Outcomes, Survey Instruments, and Service Learning Research

This section describes specific instruments that can be used to measure civic learning outcomes based on the political science theories discussed earlier in the chapter. Following a brief description of the instruments, this section introduces specific civic learning outcomes, aligns those outcomes with the relevant theories, and identifies which of the instruments would be useful in measuring those outcomes.

The Civic Attitudes and Skills Questionnaire (CASQ) was developed by Moely, Mercer, Ilustre, Miron, and McFarland (2002). The instrument contains six subscales measuring the following outcome categories: civic action, interpersonal and problem-solving skills, political awareness, leadership skills, social justice attitudes, and diversity attitudes.

From The Center for Research on Civic Learning and Engagement Index of Civic and Political Engagement, Andolina, Keeter, Zukin, and Jenkins (2003) developed an Index of Civic and Political Engagement as part of a research project undertaken for the Center for Information and Research on Civic Learning and Engagement (CIRCLE). The index contains four sets of questions used to create subscales for the following categories: civic behavior, electoral behavior, political voice, and attentiveness.

Indexes of Tolerance

Putnam (2000) created "Indexes of Tolerance for Racial Integration, Gender Equality, and Civil Liberties" (p. 353). The indexes measure tolerance for racial integration, tolerance for feminism, and tolerance for civil liberties. In the PEP, Beaumont, Colby, Ehrlich, and Torney-Purta (2006) developed pretest and posttest questionnaires to measure college students' civic and political engagement. The questionnaire contains several subscales, including knowledge and understanding; skills; identity, values, and norms; interest and motivation; efficacy; and action and involvement. Indicators of tolerance are identified in the skills of collaboration subscale. The complete questionnaire can be requested from Beaumont (beaumont@polisci.umn.edu).

The Social Capital Index

One way of measuring civic values and dispositions is to identify individuals' commitment to building and sustaining social capital, those social networks and communal bonds based on norms of trust and reciprocity. Putnam's (2000) social capital index contains measures of community organizational life, engagement in public affairs, community volunteerism, informal sociability, and social trust.

Theories, Outcomes, and Measures

Table 2.2.4 summarizes the civic learning outcomes derived from the political theories discussed in this chapter. These outcomes are presented as knowledge, skills, and values. Following each outcome, there is a parenthetical reference to existing quantitative instruments described previously that can be used to measure the outcomes. It should be noted that none of the scales referenced previously and in Table 2.2.4 contain measures of civic and political knowledge. The author recommends that those interested in creating their own political knowledge scales review the U.S. Department of Education's *NAEP Civics Report Card for the Nation* (1999) for a description of political

TABLE 2.2.4

Political Theories, Outcomes, and Relevant Evaluation Instruments

Political Theory	Knowledge	Skills	Values
Rawls's Liberal Theory of Justice	Identifies civil liberties and rights protected by the Bill of Rights and the 14th Amendment Identifies political, social, and economic inequalities Explains sources of inequalities	Political and community engagement skills commensurate with emphasis on protecting principles of liberty and equality; for example, acquires political information, evaluates political information, communicates political views through a variety of media (CIRCLE, Political Voice subscale; PEP Political Influence and Action and Political Analysis and Judgment Scales) Identifies multiple access points for promoting political change (PEP Contextual Efficacy Scale)	Expresses a commitment to redress inequalities and injustices Commitment to democratic government Commitment to equality of opportunity and political representation (CASQ, Diversity Scale; Indexes of Tolerance) Negative response to merit-based justifications for political and social inequality (CASQ Social Justice Scale)
Civic Republicanism	Identifies civic responsibilities consistent with membership in democratic society, e.g., voting, jury duty. Identifies belonging to various political, social, and ethnic communities Defines *the public good*	Volunteering and community service (CASQ, Civic Action Scale; CIRCLE Civic Behavior subscale; Social Capital Index, measures of "community organizational life" and "community volunteerism") Political engagement (CIRCLE Electoral Behavior subscale; PEP Expectations for Future Political Action Scale; Social Capital Index, measures of "engagement in public affairs")	Willingness to place public interests over private interests Commitment to the norm of reciprocity (CASQ, Social Justice and Diversity Attitudes Scales)

Feminism/ Multiculturalism	Accurately summarizes histories of oppressed groups	Consciousness raising (PEP Skills of Teamwork and Collaboration and Leadership and Communication Scales and PEP Contextual Efficacy Scale)	Expresses commitment to tolerance of individual and group differences (CASQ, Social Justice and Diversity Attitudes Scales; Indexes of Tolerance)
	Recognizes reality of historical oppression.	Acts individually or in concert with others to correct injustices based on race, ethnicity, religion, gender, and/or sexual orientation (PEP Skills of Teamwork and Collaboration and Leadership and Communication Scales)	Expresses commitment to equal political representation of groups (CASQ, Social Justice and Diversity Attitudes Scales; Indexes of Tolerance)
	Identifies strategies of individual and group resistance to oppression	"Popular" research skills; in other words, can identify communal sources of knowledge and expertise	Expresses commitment to solidarity with oppressed groups (CASQ, Social Justice and Diversity Attitudes Scales)
		Models democratic behavior in organizational settings (CASQ, Interpersonal and Problem-Solving Skills Scale; PEP Skills of Teamwork and Collaboration and Leadership and Communication Scales)	
		Can create coalitions among diverse groups	
		Note: The PEP subscales are based on respondents' self-assessments in Likert scale-measured responses to the following items:	
		PEP Teamwork and Collaboration Subscale	
		Ability to reach a compromise	
		Help diverse groups work together	
		Deal with conflict when it comes up	
		Talk about social barriers such as race	
		PEP Leadership and Communication Subscale Items	
		Articulate my ideas and beliefs to others	
		Assume the leadership of a group	
		Make a statement at a public meeting	

(Continues)

TABLE 2.2.4. (Continued)

Political Theory	Knowledge	Skills	Values
		PEP Contextual Efficacy Subscale Working with others, how hard would it be for you to accomplish the following? Getting the town government to build an addition to the local senior center Influencing a state policy or budget decision Influencing the outcome of a local election Organizing an event to benefit a charity Starting an after-school program for children whose parents work Influencing decisions about who teaches on your campus. The CASQ scales are based on respondents' self-assessments in Likert scale-measured responses to the following items: CASQ: Interpersonal and Problem Solving Skills I can listen to other people's opinions. I can work cooperatively with a group of people. I can think logically in solving problems. I can communicate well with others. I can successfully resolve conflicts with others. I can easily get along with people. I try to find effective ways of solving problems. I try to place myself in other's positions to try to understand them. I find it easy to make friends. I can think analytically in solving problems. I try to place myself in the place of others in trying to assess their current situation. I tend to solve problems by talking them out.	

and civic knowledge outcomes and the National Center for Education Statistics' (n.d.) website to review sample items used in the *Civics Report Card*.

Conclusions and Questions for Future Research

One may draw several inferences from Table 2.2.4 about the relationship between civic-learning outcomes derived from political science theory and existing quantitative tools. First, many of the outcomes derived from political science theory can be measured with existing quantitative tools or by adapting existing tools to better fit a specific theory. Second, there are opportunities for service learning researchers to develop new scales to measure the specific sets of outcomes related to specific theoretical frameworks. For example, scales based on political knowledge outcomes are needed, as are procedures or protocols that can provide for direct observation of civic skills and behaviors. Third, none of the instruments summarized in this chapter focus on political and civic knowledge, but rather self-reports of skills, values and dispositions, and intentions (see chapter 3.5).

This last inference is disturbing. This is particularly so within the political science discipline, for, as Delli Carpini and Keeter (2000) point out, political scientists are most likely "to embrace a teaching philosophy that dictates transmitting knowledge and cultivating a critical perspective rather than encouraging participation" (p. 635). Consequently, such instructors are not likely to integrate service learning if there is little evidence of its positive impact on political knowledge and a critical perspective on politics. As a result, a topic that deserves greater consideration within service learning research is the degree to which service learning contributes to participants' political knowledge.

Another topic that deserves greater consideration is the kind of political knowledge students need for effective civic engagement. Does it matter whether students know how many justices sit on the Supreme Court or the names of their senators and representatives? Is it more important that students know what government agencies address issues of concern to them and how to contact and put pressure on those agencies? Is it more important that students know political facts or that they have an understanding of social issues and political processes? The theories reviewed in this chapter allow researchers to address these questions. For example, liberal theorists would tend to emphasize facts and a basic understanding of processes, particularly voting. Civic republicans would emphasize processes that bring citizens together to address common goals, and critical theorists would emphasize knowledge of rights and processes that can be applied in the pursuit of social justice and social change.

Some of the outcomes derived from the political science theories discussed in this chapter are more appropriate for *political* engagement and others more appropriate for *civic* engagement. In their study of voluntary activity in the United States, Verba, Schlozman, and Brady (1995) make a distinction between political participation and civic participation. They define *political participation* as an "activity that has the intent or effect of influencing government action—either directly by affecting the making of public policy or indirectly by influencing the selection of people who make those policies" (p. 38). Civic participation involves those voluntary activities that occur outside the realm of politics. However, they also note that the distinction between political and civic is not always precise or clear. For example, according to the authors volunteering for an organization that not only provides direct service to individuals but also advocates for those individuals to government officials is a form of political engagement. Because of this overlap, it is not always easy to delineate among the knowledge, skills, dispositions, and values needed for activities that are primarily political and those that are primarily civic. Likewise, some combination of political knowledge, skills, dispositions, and values will be necessary for effective civic engagement and vice versa. Consequently, researchers applying the political science theories described in this chapter should focus on those outcomes that are salient to their specific object of study and the theory upon which their research is based.

Another point related to political knowledge also emerges from my review of the literature and exiting instruments, namely determining how students' political knowledge should be measured. In addition to the results of tests of students' knowledge that could be course-specific or general, researchers can use student reflections on service learning experiences and focus-group analyses to measure the relationships between students' political knowledge and their service experiences. Furthermore, none of the theorists discussed here, except for Gutmann (1999), make an explicit appeal for formal political and civic education. Yet they believe that citizens can develop the attributes each theorist requires. Consequently, researchers who do not specialize in political science or history should reject the assumption that either content specialization in those disciplines is required to measure civic and political knowledge or that such knowledge is not required for the development of democratic citizens.

Hepburn, Niemi, and Chapman (2000) offer another set of research questions related to service learning and political science, particularly in regard to students' civic attitudes. They ask what "content, service placements, and time commitment actually contribute to positive changes in democratic attitudes" (p. 621). Of course, to respond to their question, one must first ask what democratic attitudes one wants to measure based on a particular political science theory.

The political science theories and survey instruments reviewed herein can assist one in identifying such attitudes. For example, based on liberal theory, one would want to assess changes in attitudes with respect to students' respect for equality in terms of liberties and rights. Based on civic republican theory, one would want to measure changes in students' definitions of and commitment to *the public good*. Based on critical theory, one would want to evaluate changes in students' knowledge of sources of social inequality and commitments to redressing such inequalities. Then one can investigate the degree to which course content, type of service placement, type and nature of reflection, and time in the placement contribute to the positive development of civic knowledge, skills, values, and attitudes as described by one's conceptual framework based on one of the political science theories discussed in this chapter.

References

Alejandro, R. (1998). *The limits of Rawlsian justice*. Baltimore, MD: Johns Hopkins University Press.

Andolina, M., Keeter, S., Zukin, C., & Jenkins, K. (2003). *A guide to the Index of Political and Civic Engagement*. College Park, MD: The Center for Information and Research on Civic Learning and Engagement.

Barber, B. R. (1992). *An aristocracy for everyone: The politics of education and the future of America*. Oxford, England: Oxford University Press.

Battistoni, R. M. (2001). *Civic engagement across the disciplines: A resource book for service-learning faculty in all disciplines*. Providence, RI: Campus Compact.

Battistoni, R. M. (2002). Service-learning in political science: An introduction. *PS: Political Science and Politics, 35*, 615–616.

Battistoni, R. M. (2013). Should political scientists care about civic education? *Perspectives on Politics, 11*, 1135–1138.

Battistoni, R. M., & Hudson, W. E. (Eds.). (1997). *Experiencing citizenship: Concepts and models for service-learning in political science*. Sterling, VA: Stylus.

Beaumont, E. (2013). Political learning and democratic capacities: Some challenges and evidence of promising approaches. In A. R. M. McCartney, E. A. Bennion, & D. Simpson (Eds.), *Teaching civic engagement: From student to active citizen* (pp. 41–56). Washington, DC: American Political Science Association.

Beaumont, E., Colby, A., Ehrlich, T., & Torney-Purta, J. (2006). Promoting political competence and engagement in college students: An empirical study. *Journal of Political Science Education, 2*, 249–270.

Beiner, R. (Ed.). (1995). *Theorizing citizenship*. Albany, NY: State University of New York Press.

Berger, B. (2009). Political theory, political science, and the end of civic engagement. *Perspectives on Politics, 7,* 335–350.

Boyte, H. (1999). Building the commonwealth: Citizenship as public work. In S. L. Elkin & K. E. Soltan (Eds.), *Citizen competence and democratic institutions* (pp. 259–278). University Park, PA: The Pennsylvania State University Press.

Campbell, D. E. (2000). Social capital and service-learning. *PS: Political Science and Politics, 33,* 641–645.

Carter, L. H., & Elshtain, J. B. (1997). Task force on civic education statement of purpose. *PS: Political Science and Politics, 30,* 745.

Daniels, N. (Ed.). (1975). *Reading Rawls: Critical studies on Rawls'* A Theory of Justice. New York, NY: Basic Books.

Davion, V., & Wolf, C. (Eds.). (2000). *The idea of a political liberalism: Essays on Rawls.* Lanham, MD: Rowman & Littlefield.

Delli Carpini, M. X., & Keeter, S. (2000). What should be learned through service-learning? *PS: Political Science and Politics,* 635–637.

Dombrowski, D. A. (2001). *Rawls and religion: The case for political liberalism.* Albany, NY: State University of New York Press.

Flatham, R. E. (1996). Liberal versus civic, republican, democratic, and other vocational educations: Liberalism and institutionalized education. *Political Theory, 96,* 4–32.

Freeman, S. (Ed.). (2003). *The Cambridge companion to Rawls.* New York, NY: Cambridge University Press.

Gaventa, J. (1999). Citizen knowledge, citizen competence. In S. L. Elkin & K. E. Soltan (Eds.), *Citizen competence and democratic institutions* (pp. 49–66). University Park, PA: The Pennsylvania State University Press.

Gutmann, A. (1999). *Democratic education.* Princeton, NJ: Princeton University Press.

Hepburn, M. A., Niemi, R. G., & Chapman, C. (2000). Service-learning in college political science: Queries and commentary. *PS: Political Science and Politics,* 617–622.

Hildreth, R. W. (2000). Theorizing citizenship and evaluating public achievement. *PS: Political Science and Politics, 33,* 627–632.

Hunter, S., & Brisbin, Jr., R. A. (2000). The impact of service learning on democratic and civic values. *PS: Political Science and Politics,* 33, 623–626.

Kukathas, C., & Pettit, P. (1990). *Rawls: A theory of justice and its critics.* Stanford, CA: Stanford University Press.

Lukes, S. (1974). *Power: A radical view.* London: Macmillan Press.

Macedo, S., Alex-Assensoh, Y., Berry, J. M., Brintnall, M., Campbell, D. E., Fraga, L. R., . . . & Galston, W. A. (2005). *Democracy at risk.* Washington, DC: Brookings Institute.

MacIntyre, A. (1984). *After virtue: A study in moral theory* (2nd ed.). Notre Dame, IN: University of Notre Dame Press.

McCartney, A. R. M., Bennion, E. A., & Simpson, D. (Eds.). (2013). *Teaching civic engagement: From student to active citizen.* Washington, DC: American Political Science Association.

Moely, B. E., Mercer, S. H., Ilustre, V., Miron, D., & McFarland, M. (2002). Psychometric properties and correlates of the Civic Attitudes and Skills Questionnaire (CASQ): A measure of students' attitudes related to service-learning. *Michigan Journal of Community Service Learning, 8*(2), 15–26.

Mulhall, S., & Swift, A. (1992). *Liberals and communitarians.* Oxford, England: Blackwell Press.

National Center for Education Statistics. n.d. *NAEP questions tool.* Retrieved from http://nces.ed.gov/nationsreportcard/itmrls/portal.asp?type=search&subject =civics

Pogge, T. W. (1989). *Realizing Rawls.* Ithaca, NY: Cornell University Press.

Putnam, R.D. (2000). *Bowling alone: The collapse and revival of American community.* New York, NY: Simon & Schuster.

Rawls, J. (1971). *A theory of justice.* Cambridge, MA: Harvard University Press.

Rawls, J. (2001). *Justice as fairness: A restatement.* Cambridge, MA: Harvard University Press.

Redlawsk, D. P., & Rice, T. (Eds.). (2009). *Civic service: Service-learning with state and local government partners.* San Francisco, CA: Jossey-Bass.

Sandel, M. J. (1982). *Liberalism and the limits of justice.* New York, NY: Cambridge University Press.

Sandel, M. J. (1984). The procedural republic and the unencumbered self. *Political Theory, 12,* 81–96.

Sandel, M. J. (1996). *Democracy's discontent: American in search of a public philosophy.* Cambridge, MA: The Belknap Press of Harvard University Press.

Schachter, H. L. (1998). Civic education: Three early American Political Science Association committees and their relevance to our times. *PS: Political Science and Politics, 31,* 631–635.

Snyder, R.C. (2001). Should political science have a civic mission? An overview of the historical evidence. *PS: Political Science and Politics, 34,* 301–305.

U.S. Department of Education. Office of Educational Research and Improvement. National Center for Education Statistics. (1999). *The NAEP civics report card for the nation.* NCES 2000-457. Washington, DC: U.S. Department of Education.

Verba, S., Schlozman, K. L., & Brady, H. E. (1995). *Voice and equality: Civic volunteerism in American politics.* Cambridge, MA: Harvard University Press.

Walker, T. (2000). The service/politics split: Rethinking service to teach political engagement. *PS: Political Science and Politics, 33,* 647–649.

Walzer, M. (1983). *Spheres of justice: A defense of pluralism and equality.* New York, NY: Basic Books.

Westheimer, J., & Kahne, J. (2004). What kind of citizen? The politics of educating for Democracy. *American Educational Research Journal, 41,* 237–269.

Young, I. M. (1990). *Justice and the politics of difference.* Princeton, NJ: Princeton University Press.

Young, I. M. (1995). Polity and group difference: A critique of the idea of universal citizenship. In. R. Beiner (Ed.), *Theorizing citizenship* (pp. 175–208). Albany, NY: State University of New York Press.

EDUCATIONAL THEORY AND STUDENT CIVIC OUTCOMES

Marcia B. Baxter Magolda and Lisa M. Boes

Collegians face an increasingly complex world as they take up adult roles during and after college. Increasing globalization, cultural clashes, and economic challenges are just a few of the major issues that require navigating multiple perspectives to function effectively in a diverse society. Higher education's emphasis on civic outcomes, exemplified by the Association of American Colleges & Universities' (AAC&U, 2015) core commitments regarding educating students for personal and social responsibility, is aimed at preparing collegians to become global citizens. Despite widespread agreement on major civic outcomes and their importance, as well as the growth of service learning courses and related civic education opportunities, collegians' progress on civic outcomes is cause for concern (Finley, 2012). Drawing on data from the Cooperative Institutional Research Program, the National Survey of Student Engagement, and the quantitative portion of the Wabash National Study, Finley concluded, "students' civic learning is neither robust nor persuasive" (p. 1).

Examining civic outcomes closely reveals one major reason collegians struggle to achieve them. AAC&U (2015) defines *civic outcomes* via five dimensions for personal and social responsibility: striving for excellence, cultivating personal and academic integrity, contributing to a larger community, taking seriously the perspectives of others, and developing competence in ethical and moral reasoning. The character traits associated with these outcomes include establishing one's own values to guide one's actions. The ability to form one's own values and beliefs through evaluating multiple perspectives, to appreciate and engage multiple perspectives, and to act interdependently within a diverse community in an ethical way are what Kegan (1994) calls demands on the mind. These are demands for complex cognitive, intrapersonal, and interpersonal capacities, or ways of making meaning.

Adult development research (Baxter Magolda, 2009; Baxter Magolda & King, 2012; Kegan, 1994) suggests that these demands on the mind are underdeveloped in most collegians (and many adults). Longitudinal studies of collegians' developmental capacities suggest that most have been socialized to uncritically follow external authority to define their beliefs, identities, and social relationships (Abes & Jones, 2004; Baxter Magolda, 2001; Baxter Magolda & King, 2012; Olson & Pizzolato, in press; Torres & Hernandez, 2007). Coupled with collegians' lack of readiness to explore power and privilege, these can lead to resistance to service learning (Jones, Gilbride-Brown, & Gasiorski, 2005). In contexts in which educators value learners' thoughts and feelings, use learners' experiences as a source of learning, acknowledge the complexity of learning, invite learners' personal authority, and learn mutually with learners, collegians began to question authority and recognize the need to develop their own perspectives (Baxter Magolda, 2009; Baxter Magolda & King, 2004, 2012; Boes, 2006; Pizzolato, 2008). High-quality service learning courses can provide such a context for student development.

Consensus is building that *self-authorship*, defined as the capacity to internally define one's beliefs, values, identies, and social relations, is the necessary developmental capacity for ethical and moral reasoning, intercultural maturity, global citizenship, and leadership (Baxter Magolda & King, 2004; Berger, 2012; Kegan & Lahey, 2009; King & Baxter Magolda, 2005). This chapter articulates the relationship between student and adult development theory and civic outcomes, and it explores how service learning courses that integrate learning partnerships with peers, faculty, and community partners can address the developmental capacities needed to foster civic outcomes.

Adult Development Theory

College student and adult development theory describes the cognitive, intrapersonal, and interpersonal transitions young adults experience as they shift from following authority uncritically to establishing their own beliefs, identities, and social relations. Kegan (1982) explicitly integrated the cognitive, intrapersonal (or identity), and interpersonal dimensions of development as elements of the same meaning-making structure to form a more "sophisticated understanding of the relationship between the psychological and the social, between the past and the present, and between emotion and thought" (p. 15). Kegan explained that meaning-making structures are a combination of elements over which persons have control (i.e., object) and elements that have control over persons (i.e., subject). *Object* is "distinct enough from us that we can do something with it" (Kegan, 1994, p. 32) whereas *subject* "refers to those elements of our knowing or organizing that we are identified with, tied to, fused with, or embedded in. We *have* object; we *are* subject" (p. 32). Growth of the mind comes from "liberating ourselves from that in which we were embedded, making what was subject into object so that we can 'have it' rather than 'be had' by it" (p. 34). Kegan (2000) argued that this growth of the mind stands at the core of *transformative learning*. Similarly, Mezirow (2000) defines *transformative learning* as

> the process by which we transform our taken-for-granted frames of refer-ence (meaning perspectives, habits of mind, mind-sets) to make them more inclusive, discriminating, open, emotionally capable of change, and reflec-tive so that they may generate beliefs and opinions that will prove more true or justified to guide action. (pp. 7–8)

Mezirow notes that this requires "participation in constructive discourse to use the experience of others to assess reasons justifying these assumptions" (p. 8).

The growth of the mind that is required to achieve civic outcomes is a shift from uncritical reliance on external authority toward *self-authorship*, or the internal capacity to craft one's beliefs, identities, and social relations. Kegan (1994) described this shift through five meaning-making structures called orders of consciousness. His second through fourth orders are most typi-cal in adult life (Berger, 2012; Drago-Severson, 2010). Persons using second order, also termed *instrumental*, meaning making (typically late adolescents and young adults) rely on external authority found in rules and regulations. Focused on their own perspectives and unable to take the perspectives of oth-ers, they follow rules to meet their needs and avoid negative consequences. The hallmark of the shift from second to third order, or *socialized meaning making*, is the ability to take others' perspectives. This yields loyalty to others beyond the self; it simultaneously involves becoming enmeshed in others' perspectives as the new source of authority. Socialized meaning-makers act in ways to meet the expectations they perceive others have of them and sacrifice their own needs in the process. The hallmark of the shift from third to fourth order, or *self-authored meaning making,* is that authority becomes internal to the self. Able to hold multiple perspectives and their own simultaneously, self-authored meaning makers craft internal criteria to guide their beliefs, identities, and social relations. Studies suggest that about one-third of adults use self-authored meaning making (Kegan, 1994; Kegan & Lahey, 2009). Less than 1% use fifth order, or *self-transforming meaning making* (Kegan &

Lahey, 2009), in which persons continually use others' perspectives to transform their own perspectives to become more expansive. The capacity of self-authorship is necessary to meet most civic outcomes, yet the capacity for self-transformation would support these outcomes more fully.

Baxter Magolda's (2001, 2009) 29-year longitudinal study of adults 18 to 47 years old reveals a more detailed portrait of this journey toward self-authorship through the college experience into middle adulthood. Baxter Magolda described this journey through three phases: uncritically following external formulas, the crossroads, and self-authorship. Her participants, 101 predominantly White, traditional-age college students at the outset of the study, uncritically followed external formulas upon entering college (Baxter Magolda, 2001). Their trust in authority figures led them to adopt authorities' perspectives for what to believe and follow authorities' vision for how to succeed. Tensions between their own and others' expectations occurred during their college years when authorities disagreed, they found it difficult to succeed following formulas uncritically, or they were encouraged to think for themselves. This led them into a crossroads. The majority of the 80 participants still remaining in the study during their senior year left college in this crossroads, struggling to navigate their emerging internal voices with external expectations (Baxter Magolda, 2001). The 70 who continued into the postcollege phase quickly encountered pressure, primarily in their work contexts, to take responsibility for their work, beliefs, identities, and social relations. Over the course of their 20s and 30s, depending on their particular circumstances, they began to listen to their internal voices, work to cultivate them, and eventually came to trust themselves to coordinate external influences based on internal criteria. Their experiences in their 30s and 40s revealed that self-authorship began when participants realized that although reality was beyond their control, they could control their reactions to it. This initial trust in their internal voices led them to build internal foundations, or philosophies of life, upon which to ground their actions. As they lived out these foundations, they secured these internal commitments. These three elements of self-authorship—trusting the internal voice, building internal foundations, and securing internal commitments—evolved in a cyclical fashion as participants returned to earlier elements when new challenges arose (Baxter Magolda, 2009). Participants using self-authored meaning making were able to navigate the complexities of their multiple adult roles and challenges.

The Wabash National Study (WNS), a longitudinal study of college students conducted 20 years after Baxter Magolda's college phase, yielded a similar portrait (Baxter Magolda & King, 2012). Nearly 1,000 annual interviews with a diverse sample of students from six different campuses revealed nuances within Baxter Magolda's three phases of external formulas, crossroads, and self-authorship resulting in a 10-positon description of this journey (Baxter Magolda & King, 2012). Three external positions describe the growing tensions with trusting authority; four crossroads positions describe constructions of internal voice upon entering the crossroads, and the movement of the internal voice to the foreground while working one's way out of the crossroads by listening to and cultivating the internal voice. Because too little data revealed self-authored meaning making by the WNS participants' senior year in college, the 10-position description relies on Baxter Magolda's original three elements of self-authorship. The WNS links meaning making to civic outcomes because it is focused on both self-authorship and liberal arts outcomes. For example, King, Baxter Magolda, and Massé (2011) found that participants who used more internal meaning making exhibited advanced levels of *intercultural maturity*, defined as "how people become increasingly capable of understanding and acting in ways that are interculturally aware and appropriate" (King & Baxter Magolda, 2005, p. 573).

Additional longitudinal studies portray nuanced versions of the journey toward self-authorship in multiple student populations. Torres's study of Latino/a students on multiple campuses revealed that students traveled through external formulas, the crossroads, self-authorship, and building an internal foundation (Torres & Hernandez, 2007). They also experienced additional developmental tasks, including recognizing how their cultural history influenced their self-authored choices, incorporating an informed Latino/a identity and corresponding cultural choices into their everyday lives, negotiating relationships based on their Latino/a identity, and recognizing and dealing with racism. Abes and Jones (2004) reported that their lesbian participants encountered additional, similar dynamics in resisting social norms. Although they also used external formulas, crossroads, and self-authored meaning making, these participants had to resist and participate in changing social norms in the process of defining their identities. Olson and Pizzolato (in press) report similar dynamics in following college students over the course of one year in a welfare-to-work program. Participants were encouraged to develop their internal voices in the college setting yet were restricted from doing as a result of the need to meet external requirements of governmental agencies. They were able to repurpose some external formulas to begin to use their voices into these contexts.

Evaluation of Existing Service Learning Research

The research agenda for service learning in the 1990s turned attention to effects on students' intellectual, moral, and citizenship development (Giles,

Honnet, & Migliore, 1991). In this chapter, we review the literature that connects service learning practice to transformative learning and adult development, with a focus on research that addresses how students learn, or the learning and developmental processes underneath civic outcomes, and the developmental capacity students bring to the experiences. Although studies support transformative learning as a means to help students achieve personal, civic, moral, and intellectual learning and development (Feinstein, 2004; Kiely, 2004), few studies make direct links between these outcomes and the developmental capacities that enable them.

Kiely's (2005) transformative learning model, drawn from longitudinal research with students participating in international service learning programs and informed by Mezirow (2000), outlines a five-step process by which experiences shape students' "sense of self, lifestyle, connection to others, view of global problems, and purpose in life" (Kiely, 2004, p. 5). One element of this pedagogical approach is experiences of *dissonance*, or *disorienting dilemmas,* in which participants experience incongruence between their frame of reference and aspects of the service learning context. The learning process and the outcomes are developmental in nature, educating students who are "more socially responsible, self-directed, and less dependent on false assumptions" (Kiely, 2005, p. 7). Those who conduct inquiry using this model would benefit from designing studies that explore the developmental capacities students bring to the service learning experience in relation to the transformational learning process and associated civic outcomes.

Studies that link developmental capacity to self-authorship, critical Whiteness, and social identity examine the ways in which sociocultural backgrounds and developmental capacity influence how students interpret service learning experiences and implications for promoting desirable outcomes (Jones & Abes, 2004; Jones, Gilbride-Brown, & Gasiorski, 2005; Jones, Robbins, & LePeau, 2011). Although not disputing positive service learning outcomes, Jones, Gilbride-Brown, and Gasiorski (2005) revealed evidence of resistance to the complexities of the service learning context exhibited even by students who were capable of the academic challenges in the course. These authors attributed students' resistance to "deeply engrained privileges, lack of exposure to those different from themselves, and absence of the developmental complexity required to recognize privilege" (p. 16). Their findings are consistent with one of the foundational philosophies that shapes service learning practice, Dewey's (1938) reflective inquiry. Dewey cautioned that not all experiences were *educative* and that some experiences could be *miseducative*, engendering callousness, leading to insensitivity and unresponsiveness, and limiting the possibility of future learning. Students' reactions to service learning experiences stem from a complex interaction of the nature of the experience and students' ability to reflect upon and make meaning of the experience from their developmental and sociocultural perspectives.

Giles (2014) also found positive outcomes associated with dissonance, but when the dissonance was high intensity and associated with a differing political perspective, students could become entrenched in their own perspectives, disrupting learning. Similarly, in their three-campus study of short-term immersion programs, Jones, Rowan-Kenyon, Ireland, Niehaus, and Skendall (2012) found that these programs placed many participants in their first intercultural learning experience. Because boundary crossing and engagement with race and culture in the community and among their peers is an important component, these authors recognized the importance of skilled facilitators who are able to manage the level of dissonance students experience and help students "navigate the sometimes intense and emotional discussion on topics such as racism, privilege, homophobia, and other compelling issues that emerge" (p. 216). The quality of facilitation in relation to the level of dissonance students experience is the bridge that promotes developmental learning and helps students "build firm ground in a new place" (Berger, 2004, pp. 345–346, as cited in Giles, 2014).

Boes' (2006) study of the relationship between students' developmental perspective and learning experiences in a community organizing course revealed that learning was mediated by participants' developmental capacity, the nature of dissonance they experienced, and the degree of support available to grow, rather than retreat, from the dissonance. The course was designed to engage students in the following overlapping spheres: (a) intellectual theories about social change and community organizing; (b) narrative explorations of personal values, identies, and relationships related to experience within the course; and (c) opportunities to create strategies and action with others in the community. Reflection papers, class discussions, and individual coaching sessions with the instructor were designed to engage students with the dissonance they experienced. The experiences of two students illustrate this finding and demonstrate ways that relationships with instructors and community partners can mediate the dissonance students may experience in service learning contexts.

The first student, Sam, came to the course primarily from a socialized meaning-making perspective. His initial goal was to recruit college students to reach out to mayors around the country to advance same-sex marriage laws. Sam preferred theory and logic over emotion and thus struggled with the narrative approach. Although he tried it, he felt out of sync with his peers and reported feeling "frustrated and misunderstood" (Boes, 2006, p. 209). He was the only student in the course who chose to pursue a national project. Although he was able to recruit other politically minded students to join his campaign, they made little collective progress. After weeks of receiving discouraging feedback, Sam met with the instructor who asked him to reflect on his goals and the extent to which a national project was realistic and suggested he consider a campus-based project. Sam left this meeting "angry and dismayed" (p. 210) noting that, "it really caught [him] off guard" (p. 209). He went to his next group meeting and said that he wanted to start over. Despite their shock that he was willing to give up a project that had been "[his] baby" (p. 210), the group decided to focus locally, and by collaborating with another campus organization, they recruited 300 students to participate in a local rally and celebration. Sam was conflicted about his new approach, stating the following:

> Wow, stuff started happening. I wrote a response paper and whoa, got [the highest grade]. Everything changed, but I still felt like . . . I wasn't really me in the [grade]. It was what [the instructor] wanted to hear. And I felt really bad about that. But then I said, you know, I'm a persistent guy. . . . So let's get back to the drawing board [and keep trying this]. And then it just sort of went from there. I started over from scratch. And I was working more from the framework, less on my organization. (Boes, 2006, p. 211)

Sam tried on a new role and a new approach to organizing out of frustration and his desire to do well in the course. He experimented with a different way to lead his project, one that aligned with the community organizing principles in the course. When Sam began doing things differently in his project, people responded differently, and it changed how he felt about the work he was doing. Although it did not feel authentic at first, the success he experienced began influencing his perspectives. Sam shared the following thoughts about how his initial intellectual approach limited his ability to engage effectively with others in the community:

> Reflecting back on [our first] meeting. . . . It was my vision. I did too much on my own that left people feeling like it was my project and I should take it from there, make them tacticians but nothing more. Where people did critique, refine, and amend the idea, they did so in the form of improving my vision. It was at once flattering and frustrating, because while I appreciated their recognition of my work, I was looking for others to embrace the idea the way I had. Missing from this puzzle was their motivation. I wanted them to take this abstract idea, as if it were not invented by me, and bring it to everyone for everyone. That, I realize now was a very arrogant plan that presumed I had stumbled upon a vision equivalent to some fundamental truth. By articulating such a specific vision, I necessarily alienated or at least devalued anyone who had a different vision for bringing about change

with respect to this issue. In short, my organization became theoretical and ceased to be functional. I was back at the beginning. (Boes, 2006, pp. 212–213)

Sam experienced a lot of dissonance in the course. He recognized that his project was different than other students', and he was not receiving positive feedback in class discussions or on his papers. When it negatively influenced his grade, he talked with the instructor and reevaluated his approach. It was a risk to change his plans; it meant moving away from the logical analytic way in which he defined himself and opened himself up to peer criticism for changing his strategy.

The second student, Stephen, came into the course with a self-authoring perspective. He joined an existing community development corporation to work on an affordable housing campaign in a low-income Hispanic neighborhood. Stephen also came to the course with an intellectual approach that produced dissonance:

> My original attraction to this class was almost entirely intellectual; I knew I wanted to write a senior thesis [on social capital] and figured this would be a good chance to get practical experience. . . . [I sought out] electoral groups geared towards political action, however, after I listened to three consecutive Hispanic community organizers, each of whom reminded me of an uncle or a cousin, talk about the work they are doing in local low-income communities, I changed course. The original intellectual interest in social capital theory that first attracted me to the class was later fed by the emotional connection to a community with a shared heritage. The emotional connection re-centered the project and allowed for my theoretical interests to reemerge. I have spent the week not only researching potential organizations, but also redesigning the pilot study for my thesis to focus on social capital in marginalized ethnic communities as opposed to political campaigns. The interplay between intellectual and emotional interests has built on itself in a refreshingly regenerative manner. (Boes, 2006, p. 217)

Stephen allowed his emotional connection to influence his thinking and plans. He also recognized the role it played in connecting to his constituents:

> When I first walked into a low-income apartment in [this neighborhood], the question [of plausibility] hit me smack in the face. How can I relate to my constituents that my concerns in their community are genuine? When the constituent turned to me and asked "So why are you in [this neighborhood]?" I did not mention needing to organize people for a class. Instead, I told her how the neighborhood reminds me of the block where my grandfather bought his first house and where my mom grew up. The

woman's expression changed immediately; my short story about my grand-father immigrating here and buying a home transformed me in her eyes. To this woman, struggling to purchase her first home, I was no longer a [college] student there to study her. Instead I became the representation of the potential she desires for her children and her grandchildren. (Boes, 2006, pp. 218–219)

Stephen acknowledged the discomfort he experienced in his outreach and was aware of the power dynamics. He drew from his family history to bridge the differences and work together on shared goals.

Stephen identified another source of dissonance, which he termed the *insider-outsider paradox*, "the tension between getting the distance necessary for a broad perspective while not staying so far away as to not have an impact" (Boes, 2006, p. 221). As an outsider, Stephen recognized that he brought fresh perspectives. He could see things and analyze the situation in ways the long-standing members could not because he was not embedded in the assumptions of the organization. But he also saw how his outsider status held him back from challenging staff members or suggesting changes. Initially, instead of confronting some of the shortcomings, he explained them away. He did not feel that as an outsider he had the right to make changes in the organization.

Near the end of the semester, Stephen scheduled a meeting with a community member who had been active in the organization for many years. When she expressed some of the same concerns that Stephen had "explained away" (Boes, 2006, p. 222) throughout the semester, it validated Stephen's experience, and he began to consider that aspects of his experience were also of an insider. At this point Stephen said, "It was like a wall inside my head fell down. I was immediately struck by the enormity of all of the disconnects that I now saw for what they truly were" (p. 222). He now understood that his own role definitions set up a dichotomy between issue-based and community-building organizing and the conceptual categories influenced how he saw himself and his willingness to intervene. He called this a tension between "distance and proximity" (p. 222).

Stephen looked back on his experience of working with an established community organization: "I struggled most of the class to try and *resolve* the tension between in-class theory and my out-of-class project. . . . By the end of the class, I started to see the *tension itself* as important and helpful. I *accepted* the dissonance instead of trying to minimize it" (Boes, 2006, p. 222).

The community organizing course provided Sam and Stephen experiences of dissonance from which they learned. For Sam, after a meeting with the instructor, he agreed to "try on" (Boes, 2006, p. 226) a new approach, but it was not one he felt was truly his own until things started changing in his project and he experienced it differently. For Stephen, the change in his understanding came through relationships with others in the community. When his community supervisor shared her frustrations, Stephen recognized his own, and he recognized that defining himself as an "outsider" (p. 226) influenced how he approached the work and what he believed was possible.

Although Stephen and Sam both found the course challenging, Stephen experienced significantly more support for the self-authored meaning-making perspective he brought into the course as well as encouragement from community members to develop an even more complex system. Although Stephen was aware of the dissonance he was experiencing throughout the semester, he still found that he could fully participate in class discussions and experiment with other course concepts in his project. Sam, on the other hand, reflected that he had "never felt more in over my head in an academic setting" (Boes, 2006, p. 227). It was out of desperation that he scheduled a meeting with the instructor. Without support for the more socialized aspects of his meaning making, he was unable to consider how he could pursue a project differently. Without clear guidelines about how to structure his project, and clear feedback about how he could correct what was not working, Sam continued to focus most of his energy on what he later described as either "elaborate procrastination" or "theoretical planning with practical goals" (p. 227). As a result, Sam felt like his learning was compacted into the last three weeks of the semester. Sam's experience at the beginning of the course risked being miseducative (Dewey, 1938). Thus even in a service learning course designed to support students, lack of explicit attention to developmental capacities reduced its effectiveness for some students.

Taken together, this evidence reveals that the outcomes of service learning are mediated by the nature of the experience, the sociocultural perspectives learners bring to the experience, learners' developmental capacity to make sense of experiences in more complex ways, educators' ability to support learners in reconstructing their perspectives, and meaningful interactions with community members. The complexity of this process warrants further research to enhance understanding of the relationships between various factors to achieve desirable civic outcomes.

Service Learning Pedagogy: Learning Partnerships

Boes' (2006) model of service learning as constructive-developmental pedagogy outlines the intersections of developmental dimensions in the learning process (see Figure 2.3.1).

Figure 2.3.1. Boes's model of service learning as constructive-developmental pedagogy.

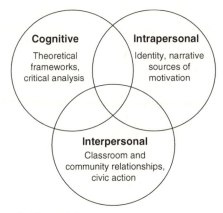

Source. Boes (2006). Adapted with permission.

Cognitive and interpersonal/behavioral domains are linked when students apply course concepts to community activities and use these experiences to evaluate and critique frameworks and theory. Cognitive and intrapersonal domains are linked when students reflect on their identity, articulate it in reflection activities, and craft a narrative account of themselves and their motivation. This blends analytical and emotional approaches and guides students in thinking about themselves and the world. The intrapersonal and interpersonal domains overlap in the behavioral connection of developing and managing relationships in the classroom and in the community. Similarly, Kiely's (2005) Transformational Service Learning Model emphasizes processing dissonance both individually and in relationships.

These dynamics are inherent in the Learning Partnerships Model (LPM; Baxter Magolda, 2009), an established model of constructive-developmental pedagogy that links developmental capacity to curricular and cocurricular design and implementation. Effectively implemented in various service learning contexts (e.g., Egart & Healy, 2004; Yonkers-Talz, 2013), the LPM offers specific guidance to help educators construct learning partnerships that embody the principles of service learning and promote the self-authorship capacity needed to achieve civic outcomes.

The LPM emerged from Baxter Magolda's 29-year longitudinal study of young adult development (2001, 2009). Synthesizing participants' insights from their college, work, and personal life experiences, Baxter Magolda described learning partnerships as the balance of three components that supported participants' growth and three components that challenged it, confirming the long-standing notion that developmental growth results from a balance of challenge and support (Piaget, 1950; Sanford, 1962). Supporting learners' development self-authorship includes the following:

- Respecting their thoughts and feelings, thus affirming the value of their voices,
- Helping them view their experiences as opportunities for learning and growth, and
- Collaborating with them to analyze their own problems, engaging in mutual learning with them. (Baxter Magolda, 2009, p. 251)

Challenging learners to develop self-authorship includes the following:

- Drawing participants' attention to the complexity of their work and life decisions, and discouraging simple solutions
- Encouraging participants to develop their personal authority by listening to their own voices in determining how to live their lives
- Encouraging participants to share authority and expertise, and work interdependently with others to solve mutual problems. (Baxter Magolda, 2009, p. 251)

The LPM promotes self-authorship in curricular and cocurricular contexts (Baxter Magolda & King, 2004; Taylor, Baxter Magolda, & Haynes, 2010), including service learning courses. Using LPM explicitly to shape an urban internship leadership program, Egart and Healy (2004) reported that students

> had integrated a view of themselves and the world that was larger and more complex than they had had before the internship began. This shift in perspective encompassed a new view of self in relation to others, to knowledge, and inwardly toward the self. (p. 144)

Egart and Healy identified the catalysts for this shift as navigating supervisor-intern relationships, experiencing independence and autonomy in their service and living contexts, encountering dissonance, and engaging in reflection—all components they intentionally framed as learning partnerships. For example, assigned written journal reflections portrayed experiences as learning opportunities and helped participants process the dissonance they encountered. Conversations about these journals with supervisors and program staff respected participants' existing perspectives and invited them to develop their own personal authority. Personalizing both written and oral reflection helped tailor this processing to the individual participant's way of making meaning.

Yonkers-Talz (2004) intentionally shaped the *Casa de Solidaridad*, an international cultural immersion program, with the LPM. He reported that "exposure to the realities of people living in poverty while living in a different culture created dissonance, challenging values and beliefs (cognitive), sense of self (intrapersonal) and relationships (interpersonal)" (p. 168). More importantly he clarified that maturity, or personal transformation, stemmed from "opportunities for personal and communal reflection, community living and experiences with poor Salvadorans, and assignments that integrate students' experience in marginal communities with academic disciplines" (p. 168). Participants kept written journals, received feedback from the director on these reflections, and regularly shared their reactions to dissonance in community conversations. Personal exchanges with the director enabled the director to welcome students' existing developmental capacities and invite them to consider more complex ones. Following up with *Casa* alumni after 10 years, Yonkers-Talz (2013) reported that the nearly 300 respondents noted significant changes in their vocational interests related to being global citizens, an "expanded imagination" (p. 76) about one's role in the world, a "solidarity with and compassion for those who are suffering" (p. 76), and meaningful personal development.

Boes' (2006) analysis of a community organizing course revealed the crucial nature of learning partnerships that connect to learners' current meaning making. The course clearly offered LPM challenges by drawing students' attention to the complexity of community organization projects, affording them substantial personal authority in their projects, and encouraging working interdependently. The support components respected students' thoughts and feelings, viewed their organizing projects as opportunities for growth, and encouraged mutual learning. However, self-authoring students fared better with the course expectations than did those using more socialized perspectives. The latter group felt overwhelmed with the challenges and needed more support to take the level of responsibility they were being offered for their learning. These insights revealed that learning partnerships must be authentically and mutually constructed, taking into account the learners' present meaning-making capacities. Berger (2012) offers excellent examples of structuring learning partnerships to link to various meaning-making capacities.

Implications and Recommendations for Future Research

Collectively, service learning research yields evidence that engaging in service learning does not guarantee achieving the civic outcomes it is intended to produce. Service learning is a high-impact practice for many students but has little positive effect, or even a negative effect, on other students. It is not a one-size-fits-all process because students' varying personal characteristics and developmental capacities influence how they experience service learning, which in turn varies widely due to multiple layers of context. The single most pressing research consideration is understanding students' existing and evolving developmental capacities and their interactions with the dynamics of the service learning context.

The theoretical foundations of service learning pedagogy support linking service learning to developmental capacity. Boes' (2006) review of these theoretical foundations revealed three principles of service learning pedagogy, each of which can be investigated through research. First, knowledge is constructivist in nature and engages students in making meaning through habits of the mind and heart. Connecting thinking, feeling, and action with reflective inquiry and negotiating relationships, particularly with diverse others, provide opportunities for students to develop complex analytic skills and opportunities for self-exploration. Second, engagement with social issues provides opportunities for dialogue and community building that promotes lifelong learning and democratic engagement. Third, the nature of learning and action through service learning participation is civic in nature. It links individual learning and transformation with social engagement and change. The missing piece in service learning is intentionally shaping the experience to simultaneously welcome students' existing developmental capacities and invite more complex capacities to emerge from the experience.

Service learning is built on introducing participants to dissonance, engaging them in reflection about that dissonance, and decentering and remapping their perspectives. Introducing dissonance and offering opportunities for reflection are necessary but insufficient conditions for decentering and remapping to yield transformation. Service learning pedagogy such as Boes's (2006) and Kiely's (2005) models provide evidence that intentionally taking existing developmental capacity into account and providing sufficient support matched to those capacities increases the likelihood of successfully navigating decentering and remapping to promote self-authorship and thus civic outcomes. More research on service learning that is shaped on the basis of participants' developmental capacity is crucial to understanding these interactions more fully. For example, if students are uncritically following external formulas, instructors can simultaneously acknowledge those formulas and invite students to consider how dissonance introduced might alter them.

Research on developmental capacity is exploring intersections of developmental capacity and social identity (e.g., race, social class, sexual orientation) (Jones & Abes, 2013; Olson & Pizzolato, in press; Torres, 2009). This research sheds light on how students frame power and privilege, how they construct their social identities in various contexts, and therefore how they might react to challenges to their power and privilege. Longitudinal research can increase understanding of how students' social identities and developmental capacities shape their approach to, interpretation of, and reaction to service learning and civic outcomes.

Based on the premise that developmental capacity is a crucial component of service learning that yields desirable civic outcomes, questions for future research include the following:

- How do students with various meaning-making capacities perceive, interpret, and react to dissonance they encounter in service learning experiences?
- How do students' constructions of their social identities influence how they navigate dissonance by decentering and remapping their perspectives?
- How can support and challenge from instructors, peers, and community partners be balanced effectively for students with varying developmental capacities (particularly socializing capacities) to yield transformational learning?
- How can the LPM be applied to understanding interactions between students and others in a service learning context?
- How can the LPM be used to prepare instructors for various roles they can assume to support student civic development in a service learning course?

Conclusion

Service learning has been hailed as a high-impact practice that promotes important civic outcomes, yet insufficient attention has been paid to its widely varying effects. Service learning experiences typically introduce participants to dissonance that has potential to promote the intellectual, intrapersonal, and interpersonal growth that undergirds civic outcomes. However, these experiences vary in their degree of support for participants' developmental capacity to engage dissonance productively. Existing service learning research emphasizes that participants who find themselves overwhelmed by dissonance resist, rather than grow from, that encounter.

Adult development theory reveals a crucial dynamic that influences the potential effect of service learning: students' developmental capacities. How students construct their beliefs, values, identities, and social relations sets the stage for how they perceive, understand, and approach dissonance they encounter in service learning. Adult development research indicates that traditional age students are more likely to use socializing meaning-making capacities than self-authoring ones, leaving them overwhelmed by the tasks of appreciating multiple perspectives, working interdependently with diverse others, and adopting a broader view of their roles in society. Unless the mismatch between developmental capacity and service learning experiences is intentionally addressed by crafting reflection activities and learning partnerships, service learning will fall short of the civic outcomes it aims to engender.

Educators shape educational practice in multiple contexts (e.g., classrooms, residence halls, orientation, intercultural programs) to intentionally engage students' current developmental capacities because these educators understand that learning outcomes hinge on particular developmental capacities. These learning partnerships integrate cognitive, intrapersonal, and interpersonal dimensions in the learning process. Shaping service learning pedagogy to both support and challenge students' existing cognitive, intrapersonal, and interpersonal developmental capacities increases the likelihood of it actually being a high-impact practice and promoting the civic outcomes so crucial to a socially just society.

References

Abes, E. S., & Jones, S. R. (2004). Meaning-making capacity and the dynamics of lesbian college students' multiple dimensions of identity. *Journal of College Student Development, 45*, 612–632.

Association of American Colleges & Universities. (2015). *Character traits associated with the five dimensions of personal and social responsibility.* Retrieved from https://www.aacu.org/node/5127

Baxter Magolda, M. B. (2001). *Making their own way: Narratives for transforming higher education to promote self-development.* Sterling, VA: Stylus.

Baxter Magolda, M. B. (2009). *Authoring your life: Developing an internal voice to navigate life's challenges.* Sterling, VA: Stylus.

Baxter Magolda, M. B., & King, P. M. (Eds.). (2004). *Learning partnerships: Theory & models of practice to educate for self-authorship.* Sterling, VA: Stylus.

Baxter Magolda, M. B., & King, P. M. (2012). *Assessing meaning making and self-authorship: Theory, research, and application.* Vol. 38, no. 3 in *ASHE Higher Education Report.* San Francisco: CA: Jossey-Bass.

Berger, J. G. (2012). *Changing on the job: Developing leaders for a complex world.* Stanford, CA: Stanford University Press.

Boes, L. M. (2006). *Learning from practice: A constructive-developmental study of undergraduate service learning pedagogy* (Unpublished doctoral dissertation). Harvard University, Graduate School of Education, Cambridge, MA.

Dewey, J. (1938). *Experience and education.* New York: Collier Books.

Drago-Severson, E. (2010). *Leading adult learning.* Thousand Oaks, CA: Corwin.

Egart, K., & Healy, M. (2004). An Urban Leadership Internship program: Implementing learning partnerships "unplugged" from campus structures. In M. B. Baxter Magolda & P. M. King (Eds.), *Learning partnerships: Theory and models of practice to educate for self-authorship* (pp. 125–149). Sterling, VA: Stylus.

Feinstein, B. (2004). Learning and transformation in the context of Hawaiian traditional ecological knowledge. *Adult Education Quarterly, 54*(2), 105–120.

Finley, A. (2012). *Making progress? What we know about the achievement of liberal education outcomes.* Washington, DC: Association of American Colleges & Universities.

Giles, D. E., Jr., Honnet, E. P., & Migliore, S. (Eds.) (1991). *Setting the agenda for effective research in combining service and learning in the 1990s.* Raleigh, NC: National Society for Internships and Experiential Education.

Giles, H. C. (2014). Risky epistemology: Connecting with others and dissonance in community-based research. *Michigan Journal of Community Service Learning, 20*(2), 65–78.

Jones, S. R., & Abes, E. S. (2004). Enduring influences of service learning on college students' identity development. *Journal of College Student Development, 45,* 149–166.

Jones, S. R., & Abes, E. (2013). *Identity development of college students: Advancing frameworks for multiple dimensions of identity.* San Francisco, CA: Jossey-Bass.

Jones, S. R., Gilbride-Brown, J., & Gasiorski, A. (2005). Getting inside the "underside" of service learning: Student resistance and possibilities. In D. W. Butin (Ed.), *Service learning in higher education* (pp. 3–24). New York: Palgrave MacMillan.

Jones, S. R., Robbins, C. K., & LePeau, L. A. (2011). Negotiating border crossing: Influences of social identity on service learning outcomes. *Michigan Journal of Community Service Learning, 17*(2), 27–42.

Jones, S. R., Rowan-Kenyon, H. T., Ireland, S. M-Y., Niehaus, E., & Skendall, K. C. (2012). The meaning students make as participants in short-term immersion programs. *Journal of College Student Development, 53,* 201–220.

Kegan, R. (1982). *The evolving self: Problem and process in human development.* Cambridge, MA: Harvard University Press.

Kegan, R. (1994). *In over our heads: The mental demands of modern life.* Cambridge, MA: Harvard University Press.

Kegan, R. (2000). What "form" transforms? A constructive-developmental approach to transformative learning. In J. Mezirow (Ed.), *Learning as transformation: Critical perspectives on a theory in progress* (pp. 35–69). San Francisco, CA: Jossey-Bass.

Kegan, R., & Lahey, L. L. (2009). *Immunity to change: How to overcome it and unlock potential in yourself and your organization.* Boston, MA: Harvard Business Press.

Kiely, R. (2004). A chameleon with a complex: Searching for transformation in international service learning. *Michigan Journal of Community Service Learning, 10*(2), 5–20.

Kiely, R. (2005). A transformative learning model for service learning: A longitudinal case study. *Michigan Journal of Community Service Learning, 12,* 5–22.

King, P. M., & Baxter Magolda, M. B. (2005). A developmental model of intercultural maturity. *Journal of College Student Development, 46*, 571–592.

King, P. M., Baxter Magolda, M. B., & Masse, J. (2011). Maximizing learning from engaging across difference: The role of anxiety and meaning making. *Equity and Excellence in Education, 44*, 468–487.

Mezirow, J. (Ed.). (2000). *Learning as transformation: Critical perspectives on a theory in progress.* San Francisco, CA: Jossey-Bass.

Olson, A., & Pizzolato, J. E. (in press). Exploring the relationship between the three dimensions of self-authorship. *Journal of College Student Development.*

Piaget, J. (1950). *The psychology of intelligence* (M. P. a. D. Berlyne, Trans.). London, England: Routledge & Kegan Paul.

Pizzolato, J. E. (2008). Advisor, teacher, partner: Using the learning partnerships model to reshape academic advising. *About Campus: Enriching the Student Learning Experience, 13*(1), 18–25.

Sanford, N. (1962). Developmental status of the entering freshman. In N. Sanford (Ed.), *The American college: A psychological and social interpretation of the higher learning* (pp. 253282). New York, NY: Wiley & Sons.

Taylor, K. B., Baxter Magolda, M. B., & Haynes, C. (2010). Miami University's collective journey toward discovery-based learning. *Learning Communities Journal, Special Issue, 2*(2), 1–26.

Torres, V. (2009). The developmental dimensions of recognizing racist thoughts. *Journal of College Student Development, 50*, 504–520.

Torres, V., & Hernandez, E. (2007). The influence of ethnic identity development on self-authorship: A longitudinal study of Latino/a college students. *Journal of College Student Development, 48*, 558–573.

Yonkers-Talz, K. (2004). A learning partnership: U. S. college students and the poor in El Salvador. In M. B. Baxter Magolda & P. M. King (Eds.), *Learning partnerships: Theory and models to educate for self-authorship* (pp. 151–184). Sterling, VA: Stylus.

Yonkers-Talz, K. (2013). *Casa de la Solidaridad: A pedagogy of solidarity* (Unpublished doctoral dissertation). University of San Francisco, School of Education, San Francisco, CA.

PHILANTHROPIC STUDIES AND STUDENT CIVIC OUTCOMES

Julie A. Hatcher

P hilanthropic studies is a growing field of study within domestic and international higher education (Mirabella & McDonald, 2012). As a multidisciplinary field, philanthropic studies provides a conceptual understanding of voluntary action of individuals and organizations, as well as the cultural traditions and norms that support philanthropy across time and cultures. Although related to nonprofit studies and nonprofit management, it values both the humanities and social science approaches to understanding the norms and traditions of philanthropy across time and cultures (Hatcher, Shaker, & Freeman, 2016). Theories from multiple disciplines, particularly the liberal arts (e.g., literature, history, economics, philosophy, political science, sociology), inform the research on and practice of philanthropy.

Philanthropy encompasses a wide range of traditions including relief, improvement, social reform, and civic engagement (Lynn & Wisely, 2006). Traditions of philanthropy are found in every culture and one of the chief aims of philanthropy across the globe is to improve society and deliver services not readily provided by either the state or the market (Payton & Moody, 2008). The scope of philanthropy is broad, and research in the field covers a range of prosocial behaviors (e.g., advocacy, charitable contributions, civic participation, social movements, volunteering), a variety of issues relevant to leadership in nonprofit and community organizations (e.g., board governance, cross-sector partnerships, fundraising, grant making, volunteer management capacity), and new forms of philanthropic action that continue to emerge within the sector (e.g., B-corps, crowd-funding, giving circles, social entrepreneurship). Powell and Steinberg (2006) summarized the scope of research that comprises the nonprofit sector, and their research handbook is one illustration of the breadth of theory that is used to understand philanthropy.

Over the past 25 years philanthropic studies has grown as a field of study in higher education. Colleges and universities offer various types of academic programs for undergraduate (e.g., certificates, minors, majors) and graduate students (e.g., MA, MPA, PhD) to address the growing interest and career opportunities within the nonprofit sector both domestically and in international contexts (Mirabella & McDonald, 2012). An innovative curricular strategy is experiential philanthropy courses in which students are responsible for reviewing proposals and making significant grants to community organizations (Campbell, 2014; Olberding, 2010). These experiential learning courses are offered across a range of disciplines (e.g., communications, history, marketing, social work), and they are designed to introduce students to philanthropy and the nonprofit sector (Olberding, 2010). Some of these courses include community service activities along with grant making, and many course characteristics are similar to service learning course design (Benenson, Moldow, & Hahn, 2014).

From the perspective of philanthropic studies, civic outcomes for students in a service learning course could include domains such as knowledge (e.g., contemporary social issues, nonprofit organizations, public policy, volunteer opportunities), skills (e.g., advocacy, collective action, grant writing, listening), dispositions (e.g., empathy, generosity, gratitude, purpose driven, social responsibility), and intentions for future voluntary action (e.g., participating on a board, donating money, volunteering) or professional behavior (e.g., career with a public purpose, employment within the nonprofit sector, pro bono service). Each of these civic outcomes is important in preparing civic-minded graduates (CMGs) and civic-minded professionals (CMPs) (Hatcher, 2008; Steinberg, Hatcher, & Bringle, 2011). In turn these civic outcomes ultimately support nonprofit and community organizations and help to enact the public purposes of higher education (Bringle, Games, & Malloy, 1999; Colby, Ehrlich, Beaumont, & Stevens, 2003; Sullivan & Rosin, 2008).

Given the focus of this volume on student civic outcomes through service learning, this chapter identifies theories from philanthropic studies that are of particular relevance to understanding volunteering. First, an analysis is provided of the distinctions between service learning and volunteering, as well as the similarities between the community activities that students complete in a service learning course compared to those activities of volunteers. Next, using the Volunteer Process model (Musick & Wilson, 2008; Snyder & Omoto, 1992), three stages of volunteering are presented that can inform research on student experiences and civic outcomes in service learning courses. In addition, based on theory and research, implications for practice are identified that could improve service learning course quality to reach civic outcomes. This conceptual approach is only one way that the field of philanthropic studies can inform research on service learning and civic engagement more broadly in higher education.

Service Learning Versus Volunteering

Service learning is often conceptualized as distinctly different from volunteering in a cocurricular setting, although both have similar goals to cultivate social responsibility among participants. Building on Sigmon's (1994) typology of service learning, Furco (1996) developed a typology to distinguish among various types of service-oriented activities (i.e., volunteering, community service, service learning, field education, internship) and how these activities range on two continuums in terms of (a) the primary intended beneficiary of the activity and (b) the overall balance between the emphasis on service and learning. From this conceptualization "volunteerism is the engagement of students in activities where the primary emphasis is on the service being provided and the primary intended beneficiary is clearly the service recipient" (Furco, 1996, p. 2).

For many years as a scholar and a practitioner working with faculty to design service learning courses, I intentionally omitted using the "V word" of "volunteer" in any discussion about service learning. This was due, in part, to defining *service learning* as a "course-based educational experience" that involves students in "organized service activities" and asks students to "reflect on the experience" to deepen academic learning and develop both "personal values and a sense of civic responsibility" (Bringle & Hatcher, 1996, p. 221). This definition concurs with Furco's (1996) assertion that service learning courses, by design, are "distinguished from other approaches to experiential education by their intention to equally benefit the provider and the recipient of the service as well as to ensure equal focus on both the service being provided and the learning that is occurring" (p. 5).

Yet by definition, *service learning* courses include community service activities, and often these activities are similar to the types of activities undertaken by volunteers, typically within nonprofit organizations (Campus Compact, 2014). Community service activities are one of the six key attributes of service learning course design (chapters 1.1 and 1.3). Well-designed service learning courses integrate community activities and relevant social issue(s) as critical dimensions for student understanding of academic content, the syllabus provides a strong rationale for the relationship of the community activities to learning outcomes, and students are asked to critically reflect upon and develop products that explore the relevance of the service experience to academic content (chapters 1.1 and 1.3). Among the range of community activities embedded within a service learning course (e.g., distributing food, tutoring youth, assisting with special events, gathering data for community-based research), most may be very similar to the activities and experiences of volunteers in community organizations (Burns, 2011; Dorado, Giles, & Welch, 2009). Service learning students are typically involved for short periods of time and provide direct services to others under the guidance of a site supervisor or volunteer manager. These service experiences can be described as episodic volunteering because they are short-term in duration and typically completed in fewer than six months (Macduff, 2005). From a community organization's perspective, there may not be a clear distinction among college students as *interns, volunteers,* or *service learners* by site supervisors because each contributes time and talent to meeting organizational goals (Gazley, Littlepage, & Bennett, 2012).

Theories and Research on Volunteering: The Volunteer Process Model

Volunteering is one of the many aspects of study within the field of philanthropic studies (Powell & Steinberg, 2006). Volunteering is valued as a vital resource for the nonprofit sector and the economy, and it contributes in important ways to social cohesion within organizations and society more broadly (Leete, 2006). Volunteering is "an intrinsically complex phenomenon" and multifaceted activity and there is no one theory that can explain why a person is willing, or may feel obligated, to give of time to help others (Hustinx, Cnaan, & Handy, 2010, p. 411).

Volunteering is usually described by scholars as unpaid work, and, as such, theories from many disciplines inform research (Musick & Wilson, 2008). Economists tend to focus on rationale choice frameworks and the "seemingly irrational behavior" (Hustinx et al., 2010, p. 420) of people giving their time to help others. Sociologists tend to focus on the contextual factors and pressures that support the normative practices of volunteering and its contribution to social cohesion and civil society (Sievers, 2010; Wilson, 2012). Psychologists may frame inquiry in terms of personal motives, situational and interpersonal influences, and developmental theory (chapters 2.1, 2.3, and 2.5). These conditions may come to bear at any given time within a social context or within a person who is volunteering, thus complicating the understanding of why a person volunteers (Leete, 2006). People may volunteer because they interact with others who are more likely to volunteer (e.g., through participation in clubs and membership associations, through attendance at faith-based organizations) and therefore they are asked more frequently to join in on a volunteer activity (Janoski, Musick, & Wilson, 1998). A person may also have one, or a combination, of the "Big 5" personality traits (i.e., consciousness, openness, emotionality, agreeableness, extraversion) that highly correlate with volunteer behavior (Hustinx et al., 2010, p. 419). Such personality traits and dispositions tend to lead to greater integration within the community organization and higher satisfaction with the volunteer experience (Snyder & Omoto, 1992). Or volunteers may have intrinsic motives to advance their own goals or extrinsic motives to assist others in need, and most likely it is a combination of both types of motives (Clary et al., 1998; Leete, 2006). Or it may be that volunteering is such a foundational part of a person's identity that not volunteering would be counter to how he or she sees him- or herself living in the world (Daloz, Keen, Keen, & Parks, 1996; Steinberg et al., 2011).

The Volunteer Process model (Musick & Wilson, 2008; Snyder & Omoto, 1992; Wilson, 2012) provides a systematic way to understand three stages of volunteering. These stages include the (a) *antecedents of volunteering*, or the qualities, dispositions, and motives of the volunteer (b) *experiences of volunteering*, or the qualities of the experience itself as the volunteer interacts with others and (c) *consequences of volunteering* for the volunteer as well as the host organization. The model is used to frame (a) what is known about the three stages of volunteering, (b) its relevance to the community activities within service learning course design, and (c) potential research questions and relevant variables to improve research on service learning and civic outcomes.

Stage One: Antecedents of Volunteering

The first stage within the Volunteer Process model is antecedents. Some college students may enroll in a service learning course with a number of prior life experiences as a volunteer; yet, for others, this may be the first time that they have been asked to contribute their time and talents through community engagement. In terms of research on service learning, these prior experiences need to be identified and accounted for in the research design (chapter 3.4). Otherwise, the outcomes of the service learning course could be due to the characteristics that students bring into the course rather than to the service learning course itself. Teasing out the value added by the service learning course is one of the basic challenges in research on service learning. The following sections provide an overview of three of the antecedents to community service activities (i.e., prior experience, volunteer motives, social environment) that are particularly relevant to research on service learning.

Prior Experience

In the past 20 years, service-oriented activities (i.e., volunteering, community service, service learning, field education, internships) have become a more evident practice within higher education (Campus Compact, 2014; Griffith, 2012), and close to half of all students now entering higher education come with prior experience in community service during their high school years (Griffith, 2012). Those who have had *prior volunteer experiences* are most likely to be willing to volunteer again. Experiences from a young age, particularly volunteering in high school-based programs, influence the likelihood that a college student will choose to participate in community service (Astin, Sax, & Avolas, 1999; Griffith, 2012).

Volunteering is typically described as a habit, and like other life habits, the propensity to volunteer develops and changes across one's life span (Musick & Wilson, 2008). Sociologists have identified a number of life cycle considerations (e.g., attending college, marriage, parenting, employment) that tend to change the patterns of volunteering (Musick & Wilson, 2008) and these are potential variables that may assist in interpreting findings and differences across groups of students in service learning courses. Rates of volunteering differ from study to study, due in part to how the question about volunteer activity is asked. Generally speaking, women volunteer at a higher rate than men (27.8% versus 21.8%); Whites volunteer at higher rates (26.4%) than Blacks (19.4%), Asians (17.9%), or Hispanics (15.5%); and those in their early 20s are the least likely (18.4%) of all age groups to volunteer (U.S. Bureau of Labor Statistics, 2015). College students volunteer at higher rates than their peers who do not attend college (Dote, Cramer, Dietz, & Grimm, 2006), and college graduates are more likely to volunteer (38.8%) than those with only some college (26.5%) or a high school diploma (15%) (U.S. Bureau of Labor Statistics, 2015).

Whether the research approach is quantitative, qualitative, or mixed-methods, gathering information on prior experience is important to account for differences in student outcomes that may be related to prior experience rather than derived from the course itself. This is most easily done by replicating the survey questions or approaches used in other studies (e.g., Astin et al. 1999; Dote et al. 2006). In our quantitative research on college students (e.g., Steinberg et al., 2011), we often use a set of survey questions that we have dubbed the "dosage effect" of prior community service experiences. In a qualitative study, we used a similar approach by asking students a series of questions about their prior experience using the CMG interview protocol (Steinberg et al., 2011). Outcomes gained in a service learning course may be different for those students who have lower versus higher levels of prior volunteer experience, and understanding this difference is one way to improve research on service learning. It may also be that service learning is particularly beneficial for underrepresented students who have had little prior experience in service-oriented activities (e.g., Lockeman & Pelco, 2013). These questions require data on prior involvement.

In terms of practice, it may be beneficial for students as an early pre-flection exercise (Eyler, 2002), individually or within a group, to identify and describe prior volunteer experiences and talk with others about what to expect at the community service site. One could then ask those with a wide range of volunteer experiences to share what they have learned about navigating their role as a volunteer. This is an informal way to prepare students to enter the community organization with additional information and gain insight from peers on how to best acclimate to the new setting.

Volunteer Motives

In this model, another antecedent of volunteering is motivation. There are many ways to evaluate why one chooses or is motivated to help another. Economists (Leete, 2006) and psychologists (Clary, Snyder, & Stukas, 1996) have explored a wide range of motives that can be categorized according to intrinsic and extrinsic benefits as well as intrinsic and extrinsic motives. Although altruism may lead a person to volunteer initially, self-interested motivations are actually more important for continued participation, and a mix of all motives is most important to volunteer persistence (Clary et al., 1998; Snyder & Omoto, 1992). Leete (2006) presents a taxonomy of various theories of volunteer motivation, and classifies motives in terms of either voluntary or obligatory action, as well as intrinsic and extrinsic motives. She describes intrinsic motivations as the satisfaction from participating in and during the activity itself, and extrinsic motivations as the satisfaction gained as a result of voluntary action. These motivations may include gaining new knowledge, fulfilling values that are important to ones' self, developing job and marketable skills, and developing and maintaining social networks (Leete, 2006). Each of these variables could be used to explore the motives of students in a service learning course, how motives may or may not change across time, and how motives may or may not moderate gains in civic outcomes (chapter 2.1).

There are many tools available to conduct research that explores volunteer motives (Bringle, Phillips, & Hudson, 2004; Simons, 2015). The Fetzer Institute (n.d.) offers a comprehensive resource guide, *Self-Report Measures for the Scientific Study of Love and Compassion: Helping Others, Volunteering, & Charitable Giving* that describes measurement tools as well as their use in prior research. The Volunteer Functions Inventory (VFI) (Clary et al., 1998) is a 30-item scale that evaluates six dimensions and values that volunteers bring with them and are seeking in the volunteer experience (i.e., understanding, social, values, protective, career, enhancement). Each of these six dimensions of the VFI can also be used as independent scales to understand motivational change across time. The VFI is frequently used in research on volunteer motives of college students (e.g., Burns, 2011; Gage & Thapa, 2012). Data gathered on motivations can be used to provide baseline information on students prior to involvement in service learning, to understand the differences that may exist among students (or student cohorts) when they enter college, or to explain under what conditions these motives may change over the course of the college experience and beyond.

In terms of service learning, Morton (1995) contends that students have a range of motives and preferences for different types of service activities (i.e., charity, project, social change), and that these preferences rarely change. He argues that the role of educators is not to change student preferences for engagement but rather to introduce students to various forms of service and work to deepen the integrity with which students engage in the type of service that they prefer. We used this conceptualization of motivation and asked entering freshmen on our campus about their preferences. Similar to Morton's interpretation, the majority of entering students preferred charity and one-time service projects, and the least preferred approach was social justice (Bringle, Hatcher, & MacIntosh, 2006; Moely, Furco, & Reed, 2008).

In terms of practice, it may be beneficial for instructors to design structured reflection activities that ask students to identify and critically evaluate various motives they may bring into the service learning course. This could be used to highlight the value of both intrinsic and extrinsic motivations, and to remind students that self-interest is an important and valid motive within service engagement. Upon course completion, one could ask students to reflect upon and identify the intrinsic benefits they have gained through service learning, or ask students to critically reflect upon why and how their motivations have remained consistent or changed as a result of participating in course activities. The degree to which motives are identified, discussed with peers, and affirmed may lead students to an increased understanding of themselves and each other, as well as increase the likelihood of aligning their own motives with volunteering in the future.

Social Context

Another antecedent to volunteering is the degree to which support is provided for volunteering through interactions and relationships with others. These interactions and relationships are formed through families, neighborhoods, peers, mentors, clubs and organizations, faith-based organizations, schools, regions of the country, and across cultures and ethnic traditions.

Research on volunteering is consistent; if one is asked to volunteer, one is more likely to volunteer, and the invitations to volunteer typically come from within social networks through formal and informal interactions (Janoski, Musick, & Wilson, 1998). Compared to 20 years ago, colleges and universities are assuming more active roles as social institutions to provide a supportive context for cultivating and sustaining voluntary action (Musick & Wilson, 2008; Sponsler & Hartley, 2013). Availability of service learning courses, either required or discretionary, is one mechanism by which higher education is asking students to volunteer.

Social contexts may influence the likelihood that a student has had prior experience as a volunteer upon enrolling in a service learning course. Therefore, students who report that they participate in clubs and organizations, attend religious services, live on campus, or have a parent or parents who volunteer may experience a service learning course differently than students without the benefits derived from such social networks. Each of these contexts plays an important role in sustaining voluntary action across time, particularly in the postgraduate years. Therefore, in exploring the relationship of service learning to civic outcomes, understanding variations in the past and current social environment of college students is relevant (chapters 2.3 and 2.5).

The social context of the campus, often described as campus climate, is increasingly seen as a key support for developing civic learning (chapters 1.2 and 3.3; Sponsler & Hartley, 2013). The Personal and Social Responsibility Inventory (PSRI, n.d.) is a campus climate survey designed to measure five dimensions including the degree to which the campus supports civic awareness and practices that support students' civic commitments. The PSRI dimension "contributing to the larger community" has a number of questions that are particularly relevant to gauging students' interpretations of their campus context and the social support they encountered during college (chapter 1.2). Presumably, those campuses that score higher on this dimension would have greater prevalence of service learning courses than campus contexts with lower emphasis on community engagement. This has yet to be explored but may be a social context factor that influences differences for student civic outcomes in service learning.

Participation in clubs and organizations during the college years is another type of social context that supports the development of civic skills as students work together to take collective action (Baggetta, 2011; Weinberg, 2005). Evidence suggests that participation in clubs and organizations contributes to the development of civic skills (Kirlin, 2003), and the associational ties contribute to civic identity development (Baggetta, 2011). We have adapted Baggetta's work to explore the associational nature of the classroom context (i.e., interactions with faculty, interaction with students, dialogue and debate with others) and its relationship to student civic outcomes (i.e., civic mindedness, understanding of nonprofit sector) in experiential philanthropy courses (Hatcher & Witkowski, 2014). Coupled with prior research on the importance of dialogue across difference (Keen & Hall, 2009), this could help to further inform how variations in the nature of the classroom context itself within a service learning course may relate to civic outcomes (chapter 1.3).

Stage Two: Experiences of Volunteering

The second stage of the volunteer process model focuses on the volunteer experience itself and includes the experiences of volunteers as they interact with others to meet the service goals of the organization (Musick & Wilson, 2008). The following section provides an overview of three dimensions of volunteering that students are likely to encounter during the community service activities (i.e., nature of the experience, volunteer management capacity, volunteer satisfaction) in a service learning course. Variations in each of these dimensions may influence the degree to which service learning contributes to student civic outcomes.

Nature of the Experience

Volunteering is distinct from informal helping and caring because it is an organized service experience, and it takes place in or on behalf of an organization (Musick & Wilson, 2008). Like work, volunteer activities can range in terms of complexity of the task and skills needed, as well as frequency of time and duration to get the task done. Cnaan, Handy, and Wadsworth (1996) identified four dimensions along which volunteer activity can be structured and ranked; these dimensions include (a) freedom of choosing participation, (b) extent of remuneration, (c) extent to which the action is structured versus informal, and (d) extent to which beneficiaries are distanced from the volunteer's personal sphere. In a similar way, Penner (2002) identifie descriptors that provide a range for volunteer activities that include (a) contextual, helping alone or with others; (b) nonobligatory versus obligatory helping, not knowing those helped or feeling a personal sense of obligation; and (c) longevity, one-time participation versus continued involvement. In terms of frequency and duration of participation, scholars now use the term *episodic volunteering*, and this type of volunteering can be described as temporary, interim, or occasional (Macduff, 2005).

These distinctions among volunteer experiences are useful to inform research on the variations in the types of experiences within a service learning course (e.g., see Mabry, 1998; Morgan & Streb, 2001; Reed, Jernstedt, Hawley, Reber, & DuBois, 2005) and how these various conditions may relate to civic outcomes. Service learning courses can include at least four types of community activities by students (Florida Department of Education, 2009): (a) direct service learning, (b) indirect service learning, (c) research service learning, and (d) advocacy service learning. These categories are not mutually exclusive, and community-based activities might involve one or more of these approaches. Future research could explore how the types of community-based activities relate to student satisfaction as well as student civic outcomes. For example, to what extent do civic outcomes vary for students who are participating on their own or as a member of a group project at the service learning site? To what extent does required or optional participation in the service activity (Griffith, 2010) or length of involvement (Mabry, 1998) influence student satisfaction and civic outcomes?

Volunteer Management Capacity

The rate of college student volunteering has increased in the past decade due in part to the involvement of colleges, universities, and national service programs (Toncar, Reid, Burns, Anderson, & Nguyen, 2006). With the increased emphasis in higher education on community engagement, staff from nonprofit organizations are working more closely with college students than they did a decade ago (Sandy, Ikeda, Cruz, & Holland, 2007). This new source of volunteers presents both opportunities and challenges for nonprofit organizations. Volunteer management capacity (VMC) includes (a) staff supervision and support of volunteering and (b) the adoption of administrative practices necessary for the management of volunteers. Having the capacity to manage volunteers increases an organization's ability to attract and retain volunteers (Garner & Garner, 2010).

Gazly, Littlepage, and Bennett (2012) present the strongest research to date using VMC as a framework to understand nonprofit staffs' perspectives on college student engagement. This research sought to address a recognized gap in the research on service learning relative to community outcomes by asking community and nonprofit leaders about their experiences in managing as well as the benefits gained by hosting college student volunteers. Using a random sample of nonprofit managers ($n = 290$), findings indicated a positive correlation between the amount of organizational investment in volunteer management and the perceived benefit that these organizations derived from college students (i.e., interns, service learning, volunteers). Gazley and colleagues recommended the need for future research to "take a comparative angle to test our propositions on understanding the best combination of campus and community volunteer management resources" (p. 1046). One could investigate the degree to which VMC occurs in service learning, and the degree to which this responsibility is effectively shared and managed by staff on campus and in community organizations. To what extent does the level of VMC influence student civic outcomes as well as outcomes for the community organization in terms of service delivery and attracting future volunteers? In what ways might long-term partnerships, rather than short-term placement sites, contribute to a shared approach in effectively managing service learning students? To what extent does service learning contribute to strengthening organizations in the nonprofit sector?

In terms of practice, having the capacity to offer screening and matching, orientation and trainings, supervision and ongoing feedback, and celebration and recognition of volunteer contributions should increase the likelihood that students will be satisfied with the community service experience (Wilson, 2012) in a service learning course. Sometimes the VMC is shared between the campus and community organization, as many campuses support and train students to assume some of these volunteer management roles; however, program evaluation and research is necessary to understand the benefits of these varied and shared approaches.

Volunteer Satisfaction

Volunteering is a form of unpaid work (Musick & Wilson, 2008), and significant attention has been given to understanding volunteer satisfaction, retention, and rewards. Volunteer satisfaction relates to the likelihood that a person will become attached to the role of a volunteer and will routinely volunteer at other organizations in the future. Volunteer satisfaction also relates to one's commitment over time to a particular organization and its mission. Research indicates that volunteers report higher levels of satisfaction when some factors were in place. Some of these factors include (a) clearly defined roles; (b) roles consistent with aspects of self-identity and volunteer motivations; (c) level of social integration, including friendships that are made through interactions with other volunteers; (d) effective volunteer supervision and management; (e.g., orientation, identifying solutions when problems arise, clear instructions); and (e) confidence that they are making a difference in the lives of those they are serving (Wilson, 2012). In contrast, dissatisfied or disgruntled volunteers typically point to factors such as (a) ambiguity in their role; (b) unrealistic expectations of the contributions they can make; (c) mismanagement and inadequate support; or (d) frustration with personal interactions with others, including volunteer or professional staff. Those who are satisfied with the level of support they received are more likely to express intention to volunteer in the future (Garner & Garner, 2010).

Volunteer satisfaction is closely related to volunteer persistence (Snyder & Omoto, 1992); therefore, attention to student satisfaction in a community service setting may contribute to the likelihood of future voluntary action as an outcome of a service learning course. This concept of volunteer satisfaction has been applied in research on the effects of college student participation in service learning on their future volunteering. For example, Tomkovick, Lester, Flunker, and Wells (2008) conducted an alumni survey on a campus that had a 30-hour service learning graduation requirement. They found the level of future volunteerism of alumni was higher when alumni (a) believed their service learning experience improved their personal development, (b) perceived their service learning experience was valuable to the organization, and (c) had a higher incidence of prior volunteer experience. Toncar and colleagues (2006) developed and evaluated the Service Learning Benefit (SELEB) Scale, a 12-item self-report measure that evaluates students' perceptions of the benefit they gain from participating in service learning courses. These benefits include practical skills, interpersonal skills, citizenship, and personal responsibility. Burns (2011) integrated the use of the SELEB Scale with the VFI to examine the relationship between satisfaction and volunteer motivation. Although the findings were not conclusive, this line of inquiry holds strong potential for understanding satisfaction among students in service learning courses, the conditions that lead to this satisfaction (e.g., alignment of service with personal motives, group project versus individual involvement, clear directions and guidance), and the implications for the role of volunteer supervision and management in creating meaningful service opportunities for service learning students.

In terms of practice, many of the sources of volunteer satisfaction or dissatisfaction are likely to be familiar to service learning educators. It may be beneficial for instructors to ask students to write about their satisfactions and frustrations within the community setting, share their perspectives with another student, and gain feedback at multiple points early in the semester. The instructor could use this information as a formative assessment of how things are going at the community host site, provide feedback to the students, and, if beneficial, work directly with the site supervisor(s) to identify potential solutions. It is not necessary to alleviate all concerns, but it may be possible to mitigate some frustrations and thereby increase the likelihood that students are more satisfied with the service experience.

Stage Three: Consequences of Volunteering

The third stage of the VMC focuses on the consequences and benefits for the volunteer, and this is the aspect of volunteering that is least understood (Musick & Wilson, 2008). Across the chapters in this volume, student civic outcomes relative to service learning have been identified and explored from various disciplinary perspectives, and many of these are consistent with the research on volunteer outcomes. Some of the civic outcomes of volunteering include social responsibility and citizenship skills (chapter 2.2), psychosocial and identity development (chapters 2.1 and 2.3), overall well-being and health (chapter 2.5), and ability to work with others across difference (chapter 2.7). Through the lens of philanthropic studies, an additional civic outcome for students will be explored: knowledge of the nonprofit sector (Anheier, 2005).

Knowledge of Nonprofit Sector

Understanding the complexities and limitations of the nonprofit sector is an important dimension for understanding public problem-solving, yet rarely do undergraduates have formal courses to learn how these organizations function in society and the variety of roles that their staff assume in terms of advocacy, education, public policy, and service delivery. Charitable nonprofits (e.g., community centers, food banks, homeless shelters, redevelopment initiatives) typically work in close collaboration with government agencies to provide direct services that are supported in part by government contracts and in part by fee-for-service and private donations. They depend on volunteers and boards of directors, are required to stay fiscally sound through strategic planning, and need effective management to enact the organization's mission. Service learning courses provide an opportunity to integrate information about nonprofits and the nonprofit sector more intentionally into the curriculum, particularly when the community partner is valued as a coeducator in terms of course design and implementation (chapter 1.3; Hatcher & Studer, 2015). Leveraging this community context in educationally meaningful ways can provide students with knowledge of volunteer opportunities, charitable giving, and careers in the nonprofit sector as well as a deeper understanding of the role that nonprofits assume in addressing social issues (e.g., education, environment, health, poverty). To date, this set of outcomes is relatively unexplored in service learning literature.

Research approaches on experiential philanthropy courses, some of which are service learning courses by design, are relevant to understanding this set of outcomes. Measures have been developed to assess both the Campus Compact *Pay It Forward* (Benenson et al., 2014) and the *Learning by Giving* (Olberding, 2010) experiential philanthropy initiatives. These measures could be used to understand the level of knowledge that students gain about philanthropy and nonprofit organizations through service learning. In our conceptualization of the constructs of CMP (Hatcher, 2008) and CMG (Steinberg et al., 2011), there are a number of domains that are evaluated, including knowledge of volunteer opportunities and the nonprofit sector. Research to date indicates participation in service learning courses is associated with students' understandings of themselves as CMGs (Steinberg et al.,

2011) as well as graduates' understandings of themselves as CMPs (Richard, Keen, Hatcher, & Pease, 2016).

In terms of practice, instructors can design service learning courses to highlight knowledge of the nonprofit sector (Hatcher & Studer, 2015). Methods include (a) using key readings (e.g., Anheier, 2005; Payton & Moody, 2008; Powell & Steinberg, 2008; Sievers, 2010) and web-based resources (see Council of Foundations, Independent Sector, Kettering Foundation, Urban Institute); (b) codesigning the course with nonprofit leaders as coeducators, both within the classroom and at the community site; and (c) using reflection strategies that highlight the assets, rather than deficiencies, of the community setting and organizational partners. In terms of research, exploring how variations in course design (e.g., use of readings, roles of community and nonprofit leaders, types of reflection strategies) may contribute to knowledge of volunteering and the nonprofit sector as well as other philanthropic outcomes (e.g., donating money, serving on boards, volunteering, working in the nonprofit sector) will clarify the value of service learning in preparing students to be active contributors within organizations and communities during and after their post-secondary education. Each of these philanthropic outcomes may also be directed back toward colleges and universities, as alumni who participated in service learning courses may be more likely to remain actively engaged with the institution over time.

Conclusion

The public purposes of higher education to prepare graduates for effective citizenship have important implications for the ways that teaching and learning takes place (Bringle et al., 1999; Colby et al., 2003), and this, in turn, has implications for how service learning courses can best be designed to enhance civic outcomes (Hatcher & Studer, 2015). The literature and research on volunteering is a valuable lens through which to explore more deeply how, why, and under what conditions service learning contributes to civic outcomes for college students. As college students are engaged in educationally meaningful service they have the opportunity to learn about the value and limitations of voluntary action, the role of nonprofit and community organizations, and approaches they can take to work with others toward the common good. This understanding, derived from well-designed experiences within communities, holds the potential for cultivating civic outcomes that contribute to the vibrancy of democratic life.

References

Anheier, H. K. (2005). *Nonprofit organizations theory, management, policy.* New York, NY: Routledge.

Astin, A. W., Sax, L. J., & Avalos, J. (1999). Long term effects of volunteerism during the undergraduate years. *Review of Higher Education, 22,* 187–202.

Baggetta, M. (2011). *Campus student movement organizations and student civic development: CBSM Section Workshop Position Paper.* Retrieved from http://cbsmpapers.web.unc.edu/files/2011/08/CBSM-Workshop-Position-Paper-1.1.pdf

Benenson, J., Moldow, E., & Hahn, A. (2014). *Engaging a new generation of philanthropists: Findings from the Pay It Forward student philanthropy initiative.* Sillerman Center for Advancement of Philanthropy, The Heller School for Social Policy and Management, Brandeis University. Retrieved from http://sillermancenter.brandeis.edu/PDFs/Engaging%20a%20New%20Generation%20Full.pdf

Bringle, R. G., Games, R., & Malloy, E. A. (1999). *Colleges and universities as citizens.* Needham Heights, MA: Allyn and Bacon.

Bringle, R. G., & Hatcher, J. A. (1996). Implementing service learning in higher education. *Journal of Higher Education, 67*(2), 221–239.

Bringle, R. G., Hatcher, J. A., & MacIntosh, R. (2006). Analyzing Morton's typology of service paradigms and integrity. *Michigan Journal of Community Service Learning, 13*(1), 5–15.

Bringle, R. G., Phillips, M. A., & Hudson, M. (2004). *The measure of service learning: Research scales to assess student experiences.* Washington, DC: American Psychological Association.

Burns, D. J. (2011). Motivations to volunteer and benefits from service learning: An exploration of marketing students. *Journal for Advancement of Marketing Education, 18,* 10–23.

Campbell, D.A. (2014). Practicing philanthropy in higher education: Cultivating engaged citizens and nonprofit sector professionals. *Journal of Public Affairs Education, 20*(2), 217–231.

Campus Compact. (2014). *Three decades of institutionalizing change: 2014 annual member survey.* Boston, MA. Retrieved from http://compact.org/initiatives/membership-survey/

Clary, E. G., Snyder, M., Ridge, R. D., Copeland, J., Stukas, A. A., Haugen, J., & Meine, P. (1998). Understanding and assessing the motivations of volunteers: A functional approach. *Journal of Personality and Social Psychology, 74,* 1516–1530.

Clary, E. G., Snyder, M., & Stukas, A. A. (1996). Volunteers' motivations: Findings from a national survey. *Nonprofit and Voluntary Sector Quarterly, 25,* 485–505.

Cnaan, R., Handy, F., & Wadsworth M. (1996). Defining who is a volunteer: Conceptual and empirical considerations. *Nonprofit and Voluntary Sector Quarterly, 25*(3), 364–388.

Colby, A., Ehrlich, T., Beaumont, E., & Stephens, J. (2003). *Educating citizens: Preparing America's undergraduates for lives of moral and civic responsibility.* San Francisco, CA: Jossey-Bass.

Daloz, L. A., Keen, C. H., Keen, J. P., & Parks, S. D. (1996). *Common fire: Lives of commitment in a complex world.* Boston, MA: Beacon Press.

Dorado, S., Giles, Jr., D. E., & Welch, T. C. (2009). Delegation of coordination and outcomes in cross-sector partnerships: The case of service learning partnerships. *Nonprofit and Voluntary Sector Quarterly, 38,* 368–391.

Dote, L., Cramer, K., Dietz, N., & Grimm, R. (2006). *College students helping America.* Washington, DC: Corporation for National and Community Service.

Eyler, J. (2002). Reflection: Linking service and learning-linking students and communities *Journal of Social Issues, 58,* 517–534.

Fetzer Institute (n.d.). *Self-report measures for love and compassion research: Helping others.* Retrieved from http://fetzer.org/sites/default/files/images/stories/pdf/selfmeasures/HELPING_OTHERS.pdf

Florida Department of Education. (2009). *Standards for service-learning in Florida: A guide for creating and sustaining quality practice.* Tallahassee, FL: Florida Learn & Serve.

Furco, A. (1996). Service-learning: A balanced approach to experiential education. In Corporation for National Service (Ed.), *Expanding boundaries: Serving and learning* (pp. 2–6). Columbia, MD: Cooperative Education Association.

Gage, R. L. & Thapa, B. (2012). Volunteer motivations and constraints among college students: Analysis of the Volunteer Function Inventory and leisure constraints models. *Nonprofit and Voluntary Sector Quarterly, 41,* 405–430.

Garner, J., & Garner, L. (2010). Volunteering and opinion: Organizational voice and volunteer retention in nonprofit organizations. *Nonprofit and Voluntary Sector Quarterly, 40,* 813–828.

Gazley, B., Littlepage, L., & Bennett, T. A. (2012). What about the host agency? Nonprofit perspectives on community-based student learning and volunteering. *Nonprofit and Voluntary Sector Quarterly, 41,* 1029–1050.

Griffith, J. (2010). Community service among a panel of beginning college students: Its prevalence and relationship to having been required and to supporting "capital." *Nonprofit and Voluntary Sector Quarterly, 39,* 884–900.

Griffith, J. (2012). A decade of helping: Community service among recent high school graduates attending college. *Nonprofit and Voluntary Sector Quarterly, 41,* 786–801.

Hatcher, J. A. (2008). *The public role of professionals: Developing and evaluating the civic-minded professional scale* (Doctoral dissertation). Retrieved from https://scholarworks.iupui.edu/handle/1805/1703

Hatcher, J. A., Shaker, G. G, & Freeman, T. M. (2016). Faculty learning communities: Taking collective action to improve teaching and learning in Nonprofit and Philanthropic Studies. *Journal of Nonprofit Education and Leadership, 6*(3), 99–114.

Hatcher, J. A., & Studer, M. L. (2015). Service-learning and philanthropy: Implications for course design. *Theory into Practice, 54*(1), 11–19.

Hatcher, J. A., & Witkowski, G. (2014, November). *Advancing the research on experiential philanthropy courses.* Paper presented at the 43rd annual Association for Research on Nonprofit and Voluntary Associations, Denver, CO.

Hustinx, L., Cnaan, R. A., & Handy, F. (2010). Navigating theories of volunteering: A hybrid map for a complex phenomenon. *Journal for the Theory of Social Behaviour, 40*, 410–434.

Janoski, T., Musick, M., & Wilson, J. (1998). Being volunteered? The impact of social participation and pro-social attitudes on volunteering. *Sociological Forum, 13*, 495–519.

Keen, C., & Hall, K. (2009). Engaging with difference matters: Longitudinal student outcomes of co-curricular service-learning programs. *The Journal of Higher Education, 80*(1), 59–79.

Kirlin, M. (2003). *The role of civic skills in fostering civic engagement* (CIRCLE Working Paper 6). The Center for Information and Research on Civic Learning & Engagement. University of Maryland.

Leete, L. (2006). Work in the nonprofit sector. In W. W. Powell & R. Steinberg (Eds.), *The nonprofit sector: A research handbook* (2nd ed., pp. 159–179). New Haven, CT: Yale University Press.

Lockeman, K. S., & Pelco, L. E. (2013). The relationship between service-learning and degree completion. *Michigan Journal of Community Service Learning, 20*(1), 18–30.

Lynn, E., & Wisely, D. S. (2006). Four traditions of philanthropy. In A. Davis & E. Lynn (Eds.), *The civically engaged reader: A diverse collection of short provocative readings on civic action* (pp. 210–217). Chicago, IL: The Great Books Foundation.

Mabry, J. B. (1998). Pedagogical variations in service learning and student outcomes: How time, contact and reflection matters. *Michigan Journal of Community Service Learning, 5*, 32–47.

Macduff, N. (2005). Societal changes and the rise of the episodic volunteer. In J. L. Brudy (Ed.), *Emerging areas of volunteering* (ARNOVA Occasional Paper Series, 2nd ed.) (Vol. 1, no. 2, pp. 51–63). Indianapolis, IN: Association for Research on Nonprofit Organizations and Voluntary Action.

Mirabella, R. M., & McDonald, M. (2012). 11 university-based education programs in nonprofit management and philanthropic studies: Current state of the field and future directions. In R. J. Burke & C. L. Cooper (Eds.), *Human resource management in the nonprofit sector: Passion, purpose and professionalism* (pp. 243–258). Cheltenham, UK: Edward Elgar.

Moely, B. E., Furco, A., & Reed, J. (2008). Charity and social change: The impact of individual preferences on service-learning outcomes. *Michigan Journal of Community Service Learning, 15*(1), 37–48.

Morgan, W., & Streb, M. (2001). Building citizenship: How student voice in service-learning develops civic values. *Social Science Quarterly, 82*(1), 154–169.

Morton, K. (1995). The irony of service: Charity, project and social change in service-learning. *Michigan Journal of Community Service Learning, 2*(1), 19–32.

Musick, M. A., & Wilson J. (2008). *Volunteers: A social profile.* Bloomington, IN: Indiana University Press.

Olberding, J. (2010). Does student philanthropy work? A study of long-term effects of the "Learning by Giving" approach. *Innovative Higher Education, 37*(2), 71–87.

Payton, R. L., & Moody, M. (2008). *Understanding philanthropy: Its meaning and its mission.* Bloomington: Indiana University Press.

Penner, L. A. (2002). Dispositional and organizational influences on sustained volunteerism: An interactionist perspective. *Journal of Social Issues, 58*, 447–467.

Personal and Social Responsibility Index. (n.d.) *About the PSRI.* Retrieved from http://www.psri.hs.iastate.edu

Powell, W. W., & Steinberg, R. (Eds.). (2006). *The nonprofit sector: A research hand book (2nd ed.).* New Haven, CT: Yale University Press.

Reed, V. A., Jernstedt, G. C., Hawley, J. K., Reber, E. S., & DuBois, C. A. (2005). Effects of a small-scale, very short-term service-learning experience on college students. *Journal of Adolescence, 28*, 359–368.

Richard, D., Keen C., Hatcher, J., & Pease, H. (2016). Pathways to adult civic engagement: Benefits of reflection and dialogue across difference in college service-learning programs. *Michigan Journal of Community Service Learning.*

Sandy, M., Ikeda, E. K., Cruz, N., & Holland, B. (2007). *Community voices: A California Campus Compact study on partnerships.* San Francisco, CA: California Campus Compact.

Sievers, B. R. (2010). *Civil society, philanthropy, and the fate of the commons.* Lebanon, NH: University Press of New England.

Sigmon, R. L. (1994). *Serving to learn, learning to serve. Linking service with learning.* Washington, DC: Council of Independent Colleges.

Simons, L. (2015). Measuring service-learning and civic engagement. In R. S. Jhangiani, J. D. Troisi, B. Fleck, A. M. Legg, & H. D. Hussey (Eds.), *A compendium of scales for use in the scholarship of teaching and learning* (pp. 102–122). Washington, DC: Society for the Teaching of Psychology, American Psychological Association.

Snyder, M., & Omoto, A. (1992). Who helps and why? The psychology of AIDS volunteerism. In S. Spacapan & S. Oskamp (Eds.), *Helping and being helped* (pp. 213–239). Newbury Park, CA: Sage.

Sponsler, L. E., & Hartley, M. (2013). *Five things student affairs professional can do to institutionalize civic engagement* (NASPA Research and Policy Institute Issue Brief). Washington, DC: NASPA—Student Affairs Administrators in Higher Education. Retrieved from http://www.naspa.org/images/uploads/main/5THINGS-AUG2013_WEB.pdf

Steinberg, K., Hatcher, J. A., & Bringle, R. G. (2011). A north star: Civic-minded graduate. *Michigan Journal of Community Service Learning, 18*(1), 19–33.

Sullivan, W. M., & Rosin, M. S. (2008). *A new agenda for higher education: Shaping a life of the mind for practice.* San Francisco, CA: Jossey-Bass.

Tomkovick, C., Lester, S. W., Flunker, L., & Wells, T. (2008). Linking collegiate service-learning to future volunteerism: Implications for nonprofit organizations. *Nonprofit Management and Leadership*, *19*(1), 3–24.

Toncar, M. F., Reid, J. S., Burns, D. J., Anderson, C. E., & Nguyen, H. P. (2006). Uniform assessment of the benefits of service learning: The development, evaluation, and implementation of the SELEB scale. *Journal of Marketing Theory and Practice*, *14* (Summer), 233–248.

U.S. Bureau of Labor Statistics. (2015). Retrieved from http://www.bls.gov/news .release/volun.nro.htm

Weinberg, A. S. (2005). Residential education for democracy. *Learning for Democracy*, *1*(2), 29–45.

Wilson, J. (2012). Volunteerism research: A review essay. *Nonprofit and Voluntary Sector Quarterly*, *41*, 176–212.

WELL-BEING AND STUDENT CIVIC OUTCOMES

Claire Berezowitz, Alisa Pykett, Victoria Faust, and Constance Flanagan

T his chapter theoretically bridges civic outcomes and the well-being of college students engaged in service learning, conceptualizing well-being across multiple levels ranging from individual to relational to collective well-being. Applying an ecological lens, we argue that civic outcomes relate to well-being across each of these levels. We begin with an exploration and deconstruction of theories of well-being in regard to indicators like individual and collective efficacy; connectedness; and social trust, as it relates to different groups of college students. Service learning provides a public space enabling students to grapple with the civic implications of social issues, deliberate and consider diverse perspectives, and engage in collective action. We put forth three research agendas, raising questions about whose well-being is being considered; how critical consciousness developed through service learning influences well-being; and what kinds of service learning contexts support individual, relational, and collective well-being. Finally, implications for the design of service learning courses are offered that advance the well-being of college students, communities, and democracy.

Ecological models from the fields of human development (Bronfenbrenner, 1977) and community psychology (Trickett, 1984) provide tools for advancing theory, research, and practice that take into account how settings and contexts influence individuals and their relationships. Using this ecological framework, well-being can be understood as both subjective and relational, and service learning can be understood as a civic setting that has the potential to foster well-being at the subjective (intrapersonal), relational (interpersonal), and collective (communal) levels. Subjective well-being involves an individual's self-evaluation of his or her own life and includes two primary dimensions: hedonic well-being, or positive emotions about one's own life, and eudaimonic well-being, or positive psychological and social functioning in life (Keyes, 2007). We are primarily concerned with eudaimonic well-being because it connects an individual's well-being and sense of purpose to the well-being of others. Relational well-being is grounded in the notion of interdependence of one's fate with the fates of others through shared engagement in civic life. In addition to subjective and relational well-being, Prilleltensky (2012) highlights the importance of community-level qualities when assessing well-being. He suggests that conditions of collective efficacy, empowerment, and fairness that lead to societal flourishing are necessary for individuals to experience both subjective and relational well-being. This triadic approach to subjective, relational, and collective well-being will frame this analysis.

The relationship between civic outcomes and well-being occurs at all three levels of analysis. For example, service learning may enhance students' well-being at the individual level due to feelings of benevolence (Flanagan & Bundick, 2011). If students engage in and discuss the service experience with fellow students and community partners, they may form collective identities and realize the interdependence of their fates with others; feelings of connectedness and collective agency develop when the group rather than the individual is the focus and such identifications with the group promote well-being (Flanagan & Bundick, 2011). Through such group processes, students also develop civic perspectives (i.e., "we're all in this together") and democratic dispositions (e.g., open mindedness, social trust) that are psychosocial resources on which they can draw during times of difficulty and uncertainty (Flanagan, 2006). Finally, by raising issues of injustice, service learning can elevate students' critical consciousness and motivate them to join with others in organizations that redress those injustices (chapter 2.6). Working with others to challenge unjust conditions can promote well-being at the intrapersonal, interpersonal, and collective levels (Prilleltensky, 2012).

Theoretical Foundations

Eudaimonia emphasizes the potential of humans to see the good in and to act in the best interests of one another. It draws from Aristotle's emphasis on virtuous behaviors as the source of human well-being and happiness (Ryan & Deci, 2001). The psychological benefits include the facilitation of relationships and satisfaction of the need to belong (Baumeister & Leary, 1995). Thriving is positively correlated with eudaimonia (e.g., being prosocial, cooperative, responsive to others). Service learning can foster eudaimonic well-being by cultivating civic dispositions like a civic identity, a collective problem-solving orientation, and critical social analysis skills.

Civic engagement among college students, of which service learning is one approach, is associated with forming civic commitments and democratic dispositions that have an enduring impact on well-being (Finlay, Flanagan, & Wray-Lake, 2011). This view of well-being and its relationship to the civic outcomes of service learning is grounded in various theories drawing from psychological subdisciplines (e.g., community, developmental, positive psychology). The theories that follow illuminate the relationships between the development of civic dispositions through service learning and college students' subjective, relational, and collective well-being.

Subjective and Relational Well-Being

Subjective well-being can be understood as self-perceived quality of life, including both cognitive judgments about and emotional reactions to life satisfaction and purpose. Manifestations of relational well-being include caring, compassionate, and supportive relationships (Evans & Prilleltensky, 2007). Various theories of well-being have emerged that bind together these notions of subjective and relational well-being, including Keyes' (2002) notion of flourishing and Schreiner's (2010) conception of thriving.

Flourishing places well-being on a multidimensional continuum of mental health. Flourishing is not simply the absence of mental illness, but rather "a state of well-being in which the individual realizes his or her own abilities, can cope with the normal stresses of life, can work productively and fruitfully, and is able to make a contribution to his or her community" (Keyes, 2007, p. 98). Keyes identifies 13 dimensions that describe flourishing, including both intrapersonal psychological (e.g., self-acceptance) and interpersonal relational (e.g., social coherence and contribution) aspects. The relational aspect of flourishing is essential because social actualization and connectedness are not possible without productive and supportive interpersonal connections; thus, service learning can enable students to understand the interdependence of self and society, thereby leading to flourishing (Hersh et al., 2009).

Schreiner (2010) described flourishing among young adult college students as *thriving*, which includes engaged learning, academic determination, positive perspective, diverse citizenship, and social connectedness. Schreiner notes that multiple pathways to thriving may be uniquely experienced by different individuals. For example, campus involvement, spirituality, and sense of community are three specific pathways to thriving that may be experienced very differently by students of color on predominantly White campuses as compared to the experiences of their Caucasian peers, who may experience greater social connectedness and optimism about their future as contributors to their thriving (Schreiner, 2010).

Keyes's flourishing and Schreiner's thriving point to a relationship between intrapersonal and interpersonal factors that involve both subjective and relational well-being. Students may feel an enhanced sense of subjective well-being as they experience increased self-efficacy, sense of purpose, or life satisfaction through the service learning experience (Reeb & Folger, 2013). At the same time, relational well-being may be enhanced through group reflections on service learning as students collectively grapple with social issues and experience both social coherence and contribution (Helliwell & Putnam, 2004). Service learning can then be viewed as a civic setting in which meaningful interactions with others and civic contributions can lead to flourishing. In the case of service learning, theories such as flourishing and thriving must be expanded to also describe social flourishing and conditions of collective well-being.

Connectedness and Social Trust

Working on public problems with fellow members of communities should positively influence well-being by fulfilling the human need to belong (Baumeister & Leary, 1995). This larger sense of community also implies personal voice and mattering, shared emotional connection, and interdependent goals (Schreiner, 2010). Service learning may enable a student to feel connected to and valued by something bigger than oneself, which has been identified as a basic human need and a precursor to well-being (Strayhorn, 2012). The civic experience of collective efficacy can increase social connectedness and reduce social isolation, thereby contributing to increased relational well-being and a sense that "we're all in this together" (Checkoway, 2011).

The "web of networks, norms, and trusting relationships that enable people to address community issues through collective action" is social capital (Flanagan, Kim, Collura, & Kopish, 2014, p. 296), which encompasses both bonding and bridging forms. Bonding social capital refers to the solidarity felt among people in tightly knit (typically homogeneous) networks, whereas bridging social capital refers to weaker ties of more heterogeneous individuals and groups (Putnam, 2000). Bridging social capital encourages growth in areas like perspective-taking, collective efficacy, and social trust. Through scaffolded service learning experiences aimed at developing perspective-taking skills and personal reflection, engaging with difference can lead to increased social trust, an indicator of social capital, among both students and community members. Social trust is essential for democracy because it reflects a belief that fellow human beings are trustworthy and fair and is positively correlated with engaging in civic affairs (Flanagan et al., 2014). Through the service learning experience of working together toward the common good, students may develop a belief in the good intentions of others.

Social connectedness and social capital may serve to moderate psychological distress of grappling with social injustices and difference (Flanagan, Faust, & Pykett, 2013). Social solidarity can mitigate individual levels of anxiety and discomfort with pressing social issues (Flanagan, 2003). Underrepresented students likely have very different experiences of service learning than majority students, particularly if the characteristics of their "home" communities are similar to the ones being served. In such instances, the majority student population may develop bridging social capital, whereas underrepresented students may develop bonding social capital instead (Putnam, 2000), resulting in different types of relational well-being for students with unique social identities. Moreover, one might expect that engaging with social issues that exist in one's home community is very different from considering less personal social injustices faced by others.

Psychological and Multilevel Empowerment

In community psychology, psychological empowerment is understood to have emotional, cognitive, behavioral, and relational components (Christens, 2012). The emotional (i.e., intrapersonal) component consists of leadership and policy competence and is measured as perceived control in various social domains of an individual's environment (Peterson et al., 2006; Zimmerman & Zahniser, 1991). The cognitive component involves critical knowledge of resources, contexts, and systems in the community, whereas the behavioral component is often conceived as civic participation itself. Finally, the relational component includes collaborative competence, bridging social divisions, facilitating the empowerment of others, and mobilizing networks.

Feelings of empowerment are correlated with engagement in community work (Christens, Peterson, & Speer, 2011), and psychological empowerment is associated with subjective well-being (Diener & Biswas-Diener, 2005). Empowerment theories refer to capacities to influence the social and political systems. The mechanism underlying this association may be that agency in sociopolitical contexts helps to prevent alienation and hopelessness (Christens & Peterson, 2012; Prilleltensky, 2008; Zimmerman, 1990). Empowerment theory also refines the notion of relational well-being by asserting that feelings of communal contribution and the development of shared identities arise from exercising social power together to influence systems (Speer & Hughey, 1995).

Using an ecological lens, empowerment theory also looks beyond individuals to the qualities of their relationships and settings (Maton, 2008; Zimmerman, 2000). Relational dynamics that promote empowerment are closely connected to relational well-being and include group resiliency, cohesion, collective efficacy, and outcome efficacy (Collura, 2015; Zimmerman, 2000). Setting-level qualities associated with empowerment include opportunities for adopting meaningful roles and the presence of participatory decision-making processes (Bond & Keys, 1993; Maton & Salem, 1995; Speer, Jackson, & Peterson, 2001). Settings that are themselves empowered have been characterized by the development and existence of organizational-level networks, policy influences, and pluralistic leadership in the allocation of resources (Peterson & Zimmerman, 2004). Such settings can advance social change efforts to improve the overall well-being of communities (Maton, 2008).

Empowerment can be valuable in understanding the relationship between service learning settings and the well-being of students and others. Given the importance of policy competence and civic participation (Christens, 2012), a service learning experience may be designed to promote these two aspects by objectively improving the lives of others and analyzing the political context in class. Without similarly empowering the community members involved in service learning through increased civic awareness and political action, service learning may reproduce disparities in well-being since well-being is promoted through collective action in settings characterized by shared decision-making and influence over policies and resources (Zimmerman, 2000). Alternatively, service learning could prove empowering in educational settings where students are predominantly residents of the local community or when the service learning experience is participatory in nature. Therefore, analyzing service learning through the lens of empowerment helps to understand the settings, power dynamics, and inequities in systems that may promote or inhibit well-being in communities.

Critical Consciousness and Well-Being

Critical consciousness provides another theoretical tool for understanding the relationship between service learning and well-being. Service learning provides an opportunity for Freirean problem-posing education and *conscientização*, or critical consciousness raising (Freire, 2000). In explaining problem-posing education, Freire suggests that people "develop their power to perceive critically the way they exist in the world with which and in which they find themselves; they come to see the world not as a static reality, but as a reality in process, in transformation" (p. 83). Through participating in justice-oriented service learning, students can discover that they can critically analyze the world and influence processes around them (chapters 1.3 and 2.6).

Building on Freire and their own work in youth political and civic development, Watts, Diemer, and Voight (2011) propose three different components of critical consciousness: critical reflection, political efficacy, and critical action. Service learning can provide opportunities for critical reflection but does not always challenge students to build political efficacy and practice critical action. Providing students with the tools to critically analyze the injustices around them without also providing them with the tools to gather with others to take action to address the injustice can have a negative impact on well-being in the form of cynicism and hopelessness. As Prilleltensky (2012) suggests, critical consciousness, critical action, and the belief that one can effect change can mitigate the threats to well-being that can accompany increased exposure to or direct experience of injustice.

Figure 2.5.1. An ecological model of justice and well-being.

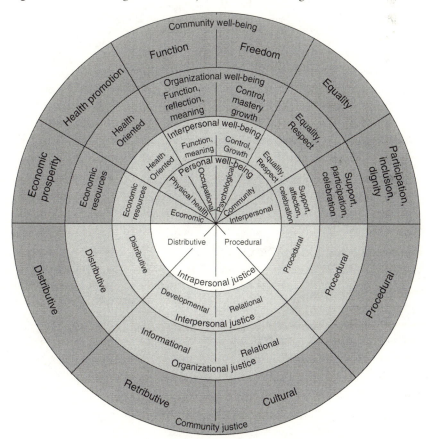

Source. Reproduced from Prilleltensky (2012, p. 11). Copyright 2012 by Springer. Reproduced with permission of Springer.

Envisioning service learning and civic outcomes from an ecological perspective that recognizes the relationship between well-being and justice, Prilleltensky's (2012) discussion on well-being as fairness provides a useful framework. He distinguishes objective well-being (material and physical needs for survival) from subjective well-being (emotional and psychological needs for thriving) and indicates that well-being is achieved through balancing these needs across multiple levels—intrapersonal, interpersonal, organizational, and community levels (see Figure 2.5.1). For Prilleltensky, justice, or fairness, resides at the core of well-being. Although positive psychology theories (Seligman, 2011) provide useful tools for those in relatively advantaged conditions, the theories fail to describe well-being for those faced daily with injustice. The experiences of well-being differ based upon whether one lives under persistent conditions of injustice or optimal conditions for justice. Drawing from Sheppard, Lewicki, and Minton (1992), Prilleltensky (2012) clarifies how individuals grapple with notions of justice: "In the end, justice is about balancing what is due me with what is due other people, institutions and communities" (p. 9). Engaging in service learning creates opportunities for critical reflection about balancing what is "due" to different people, the processes by which people receive what is due, and one's own position of relative privilege.

Existing Research and Future Directions

Next, we explore existing research linking service learning with the previously articulated theories related to individual, relational, and collective well-being. Building on the extant literature, we suggest a future research agenda related to the design of service learning courses and the relationship between these different dimensions of well-being for different populations of students. Broadly, future research on service learning, well-being, and civic outcomes should explore (a) whose well-being is promoted through service learning; (b) what relationships might exist between critical consciousness and well-being; and (c) how contexts and settings are connected to individual, relational, and collective well-being. In addition, Table 2.5.1 presents specific research questions that build on the previously articulated theories and identified research or gaps within the existing research.

Well-Being for Whom?

Research exists linking service learning experiences to dimensions of well-being, primarily at the level of individual subjective well-being. Astin, Vogelgesang, Ikeda, and Yee (2000) compared the effects of service learning

TABLE 2.5.1
Research Agenda Linking Well-Being and Civic Outcomes of Service Learning

Levels of Well-Being	Potential Research Questions
Individual (i.e., intrapersonal)	• How do the service learning experiences of under-represented students influence their individual levels of subjective well-being? Does this vary over time? • What is the impact of service learning on the personal well-being of individuals in communities in which the service learning occurs? • How does the context in which service learning occurs influence students' levels of subjective well-being? • How and under what conditions does service learning elevate students' levels of critical consciousness? Can "troubling" experiences that potentially lower levels of subjective well-being eventually result in higher levels of relational or collective well-being in the long run?
Relational (i.e., interpersonal)	• Does the context in which service learning occurs influence the relational well-being of both students and those with whom they engage in the community? Does this vary based upon relative privilege or lack thereof? • What qualities of empowering service learning settings elevate levels of relational well-being and increase social trust among participants? • Do all groups of students experience changes in relational well-being similarly or are there differences based upon one's intersecting social identities in relation to the community in which service learning occurs?
Collective (i.e., communal)	• How does service learning influence social trust and collective well-being in communities in which service learning occurs? • Can service learning advance well-being as justice by elevating levels of critical consciousness among privileged groups? • How do strategic campus-community partnerships contribute to service learning settings that support collective well-being?

versus community service on the cognitive and affective development of college students and found positive effects for academic performance, civic values, self-efficacy, leadership, choice of a service career, and plans to participate in service after college. Students reported increased awareness of the world and of personal values, indicating higher eudaimonic subjective well-being. Furthermore, by applying Schreiner's (2010) theory of thriving, one might study whether service learning leads to thriving through enhanced subjective and relational well-being in combination with academic engagement. Enhanced self-efficacy is embodied in Keyes' psychosocial flourishing, yet the study by Astin and colleagues (2000) would have been richer had it also captured changes in collective efficacy and relational well-being among students who participate in service learning.

Astin and colleagues (2000) emphasized that the opportunity to reflect on a service learning experience with other students and the instructor was an important component of service learning, yet how might the group processing differ for underrepresented students in service learning courses? The relative social support a student receives could be diminished if other students in the class cannot identify with a particular student's experience. Moreover, research has found that student-teacher relationships have greater benefits for White students than students of other races/ethnicities (Schreiner, 2010). If so, then how does the relationship with the instructor shape the experiences of underrepresented students of color as compared to their racial/ethnic majority peers? At the same time, Lockeman and Pelco (2013) found that underrepresented and low-income students who participated in service learning courses had higher degree completion rates than underrepresented students who did not participate in service learning. Thus, service learning courses may contribute to intrapersonal and interpersonal factors related to persistence (e.g., efficacy).

Positive associations have been found between happiness, or subjective well-being, and other-oriented values (Post, 2005). For service learning, the association with well-being has been attributed to the following: Service learning is psychologically rewarding in and of itself, participation in civil society is socially reinforced, humans are biologically predisposed to engage in altruistic behavior, and experiencing relative privilege can induce feelings of gratitude (Flanagan & Bundick, 2011). Eyler (2011) reviewed studies comparing students who participated in service learning with those who did not and found that connectedness to a larger community, political efficacy, and future intent to participate in community life were gains associated with service learning. Do these constructs (e.g., other-oriented, sense of community, efficacy) have different meanings and implications depending on one's social background and relative level of privilege?

Questions remain regarding the impact of service learning on the relational well-being of underrepresented students who come from the very kinds of communities that university programs are serving. After controlling for both college environment and student characteristics, Astin and Sax (1998) found that 38% of more than 3,000 college students surveyed engaged in service in order to "work with people who are different than me" (p. 255). Future research should consider who the dominant and subordinate groups are in service learning contexts in order to understand the subjective and relational well-being of participants. Considering relational well-being as not only an outcome but also a process, Kiely (2005) found that contextual border crossing was important to transformational service learning, yet students with marginalized social identities experienced the developmental decentering that occurs during the process of crossing social and contextual borders differently than their peers with dominant identities (Jones, Robbins, & LePeau, 2011).

Reeb and Folger (2013) note a void in the service learning literature on community-level outcomes. How are individual people, networks of individuals, and communities influenced by service learning courses and how does this work influence their collective well-being? Are those who engage in service learning activities merely participants or fully partners in the experience? What are the implications of the former versus the latter in relation to the collective well-being? What differentiates service learning experiences that lead to empowered communities from those that do not? Future research should consider the unique experiences of subjective, relational, or collective well-being for different agents engaged in service learning partnerships (e.g., service-providers, administrators, corporate partners, neighborhoods).

Finally, Bowman, Brandenberger, Lapsley, Hill, and Quaranto (2010) found participation in service learning during college was related to later adult psychosocial flourishing, including personal growth, purpose in life, life satisfaction (hedonic well-being), and environmental mastery. Other longitudinal work indicates that young adults' civic engagement (i.e., voting, community volunteer service, involvement in social action/solidarity groups, endorsement of civic trust) were predicted by relationships to family and community in adolescence (Duke, Skay, Pettingell, & Borowsky, 2009). An opportunity remains to study the long-term well-being of community members, not solely students, who engage with service learning projects. In addition, longitudinal research has focused largely on individual-level outcomes, and future research can explore the long-term impact of such experiences on students' relational and/or collective well-being. For example, how do civic outcomes of service learning (e.g., collective problem-solving and action) influence the long-term collective well-being of the communities involved? Levine's (2008) work demonstrated that long-term individual civic capacity and community capacity require more than service. Future research could also explore the difference in civic outcomes and well-being between groups that engage in service learning and those that participate in other civic activities, such as collaborative deliberation or community problem-solving.

Well-Being and Justice

Service learning students may encounter conditions of injustice, which has ramifications for well-being across multiple levels. Do students develop a stronger sense of mattering and a more connected sense of community through activities that contribute to the common good? What about students in the classroom who identify more with the community in which the service learning project takes place than with their classmates who see the community as "other people"? Alternatively, might a student, in grappling with injustice and privilege for the first time or in new ways, experience emotional distress? If so, how can that be effectively managed (chapters 2.3 and 2.7)?

Because service learning activities often address the critical issues or unmet needs of groups, these activities can surface justice issues at the intrapersonal, interpersonal, group, and community levels. The individual experiences of students are likely to vary widely according to the conditions of justice or injustice under which they live based on their social position and identities along dimensions of race, gender, and class. When confronted with conditions of injustice through service learning experiences, students can develop critical consciousness and take critical action to address the injustice, which can lead to well-being across ecological levels (Prilleltensky, 2012). Alternatively, students can feel benevolence without becoming aware of the social injustice at the root of the problem. In other words, service learning courses may reproduce conditions of injustice at the individual and community levels, potentially giving rise to harmful assumptions, indifference, or cynicism. At the same time, research can investigate how service learning that attends to critical reflection, political efficacy, and critical action has the potential to facilitate growth in students' interpretations of social issues, commitments to social justice, understandings of privilege, and intentions to personally effect change (Butin, 2007; Jones, Robbins, & Lapeau, 2011; Mitchell, 2007).

Issues of justice and empowerment appear in the literature linking service learning to student well-being. Seider, Rabinowicz, and Gillmor (2011) found that students who participated in social justice–focused service learning experiences demonstrated a significant shift toward a structural understanding of poverty when compared with peers in the control group. Based upon interviews with participants, the program's efficacy came from the combined effects of students' personal conversations with individuals at their service sites and the theoretical frameworks explored through weekly discussions of readings.

Christens, Collura, and Tahir (2013) studied civic hopefulness and critical consciousness among people engaged in community organizing and grassroots advocacy. Using latent-class analysis—a person-centered methodological approach—they identified subgroups based on levels of cognitive and emotional empowerment. Four clusters emerged in the analysis of 1,322 people engaged in community work: critical but alienated, uncritical but hopeful, uncritical and alienated, and critical and hopeful. They then examined the relationships between the subgroups and other variables, such as social capital, psychological sense of community, and psychological well-being. This study could be replicated in service learning to explore potential pathways among subgroups, helping to guide the creation of settings that foster critical hopefulness.

Research is needed that explores levels of critical consciousness or psychological empowerment and well-being at multiple time points across a service learning course, as well as throughout the college experience. Diemer Rapa, Park, and Perry (2014) developed a critical consciousness scale that has three dimensions (i.e., critical reflection, political efficacy, critical action). Psychological empowerment has been conceptualized with four different components (emotional, cognitive, relational, and behavioral) (Christens, 2012). Future research could explore the relationships among the components at different points throughout the semester, when examining particular social issues, or using certain pedagogical approaches. For example, researchers could employ a mixed-methods, person-centered study using critical consciousness (Diemer et al., 2014) or psychological empowerment (Christens, Peterson, & Speer, 2014) scales and a qualitative analysis of student reflection products and observations of course discourse. Do students who start with a higher level of critical consciousness, or one dimension of critical consciousness, have different pathways to well-being than those who start with lower levels? What is the relationship between well-being and critical consciousness at different times throughout the semester? What about at the course level? Or in relation to different college experiences? Do the pathways of students in particular courses differ in meaningful ways from other courses or types of service activities?

Contexts of Service Learning

Although the context in which service learning occurs varies widely, data on contexts and settings are not often systematically collected and analyzed (chapter 2.7). Such lack of focus on rich contexts may be a product of the drive to justify service learning by demonstrating its impact on students and communities (Kiely, 2005). Contexts (e.g., the history, characteristics, dynamics of educational institutions) and processes (e.g., classroom design, pedagogical approach, programmatic norms) may mediate the relationship between service learning and well-being for various constituencies (i.e., students, communities, instructors, service site supervisors). Such features are captured in pedagogical models, such as Mitchell's (2008) comparison of traditional and critical service learning in classroom and community settings. Additionally, rich qualitative exploration has focused on the influence of social justice pedagogy (e.g., Kiely, 2005; Seider et al., 2011) but is not yet explicitly connected to well-being at different levels.

Some systematic research on service learning contexts examines well-being and broader institutional characteristics like religiosity and institutional climate (Kuh & Umbach, 2004; Whitt, Edison, Pascarella, Terenzini, & Nora, 2001). Astin and Sax (1998) controlled for contextual effects in their study on the impact of service on college student well-being. Often, however, studies do not systematically consider the important role of contextual or interactional effects. Alternatively, research could focus on the mechanisms by which these different contextual factors influence experiences of service learning and well-being. For example, critical institutions might advance well-being through service learning in part because students collaborate with community members on campaigns to advance policy change by empowering communities and promoting relational well-being across participants. A critical institution could support educators implementing this type of service learning experience, thereby enhancing the eudaimonic well-being of the course's instructor. Therefore, future service learning research should systematically collect and use data about institutional contexts in analyses of service learning and well-being (chapter 3.3).

The lack of systematic analyses of service learning settings and their role in the relationship between service learning and well-being may also be due to a lack of effective multilevel theoretical frameworks and methodological approaches for assessment beyond individual level outcomes (chapters 3.3, 3.4, and 3.5). Multilevel theoretical frameworks, such as empowerment theory and theories of well-being, offer opportunities to apply conceptual frameworks to setting-level analyses. The application of an empowerment framework to service learning research and practice could encourage ecologically oriented research questions that involve systematically analyzing setting level data, such as whether service learning settings that target and influence policy are more effective at promoting relational well-being than other types of engagement. One also could systematically examine whether resource allocation in settings influences collective efficacy and well-being, thereby testing models where funding allocations are determined by communities and how this influences the construction of shared identity or feelings of communal contribution.

Reflecting on years of multilevel research in schools, Seidman (2012) observed the challenges related to the primacy of psychometric data in ecologically oriented analyses. Although individual level data are important, Seidman (2012) notes that "psychological assessment methods (psychometrics) do not always match the demands of ecological conceptualizations and questions that are embedded in a multiple levels of analysis framework" (p. 6). Therefore, research on service learning and well-being needs to consider assessment methods that look beyond psychometric data to capture the setting features and processes, including dynamic processes of decision-making, distribution of resources that inform agendas and decisions, patterns of interaction over time, relational experiences and culture, and human resources (Seidman & Tseng, 2011). To this end, service learning research can incorporate methods such as self-reports of setting norms, assessment of social networks, and behavioral observation of interactions and practices across different service learning settings on civic outcomes.

Implications for Practice

Given the multiple dimensions of well-being that are at stake for individuals, networks of individuals, and entire communities through service learning courses, it is imperative that service learning programs are designed and implemented to facilitate these multiple dimensions of well-being. At the individual level, the very notion of "service" learning can be problematic since it implies a division between a "recipient" and a service "provider." As an alternative, language such as "community-engaged learning" implies a more equitable distribution of power between college students and community partners. Additionally, the subjective and relational well-being of all students, not just the majority students in a course, must be considered in the design of both personal and public reflections. Explicit opportunities to engage with difficult questions about social identities and relational dynamics of the service learning experience through public reflection with others, as opposed to individual private reflection, necessitates that service learning and subsequent reflection activities be well-facilitated by skilled instructors and/ or community partners.

Currently, institutional oversight of service learning courses is limited, and seldom are courses intentionally designed to fit sequentially within a developmental program of study. Service learning practitioners and institutions of higher education would do well to scaffold service learning courses and experiences throughout a student's educational experience. By providing experiences leading up to and following a service learning course, service learning can facilitate civic outcomes at the individual, relational, and collective levels. In the context of service learning, civic outcomes have the potential to parallel the multiple dimensions of well-being. At the individual level, service learning fosters civic-minded graduates who have the knowledge, skills, and dispositions to improve communities (Steinberg, Hatcher, & Bringle, 2011). At the interpersonal level, students and community members engage in collective action and reflection while strengthening social ties and trust. At the collective level, reciprocal community-campus partnerships can lead to the more equitable access to conditions for the flourishing for all. Empowered civic contexts facilitate the well-being of both students and community partners, and further research is needed to determine the effectiveness of specific types of service learning settings (e.g., those that aim to influence policies, setting-level power structures) at promoting relational and collective well-being as compared to other forms of community-based activities (e.g., cocurricular volunteering).

Although service learning often involves working to improve the lives of others in communities, empowerment theory suggests that those who are most negatively affected by social and political systems must be their own agents in changing the systems that advance their well-being, as opposed to remaining recipients of services driven by college students' developmental needs. By empowering individuals in different community settings, service learning can foster an understanding of power dynamics and inequities in systems that may promote or inhibit collective well-being. Service learning courses can be designed and implemented to empower everyone involved by ensuring that the entire process is participatory in nature, encouraging students and community members to explore and articulate power dynamics, and teaching students to adopt a collective orientation of "we," rather than "us and them."

Finally, many college courses are time limited, and relationships with community partners often take much longer to develop. If the well-being of college students as well as the collective well-being of communities and partners is to be considered, then ample time and resources are required to develop and deepen strategic partnerships that cultivate understanding and trust. Participatory and empowering approaches to service learning should be provided not only for students to engage with social issues to develop critical consciousness but also to participate in collective action to address instances of injustice and develop a sense of collective efficacy over time. This can occur by providing students with multiple opportunities (internships, volunteering, research, employment) to stay engaged with an issue or a community for a longer period of time that extends beyond the academic semester. This also has implications for the long-term partnerships that can be developed between faculty and community partners as coeducators.

Conclusion

If well-being is conceptualized as a multidimensional, multilevel process, then future research on service learning can benefit from exploring the relationships among civic outcomes, the emergent psychological and social processes that constitute well-being, and the features of settings and relationships that promote well-being. Important research questions must address whose well-being is at stake and through what kinds of relationships and processes. A mixed-methods approach may demonstrate directionality and examine mechanisms that link civic outcomes of service learning to relational and collective well-being. Future research would do well to assume a longitudinal and multidirectional approach to studying service learning civic outcomes, recognizing that, in the short term, service learning may in fact lower students' levels of subjective well-being, whereas in the long term, relational and collective well-being may lead to a more enduring form of well-being for students and communities (Flanagan, Faust, & Pykett, 2014).

References

Astin, A. W., & Sax, L. J. (1998). How undergraduates are affected by service participation. *Journal of College Student Development, 39*, 251–263.

Astin, A. W., Vogelgesang, L. J., Ikeda, E. K., & Yee, J. A. (2000). *Executive summary: How service learning affects students.* Los Angeles, CA: Higher Education
Research Institute, University of California, Los Angeles.

Baumeister, R. F., & Leary, M. R. (1995). The need to belong: Desire for interpersonal attachments as a fundamental human motivation. *Psychological Bulletin,
117*, 497–529.

Bond, M. A., & Keys, C. B. (1993). Empowerment, diversity, and collaboration:
Promoting synergy on community boards. *American Journal of Community Psychology, 21*, 37–57.

Bowman, N., Brandenberger, J., Lapsley, D., Hill, P., & Quaranto, J. (2010). Serving
in college, flourishing in adulthood: Does community engagement during the
college years predict adult well-being? *Applied Psychology: Health and Well-Being,
2*, 14–34.

Bronfenbrenner, U. (1977). Toward an experimental ecology of human development.
American Psychologist, 32, 513–531.

Butin, D. W. (2007). Justice-learning: Service-learning as justice-oriented education.
Equity & Excellence in Education, 40, 177–183.

Checkoway, B. (2011). New perspectives on civic engagement and psychosocial well-being. *Liberal Education, 97*, 6–11.

Christens, B. D. (2012). Toward relational empowerment. *American Journal of Community Psychology, 50*, 114–128.

Christens, B. D., Collura, J. J., & Tahir, F. (2013). Critical hopefulness: A person-centered analysis of the intersection of cognitive and emotional empowerment. *American Journal of Community Psychology, 52*, 170–184.

Christens, B. D., & Peterson, N. A. (2012). The role of empowerment in youth development: A study of sociopolitical control as mediator of ecological systems' influence on developmental outcomes. *Journal of Youth and Adolescence, 41*, 623–635.

Christens, B. D., Peterson, N. A., & Speer, P. W. (2011). Community participation and psychological empowerment testing reciprocal causality using a cross-lagged panel design and latent constructs. *Health Education & Behavior, 38*, 339–347.

Christens, B. D., Peterson, C. H., & Speer, P. W. (2014). Psychological empowerment in adulthood. In T. Gullotta & M. Bloom (Eds.), *Encyclopedia of primary prevention and health promotion* (pp. 1766–1776). New York: Springer.

Collura, J. (2015, July). *Building youth empowerment.* Paper presented at the Ohio Promoting Wellness and Recovery Conference, Athens, OH.

Diemer, M. A., Rapa, L. J., Park, C. J., & Perry, J. C. (2014). Development and validation of the critical consciousness scale. *Youth & Society.* Advance online publication. doi: 10.1177/0044118X14538289.

Diener, E., & Biswas-Diener, R. (2005). Psychological empowerment and subjective well-being. In D. Narayan (Ed.), *Measuring empowerment: Cross-disciplinary perspectives* (pp. 125–140). Washington, DC: The World Bank.

Duke, N. N., Skay, C. L., Pettingell, S. L., & Borowsky, I. W. (2009). From adolescent connections to social capital: Predictors of civic engagement in young adulthood. *Journal of Adolescent Health, 44*, 161–168.

Evans, S. D., & Prilleltensky, I. (2007). Youth and democracy: Participation for personal, relational, and collective well-being. *Journal of Community Psychology, 35*, 681–692.

Eyler, J. (2011). What international service learning research can learn from research on service learning. In R. G. Bringle, J. A. Hatcher, & S. G. Jones (Eds.), *International service learning: Conceptual frameworks and research* (pp. 225–242). Sterling, VA: Stylus.

Finlay, A. K., Flanagan, C., & Wray-Lake, L. (2011). Civic engagement patterns and transitions over 8 years: The AmeriCorps national study. *Developmental Psychology, 47*, 1728–1743.

Flanagan, C.A. (2003). Trust, identity, and civic hope. *Applied Developmental Science, 7*, 165–171.

Flanagan, C. A. (2006). Public scholarship and youth at the transition to adulthood. *New Directions for Teaching and Learning, 105*, 41–50.

Flanagan, C. A., & Bundick, M. (2011). Civic engagement and psychosocial well-being in college students. *Liberal Education, 97,* 20–27.

Flanagan, C. A., Faust, V., & Pykett, A. (2013). Educating the public in the spirit of the land-grant university. *The Journal of General Education, 62,* 247–257.

Flanagan, C. A., Kim, T., Collura, J., & Kopish, M. A. (2014). Community service and adolescents' social capital. *Journal of Research on Adolescence, 25,* 295–309.

Freire, P. (2000). *Pedagogy of the oppressed* (30th anniversary ed.). New York: Continuum.

Helliwell, J. F., & Putnam, R. D. (2004). The social context of well-being. *Philosophical Transactions of the Royal Society of London, Series B, 359,* 1435–1446.

Hersh, R. H., Bundick, M., Keeling, R., Keyes, C., Kurpius, A., Shavelson, R., Silverman, D., & Swaner, L. (2009). A well-rounded education for a flat world. *Educational Leadership, 67,* 50–53.

Jones, S. R., Robbins, C. K., & LePeau, L. A. (2011). Negotiating border crossing: Influences of social identity on service-learning outcomes. *Michigan Journal of Community Service Learning, 17*(2), 27–42.

Keyes, C. L. (2002). The mental health continuum: From languishing to flourishing in life. *Journal of Health and Social Behavior, 43,* 207–222.

Keyes, C. L. (2007). Promoting and protecting mental health as flourishing: A complementary strategy for improving national mental health. *American Psychologist, 62,* 95–108.

Kiely, R. (2005). A transformative learning model for service-learning: A longitudinal case study. *Michigan Journal of Community Service Learning, 12*(1), 5–22.

Kuh, G. D., & Umbach, P. D. (2004). College and character: Insights from the national survey of student engagement. *New Directions for Institutional Research, 122,* 37–54.

Levine, P. (2008). The case for "service." *Philosophy & Public Quarterly, 28,* 2–8.

Lockeman, K. S., & Pelco, L. E. (2013). The relationship between service-learning and degree completion. *Michigan Journal of Community Service Learning, 20*(1), 18–30.

Maton, K. I. (2008). Empowering community settings: Agents of individual development, community betterment, and positive social change. *American Journal of Community Psychology, 41,* 4–21.

Maton, K. I., & Salem, D. A. (1995). Organizational characteristics of empowering community settings: A multiple case study approach. *American Journal of Community Psychology, 23,* 631–656.

Mitchell, T. D. (2007). Critical service-learning as social justice education: A case study of the Citizen Scholars Program. *Equity & Excellence in Education, 40,* 101–112.

Mitchell, T. D. (2008). Traditional vs. critical service-learning: Engaging the literature to differentiate two models. *Michigan Journal of Community Service Learning, 14*(2), 50–65.

Peterson, N. A., Lowe, J. B., Hughey, J., Reid, R. J., Zimmerman, M. A., & Speer, P. W. (2006). Measuring the intrapersonal component of psychological empowerment: Confirmatory factor analysis of the sociopolitical control scale. *American Journal of Community Psychology, 38*, 287–297.

Peterson, N. A., & Zimmerman, M. A. (2004). Beyond the individual: Toward a nomological network of organizational empowerment. *American Journal of Community Psychology, 34*, 129–145.

Post, S. G. (2005). Altruism, happiness, and health: It's good to be good. *International Journal of Behavioral Medicine, 12*, 66–77.

Prilleltensky, I. (2008). The role of power in wellness, oppression, and liberation: The promise of psychopolitical validity. *Journal of Community Psychology, 36*, 116–136.

Prilleltensky, I. (2012). Wellness as fairness. *American Journal of Community Psychology, 49*, 1–21.

Putnam, R. D. (2000). *Bowling alone: The collapse and revival of American community.* New York: Simon & Schuster.

Reeb, R. N., & Folger, S. F. (2013). Community outcomes of service learning. In P. H. Clayton, R. G. Bringle, & J. A. Hatcher (Eds.), *Research on service learning: Conceptual frameworks and assessment* (Vol. 2B, pp. 389–418). Sterling, VA: Stylus.

Ryan, R. M., & Deci, E. L. (2001). On happiness and human potentials: A review of research on hedonic and eudaimonic well-being. *Annual Review of Psychology, 52*, 141–166.

Schreiner, L. A. (2010). The "thriving quotient": A new vision for student success. *About Campus, 15*, 2–10.

Seider, S. C., Rabinowicz, S. A., & Gillmor, S. C. (2011). Changing American college students' conceptions of poverty through community service learning. *Analyses of Social Issues and Public Policy, 11*, 105–126.

Seidman, E. (2012). An emerging action science of social settings. *American Journal of Community Psychology, 50*, 1–16.

Seidman, E., & Tseng, V. (2011). Changing social settings: A framework for action. In M.S. Aber, K. I. Maton, & E. Seidman (Eds.), *Empowering settings and voices for social change* (pp. 12–37). New York: Oxford University Press.

Seligman, M. E. P. (2011). *Flourish: A visionary new understanding of happiness and well being.* New York: Free Press.

Sheppard, B. H., Lewicki, R. J., & Minton, J. W. (1992). *Organizational justice: The search for fairness in the workplace.* New York: Lexington Books.

Speer, P. W., & Hughey, J. (1995). Community organizing: An ecological route to empowerment and power. *American Journal of Community Psychology, 23*, 729–748.

Speer, P. W., Jackson, C. B., & Peterson, N. A. (2001). The relationship between social cohesion and empowerment: Support and new implications for theory. *Health Education & Behavior, 28*, 716–732.

Steinberg, K., Hatcher, J. A., & Bringle, R. G. (2011). A north star: Civic-minded graduate. Michigan Journal of Community Service Learning, 18(1), 19-33.

Strayhorn, T. L. (2012). *College students' sense of belonging: A key to educational success for all students.* New York: Routledge.

Trickett, E. J. (1984). Toward a distinctive community psychology: An ecological metaphor for the conduct of community research and the nature of training. *American Journal of Community Psychology, 12,* 261–279.

Watts, R. J., Diemer, M. A., & Voight, A. M. (2011). Critical consciousness: Current status and future directions. In C. A. Flanagan & B. D. Christens (Eds.), Youth civic development: Work at the cutting edge. *New Directions for Child and Adolescent Development, 134,* 43–57.

Whitt, E. J., Edison, M. I., Pascarella, E. T., Terenzini, P. T., & Nora, A. (2001). Influences on students' openness to diversity and challenge in the second and third years of college. *Journal of Higher Education, 72,* 172–204.

Zimmerman, M. A. (1990). Toward a theory of learned hopefulness: A structural model analysis of participation and empowerment. *Journal of Research in Personality, 24,* 71–86.

Zimmerman, M. A. (2000). Empowerment theory. In J. Rappaport & E. Seidman (Eds.), *Handbook of community psychology* (pp. 43–63). New York: Springer US.

Zimmerman, M. A., & Zahniser, J. H. (1991). Refinements of sphere-specific measures of perceived control: Development of a sociopolitical control scale. *Journal of Community Psychology, 19,* 189–204.

CRITICAL THEORIES AND STUDENT CIVIC OUTCOMES

Tania D. Mitchell and Colleen Rost-Banik

Community engagement strategies in higher education wrestle with the tension of effectively supporting student learning and contributing to meaningful community and economic development. Some (Butin, 2010; Hayes & Cuban, 1997; Mitchell, 2008) suggest that this tension can be mitigated with a focus on the liberatory aims of community engagement. Critical theories, which explore social identity, critique systems of power, and develop community, have important connections to community engagement but are frequently underutilized in service learning research. This chapter explores critical theories, provides an overview of how critical theories are used in research, and identifies potential perspectives to improve service learning research. The challenge of civic outcomes, when viewed through critical theories, will also be a focus of our discussion.

What Are Critical Theories?

Bohman (2015) explains that *critical theory* has both "a narrow and a broad meaning" (para. 1). This narrow meaning is generally attributed to the philosophical tradition of the Frankfurt School, including the theorists Habermas (1971) and Horkheimer (1972), with their focus on human emancipation and democratic participation. The Frankfurt thinkers, argues Agger (2013), imagined "a society of praxis" (p. 89) where limits on democracy were challenged and members of society were able to exercise freedom. Missing in this interpretation, however, is attention to issues of identity, which Fraser (1995) calls "a serious deficiency" (p. 22). Even as critical theory seeks human emancipation, it rarely accounts for the ways that particular knowledge and resources are privileged and, therefore, who gets to participate in the project of democracy.

The broad meaning of critical theory highlights its transformative focus. Through a mutual aim "to explain and transform *all* the circumstances that enslave human beings," many critical theories have emerged (Bohman, 2015, para. 1, emphasis in original). These include critical race theory (CRT), feminist theories, queer theory, postmodernism, poststructuralism, and postcolonialism among others (Agger, 2013; Bohman, 2015; Kincheloe & McLaren, 2005). These critical theories largely seek to address issues of identity, explaining and challenging the structural and hierarchical oppression faced by marginalized peoples.

For this chapter, we rely on Kincheloe and McLaren's (2005) definition of *critical theories* as those "concerned in particular with issues of power and justice and the ways that the economy; matters of race, class, and gender; ideologies; discourses; education; religion and other social institutions; and cultural dynamics interact to construct a social system" (p. 306). Critical theories seek to build awareness and understanding of oppression as it exists and to "demonstrate the possibility of a qualitatively different future society" (Agger, 2013, p. 5). Key to the critical theories we explore in this chapter is their activist orientation. These theories "not only [try] to understand our social situation, but to change it . . . to transform it for the better" (Delgado & Stefancic, 2001, p. 3). This understanding of critical theories makes clear their relevance to civic outcomes in service learning research. Critical theories focus on power and identity as they shape and influence participation in a community (Young, 1990) and serve as important tools for analysis to understand both the context and potential of service learning to advance social justice.

It is beyond the scope of this chapter to offer significant insights into each of the critical theories encompassed in the broad meaning of the word, but we aim to provide brief conceptualizations of four key theories that have influenced—and can potentially influence—service learning research of civic outcomes.

Critical Race Theory

CRT is focused on "studying and transforming the relationship among race, racism, and power" (Delgado & Stefancic, 2001, p. 2). It is most distinguished by its recognition of racism as "ordinary, not aberrational" in the "everyday experience of most people of color in this country" (p. 7). This acknowledgment means accepting that racism not only is "difficult to cure" but also "large segments of society have little incentive to eradicate it" (p. 7). CRT critiques claims of colorblindness and neutrality and instead advances a thesis of social construction, rejecting biological or genetic characteristics

of race for a recognition of race as "products of social thought and relations" (p. 7). The process of "differential racialization" (p. 7), whereby racial
groups' experiences in this country are shaped profoundly by shifting needs
in the dominant discourse, demonstrates this social construction. From
the internment of Japanese Americans during World War II to the "model
minority," from hardworking individuals in search of the "American dream"
to "illegals," minoritized groups are differently racialized and, thereby, "rendered minorities in particular situations and institutional environments
that sustain an overrepresentation of Whiteness" (Harper, 2012, p. 9). Thus,
CRT seeks to challenge the minimization of racism in society (Bonilla-
Silva, 2009). It requires attention to issues of race and racism and seeks to
uplift the narratives of people of color to recount how race and racism are
experienced.

Feminisms

Feminisms is a diverse set of theorizing about the role and place of women in
society. It is frequently classified in "waves" with the first wave encompassing
the work to include women in the construct of democracy (e.g., the right
to vote) and the second wave focused on critiquing and challenging the
consistent subjugation and devaluing of women's contributions. The second
wave, believed to have "enshrined the hegemony of the White, middle-class,
heterosexual woman, relegating other women to the margins of feminist
politics" (Hekman, 2000, p. 290), ushered in the third wave of feminism,
which seeks to challenge this "long and painful legacy of its exclusions" (Davis,
2008, p. 70). Third wave feminism recognizes the diversity of women and
embraces intersectional analyses of social issues and concerns (Agger, 2013;
Baumgardner & Richards, 2000; Crenshaw, 1989; Walker, 1992). Feminisms,
like most critical theories, are concerned with issues of power and identity.
Questions of political power (e.g., voting, representation in government),
social power (e.g., the oppressive nature of patriarchy), economic power (e.g.,
equal pay, distribution of reproductive labor), as well as issues of personal
autonomy (e.g., reproductive choice) tend to frame most feminist theories.
Feminist thinking, especially from an intersectional perspective, requires an
analysis that begins from one's own social location (Davis, 2008) and stipu-
lates that social transformation requires change both in the home and in
institutions (Agger, 2013; Davis, 2008; Okin, 1989).

Queer Theory

Queer theory emphasizes the fluid nature of gender and sexuality (Agger,
2013; Meyer, 2007). It reveals "how gender operates as a regulatory construct
that privileges heterosexuality and, furthermore, how the deconstruction of

normative models of gender legitimates lesbian and gay subject positions" (Jagose, 1996, p. 83). As with other critical theories, queer theory "complicates questions of identity and power" (Perez, 2005, p. 173). Dasgupta (2009) explains that queer theory has shifted from establishing or claiming identity ("I'm gay!") to a process of identity construction ("This is how I perform gayness"). This idea of performance is a central concept of queer theory put forward by Butler (1988) who explained that "the various acts of gender creates the idea of gender, and without those acts, there would be no gender at all" (p. 522). Butler continues, "The authors of gender become entranced by their own fictions whereby the construction compels one's belief in its necessity and naturalness" (p. 522). Queer theory, therefore, troubles "the normative and its attendant regimes" (Perez, 2005, p. 175) and upends "recognizable and categorizable identities" (Phillips, 2009, p. 7) through an analysis of power and attention to the discourses and institutions that are seen as normal rather than marginal (Stein & Plummer, 1994; Warner, 1999).

Kumashiro (2003) argues "that norms of society *require* the existence of things queer" (p. 367, emphasis in original). In order for something to be deemed normal, another thing must be considered abnormal, or in contrast to what has been normalized. Queer theory seeks to challenge these binaries with recognition that identity is performed according to what individuals come to understand and believe is "socially and culturally relevant" (Agger, 2013, p. 104). The performative nature of identity means that these categories are unstable and insufficient with the possibility of plural, and potentially contradictory, meanings (Abes, 2008; Phillips, 2009). This rejection of bifurcation means that "the concept of queer truly seeks to . . . disrupt and challenge traditional modes of thought and, by standing outside them, examine and dismantle them" (Meyer, 2007, p. 26).

Poststructuralism

Poststructuralism engages language, discourses, subjectivity, social relations, and institutions to understand dimensions and dynamics of power as well as to identify and strategize opportunities for change (Britzman, 2003; Davies, 2003; Foucault, 1983; Gavey, 1989). It raises "critical concerns about what it is that structures meanings, practices, and bodies, about why certain practices become intelligible, valorized, or deemed as traditions while other practices become discounted, impossible, or unimaginable" (Britzman, 2003, p. 246). The emphasis on subjectivity acknowledges the role of society on "individual practices and experiences" (Alcoff, 1988, p. 416). Foucault (1983) explains:

> This form of power applies itself to immediate everyday life which categorizes the individual, marks him by his own individuality, attaches him to

his own identity, imposes a law of truth on him which he must recognize and which others have to recognize in him. It is a form of power which makes individuals subjects. (p. 212)

In other words, "subjects cannot be uncoupled from the conscious and unconscious discourses that fashion how subjects become recognized and misrecognized" (Britzman, 2003, p. 252). Davies (2003) further explains that the structures of the social world and the place of power in society leave many without the ability to exercise full agency.

Poststructural theories recognize that knowledge is a construct maintained and upheld by those with power; therefore, poststructuralism welcomes a "plurality of meanings" to displace and disrupt the dominant knowledges that oppress (Gavey, 1989, p. 462). Because it rejects single-cause explanations for experiences of and/or with oppression, poststructuralism embraces complexity and contradictions that shape the conditions of people's lives. Poststructuralist analyses focus "on the way each person actively takes up the discourses through which they and others speak/write the world into existence" (Davies, 2003, p. 14). Transformation is a project of disrupting and deconstructing the discourses that inform, influence, and shape the subject (Foucault, 1983; Lather, 2007).

After this brief overview of critical theories, we turn to the ways these theories have been linked to service learning practice and research.

Connections Between Critical Theories and Service Learning

Several authors highlight the compatibility of critical theories and service learning, with Cunningham and Vachta (2003) lauding the combination as "organic, critical praxis in the best sense" (p. 35). Service learning can engage students in work to transform their understandings of community concerns and the solutions enacted to remedy them. Designed to support students in learning academic concepts and how those concepts are experienced in the "real world," service learning can help students develop "a more critical perspective on the forms of domination inherent in their own histories, knowledge, and practices, and learn to value alternative forms of knowledge" (Hayes & Cuban, 1997, p. 75).

These combinations of service learning practice and critical theories focus on issues of power and identity and their implications for community engagement. For example, Donahue and Luber (2015) believe queer theory encourages thinking "about reciprocal relationships in service learning, where borders between providers and recipients of service as well as between learning and teaching are blurred" (p. 212). Hayes and Cuban (1997) invoke critical postmodern theory to explain how "service-learning prompts students to understand their own culture in new ways, appreciate cultural differences, become more critically aware of social inequities and power relations, and envision a more democratic society" (p. 72). In this way, service learning can be "sites of potential resistance to social inequities as well as sites of creative change and possibility" (Hayes & Cuban, 1997, p. 76).

Although critical theory and service learning may be compatible, connections between them cannot and should not be assumed. Bubriski and Semann (2009), for example, critique service learning as contradictory to feminisms because it "reproduces sexist social relations" and "relegate[s] women primarily to caregiving and clerical work" (p. 94). Novek (1999) questions the service aspects of service learning as too often "problematically linked" to "disempowering" work in the community (p. 236). Challenging this problematic link, Gilbride-Brown (2011) contends that much of the "transformational narrative" captured by student outcome research that "speak[s] to highly positive outcomes around reduction of stereotyping, increased capacity for advocacy, citizenship development, and increased tolerance" is best characterized as "theoretical gazing" (p. 29). These outcomes do little to "foreground the voices of underrepresented people and make explicit the impact of race and social class inequality" as critical theories would require (p. 27).

Approaches to service learning research framed by critical theories seek to equalize power, question binaries, challenge assumptions, and recognize the central role of identity in understanding the "lived realities" of stakeholders in service learning relationships. Hurst (2014) explains that feminist approaches to service learning resist the "positivist assumptions" of community service's transformational narrative, instead exploring ways "relations of privilege and oppression are productive sites to contextualize the service learning relationship" (p. 336). Mitchell (2008) frames critical service learning as an intentional practice with "an explicit social justice aim" (p. 50). Similarly, Butin's (2007) justice learning is an antifoundational approach guided by critical theory that seeks to disrupt "unacknowledged binaries" (p. 180). This attention to "lived reality, culture, race, class, and gender experiences," according to Veloria (2015), "pushes the binary of content and social context" (p. 139) to benefit students' engagement in and with communities. These critical approaches create the possibility to build the awareness and understanding of structural oppression and to practice "the qualitatively different" relationships critical theories strive to create (Agger, 2013, p. 5). Through this attention—and intention—instructors can create the critical praxis Cunningham and Vachta (2003) believe is possible.

Exploring qualitative, quantitative, and mixed method designs, the next two sections consider how critical theories have been translated into critical research methodologies.

Critical Research

According to Martínez-Alemán (2015), the goal of applying critical theories to research is the development of interdisciplinary approaches geared toward solving "those problems that are the consequence of domination within and across human communities" (p. 7). As a "transformative endeavor," critical research is progressive and fearless. "Inquiry that aspires to the name 'critical' must be connected to an attempt to confront the injustice of a particular society or public sphere within the society" (Kincheloe & McLaren, 2005, p. 305). A commitment to social justice is a key attribute of critical researchers. In choosing a critical approach, scholars are aiming to build understanding of the multiple dimensions of structural inequality. It is an empowerment-centered research frame that "attempts to expose the forces that prevent individuals and groups from shaping the decisions that crucially affect their lives" (Kincheloe & McLaren, p. 308). The most important outcome of critical research in higher education is a "framework for pragmatic change" that will redress issues of inequality, oppression, and exclusion (Martínez-Alemán, 2015, p. 6).

However, Martínez-Alemán (2015) cautions that critical theories are often "deployed haphazardly" (p. 7) with methodologies that have tenuous links, at best, to the theoretical frameworks claimed. "Critical race theory research, for example, often catapults the articulation of critical theory in order to apply methods designed to identify racial and ethnic discrimination or subjugation" rather than utilizing methods, like counterstories, that emerge from the theory (Martínez-Alemán, 2015, p. 7). Gilbride-Brown (2011) explains that quantitative research in service learning has generated a narrative of positive transformation in students around issues of stereotyping and injustice, but the few studies in service learning that explicitly pay attention to the "racialized systems of privilege and power" show mixed results regarding students' understanding of race and racism when examined quantitatively and negative results including "silence, lack of salience, and commitment to colorblindness" when examined qualitatively (p. 33).

Some studies using critical race theory focus on issues of race and racism in service learning experiences (Gilbride-Brown, 2008; Shabbaz & Cooks, 2014; Verjee, 2012).

Gilbride-Brown (2011) challenges "a long-standing colorblind stance in service-learning" and uses CRT to center the voices of Black students participating in a community engagement project (pp. 34–35). In her research, a critical qualitative framework was used to understand the experiences of students in a service learning experience with a racially homogenous classroom space (Gilbride-Brown, 2008). Her analyses offer a unique and complicated picture that "[speaks] against a 'neat' read of the ways these students of color experienced service-learning as a critical pedagogy" (p. iii). She contests the "individualistic, 'server-centered' discourse inscribed by Whiteness [that] dominates how researchers and practitioners think about service-learning" (p. 138) and suggests that utilizing critical theories to guide service learning research and practice reveals complexities that might lead to a more justice focused praxis (Gilbride-Brown, 2008).

Shabazz and Cooks (2014) apply a CRT framework to understand how students in a media studies course frame problems in a community. They found that relationships built by the college students with middle school students and teachers helped students to "be more reflexive about deficits and assets based on privileges and social inequities" (para. 48). As advocated by CRT, their stories, "rather than reciting facts about poverty and school failure," helped the students understand the lived experiences of the young people they worked with and facilitated a clearer understanding of structural deficits and community assets (Shabazz & Cooks, 2014, para. 48).

Verjee's (2012) study explores the experiences of women of color to "create a vision for service-learning engagement that would foster respectful and mutually beneficial partnerships" (para. 3). She suggests that institutions must explore more fully the "practices of domination" that structure relationships and argues "the project of service-learning engagement must be led by communities affected by systemic marginalization in their desire for societal transformation" (para. 62). Through engaging the counterstories of women of color, Verjee (2012) contends that higher education can understand the ways it must "change internally" to begin "the work . . . that would enable colleges and universities to create outstanding partnerships to address and solve local, national, and global injustices" (para. 66).

Responding to Gilbride-Brown's (2011) call for more interrogation into service learning's "White-dominated, individualistic, and meritocratic ideologies" (p. 39), research that utilizes CRT challenges the narrative of service learning as a universal good (Gilbride-Brown, 2008) and creates space for critique and transformation that can build a pedagogy responsive to structural conditions of race and racism both on and off campus. In this way, CRT "challenges privileged discourses and provides voice to historically marginalized and oppressed people, strengthening the social, political, and cultural survival and traditions of resistance" (McCoy & Rodricks, 2015, p. 40).

Critical Research Methodologies

The qualitative focus of critical research methods is often critiqued as a weakness of critical theories. The emphasis on counterstories and narratives is meant to honor the knowledge held and developed in marginalized communities. Yet, it has also generated opportunities to dismiss these research methods as less rigorous than quantitative designs. Specifically, Bernal (2002) contends that argument "against using personal stories and narratives is a critique against alternative ways of knowing and understanding and is basically an argument over subjectivity versus objectivity" (p. 119).

In terms of our literature review, examples of service learning research that employ critical theories were entirely qualitative in approach. For example, Jones, LePeau, and Robbins (2013) reanalyzed qualitative data (interviews and student papers) using a critical theory anchor to "read" their data differently. They desired, through this new reading, to understand "how participants construct knowledge within systems of power and how this knowledge can be transformed to incite social justice initiatives" (p. 220). As critical theories aim to "expose the forces that prevent individuals and groups from shaping the decisions that crucially affect their lives" (Kincheloe & McLaren, 2005, p. 308), Jones and colleagues ended their study questioning the efficacy of the service learning experience (in this case an alternative break trip) "to facilitate all students' learning" about structural injustice (Jones et al., 2013, p. 233). They caution that their findings should "lead educators to consider that what we end up knowing about service-learning is influenced by the students who participate in service-learning programs" (p. 233), leading practitioners to question not only curriculum design but also issues of recruitment and access that may allow for more diverse participation in these types of programs.

Shabazz and Cooks (2014) advocate for critical theories in service learning research because research conducted exclusively from dominant perspectives without attention to the experiences or voices of marginalized people "too often fails to regard its own biases and exclusions, and more so the epistemological assumptions which frame what counts as teaching and research of and for the community" (para. 25). A critical research methodology not only illuminates experiences of groups too often ignored in service learning research but also creates opportunities to critique the frameworks for service learning experiences that reinforce, rather than challenge, systems and structures that prevent people from being able to exercise full participation in our democracy.

Despite the qualitative focus of methodologies emerging from critical theories, Stage (2007) argues that there is a space for critical theories in quantitative research. Recognizing that critical research is aimed at uncovering assumptions and contradictions that constrain people from actualizing their full potential, Stage argues that "as quantitative researchers we are uniquely able to find those contradictions and negative assumptions that exist in quantitative research frames" (p. 6). Through qualitative methods, like interviews and observations, "traditional critical researchers" (p. 9), according to Stage, use the narratives and lived experiences of marginalized people to show how injustice manifests. However, "the critical quantitative researcher," she explains, "uses analysis of sociological and economic processes to demonstrate that for particular population groups, some widely accepted models and assumptions are inaccurate" (p. 10). In summation, Stage identifies two tasks for critical quantitative researchers: "Use data to represent educational processes and outcomes on a large scale to reveal inequities and to identify social or institutional perpetuation of systematic inequities in such processes and outcomes" (p. 10). We could not identify any research on service learning or community engagement that met the two tasks of critical quantitative research as Stage outlines them.

Martínez-Alemán (2015) calls for methodological flexibility in employing critical theory in educational research. A mixed-methods approach to critical research may offer a research design that captures both the stories and emphasizes their significance. "The qualitative studies provide details on how subtle experiences color students' lives; the quantitative studies provide the persuasion of numbers" (Stage, 2007, p. 12). Teddlie and Tashakkori (2009) advocate for a qualitative dominant mixed-method design to employ critical theory in research. This process emphasizes the qualitative phase and uses quantitative measures as support. Stage (2007) suggests that through mixed methods "the critical work of educational researchers is more complete" (p. 12).

The application of critical methodologies to service learning research is limited but necessary if we are to "go beyond simplistic understandings" of this pedagogy and its impact (McCoy & Rodricks, 2015, p. 70). The next section explores civic outcomes and their connections to critical theories to consider how this nexus might inform service learning research.

Troubling Civic Outcomes

Because critical theories foreground issues of power, we must question who and what informs our conceptions of the civic and of civic outcomes. Using critical theories requires examining why certain actions are viewed as civic participation within service learning practice (e.g., volunteering at a soup kitchen, tutoring, mentoring) whereas others are not (e.g., protesting, fighting for a living wage for workers on campus, enacting resistance against immigrant deportation). Despite critical theories' influence, service learning has not been focused on dismantling social and economic structures, and even when students engage in resistance, these efforts are often not considered civic action by their institutions (Heinecke, Cole, Han, & Mthethwa, 2016). In this section we use critical theories to trouble the assumptions of civic outcomes, particularly how knowledge, values, and skills are identified and framed as well as how delineations of achievement are marked.

Although there is opportunity, as Stage (2007) suggests, to use quantitative research to make large-scale inequities for certain groups transparent, the rubrics and scales used to operationalize and measure civic outcomes, at least as currently designed, do not reflect the spirit and aims of critical theories. Critical theories challenge the ways in which oppressive systems operate and emphasize collective approaches to change. Rubrics and scales designed to measure civic outcomes do not call attention to oppressive systems, nor do they focus on collective efforts.

Take, for example, the Civic Engagement VALUE rubric developed by the Association of American Colleges & Universities (AAC&U), a tool for evaluating students' competency in civic engagement based on their knowledge, values, skills, and motivation "to make a difference in the civic life of our communities" (AAC&U, 2010, p. 1). Critical theories require researchers to examine the definition of *civic life* offered in the rubric. Further described as the "public life of the citizen concerned with the affairs of the community and nation as contrasted with private or personal life, which is devoted to the pursuit of private and personal interests" (p. 1), this definition offers a *civic ideal* that overlooks the connections between private and personal interests forged by the impacts of policies in both public and private spheres. For instance, undocumented students' private lives are dramatically influenced by their ability to work or attend college. Low-income students' "private" interests or responsibilities may require full-time work and limit leisure time to engage publically. Conversely, students with social and economic privilege are likely to have more time to participate in *public life* as defined by the rubric. With this critical reading of the civic ideal, we offer examples of how critical theories challenge the assumptions of knowledge, values, and skills within the Civic Engagement VALUE rubric.

The Civic Engagement VALUE rubric presumes that the knowledge representative of students' progress stems from the university and academic discipline where "relevant connections" are made between civic engagement and students' "participation in civic life, politics, and government" (AAC&U, 2010, p. 2). However, community engagement involves multiple perspectives and stakeholders. Privileging knowledge framed by academic disciplines hides several inherent assumptions about norms of evaluation. Because instructors, believed to be experts in the discipline, are tasked as evaluators of students' civic outcomes, the rubric does not offer space for students to evaluate themselves. Instead, the instructor holds the power, deciding how *knowledge* is defined and measured. Additionally, the rubric ignores community members, who may have different values and perceptions in the evaluation of students' capabilities. It does not consider the impacts, implications, and involvement of the community in the development of service learning students. Critical theories would encourage dialogue with community members and students as well as ongoing formative feedback to engage multiple ways of knowing. Service learning research informed by critical theories should consider the whole experience—not just concepts and ideas learned in the classroom, but interactions and experiences that informed those understandings in the community (Patton, Harper, & Harris, 2015).

Similarly, the rubric's framing of knowledge privileges disciplinary approaches to "analyz[ing] knowledge" and "mak[ing] relevant connections to civic engagement" (AAC&U, 2010, p. 2). A poststructural stance that knowledge is partial (Lather, 2007), alongside CRT and queer theory recognitions of the White, Western, heteronormative foundations of most disciplines, calls into question whether disciplinary knowledge can reflect or support the lived experiences of racially marginalized students or communities (Kumashiro, 2002; Mills, 1997; Scheurich & Young, 1997; Smith, 2012). How might disciplines dismiss antiracist, antisexist, and antiheteronormative approaches that demonstrate resistance and resilience? How are instructors, trained in these disciplines, equipped to measure students' level and application of knowledge in ways that recognize and challenge the hegemonic boundedness of the disciplines? Further, the Civic Engagement VALUE rubric does not acknowledge indigenous, cultural, or community knowledge and practices that can offer frameworks for analysis. Critical theories recognize that knowledge also flows from communities and sources outside of the particular academic disciplines and the experts within them (Moll, Amanti, Neff, & Gonzalez, 1992).

Within the Civic Engagement VALUE rubric, the Diversity of Community and Cultures outcome scaffolds student learning, beginning with awareness of one's own attitudes and beliefs and building to adjusting one's "attitudes and beliefs because of working within and learning from diversity of communities and cultures" (AAC&U, 2010, p. 2). Even as we agree that students should have an awareness of self and others, the rubric disregards power relationships that exist between service learners and community members. Todd (2011) asserts that approaching difference as an opportunity to gain knowledge about the other "implicitly [denies] that racism is largely a problem of unequal distribution of power, of which lack of knowledge and understanding may be a symptom but not the root cause" (p. 125). Knowing that the assumed service learner is White (Butin, 2006; Green, 2003), and that the majority of service learning research (and most higher education research) takes place at predominantly White institutions (Seider, Huguley, & Novick, 2013), it is important to acknowledge the unequal power relations inherent in service learning (Peterson, 2009). Critical theories contend that White people long to distance themselves from the entanglements of racism (Schick, 2000; Todd, 2011). Civic outcomes informed by critical theories might interrogate how service learning "is complicit in reproducing Whiteness through providing access to a space for an ethical White subject who can legitimately know and intervene in the lives of racialized others, which in itself reasserts privilege" (Todd, 2011, p. 130). The Civic Engagement VALUE rubric does not acknowledge structural injustice or the ongoing marginalization that targets particular communities. The rubric does not create an opportunity to interrogate how service learners may challenge or change their understanding of structural injustice, or the role of civic action in changing those unjust circumstances. Critical theories would envision these as civic outcomes to be developed and assessed through service learning research.

One of the skills identified in the civic action and reflection dimension of the Civic Engagement VALUE rubric is leadership. This skill is optimized when a student "demonstrates independent experience and shows initiative in team leadership of complex or multiple civic engagement activities, accompanied by reflective insights or analysis about the aims and accomplishments of one's actions" (AAC&U, 2010, p. 2). A feminist and CRT perspective considers the privileged positions of students relative to the community served. The experience of leadership in the context of working with people who are different than them must be complicated. Todd (2011) argues that students are often prepared with the "techniques, practices, and knowledge that can be used to produce socially just outcomes for others who are perceived as being able to benefit from these interventions" (as cited in Todd, 2011, p. 121), but they must also be able to interrogate the ways in which their actions can be implicit in socially unjust systems. A civic outcome that respects community agency, emphasizes collaboration, recognizes power dynamics, and is informed by the legacies of racism, colonialism, and sexism that contribute to structural inequalities would bring a critical theoretical perspective to understanding leadership. Positioning service learning research to explore issues of power in community–university partnerships as well as students' understanding of their collective power with others in these interactions would reflect a critical approach (Pusser, 2015).

Critical theories can also inform service learning research through their emphasis on destabilizing norms, which complicates assessing civic outcomes. Using a rubric as a frame of measurement focuses on specific delineations of achievement, deemphasizing the fluidity that students are likely to display based on the complexity of situational contexts in service learning (see chapter 2.6). Even though students might show a particular capacity in one setting does not mean that the knowledge, values, or skills will neatly transfer to another setting (Diemer, McWhirter, Ozer, & Rapa, 2015). Each engagement with the community is context-specific and will not yield the same results. Poststructural theory contends people can simultaneously hold multiple and contradictory positions (Britzman, 2003; Lather, 2007); thus, while a student might be at the capstone level of engagement in the dimension of diversity of communities and cultures in one setting, that same student might only demonstrate the benchmark level in another context. In research on students' civic outcomes, it might be useful to consider how multiple and contradictory perspectives and locations can be captured.

By examining how critical theories complicate the civic outcomes identified in the AAC&U Civic Engagement VALUE rubric, we illuminate ways these theories raise questions that disrupt the status quo and create liberatory possibilities for service learning research and practice.

Toward Critical Service Learning Research

Martínez-Alemán, Pusser, and Bensimon (2015) see critical theories offering scholars and researchers the opportunity "to explain and decode inequitable social relations and action in higher education" (p. 2). The application of critical theories to service learning research can uniquely position researchers to explore these inequities within institutions, as well as in the communities, where engaged learning experiences are cocreated by students and community residents. This affords an opportunity to consider the ways institutions of higher education, through community engagement experiences, both challenge and reinforce conditions that create structural inequities.

There is a dearth of research on marginalized voices in service learning. Participants in most studies are predominantly White, economically privileged, traditionally aged students. Students of color are usually grouped together as "non-White," consolidating Black, Latino, Asian American, Pacific Islander, and Native American experiences and reporting as if they were a homogenous "Other." Service learning studies rarely ask for demographic variables like sexual orientation or (dis)ability, so little is known about the experiences of these students. A more critical service learning research approach would seek to explore the perspectives of these marginalized students in order to understand the possibilities of service learning to "foster greater social freedom" for them (Martínez-Alemán et al., p. 2). This would mean that survey research would ask for these demographic variables, and analyses would disaggregate them to ensure that the multiplicity of student experiences was explored and reported.

Critical service learning research should explore students' awareness and understanding of oppression, their understandings of power, the realities of structural inequalities, and the lived experiences of marginalized peoples. Critical service learning research would bring forth voices of diverse learners and community members, showing the nuances, contradictions, and multiplicities that occur as people from disparate backgrounds meet and form temporary relationships through service learning. Service learning research informed by critical theories would interrogate pertinent perspectives like that of Sperling (2007), who questions White, middle-class students engaging in service with youth of color. Asserting that service learning practitioners should seek parents' permission to have their young children teaching White college students not to be racist, Sperling challenges the transformational discourses perpetuated by service learning research. Critical service learning research would explore how these interactions might unfairly burden youth of color and their families.

Using critical theories as a framework for service learning research, a dialogical process of understanding civic outcomes would be worthwhile. This process would identify civic outcomes that emerge from the lived experiences of communities' stakeholders, engaging community members and various stakeholders in defining the civic possibilities and outcomes that need to be better understood. Critical research can engage counterstories of service learning—those of marginalized students, of constituent communities, of organizations, and social movements working for community change but not engaged in service learning. Research can also include a focus on collective civic vision and change rather than individual attitudes, behaviors, and outcomes.

This chapter has demonstrated the potential for critical theories to inform and enhance service learning research. Although it seems counter-intuitive to the critical theories in this chapter, the following list of guiding questions is offered when applying critical theories that can inform the development, implementation, analysis, and reporting on civic outcomes in service learning research.

- How might a researcher incorporate the knowledge of community partners and students when defining and assessing *civic outcomes*?
- How are the power relationships embedded in systems and structures within civic outcomes being addressed? How can a researcher interrogate the racism, classism, sexism, heterosexism, ableism, and other forms of oppression when examining students', instructors', and the institution's relationships with various community stakeholders? How can a researcher interrogate them within the classroom, department, or campus?
- How can a researcher view, assess, and write about civic skills like leadership from multiple perspectives? Have students been offered a way of connecting with the community that does not assume they take leadership roles but instead work alongside to learn with and from community members?
- Where has a unitary/simplistic narrative about students' civic outcomes been created and how might this be complicated through additional analyses? When looking at all the data, is there a more nuanced counterstory to tell?
- How has the researcher addressed minoritized identity categories (e.g., race, class, gender, ability, sexual orientation, religion, citizenship status)? Has the data been appropriately disaggregated so that there are more than two categories within any particular identity? How can pertinent information about civic outcomes for students who are often marginalized be presented and summarized?

Service learning research should be taking a critical, reflexive look at the work service learning does in communities and investigate if, when, and how social change occurs. This examination should be informed from a community level, not simply with individual students or from the perspective of the college or university. Service learning research informed by critical theories requires asking new and different questions about service learning practice, its outcomes, and its stakeholders. Most service learning research has opted to focus on topics that champion the cause of service learning at the expense of identifying and exploring the ways that service learning practice has reinforced the stereotypes and inequalities that the pedagogy can challenge. Martínez-Alemán and colleagues (2015) suggest that critical research in higher education is "[d]esigned to effect democratic change"; invoking critical theory in research "detects democratic inconsistencies so that our practices and policies can better serve democratic society" (p. 2). This aim of critical research in higher education is undeniably consistent with the aims of service learning. A service learning research agenda informed by critical theories supports service learning in its dual aims of facilitating student and community development and provides a more complete picture of the impacts and implications of service learning practice.

References

Abes, E. S. (2008). Applying queer theory in practice with college students: Transformation of a researcher's and participant's perspectives on identity, a case study. *Journal of LGBT Youth, 5*(1), 57–77.

Agger, B. (2013). *Critical social theories: An introduction.* Oxford: Oxford University Press.

Alcoff, L. (1988). Feminism versus post-structuralism: The identity crisis in feminist theory. *Signs, 13,* 405–436.

Association of American Colleges & Universities. (2010). *Civic engagement VALUE rubric.* Washington, DC: Author.

Baumgardner, J., & Richards, A. (2000). *Manifesta: Young women, feminism, and the future.* New York, NY: Farrar, Straus & Giroux.

Bernal, D. D. (2002). Critical race theory, Latino critical theory, and critical raced-gendered epistemologies: Recognizing students of color as holders and creators of knowledge. *Qualitative Inquiry, 8*(1), 105–126.

Bohman, J. (2015). Critical theory. In E. N. Zalta (Ed.), *The Stanford encyclopedia of philosophy.* Retrieved from http://plato.stanford.edu/archives/spr2015/entries/critical-theory/

Bonilla-Silva, E. (2009). *Racism without racists: Colorblind racism and the persistence of racial inequality in the United States* (3rd ed.). Lanham, MD: Rowman & Littlefield.

Britzman, D. P. (2003). *Practice makes practice: A critical study of learning to teach.* Albany, NY: State University of New York Press.

Bubriski, A., & Semaan, I. (2009). Activist learning vs. service learning in a Women's Studies classroom. *Human Architecture: Journal of the Sociology of Self-Knowledge, 7*(3), Article 8. Retrieved from http://scholarworks.umb.edu/humanarchitecture/vol7/iss3/8

Butin, D. W. (2006). The limits of service-learning in higher education. *The Review of Higher Education, 29,* 473–498.

Butin, D. W. (2007). Justice-learning: Service-learning as justice-oriented education. *Equity & Excellence in Education, 40,* 177–183.

Butin, D. W. (2010). *Service-learning in theory and practice: The future of community engagement in higher education.* New York, NY: Palgrave-Macmillan.

Butler, J. (1988). Performative acts and gender constitution: An essay in phenomenology and feminist theory. *Theatre Journal, 40,* 519–531.

Crenshaw, K. (1989). Demarginalizing the intersection of race and sex: A Black feminist critique of antidiscrimination doctrine, feminist theory, and antiracist politics. *University of Chicago Legal Forum, 14,* 538–54.

Cunningham, K., & Vachta, K. E. (2003). Critical currents in community service learning and community-based research: History, theory, and practice. *Journal of Applied Social Science, 20*(2), 23–41.

Dasgupta, S. (2009). Words, bodies, times: Queer theory before and after itself. *borderlands, 8*(2), 1–20. Retrieved from http://www.borderlands.net.au/vol8no2_2009/dasgupta_words.pdf

Davies, B. (2003). *Shards of glass: Children reading & writing beyond gendered identities.* Cresskill, NJ: Hampton Press.

Davis, K. (2008). Intersectionality as buzzword: A sociology of science perspective on what makes a feminist theory successful. *Feminist Theory, 9*(1), 67–85.

Delgado, R., & Stefancic, J. (2001). *Critical Race Theory: An introduction.* New York, NY: New York University Press.

Diemer, M. A., McWhirter, E. H., Ozer, E. J., & Rapa, L. J. (2015). Advances in the conceptualization and measurement of critical consciousness. *Urban Review, (47)*5, 809–823.

Donahue, D. M., & Luber, M. (2015). Queering service learning: Promoting antioppressive action and reflection by undoing dichotomous thinking. In J. C. Hawley (Ed.), *Expanding the circle: Creating an inclusive environment in higher education for LGBTQ students and studies* (pp. 209–224). Albany, NY: State University of New York Press.

Foucault, M. (1983). Why study power: The question of the subject. In H. L. Dreyfus & P. Rabinow (Eds.), *Michel Foucault: Beyond structuralism and hermeneutics* (2nd ed., pp. 208–226). Chicago, IL: University of Chicago Press.

Fraser, N. (1995). What's critical about critical theory? In J. Meehan (Ed.) *Feminists read Habermas: Gendering the subject of discourse* (pp. 21–55). New York: Routledge.

Gavey, N. (1989). Feminist poststructuralism and discourse analysis: Contributions to feminist psychology. *Psychology of Women Quarterly, 13,* 459–475.

Gilbride-Brown, J. (2008). *(E)racing service-learning as critical pedagogy: Race matters.* (Dissertation). Retrieved from https://etd.ohiolink.edu/ etdc/view?acc_num=osu1226014242

Gilbride-Brown, J. (2011). Moving beyond the dominant: Service-learning as a culturally-relevant pedagogy. In T. Stewart & N. Webster (Eds.), *Exploring cultural dynamics and tensions within service-learning* (pp. 27–44). Charlotte, NC: Information Age Publishing.

Green, A. E. (2003). Difficult stories: Service-learning, race, class, and Whiteness. *College Composition and Communication, 55,* 276–301.

Habermas, J. (1971). *Knowledge and human interests.* Boston, MA: Beacon Press.

Harper, S. R. (2012). Race without racism: How higher education researchers minimalize racist institutional norms. *Review of Higher Education, 36*(1), 9–29.

Hayes, E., & Cuban, S. (1997). Border pedagogy: A critical framework for service learning. *Michigan Journal of Community Service Learning, 4,* 72–80.

Heinecke, W. F., Cole, R., Han, I., & Mthethwa, N. (2016). Student activism as civic engagement: Challenging institutional conditions for civic leadership at

University of Virginia. In K. M. Soria & T. D. Mitchell (Eds.), *Civic engagement and community service at research universities: Engaging undergraduates for social justice, social change, and responsible citizenship* (pp. 219–239). New York, NY: Palgrave Macmillan.

Hekman, S. (2000). Beyond identity: Feminism, identity, and identity politics. *Feminist Theory, 1*, 289–308.

Horkheimer, M. (1972). *Critical theory.* New York, NY: Seabury Press.

Hurst, R. A. J. (2014). A "journey in feminist theory together": The doing feminist theory through digital video project. *Arts & Humanities in Higher Education, 13*, 333–347.

Jagose, A. (1996). *Queer theory: An introduction.* New York: New York University Press.

Jones, S. R., LePeau, L. A., & Robbins, C. K. (2013). Exploring the possibilities and limitations of service-learning: A critical analysis of college student narratives about HIV/AIDS. *The Journal of Higher Education, 84*, 213–238.

Kincheloe, J. L., & McLaren, P. (2005). Rethinking critical theory and qualitative research. In N. K. Denzin & Y. S. Lincoln (Eds.), *The Sage handbook of qualitative research* (3rd ed., pp. 303–342). Thousand Oaks, CA: Sage.

Kumashiro, K. K. (2002). *Troubling education: Queer activism and antioppressive pedagogy.* New York, NY: Routledge.

Kumashiro, K. K. (2003). Queer ideals in education. *Journal of Homosexuality, 45*, 365–367.

Lather, P. (2007). *Getting lost: Feminist efforts toward a double(d) science.* Albany, NY: State University of New York Press.

Martínez-Alemán, A. M. (2015). Critical discourse analysis in higher education policy and research. In A. M. Martínez-Alemán, B. Pusser, & E. M. Benison (Eds.), *Critical approaches to the study of higher education: A practical introduction* (pp. 7–43). Baltimore, MD: Johns Hopkins University Press.

Martínez-Alemán, A. M., Pusser, B., & Bensimon, E. M. (2015). Introduction. In A. M. Martínez-Alemán, B. Pusser, & E. M. Bensimon (Eds.), *Critical approaches to the study of higher education* (pp. 1–6). Baltimore, MD: Johns Hopkins University Press.

McCoy, D. L., & Rodricks, D. J. (2015). Critical race theory in higher education: 20 years of theoretical and research innovations. *ASHE Higher Education Report, 41*(3), 1–117.

Meyer, E. J. (2007). "But I'm not gay": What straight teachers need to know about queer theory. In N. M. Rodriguez & W. F. Pinar (Eds.), *Queering straight teachers: Discourse and identity in education* (pp. 15–29). New York, NY: Peter Lang.

Mills, C. W. (1997). *The racial contract.* Ithaca, NY: Cornell University Press.

Mitchell, T. D. (2008). Traditional vs. critical service-learning: Engaging the literature to differentiate two models. *Michigan Journal of Community Service Learning, 14*(2), 50–65.

Moll, L. C., Amanti, C., Neff, D., & Gonzalez, N. (1992). Funds of knowledge for teaching: Using a qualitative approach to connect homes and classrooms. *Theory into Practice, 31*(2), 132–141.

Novek, E. M. (1999). Service-learning is a feminist issue: Transforming communication pedagogy. *Women's Studies in Communication, 22,* 230–240.

Okin, S. M. (1989). *Justice, gender, and the family.* New York, NY: Basic Books.

Patton, L. D., Harper, S. R., & Harris, J. (2015) Using critical race theory to (re) interpret widely studied topics related to students in US higher education. In A. M. Martínez-Alemán, B. Pusser, & E. M. Bensimon (Eds.), *Critical approaches to the study of higher education* (pp. 193–219). Baltimore, MD: Johns Hopkins University Press.

Perez, H. (2005). You can have my brown body and eat it, too! *Social Text, 23*(3–4), 171–191.

Peterson, T. H. (2009). Engaged scholarship: Reflections and research on the pedagogy of social change. *Teaching in Higher Education, 14*(5), 541–552.

Phillips, C. (2009). Difference, disagreement and the thinking of queerness. *borderlands, 8*(2), 1–17. Retrieved from http://www.borderlands.net.au/vol8no2_2009/phillips_difference.pdf

Pusser, B. (2015). A critical approach to power in higher education. In A. M. Martínez-Alemán, B. Pusser, & E. M. Bensimon (Eds.), *Critical approaches to the study of higher education* (pp. 59–79). Baltimore, MD: Johns Hopkins University Press.

Scheurich, J. J., & Young, M. D. (1997). Coloring epistemologies: Are our research epistemologies racially biased? *Educational Researcher, 26*(4), 4–16.

Schick, C. (2000). Keeping the ivory tower white: Discourses of racial domination. *Canadian Journal of Law & Society, 15*(2), 71–90.

Seider, S., Huguley, J. P., & Novick, S. (2013). College students, diversity, and community service learning. *Teachers College Record, 115*(3), 1–44.

Shabazz, D. R., & Cooks, L. M. (2014). The pedagogy of community service-learning discourse: From deficit to asset mapping in the re-envisioning media project. *Journal of Community Engagement and Scholarship, 7*(1). Retrieved from http://jces.ua.edu/the-pedagogy-of-community-service-learning-discourse-from-deficit-to-asset-mapping-in-the-re-envisioning-media-project/

Smith, L. T. (2012). *Decolonizing methodologies: Research and indigenous peoples.* New York, NY: Zed Books.

Sperling, R. (2007). Service-learning as a method of teaching multiculturalism to White college students. *Journal of Latinos and Education, 6,* 309–322.

Stage, F. K. (2007). Answering critical questions using quantitative data. *New Directions for Institutional Research, 133,* 5–16.

Stein, A., & Plummer, K. (1994). "I can't even think straight": "Queer" theory and the missing sexual revolution in sociology. *Sociological Theory, 12*(2), 178–187.

Teddlie, C., & Tashakkori, A. (2009). *Foundations of mixed methods research: Integrating quantitative and qualitative approaches in social and behavioral sciences.* Los Angeles, CA: Sage.

Todd, S. (2011). "That power and privilege thing": Securing Whiteness in community work. *Journal of Progressive Human Services, 22*(2), 117–134.

Veloria, C. N. (2015). "Maybe this is because of society?": Disrupting and engaging discourses of race in the context of a service-learning project. *Humanity & Society, 39,* 135–155.

Verjee, B. (2012). Critical race feminism: A transformative vision for service-learning engagement. *Journal of Community Engagement and Scholarship, 5*(1). Retrieved from   http://jces.ua.edu/critical-race-feminism-a-transformative-vision-for-service-learning-engagement/

Walker, R. (1992, January/February). Becoming the third wave. *Ms.,* 39–41.

Warner, M. (1999). *The trouble with normal: Sex, politics, and the ethics of queer life.* Cambridge, MA: Harvard University Press.

Young, I. M. (1990). *Justice and the politics of difference.* Princeton, NJ: Princeton University Press.

BOUNDARY ZONES, ACTIVITY THEORY, AND STUDENT CIVIC OUTCOMES

Janice McMillan

The world is increasingly complex and uncertain (Barnett, 2004), and levels of global inequality are rising (Shatkin, 2007). Given this, many educational philosophers and observers have called upon universities to play a more active role in adequately preparing students for today's super-complex world (Barnett, 2004) and to assist in building more civic-minded global citizens (Nussbaum, 2007; Palmer, 2007). Within this context, how do we rethink the way in which we educate college students? How do we reconceptualize our work as service learning educators, a particularly complex practice and set of activities that straddles university–community boundaries?

This chapter discusses the role of service learning in civic learning from the perspective of a university located in the global South, in South Africa. Attention is given to the role of cultural and historical context in shaping an understanding of what is meant by civic outcomes. A concept like *civic-minded graduate* (Steinberg, Hatcher, & Bringle, 2011) has universal meanings as well as local significance and interpretations (Hatcher, McIlrath, McMillan, & McTighe Musil, 2014). As such, there is a need to frame understandings of civic-mindedness so that students can enact it in various cultural contexts and in appropriate ways. Educators need to be intentional when designing community-engaged learning opportunities and curricula for civic outcomes (chapters 1.2 and 1.3). This intentionality must also be informed by the cultural and historical context. In this chapter, I use the concept of "learning service" (Boyle-Baise et al., 2006, p. 17), and the work of Barnett

(2004, 2009) in terms of *being* and *engagement* to illuminate the potential role of service learning to develop civic outcomes for students.

Additionally, I draw on activity theory (Engeström, 1996, 1998) and my previous work (McMillan, 2008, 2011) to suggest that framing service learning as *boundary work* develops new lines of inquiry into the relationship between service learning and civic outcomes. This implies the need to understand how and under what conditions students interact with others through community-based activities in this *boundary zone*. In order to do this, the unit of analysis needs to shift from individualized practices of students, faculty, and community partners toward the boundary zone itself and to developing conceptual tools that can illuminate the complex practices and interactions that occur at this nexus. Activity theory is useful in this regard because it provides a conceptual framework for understanding practice in complex contexts. By way of conclusion, research questions are suggested to highlight new ways to think about and explore service learning and its relationship to civic outcomes in our ever-changing global context. This analysis has important implications for how service learning can be studied and understood across the diverse ways in which it is implemented and for how cultural, political, social, and historical context shapes its nature and outcomes.

Higher Education and Civic Outcomes: Importance of Context

We, and our students, live in an age of super-complexity in which the world is increasingly unknowable, disruptive, unequal, and disturbing (Gredley, 2015; Mayo, 2012). We are constantly assailed by difficult questions, competing priorities, and a multiplicity of choices and options. In South Africa and in the world more broadly, we see and experience this daily in the urgent, complex, and heated debates around immigration, poverty, inequality, democracy, justice, responsibility, and restitution (Gredley, 2015). The role of the university in the education of students is under intense scrutiny in our current contested and very unequal world. A quote from a student at the University of Cape Town reflects a response to some of these concerns:

> I think that we should ask the question about poverty differently, precisely because changing the questions challenges our perceptions of the problem. That is important because our perceptions are often part of the problem: we disable/passify [*sic*] people we think are helpless victims of poverty, but by focusing on these people, we let wealthier people off the hook, because they do not feature as part of the problem's definition or solution. (forum post of a student on a global citizenship program at the University of Cape Town, 2012)

Palmer (2007) and Nussbaum (2002, 2007) insist higher education should humanize students. Palmer (2007) urges universities to "uproot the myth of 'value-free' knowledge" (p. 1) and Nussbaum (2002) suggests that, because higher education is producing the next generation of citizens, we need to ask ourselves about the kinds of values, dispositions, and attributes students hold as they go out into the world after their studies. In particular, she offers the following about the role of universities in cultivating humanity in students:

> We need to produce citizens who have this education while they are still young, before their imaginations are shackled by the weight of daily duties and self-interested plans. . . . [We need] Socratic citizens who are capable of thinking for themselves, arguing with tradition, and understanding with sympathy the conditions of lives different from their own. . . . That is the cultivation of humanity. (Nussbaum, 2002, pp. 301–302)

Higher education in South Africa is also responding to these pressures (Thomson, Smith-Tolken, Naidoo, & Bringle, 2011). For many, given our apartheid past, whether looking at issues from a global or local standpoint, education in South Africa requires engaging with social justice issues. Leibowitz and colleagues (2012) argued that educating students for citizenship includes attributes such as "compassion, criticality and a sense of responsibility" that enable people to contribute toward "civic reconciliation and transformation" (p. xi). Soudien (2006) takes the context of the South African city as a critical site "in the making of the modern citizen" (p. 104). In the relationship between education and citizenship, he argues that there are two positions. The first is that we need to teach young people their history and culture in order to "build their dignity and feelings of self-worth" (p. 114). The second is that education needs to provide young people with the "high skills knowledge—the cultural capital—that will enable them to operate within the complexity of a globalized world" (p. 114). As challenging as it is, Soudien believes it is necessary to give students *both* a sense of self and of local history, as well as a connection to kinds of knowledge that can enable them to understand the complexity of the global issues.

On South African campuses, students as well as some staff, in particular (but not limited to) Black staff and students, are demanding new frameworks for fundamental institutional change. Starting at the University of Cape Town, and later spreading to other campuses, the recent calls have been for change beyond transforming the demographics of the student body. The calls are for fundamental transformation of higher education, what some are calling the "decolonisation [sic] of the curriculum" (Dei, 2014, p. 170), a complex phrase with many interpretations. These calls link with Soudien's stance on the kinds of knowledge needed in higher education today, particularly the concern with understanding history and culture in order to, in Soudien's words, "build . . . dignity and feelings of self-worth" (2007, p. 114).

Dei (2014) argues decolonization of the curriculum involves three central tenets: multicentricity, indigeneity, and reflexivity (p. 171). *Multicentricity* involves "cultivating multiple ways of knowing while working with the idea of multiple centres of scholarship" (p. 171). *Indigeneity* is concerned "both about identity and a process of coming to know" (p. 171). Such a concern sees "students as active knowers . . . [and] indigenous education should reflect the lived experience and life situation of our students" (p. 171). Of particular relevance to this chapter and to pedagogy is Dei's concept of *reflexivity*. For him, reflexivity

> means to reconnect individual and environment, self and society, identity and reality in social and scientific inquiry. [E]very discipline . . . should include the interrogation of interconnectivity of the self and the external world, and our responsibilities to our social, physical, and ecological environment. (p. 172)

Reflexivity takes into account the environment, the society, and thus the cultural context in which the activity occurs.

The three features of a decolonized curriculum outlined by Dei (multicentricity, indigeneity, reflexivity) have bearing on how I think about service learning and its relationship to civic outcomes, particularly in postcolonial contexts of extreme inequality. Given that the global context is reflecting growing inequality and increasing instability and conflict (Mayo, 2012), and the fact that students are increasingly diverse and from varying contexts in our institutions (see www.iapo.uct.ac.za/iapo/intstud/statistics for information at the University of Cape Town), I think these three tenets have bearing on education and learning more globally.

How can educators integrate these tenets into curricular design, particularly to address growing inequalities and instability? Over the past three decades, service learning has emerged as one possible practice to help students and instructors think in new ways about the public purposes of their education. Having been involved in the field for more than 15 years, I believe that service learning can provide some of the answers to these challenges. Considering, however, the extreme inequality in the context within which I work, I have felt the need to think more critically about service learning's role in helping to develop civic outcomes in students. I argue that there is not a clear and simple relationship between service learning and acting more civically in the world. Simply knowing about the nature of our society with its inequalities and complexities does not position or prepare students to become more caring and capable citizens, or more able to deal with complex situations. Service learning can be a useful starting point, but it is not sufficient. In particular, we need to bring historical and cultural context into the picture when thinking about how this is best done. Dei's perspective on the importance of decolonization of the curriculum provides an important framework and challenges us to think in new ways about service learning pedagogy. This has implications for both curriculum design and research.

Service Learning as Transformative Practice

Many scholars argue that service learning is a transformative pedagogy. In a seminal study, Eyler and Giles (1999) identify several ways in which service learning transforms students. Drawing on empirical research from two national studies in the U.S. using surveys and in-depth interviews, they show how students commented on personal, intrapersonal, and interpersonal learning. Some students even "leave service learning with a new set of lenses for seeing the world" (p. 129). For some students, service learning "is not about accumulating more knowledge but seeing the world in a profoundly different way, one that calls for personal commitment and action" (p. 129).

Engberg and Fox (2011) look at the relationship between undergraduate service learning and "global perspective-taking" and argue for "significant associations between service-learning and aspects of cognitive, intrapersonal, and interpersonal development" (p. 85). Although many students struggle to sustain such transformations, Kiely (2004) argues that service learning has transformative potential if we look at students' experiences longitudinally and some years after they complete their collegiate service experiences.

Other authors, however, are more critical of service learning's potential as a transformative practice. Curricula and pedagogy are in fact often ambiguous, with many scholars agreeing the field is conceptually and pragmatically diverse. Some argue that service learning is not inherently transformative (Camacho, 2004), nor does it focus explicitly on students' own sense of the world and their self (e.g., Butin, 2003; Mitchell, 2008). Scholars have asked important questions about power and privilege in the service relationship (see chapter 2.6; Green, 2001; Prins & Webster, 2010), inequitable paradigms that operate in service relationships (Morton, 1995), relationships that "cross borders" (Hayes & Cuban, 1997; Skilton-Sylvester & Erwin, 2000), and key processes in the partnership such as mutuality and reciprocity (d'Arlach, Sanchez, & Feuer, 2009; Henry & Breyfogle, 2006; Keith, 2005).

For service learning to be transformative, we must consider both cultural and historical contexts in curricular design (Hatcher & Erasmus, 2008). Because contexts play a role in shaping curriculum, pedagogy, and learning, it is important that we acknowledge them in consideration of student civic outcomes as well. Hatcher (1997), for instance, argues that the historical context in which Dewey—one of the main philosophical and educational influences on the service learning field—was writing is essential to understanding the moral dimensions of Dewey's philosophy of education. Deans (1999) also argues for the importance of understanding the context and history against which educational interventions take place. He looks at the work of both Dewey and Paulo Freire (1970) and contends that the conditions in the context out of which Dewey was writing—end of the nineteenth century—are very similar to present-day inequities in society. Additionally, Deans argues that many draw on Freire's work because it resonates well with many of the goals of service learning. Freire's work in the 1960s, 1970s, and 1980s is based on his experiences in Brazil. Freire (1970) argues for an educational theory and approach based on a critical understanding of power and the dialectical relationship between word (language or text) and world (cultural context). Freire, influenced by neo-Marxism, emphasizes the need to challenge oppressive structures in both schools and society. His position underscores the potential for personal and political transformation through dialogue, articulates the action-reflection dialectic of praxis, and encourages the development of critical consciousness (Deans, 1999). Freire's work in particular has been useful for service learning educators in South Africa (Daniels, 2013; Petersen & Osman, 2013).

Learning Service

Translating broad concepts such as those found in the work of Dewey, Freire, and even Dei is not easy. Their ideas challenge educators in higher education in fundamental ways, especially around issues of transformation, knowledge, and, in the case of Freire in particular, collective social action. It is important therefore to be deliberate in how we, as both educators and scholars, think about service learning practice. To do so requires quite a different stance. Boyle-Baise and colleagues (2006) ask the question:

> What might happen if, instead [of learning about something other than service through service] an *exploration of service itself* grounded classroom studies and fieldwork, fostering explicit consideration and critique of ethics, standards and distinctive forms of learning through work with others? (p. 17; emphasis added)

Boyle-Baise and her students write about an experience in a course in which the learning was directly about service itself. By using the term *learning service,* the service experience is recast "as something to be studied, as well as something to be done" (p. 17). Thus, service as an object of interest itself enables "students to envision activism as a means of civic engagement" (p.18). By looking at distinctive forms of service (e.g., multicultural service learning, service as accompaniment) students were confronted with asking questions of themselves about how and why they participate in service activities. This was an important process and critical in developing a sense of self and the civic, social, and historical context of service:

> When service itself was the object of examination, we could ponder it as a person, place and thing. . . . [W]e directed our whole attention to making meaning of service, rather than to learning something else through service, as is often the case. . . . We stepped back from it and studied its distinctive forms, underlying ethics, and different qualities. (p. 22)

Through this process, the students became interested in understanding their *own values* toward the practice and toward different forms of service. In other words, a key role for service learning in higher education might be to help students "learn service" through which process they are afforded the opportunity to disrupt their preconceived notions of service, interrogate their positionality in regard to community service activities, and continually criticize their perceptions and actions (Boyle-Baise et al., 2006). Boyle-Baise and colleagues (2006) thus challenge us to think more deeply about the nature of service itself.

Engaging Being

Another conceptual lens for transformative learning emphasizes the importance of "being" over "doing." Barnett and Coate (2005) explore what curricula might be useful to frame learning in a complex world. To explore this, they looked at curricula in five subject areas across six institutions of higher education in the United Kingdom, with a specific focus on the relationship between three domains or components of curriculum: knowing, doing, and being. Barnett makes the distinction between knowledge and knowing, with knowledge understood as a set of understandings of the world and knowing being the process of developing one's ideas or individual worldviews (Barnett, 2009, p. 432; see also chapter 2.3). The process of coming to know, therefore, brings forth dispositions, qualities, or aspects of being human (Gredley, 2015). Likewise, *doing* is less about learning practical skills and more about learning how to learn—the ability to act in the moment—for a world in a state of flux (Barnett & Coate, 2005). In reconceptualizing knowledge as knowing and skills as doing, Barnett foregrounds *being* as fundamental to all aspects of learning so that the student—as person—is no longer artificially divided from learning (Barnett, 2009).

Based on their research, Barnett and Coate (2005) argue that with knowledge changing rapidly and with skills often becoming redundant just as quickly, we need to give more attention in higher education to *being*. In preparing students for the twenty-first century, the authors argue that, although knowledge and skills are important, they need to be augmented through developing students' dispositions and qualities—aspects of being (Gredley, 2015, p. 24). This has implications for thinking about pedagogy, particularly service learning. A curriculum for being "can only be brought off consistently, can only engage the students . . . if engagement is present in the *pedagogical relationship*" (Barnett & Coate, 2005, p. 128; emphasis added). This then, also implies that teachers have to rethink their roles and how they enact their pedagogy. Linking the two concepts brings up the issue of ontology as key in thinking about both curriculum and pedagogy. As Barnett argues:

> the way forward lies in constructing and enacting a pedagogy for human being . . . . Learning for an unknown future has to be a learning understood neither in terms of knowledge or skills but of human qualities and dispositions. Learning for an unknown future calls, in short, for an *ontological turn*. (Barnett, 2004, p. 247; emphasis added)

Given the foregoing, what tools might help us in our work and our research to better understand and design for being? How might a lens that focuses on the relationship between *learning for being* and the broader cultural and historical contexts in which such learning is located, assist in framing and understanding civic outcomes?

Service Learning Boundary Zones: Challenges for Curriculum and Pedagogy

In previous work (McMillan, 2008, 2011), I have explored service learning as a form of boundary work taking place in boundary zones at the nexus of the complex but interrelated contexts of the university and the community. In my research, I explored the complex interactions that take place in service learning partnerships, which in turn generated new insight into questions of curriculum and pedagogy. In thinking about service learning and civic outcomes, therefore, I believe that understanding what it takes to do boundary work is useful as a civic outcome in itself—for students and educators alike. Understanding service learning as boundary work adds to the current work on civic outcomes. In particular, it is a useful space to understand the relationships among knowing, doing, and being (Barnett & Coate, 2005).

Scholars have explored service learning as a form of border pedagogy (Hayes & Cuban, 1997; Keith, 2005; Skilton-Sylvester & Erwin, 2000; Taylor 2002), drawing largely on work in critical pedagogy and critical postmodernism (Anzaldua, 1987; Giroux, 1992). However, none of these studies directly look at what happened in the borderland itself (i.e., at the activities through which service learning plays itself out in this space). Rather, in most cases, the research focused on analyzing students' experiences using interviews and surveys after they have completed their service learning course. If we are to understand the relationship between pedagogy and civic outcomes, I think we need a better understanding of what actually happens in the boundary zone. This is the site where both curriculum and pedagogy are shaped. In addition, boundary work is a complex practice, and instructors need to be committed to enter into new spaces to do this work well and to prepare and support students.

Boundary Zones as Activity Systems

To understand the boundary zone requires a shift in what constitutes our unit of analysis. We need to move from looking at individualized service learning practices toward focusing on the boundary zone at the university-community nexus itself (McMillan, 2009). Shifting to focus on an additional unit of analysis is useful if one wants to open up new avenues for research. Recent work by Weerts and Sandmann (2010) on boundary-spanning roles in research universities, Ramaley (2014) on wicked problems and boundary spanning, and Romero (2014) on the use of activity theory to explore bus riding as a metaphor for boundary spanning are all very positive moves in this line of inquiry.

In a South African context, Winberg (2006) describes the usefulness of understanding transaction spaces. She argues that these spaces are a key to understanding the "articulations between higher education and its contexts in the South African situation" (p. 165) and "emergent transaction spaces" (p. 165) are important sites for negotiation among participants from a range of academic and nonacademic contexts. Drawing on the work of Nowotny, Scott, and Gibbons (2001), she makes the argument that "'transaction spaces' provide the means and processes by which macro, meso, and micro concerns can 'speak to' higher education—as well as the means by which educators can 'talk back' to other contexts" (Winberg, 2006, p. 164). Transaction spaces can be understood as the spaces or opportunities opened up in the boundary zone for negotiation among participants across complex contexts.

Camacho (2004) has also pointed toward the challenges of engaging in the boundary zone through her work on service, power, and privilege. She refers to the space created through engagement between the university and its community partners as a "contact zone" (p. 32). She argues that this is not inherently an equal space, and we need to understand the historical power relations between universities and communities. In addition, communities are often in a "liminal social status" (p. 37) due to the power that universities have in such relationships.

Activity Theory

In my own work, I have drawn on activity theory (AT) and the work of Engeström (1996, 1999) to understand service learning as boundary work (McMillan, 2008, 2011). Although it is beyond the scope of this chapter to discuss this theoretical framework in depth, it is useful for future research to highlight briefly why this is a useful framework to think about civic outcomes. AT facilitates an understanding of learning as a social practice, a practice located in particular social, cultural, and historical contexts. Teaching and learning could be considered such a system and therefore, so too can service learning. As an activity system, service learning can be represented as shown in Figure 2.7.1.

Understanding an activity system means understanding the constituent elements of such a system but perhaps more importantly, understanding how the elements relate to and influence each other through joint activities. The *subjects* are individuals or subgroups engaged in an activity and from whose perspective you wish to understand the activity system. In this case, because I am discussing civic outcomes for students through service learning, they would be the subject of the system. The *object* is the raw material on which the subject brings to bear various tools (e.g., learning about a social issue, doing community service). *Tools*, material and/or conceptual (Cole, 1996), mediate subjects' action upon objects—that is, they mediate or facilitate the subjects' ability to achieve outcomes (e.g., a concept, a computer, a text). In the case of a service learning course, tools could be questionnaires, concepts, or processes such as critical reflection. When viewed through the lens of AT, with its emphasis on cultural and historical contexts, tools take on a special significance (see McMillan, 2008). The *community* is the broader or larger group interacting in the service learning activity and of which the subject or subjects are a part (e.g., students and community). The *division of labor* refers to the power relations and different roles that are evident in an activity. *The rules* operating in any activity are broadly understood as not only formal and explicit rules governing behavior but also unwritten and tacit, often referred to as norms, routines, habits, values, and conventions (Engeström, 1996; Russell, 2002).

Figure 2.7.1. A service learning activity system.

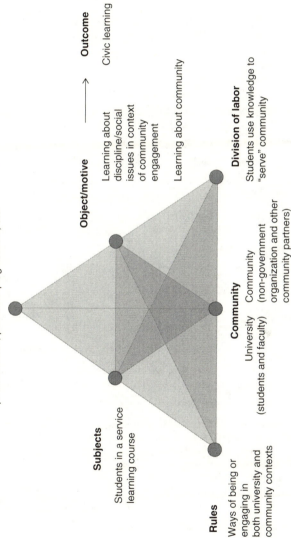

Mediating tools

Concepts, critical reflection,
questionnaires, partnership agreement, etc.

Object/motive

Learning about
discipline/social
issues in context
of community
engagement

Learning about community

Outcome

Civic learning

Subjects

Students in a service
learning course

Community

University
(students and faculty)

Community
(non-government
organization and other
community partners)

Division of labor

Students use knowledge to
"serve" community

Rules

Ways of being or
engaging in
both university and
community contexts

Figure 2.7.2. Service learning as an activity system in the boundary zone.

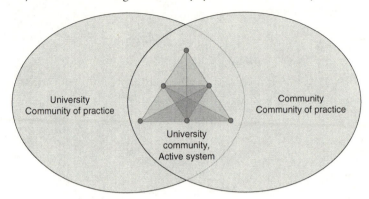

I use AT to understand and illuminate how situational factors shape students' actions in the context of a service learning course. Through this lens, service learning is located as an activity system at the nexus of the university and community (i.e., located in a boundary zone; see Figure 2.7.2).

For many, boundary zones are often spaces of challenge, contestation, and creative dissonance. Camacho's (2004) work highlights the feelings of "discomfort" (p. 39) many students experience in this space, but also the opportunities for deep learning. In my own research (McMillan, 2008), I observed students and community partners engaging in joint service learning activities. I collected "thick descriptions" (Geertz, 1973, p. 3) of what was happening and these, together with students' reflective journals, became my main sources of data. AT was helpful in rendering two features of service learning that could explain potential, even inherent, tensions in the boundary zone: the *expanded and diverse community,* and the *dual but interrelated object.*

The first feature of service learning courses is the expanded and diverse community (or communities) in which they function. These courses involve instructors and students in an expanded, more diverse learning community than the traditional university-based classroom context. The learning context in service learning also includes an outside community. Ways of engaging the outside community in turn are linked to different histories in which specific and different kinds of knowledge and ways of knowing are valued, all of which can challenge students, and thereby the service learning activity system as a whole, in significant ways.

The second feature of service learning courses is a dual but interrelated object. This refers to the fact that there are both learning *and* service goals to be achieved through service learning. Service learning is inherently about not only student learning but about some form of community *benefit* as well. In other words, although distinct, service and learning are inseparable as it is through the service that the students learn, and it is through the learning that service is rendered. This can set up an inherent tension in service learning because students and community often have very different schedules, pressures, and requirements in meeting these outcomes. This can influence the other dimensions of the activity system and result in an outcome that challenges the way in which students understand learning. Making sense of such tensions is important, and this understanding can lead to different civic outcomes.

Navigating the Boundary Zone

When we understand service learning as a cultural and historical activity system located in a boundary zone, then tensions and contradictions are inherently part of service learning practice. Identifying such tensions can assist in designing our pedagogy for being and for transformative learning, resulting in various kinds of civic outcomes. This might include opportunities for emphasizing Dei's three features of a decolonized curriculum (i.e., multicentricity, indigeneity, reflexivity). Practical examples of this include valuing community knowledge through joint designing of curriculum, understanding both students and community as active knowers, and respecting the different contexts that shape the service learning partnership.

Camacho (2004) also speaks to some of these features in her work on understanding and making visible the power relations that operate in service learning boundary zones. She argues that although these are often contested spaces, boundary zones can also offer the possibility of engagement. For this to occur, the learning experience has to focus explicitly on the power relationships between server and served through which lens such courses can be "catalyst[s] for examining the important issue of subjectivity" (p. 31). Furthermore, if we use these spaces and the experiences that happen in them as a focus for deep critical reflection—a key tool in a service learning activity system—students can begin to see beyond stereotypes and single stories, which can be an empowering context for both university and community (Camacho, 2004). A student in the global citizenship program at the university where I work, drawing on Camacho's work and trying to make sense of the importance of relationships in service, reflected as follows:

> I wrote in a previous blog that being at [NGO] made me aware of "my Whiteness." In most of the community service I have ever done, I have felt "different" in some way to the people I am serving. Which I suppose, isn't odd, because I am. But often, this is an uncomfortable feeling. (But) as Camacho (2004) notes, it is in allowing ourselves to be in that space of

discomfort that we learn, and that we are helpful. *If we sit in that space quietly and with stillness, perhaps we can cross through it and enter a space where people are not so different, where people are people trying to reach other people.* (CT blogpost, August 2012; emphasis added)

The kind of sensitivity and insight this student demonstrates about relationships in service learning is evidence of the kind of civic learning we would like our students to achieve.

In terms of understanding service learning through the lens of boundary work, this brings us to the role of *boundary workers* (McMillan, 2011, p. 554), actors who mediate across these complex boundaries in contexts of challenge and difference. In service learning, these could potentially be students, community members, or instructors. I have focused mainly on the role of instructors in my work, as have Weerts and Sandmann (2010). Because there is a purpose to the activity, boundary workers need to assist participants to make new connections across activity systems, enable coordination, and open new possibilities for meaning and therefore learning (Wenger, 1998). A boundary worker is a complex role involving "processes of translation, coordination and alignment between perspectives" (Wenger, 1998, p. 109). Boundary workers often need to address conflicting interests, which in turn requires legitimation on both sides of the boundary.

Such processes can challenge identity in significant ways for both students and instructors. Following Holland, Lachicotte, Skinner, and Cain (1998), who draw on AT to look at identity, I have come to understand that identities "are lived in and through activity and so must be conceptualized as they develop in social practice" (p. 5). Following Gibbons (2005) and Camacho (2004), working in the boundary zone is thus difficult and challenging work. In order to understand better the relationship between civic outcomes and service learning, we need to explore student experiences in the zone as well as the challenges instructors encounter as boundary workers in designing for transformative learning and navigating this space.

Questions for Future Research

Drawing on AT, there are a number of questions and lines of inquiry to explore the relationships between service learning courses and student civic outcomes. Such questions can contribute to understanding how to work deliberately to support students to understand their roles as boundary workers in a particular cultural and historical context at a particular time. We need to ask these questions about the boundary zone and about the various boundary workers in service learning.

First, in working toward developing a better understanding of the nature of the boundary zone, some of the questions to address include the following:

- In what ways is the boundary zone a place of discomfort for students and educators? In what ways is it potentially a transformative space for developing civic outcomes?
- How do different historical, cultural, or other contexts shape service learning practice and outcomes? How do we bring attention to context into our thinking about curriculum and pedagogy?
- How does the boundary zone, and roles necessary to navigate effectively within this space, shape civic outcomes, for students, educators, community partners, or residents?
- In what ways do different aspects of the boundary zone (e.g., rules, tools, roles) act to disrupt or transform effective work in service learning activities?
- What elements of service learning facilitate learning for knowing, doing, and being in a boundary zone?
- What are the implications for curricula and pedagogy if boundary work is an important civic outcome for students, educators, and community partners?
- If critical reflection is an important tool in service learning, how can AT be a useful framework to generate critical reflection activities for students to achieve the civic learning outcomes?
- Can analyzing service learning as an activity system taking place in a boundary zone create possibilities for facilitating some of the fundamental changes Dei (2014) identifies for curriculum and pedagogy: multicentricity, indigeneity, and reflexivity?

Second, in working to have a better understanding of the role of boundary workers in service learning, some of the questions to address include the following:

- How do boundary workers mediate the development of civic outcomes in themselves and others?
- Are students, instructors, and community partners all boundary workers? If so, what are the skills, knowledge, values, and attitudes required to enact this role of boundary worker successfully?
- Are the skills, values, and knowledge the same for different actors in the service learning partnership/course?
- Do skills, values, and knowledge differ across national and local contexts or can we identify common dimensions across varying contexts?

Conclusion

> Boundary work needs to be facilitated and managed and to do this specific knowledge and skills are required. . . . Engagement as a core value will be evident in the extent to which universities do actually develop the skills, create the organisational forms and manage tensions that will inevitably arise when different social worlds interact . . . . [T]o embrace this form of engagement entails that universities themselves be prepared to participate in those potential transaction spaces in which complex problems and issues will be initially and tentatively broached. (Gibbons, 2005, pp. 11–12)

The ability to "manage tensions" that emerge as a result of "different social worlds interact[ing]" is not easy. This is particularly the case when one understands practices and identities as historically and culturally located. However, taking up this challenge is important. In our increasingly unequal and divided world, we need to reimagine civic outcomes in ways that do justice to both context-specific practices and realities, and the broader project of the role of service learning in civic learning. This approach requires not only that students reexamine assumptions and views of the worlds but also the same tenacity and proactivity from researchers, curriculum designers, and educators alike.

References

Anzaldua, G. (1987). *Borderlands/la frontera: The new mestiza*. San Francisco, CA: Aunt Lute Books.

Barnett, R. (2004). Learning for an unknown future. *Higher Education Research and Development, 23*, 247–260.

Barnett, R. (2009). Knowing and becoming in the higher education curriculum. *Studies in Higher Education, 34*, 429–440.

Barnett, R., & Coate, K. (2005). *Engaging the curriculum in higher education*. Berkshire, England: SRHE and Open University.

Boyle-Blaise, M., Brown, R., Hsu, M.-C., Jones, D., Prakash, A., Rausch, M., Vitols, S., & Wahlquist, Z. (2006). Learning service or service learning: Enabling the civic. *International Journal of Teaching and Learning in Higher Education, 18*(1), 17–26.

Butin, D. W. (2003). Of what use is it? Multiple conceptualizations of service learning within education. *Teachers College Record, 105*, 1674–1692.

Camacho, M. (2004). Power and privilege: Community service learning in Tijuana. *Michigan Journal of Community Service Learning, 10*(3), 31–42.

Cole, M. (1996). *Cultural psychology: A once and future discipline*. Cambridge, MA: Harvard University Press.

Daniels, D. (2013). Advancing a transformative learning approach in teacher education through service learning. In N. Petersen & R. Osman (Eds.), *Service learning in South Africa* (pp. 186–205). Cape Town, South Africa: Oxford University Press.

d'Arlach, L., Sanchez, B., & Feuer, R. (2009). Voices from the community: A case for reciprocity in service-learning. *Michigan Journal of Community Service Learning, 16*(1), 5–16.

Deans, T. (1999). Service-learning in two keys: Paulo Freire's critical pedagogy in relation to John Dewey's pragmatism. *Michigan Journal of Community Service Learning, 6*(1), 15–28.

Dei, G. J. (2014). Indigenizing the curriculum: The case of the African university. In G. Emeagwali & G. J. Dei (Eds.), *African indigenous knowledge and the disciplines* (pp. 165–180). Rotterdam, Netherlands: Sense Publishers.

Engberg, M. E., & Fox, K. (2011). Exploring the relationship between undergraduate service-learning experiences and global perspective-taking. *Journal of Student Affairs Research and Practice, 48*(1), 85–105.

Engeström, Y. (1996). *Perspectives on activity theory.* Cambridge: Cambridge University Press.

Engeström, Y. (1999). Innovative learning in work teams: Analysing cycles of knowledge creation in practice. In Y. Engeström, R. Miettinen, & R. L. Punamki (Eds.), *Perspectives on activity theory* (pp. 377–404). Cambridge: Cambridge University Press.

Eyler, J., & Giles, Jr., D. E. (1999). *Where's the learning in service-learning?* San Francisco, CA: Jossey-Bass.

Freire, P. (1970). *Pedagogy of the oppressed.* London: Penguin Books.

Geertz, C. (1973) *The interpretation of cultures.* New York: Basic Books.

Gibbons, M. (2005, March). *Engagement with the community: The emergence of a new social contract between society and science.* Paper presented at the Griffith University Community Engagement workshop, South Bank campus, Queensland, Australia.

Giroux, H. (1992). *Border crossings: Cultural workers and the politics of education.* New York: Routledge.

Gredley, S. (2015). Learning through experience: Making sense of students' learning through service learning. *South African Journal of Higher Education, 29*(3), 200–243.

Green, A. (2001). "But you aren't white": Racial perceptions and service-learning. *Michigan Journal of Community Service Learning, 8*(1), 18–26.

Hatcher, J. A. (1997). The moral dimensions of John Dewey's philosophy: Implications for undergraduate education. *Michigan Journal of Community Service Learning, 4*(1), 22–29.

Hatcher, J. A., & Erasmus, M. (2008). Service-learning in the United States and South Africa: A comparative analysis informed by John Dewey and Julius Nyerere. *Michigan Journal of Community Service Learning, 15*(1), 49–61.

Hatcher, J. A., McIlrath, L., McMillan, J., & McTighe Musil, C. (2014, December). *Developing civic-minded graduates: Cross-cultural perspectives.* Paper presented at Talloires Network Leaders Conference, Stellenbosch, South Africa.

Hayes, E., & Cuban, S. (1997). Border pedagogy: A critical framework for service-learning. *Michigan Journal of Community Service Learning, 4*(1), 72–80.

Henry, S., & Breyfogle, M.L. (2006). Toward a new framework of "server" and "served": De(and re)constructing reciprocity in service-learning pedagogy. *International Journal of Teaching and Learning in Higher Education, 18*(1), 27–35.

Holland, D., Lachicotte, Jr., W., Skinner, D., & Cain, C. (1998). *Identity and agency in cultural worlds*. Cambridge, MA: Harvard University Press.

Keith, N. (2005). Community service learning in the face of globalization: Rethinking theory and practice. *Michigan Journal of Community Service Learning, 11*(2), 5–24.

Kiely, R. (2004). A chameleon with a complex: Searching for transformation in international service learning. *Michigan Journal of Community Service Learning, 10*(2), 5–20.

Leibowitz, B., Swartz, L., Bozalek, V., Carolissen, R., Nicholls, L., & Rohleder, P. (Eds.). (2012). *Community, self and identity*. South Africa: Human Sciences Research Council Press.

Mayo, M. (2012). Preface. In B. Hall, D. Clover, J. Crowther, & E. Scandrett (Eds.), *International issues in adult education, Vol 10: Learning and education for a better world* (pp. vii–viii). Rotterdam: Sense Publishers.

McMillan, J. (2008). *What happens when the university meets the community? An analysis of service learning as "boundary work" in higher education*. Unpublished PhD dissertation. Department of Sociology, Graduate School of Humanities, University of Cape Town, South Africa.

McMillan, J. (2009, June). *Illuminating "transaction spaces" in higher education: Service learning, "boundary work" and "boundary workers."* Paper presented at the Knowledge and Curriculum in Higher Education Symposium, University of Cape Town, South Africa.

McMillan, J. (2011). What happens when the university meets the community? Service learning, boundary work and boundary workers. *Teaching in Higher Education, 16*, 553–564.

Mitchell, T. (2008). Traditional vs. critical service-learning: Engaging the literature to differentiate two models. *Michigan Journal for Community Service Learning, 14*(2), 50–65.

Morton, K. (1995). The irony of service: Charity, project and social change in service learning. *Michigan Journal of Community Service Learning, 2*, 19–32.

Nowotny, H., Scott, P., & Gibbons, M. (2001). *Re-thinking science: Knowledge and the public in an age of uncertainty*. Cambridge, England: Polity Press.

Nussbaum, M. (2002). Education for citizenship in an era of global connection. *Studies in Philosophy and Education, 21*, 289–303.

Nussbaum, M. (2007). Cultivating humanity and world citizenship. Cambridge, MA: Forum for the future of higher education. Retrieved from http://net.educause.edu/ir/library/pdf/ff0709s.pdf

Palmer, P. J. (2007). A new professional: The aims of education revisited. *Change: The Magazine of Higher Learning, 39*(6), 6–13.

Petersen, N., & Osman, R. (2013). An introduction to service learning in South Africa. In N. Petersen & R. Osman (Eds.), *Service learning in South Africa* (pp. 2–32). Cape Town, South Africa: Oxford University Press.

Prins, E., & Webster, N. (2010). Student identities and the tourist gaze in international service-learning: A university project in Belize. *Journal of Higher Education Outreach and Engagement, 14*(1), 5–32.

Ramaley, J. (2014). The changing role of higher education: Learning to deal with wicked problems. *Journal of Higher Education Outreach and Engagement, 18*(3), 7–22.

Romero, D. (2014). Riding the bus: Symbol and vehicle for boundary spanning. *Journal of Higher Education Outreach and Engagement, 18*(3), 41–54.

Russell, D. (2002). Looking beyond the interface: Activity theory and distributed learning. In M. Lea & K. Nicoll (Eds.), *Distributed learning: Social and cultural approaches to practice* (pp. 64–82). London, England: Routledge Falmer and The Open University.

Shaktin, G. (2007). Global cities of the South: Emerging perspectives on growth and inequality. *Cities, 24*(1), 1–15.

Skilton-Sylvester, E., & Erwin, E. (2000). Creating reciprocal learning relationships across socially-constructed borders. *Michigan Journal of Community Service Learning, 7*(1), 65–75.

Soudien, C. (2006). The city, citizenship and education. *Journal of Education, 40,* 103–118.

Steinberg, K. S., Hatcher, J. A., & Bringle, R. G. (2011). Civic-minded graduate: A north star. *Michigan Journal of Community Service Learning, 18*(1), 19–33.

Taylor, J. (2002). Metaphors we serve by: Investigating the conceptual metaphors framing national and community service and service-learning. *Michigan Journal of Community Service Learning, 9*(1), 45–57.

Thomson, A. M., Smith-Tolken, A., Naidoo, A. V., & Bringle, R. G. (2011). Service learning and civic engagement: A comparison of three national contexts. *Voluntas, 22,* 214–237.

Weerts, D. J., & Sandmann, L. R. (2010). Community engagement and boundary-spanning roles at research universities. *Journal of Higher Education, 8,* 632–657.

Wenger, E. (1998). *Communities of practice: Learning, meaning and identity.* Cambridge, England: Cambridge University Press.

Winberg, C. (2006). Undisciplining knowledge production: Development driven higher education in South Africa. *Higher Education, 51,* 159–172.

PART THREE

CONDUCTING RESEARCH ON SERVICE LEARNING AND STUDENT CIVIC OUTCOMES

QUANTITATIVE RESEARCH ON SERVICE LEARNING AND STUDENT CIVIC OUTCOMES

Dan Richard

Quantitative methods address research questions using objective, numerical, and statistical techniques. To explore these techniques further, first, this chapter addresses the origins and foundations of quantitative methods and emphasizes the role of theory in research design and measurement. Second, this chapter identifies key elements of high-quality quantitative research and outlines a continuum of research design across programs of research. Third, this chapter presents some advances in quantitative methods such as structural equation modeling and meta-analysis, and provides implications for practice. This chapter also offers recommendations and examples to improve quantitative research in civic engagement and service learning to better understand the extent to which teaching strategies, community-based service, relationships, and reflection activities contribute to civic outcomes.

The Value of Quantitative Research

Many love to hate quantitative methods. An informal survey of opinions about quantitative methods at any service learning conference often elicits impassioned reactions. Some will dismiss quantitative research as "not relevant" to service learning practice, suggesting that quantitative research is too specific in its measures and methods to generalize to a given carefully designed and locally implemented service learning program. Others view quantitative methods as an unnecessarily rigid approach that wastes energy by trying to predetermine and structure the nature of outcomes for a service learning pedagogy that can have a variety of relevant student outcomes. Then there are the devotees who value quantitative methods as the single solution to enhancing understanding of educational pedagogies. Service learning researchers face an important question, "How can we appropriately incorporate quantitative research methods to improve understanding and practice of service learning pedagogies?"

Quantitative methods involve quantitative research designs and quantitative measures. In sum, quantitative research designs are used to test hypotheses. More fully, quantitative designs focus on systematic controls and comparisons with careful measurement to settle theoretically relevant hypotheses, all with the goal of testing causal claims about the relationships among constructs. The term *quantitative designs* typically refers to experimental and quasi-experimental designs (Shadish, Cook, & Campbell, 2002). As a category, quantitative measures involve assigning numerical representations to the ways in which constructs (e.g., self-esteem, civic agency) change or vary over units of study (e.g., college students) or over time (Trochim, 2005). Not all quantitative research designs use quantitative measures to test their hypotheses. In addition, researchers can employ quantitative measures without using designs that test causal hypotheses. Despite these fine distinctions, researchers often use quantitative designs and quantitative measures in tandem, in part because they share common ontological (i.e., the nature of truth) and epistemological (i.e., methods of knowing) foundations (Bringle, Reeb, Brown, & Ruiz, 2015; Van de Ven, 2007).

Origins and Foundations

Quantitative methods have their origin among the natural and physical sciences where precise measurement of constructs, control over extraneous variables, and systematic manipulation of conditions permit drawing causal conclusions from generated evidence. In the social and behavioral sciences, within which service learning and other educational research exists, researchers often are constrained, either by ethics or practical concerns, from exerting high levels of experimental control over their subjects of study (e.g., college students). For example, it would be impractical and unethical to randomly assign students to an academic major to determine the unique impact this variable has on civic outcomes. In the natural and physical sciences, experiments can place careful controls over the objects of study (e.g., measuring voltage across circuits in a closed system). It is impractical for researchers studying human behavior to place such a high level of control over the objects of study. The result is that any intervention (e.g., service learning course or program) that attempts to influence human behavior (e.g., civic engagement, prosocial behavior) must account for numerous influential factors on the target behavior that are outside of experimenter control (e.g., whether students are tired, whether students have prior volunteer experience). Such influential factors confound and mask outcome differences and make detecting causal relationships difficult (McClelland & Judd, 1993).

As scientists moved from using quantitative methods to test theories about the natural and physical world to testing theories about human behavior, the underlying assumptions about the nature of evidence became an issue of debate (see Bringle et al., 2015). Researchers began to make distinctions between "hard" sciences that tend to use mathematical representations of reality and "soft" or social sciences that tend to use verbal language to represent reality (Cohen, 1980). Researchers in the natural and physical sciences (e.g., chemistry, physics) tend to adopt a positivist approach. According to the positivist philosophy, truth can be known, and quantitative measurements of true values bring precision. In contrast, in the social sciences, constructivist approaches began to emerge (Gergen, 1985), viewing truth as a social construction of the people who perceive and understand it. Postpositive philosophies attempt to establish a middle ground between positivists and social constructivists, relying on multiple methods and theories to triangulate evidence and truth (Van de Ven, 2007).

Quantitative methods originate from the hard, natural sciences and qualitative methods originate from the soft, social sciences. Many argue that service learning has roots in the social sciences, where the values of justice, inclusiveness, and mutual participation in the construction of knowledge associated with service learning are well aligned with qualitative research methods (e.g., Dewey, 1933; Freire, 1972; see Deans, 1999; Giles & Eyler, 1994a, for reviews). Quantitative methods, however, have had solid representation in educational research (U.S. Department of Education, 2003). Currently, service learning researchers come from a variety of disciplines. Service learning researchers trained among positivistic and postpositivistic philosophies, thus, tend to use quantitative methods, whereas those trained in constructivist philosophies tend to use qualitative methods. When conducted with scientific rigor, a variety of approaches can contribute to the development and refinement of theories related to service learning and civic engagement (Steinberg, Bringle, & McGuire, 2013).

The Theory Imperative

Quantitative researchers attempt to contribute to broad, generalizable knowledge about the nature of reality (Black, 1999). Researchers use theory (i.e., conceptual frameworks about reality) to construct testable hypotheses about the relationship between causal variables (e.g., service learning courses) and outcomes (e.g., civic engagement). Theory guides the formulation of research questions, the selection of appropriate measures, and the interpretation of obtained results (Bringle & Hatcher, 2000). Bringle (2003) highlights the importance of theory in providing an explanation as to *why* a particular service learning intervention resulted in a particular outcome as opposed to describing *that* an intervention resulted in an outcome. Theoretical explanations allow the outcomes of research potentially to be generalized to other contexts and settings (if the theory holds under future research and scrutiny).

Essential Elements of Quantitative Methods

Quantitative methods represent a range of techniques devoted to careful measurement and carefully constructed designs that allow for comparative statements (inferences) about the relationships among variables. The goal of quantitative methods is to demonstrate an effect of some variable (e.g., participating in service learning, type of reflection activity) on desired outcomes and to establish the conditions under which those effects are realized. Brown (2011), for example, randomly assigned psychology students to either a community service group or a research group. Both groups of students investigated topics related to community issues (e.g., homelessness) and related those topics to the course content through reflection exercises. Only the community service group, however, had direct human contact (in the context of service) with persons experiencing homelessness. Students in the community service group showed a decrease in preferences for social dominance over outgroup members during the 10-week course, whereas those students in the research group did not. Brown further illustrated that an increase in empathic concern on the part of the community service group was largely responsible for the decrease in social dominance preferences. This study represents many of the dimensions of excellence in quantitative research design.

Quantitative methods have a few key elements that allow researchers to make strong inferences from quantitative results. Table 3.1.1 provides a description of these key elements. Quantitative methods rely on the ability to assign numerical quantities to constructs (i.e., concepts of interest to the research question; e.g., amount of reflection). Assigning quantities to a construct enables the researcher to make distinctions among units (e.g., students, instructors, institutions) using numerical distinctions.

Inherent in this process is the notion of *variability*, that is, the idea that constructs vary across people, across time, or across settings. Astin, Vogelgesang, Ikeda, and Yee (2000), for example, categorized graduates' commitment to racial understanding on a scale from *essential* (4) to *not important* (1). These assigned numbers did not completely identify or completely characterize the true commitment graduates had to racial understanding. Rather the numbers provided a convenient and numerical summary for making

TABLE 3.1.1
Key Elements of Quantitative Research

Element	Description
Constructs and Quantities	Defines constructs and assigns numerical quantities to make distinctions among units across numerical dimensions
Comparison	Compares outcomes across conditions through counterfactuals, "What would have happened differently if . . . ?"
Reproducibility	Focuses on repeatability, the likelihood of finding similar results given similar conditions and constraints
Statistical Analysis	Uses numerical, mathematical, and probabilistic statements to establish the magnitude and trustworthiness of results

distinctions among graduates who reported higher levels or lower levels of commitment to racial understanding. It is important, therefore, when using quantitative approaches, to identify *how* things vary over people, time, or settings. This identification process involves a clear understanding of the nature of the construct, usually presented within a theoretical framework, as well as procedures for measuring the construct that allow the capturing of changes over time and the identification of differences across individuals in numerical form.

Given that measured constructs are likely to vary over time or among individuals, quantitative designs emphasize comparison or a *counterfactual*. A counterfactual is a condition in which the researcher identifies *what would have happened if . . .* (Rubin, 1974; Shadish et al., 2002). As Rubin (1974) explains, someone with a headache two hours after drinking a glass of water might ask, "What would have happened had I taken two aspirin with a glass of water two hours earlier?" (p. 689). The counterfactual establishes a comparison condition to which one can compare outcomes (headache or no headache) under different conditions (aspirin or no aspirin). Strage (2000), for example, compared learning outcomes of students who had completed a service learning course in developmental psychology with students from three prior semesters who completed the same course without the service learning component. This non-service learning comparison group served as a counterfactual as to what levels of learning outcomes were obtained when no service learning existed in the course. Stronger counterfactuals included in quantitative designs allow for clearer estimates of service learning's effects and results in stronger causal inferences. Causal links based on clear counterfactuals allow researchers to infer that the service learning component of the course actually had the effect rather than something else causing it, like the teaching style of the instructor, level of peer-to-peer interaction, or the types of students taking the course.

Once a researcher establishes that an effect of the service learning experiences was likely, quantitative researchers are interested in the repeatability of findings (i.e., the likelihood of finding similar results given similar constraints or conditions). Finding replicable results is no easy task, as researchers recently discovered through a large-scale attempt to replicate behavioral research (Open Science Collaboration, 2015). Researchers found that only about 38% of previous research findings replicated when tested under carefully reconstructed conditions. The emphasis on reproducible findings has its foundation in the premise that trustworthy findings are ones that can be demonstrated over and over again (Robinson & Levin, 1997). Replicable findings are more likely to have implications for practice, as trustworthy findings more likely have generalizability to other settings.

This is not to say that choosing a quantitative design automatically makes one's findings replicable. Because the strength of quantitative methods is in their specificity of measurement and design, and the social and behavioral sciences deal with complex human behavior (Brunswik, 1955), educational researchers and other social scientists deal in probabilistic statements rather than in certainty. Results in service learning research, thus, cannot be exactly replicated, only approximately replicated. The extent of the reproducibility of the effects leads to greater confidence that the underlying causal patterns can be trusted as valid. In quantitative research, concerns about reproducibility are addressed in clearly articulated research methodology and instrumentation, measurement reliability (Henson, 2001), and clear estimation of effects.

With an emphasis on trustworthy and replicable findings, quantitative research employs statistical analysis to provide objective estimates of effect magnitude and estimates of the likelihood of repeating the research findings, all things being equal. Statistical analyses can range from rudimentary comparisons across groups on measures of civic outcomes to longitudinal designs and sophisticated structural equation models that compare different hypotheses of complex patterns among measured variables (chapter 3.4). Engberg and Hurtado (2011), for example, using data from students across 10 institutions of higher learning, determined that the impact of structural diversity and positive experiences with other racial groups increased a preference for pluralistic orientations among White students but not among students of other racial and ethnic groups. Despite the simplicity or complexity of the analysis, most statistical tests rely on the basic components of model comparison (i.e., which model best fits the data) and likelihood estimates that the results would be due to chance (i.e., that the differences or patterns observed could have been produced from a random process as opposed to a causal process).

In summary, quantitative methods are powerful tools of research measurement, design, and analysis to understand the relationship between service learning and civic outcomes. Quantitative methods focus on discovering generalizable patterns across units (e.g., individuals, programs, institutions) and allow for robust and efficient summaries of variations in construct measurements across units of interest. As an illustrative example, Simons and Cleary (2006) employed a pretest-posttest design to observe changes in measurements of political awareness, diversity attitudes, and civic engagement following participation in service learning experiences. The pretest established a counterfactual (i.e., what would the levels of civic outcomes be had students not participated in service learning?) that allowed researchers to estimate quantitative differences among measurements from pretest and posttest responses by students. The improvements observed in student civic engagement were likely due to the service learning experiences and not to preexisting levels of civic engagement because measures of civic engagement at the pretest stage (i.e., before the service learning experiences) served as a baseline upon which to compare posttest results. Although the presence of a pretest does not rule out all alternative explanations (see Shadish et al., 2002), quantitative designs allow researchers to carefully construct these important comparisons and measurements to strengthen causal inference.

The Research Design Continuum

Traditional conceptions founded in positivistic philosophies regard quantitative and "true" experimental designs as having more value than qualitative designs because quantitative designs provide the most rigorous, scientific approach to making causal inferences. Figure 3.1.1 represents this hierarchical approach in which quantitative experimental designs are presented as the scientific ideal. The figure presents three types/categories of quantitative research approaches that vary in the extent of experimental control one can exert over the implementation of treatment approaches (e.g., the implementation of a service learning program) and the extent to which one is able to randomly assign research participants to treatment levels (e.g., short-term versus long-term service, interaction with community residents versus no interaction, private reflection versus group dialogue).

Instead of viewing qualitative and quantitative research designs as hierarchical, social scientists (Mortensen & Cialdini, 2010) and educational researchers (Newman & Benz, 1998), specifically, have offered a research continuum in which different research designs are interactive components in a

Figure 3.1.1. The hierarchical approach to quantitative design.

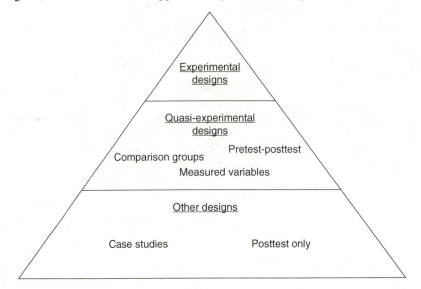

continuum of knowledge building. According to this view, different research designs address different types of questions, yet research conducted using different designs informs other types. Although most researchers are trained within disciplines and traditions that are more inclined to adopt either quantitative or qualitative designs (chapter 3.2), as knowledge and theory advance within a body of research, different methodologies are necessary to answer important theoretical and practical questions.

Service learning researchers, thus, can choose from a variety of research designs that will not meet the controlled experiment ideal. Quasi-experimental designs employ some elements of experimental control, such as nonrandomized comparison groups, multiple measurements, or modified interventions, but fall short of high levels of control in true experiments. In fact, quasi-experimental designs represent the majority of quantitative research in the service learning field. Kendrick (1996), for example, compared students who, by happenstance or by choice, enrolled in a service learning section of a sociology course to students who were enrolled in a non-service learning section of the same course. At the end of the semester, students in the service learning section reported greater self-efficacy, social responsibility, and learned more course concepts than did students in the non-service learning section. Because differences in learning outcomes between sections could have been explained by prior student individual differences (as these initial differences were not randomly dispersed between course sections), the extent to which the researchers could offer the explanation that service learning was the cause of the learning outcomes was limited. The causal relationship between the service learning and beneficial outcomes would need to be further supported by other means. Kendrick, thus, noted that over 80% of the students were not initially aware of the service learning component of the course prior to registration and that only a few students dropped or switched sections. This additional supportive evidence further strengthened the claim that student learning outcomes were a function of the service learning component of the course.

No research design is perfect, but research designs can be crafted to answer specific questions of interest as a theory or focus area is fully explored and investigated. As programs of research progress, however, they rely on a variety of research designs to answer a variety of questions (Newman & Benz, 1998). Researchers occasionally will use controlled experiments (sometimes in laboratory settings) to test theoretical foundations (Mook, 1983). At other times in the research process, researchers inquire about the boundary conditions and test the generalizability of previous findings. Bringle, Clayton, and Hatcher (2012) address different dimensions of the research process and the central role of theory in that process. Figure 3.1.2 provides an alternative

Figure 3.1.2. The research design continuum.

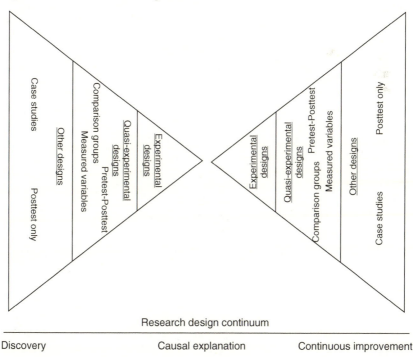

Research design continuum

Discovery   Causal explanation   Continuous improvement

perspective to the hierarchical approach to research design, offering instead a research design continuum, where the focus of the research changes over a program of research, from discovery, causal explanation, and implementation. Each stage of the continuum involves different questions (see Table 3.1.2) and tends to use particular quantitative and qualitative methods to address those questions. Tashakkori and Creswell (2007) provide an explanation of how these research questions can be integrated for mixed methods designs. Each of these stages is described in Table 3.1.2, with a focus on those stages that typically involve quantitative methods.

TABLE 3.1.2
The Research Design Continuum

Focus of Research	*Example Research Questions*	*Typical Research Designs*
Discovery	What is the construct? How does it work? What are the benefits? Who is affected?	Qualitative
Definition of *Construct* and *Variables*	What is the specific definition? What are the distinctions? What other ideas are associated with the construct?	Quasi-Experimental (Correlational Designs)
Causal Explanation	Can we isolate the effect? What is the magnitude of the effect? Can the effect be distinguished from other effects? What is the causal relationship?	Experimental
Understanding Boundary Conditions	What are the limits of the effect? Under what specific conditions does the effect appear or disappear?	Experimental & Quasi-Experimental
Implementation	Does the effect work across situations or across different groups? Will the effect be observed in the field? Why or why not?	Quasi-Experimental
Continuous Improvement	How does it work in particular situations? Are particular people affected? How can we improve? What's missing?	Qualitative
Discovery . . .		

Discovery

Progress in a research program begins in the discovery stage with the identification of a topic of interest. Research questions focus on what, when, who, and how. These questions demand careful exploration and are informed by existing and newly developed theory in the field (Giles & Eyler, 1994b). Qualitative methods tend to fit the research questions at this stage. Once a topic has been identified and explored adequately in the discovery phase, researchers often move to refine definitions and make distinctions among the concept of interest and other related ideas that already exist in the field associated with identified theories.

Definition

In the definition stage, correlational designs and other quantitative methods are used to help make explicit and distinguish constructs and definitions of interest from other constructs and associated definitions. Researchers address the reliability and validity of measures at this stage (see Steinberg et al., 2013, for a list of approaches). Moely, Mercer, Ilustre, Miron, and McFarland (2002), for example, developed the Civic Attitudes and Skills Questionnaire (CASQ), a measure of civic attitudes, skills, and behavioral intentions to engage in civic action. Because the researchers were interested in defining this construct in such a way as to be generalizable, they collected large samples of students (over 700 per sample) across a variety of backgrounds. The researchers established the reliability of the CASQ scale using statistical techniques of factor analysis and internal consistency estimates. They also addressed convergent validity, showing that measures of the CASQ were correlated with similar measures of civic attitudes, and discriminant validity, showing that several subscales of the CASQ were not correlated with social desirability response bias. The CASQ subsequently has been used in numerous studies of service learning and civic attitudes.

Similarly, Steinberg, Hatcher, and Bringle (2011) used existing theory in the civic learning literature to construct a measure of the civic-minded graduate (CMG), the intersection of identity, educational experiences, and civic experiences. Using three separate studies, Steinberg and colleagues addressed the reliability of the CMG measure (with factor analysis and internal consistency estimates) and provided evidence for the validity of the scale. The researchers demonstrated the convergent validity of the CMG scale by correlating CMG scores with independently rated narrative responses to face-to-face interviews. Discriminant validity was supported in that CMG scores were not correlated with socially desirable responses. Bringle and Hahn (2015) reported on subsequent research that found CMG to be correlated with components of its conceptual framework of knowledge, skills, dispositions, and intentions. Careful quantitative methods employed by such researchers in the definition stage, using mostly quasi-experimental (correlational) designs allows other researchers at other stages to effectively measure civic outcomes and compare them in relation to other theoretically important interventions and outcomes.

Causal Explanation

In the causal explanation stage, quantitative methods can establish that a causal relationship exists between causes and effects (e.g., that service learning results in civic engagement) and determine the magnitude and direction of these effects. In order to establish that an effect exists, one must focus on controlling for alternative explanations of the effect. Controlling for alternative explanations usually includes random assignment to control groups or other forms of comparison groups to establish that the intervention (e.g., service learning) and not something else (e.g., teaching style) produces a defensible effect on the outcome of interest (e.g., civic attitudes).

Vogelgesang and Astin (2000), for example, established that the effect of service learning exists on a variety of outcomes (e.g., commitment to activism), and they provided corrected effect size estimates (standardized regression coefficients) to compare the *relative* effects of participating in service during college disconnected from the classroom (called "generic" service, p. 25) to "course-based" (p. 25) service learning in which service was associated and integrated with coursework. Vogelgesang and Astin used a large sample size (over 22,000 students from different institution types), which helped strengthen the claim that the findings would generalize to a variety of settings and students. In addition, they used statistical techniques (structured hierarchical regression analyses) to control for plausible alternative explanations (e.g., self-efficacy) for why students participating in different types of service showed greater civic outcomes (e.g., commitment to activism) compared to students with no service involvement. The use of careful research design (i.e., identifying comparison groups) and using quantitative analyses to control for alternative explanations enhanced the causal claim that service learning leads to positive civic outcomes.

In this stage, researchers also address the necessary and sufficient conditions under which demonstrated effects operate. Mediation analysis, a statistical technique popularized by Baron and Kenny (1986; as cited in Zhao, Lynch, & Chen, 2010) allows researchers to determine if interventions (e.g., service learning) have their effects through intermediating variables. Gallini and Moely (2003), for example, demonstrated that the effect service learning courses had on college student retention in the first academic year was mediated by increasing student perceptions of academic engagement and academic challenge. That is to say, if college students participating in service learning in their first year do not show increases in perceptions of academic engagement and academic challenge, the students are not likely to be retained.

Understanding Boundary Conditions

Once a causal association is established, researchers attempt to determine the boundary conditions under which the effect is enhanced or diminished. In the understanding boundary conditions stage, researchers test if changes in features of the intervention, or with different groups, either magnify or reduce previously demonstrated results. Using a quasi-experimental (correlational) design, Hatcher, Bringle, and Muthiah (2004) demonstrated that quality of the educational experiences in service learning courses was associated to a greater extent with the quality of reflection activities than with the amount of reflection activities. Also testing boundary conditions, Mabry (1998) found that changes in civic attitudes as a function of participating in service learning experiences were greatest among students who reported having frequent or sustained contact with the beneficiaries of service as compared to students who had little or no contact with beneficiaries. Contact with service beneficiaries thus modified, moderated, or enhanced the effect of service learning experiences.

Implementation

In the implementation stage, researchers and practitioners test the ideas and models established in previous stages in a variety of teaching and learning environments to establish the practical value of the effect and its ecological validity (Brunswik, 1955). In this stage, researchers explore whether particular educational practices are suitable in different contexts and with different individuals. Researchers might explore other associated themes that emerge when theoretical concepts are applied to different contexts. The most common research design in this stage is the case study or program evaluation (chapter 3.6). With the additional elements of quantitative design, and with the connection to theoretically relevant constructs, program evaluation studies at the implementation stage can support or inform theory (see Bringle et al., 2013).

Continuous Improvement

In the continuous improvement stage, researchers explore *how* certain practices might need to be modified in different situations, which leads to asking additional questions that might challenge or fine-tune existing theories and models. Researchers also might address what themes have been missed from previous research. Qualitative research designs tend to be the norm in this stage (chapter 3.2); however, quantitative methods can be used to determine if improvements in service learning activities result in improved outcomes. New discoveries emerge as knowledge about empirically supported theories are applied to the learning context. These new discoveries start the research process over again (see Table 3.1.2).

Improving Quantitative Research on Civic Outcomes

In educational research and service learning specifically, true experimental designs are rarely used (Brown, 2011), even though the U.S. Department of Education takes the position that scientifically based research is imperative for improving the knowledge base of teaching and learning (U.S. Department of Education, 2003). Shadish and colleagues (2002) provide a variety of ways that researchers can control for alternative explanations and improve the strength of a causal claim when true experimental designs are not possible. One option for improving causal inference in quasi-experimental designs involves using various forms of assignment other than random assignment, such as cut-off based assignment or matching. As a way of statistically blocking or matching students on preexisting individual differences, Astin and Sax (1998) used hierarchical regression to statistically control for preexisting differences (e.g., materialistic values) among those who self-selected to engage in service versus those who did not select to serve. This statistical technique allowed the researchers to estimate the effects of service learning on important outcomes such as civic responsibility while controlling for the effects of these preexisting differences among volunteers and nonvolunteers. Another strategy involves the use of multiple measurement periods or multiple measures, such as longitudinal designs or nonequivalent dependent variables (chapter 3.4). Laird, Engberg, and Hurtado (2005), for example, used a longitudinal design to measure and control for previous diversity course enrollment in estimating the effects of current enrollment in diversity courses on future social activism engagement.

Other options include using nonequivalent groups or regression extrapolation instead of true control groups to establish clear counterfactuals (i.e., what would have happened if . . . ?). Researchers also might use different forms of treatment implementation, such as repeated treatment designs or switching replications (i.e., the control group receives the treatment after a delay) to improve causal inference. McCarthy and Tucker (2002), for example, used a modified version of the Solomon Four Group Design (Solomon, 1949) to employ pretests, service learning, and lecture at different time periods across different groups to control for pretest sensitization effects and to estimate the effects of service learning independent of and in combination with class lecture. The implementation of multiple control groups improved causal inference by observing a pattern of results across groups that could only be explained by an interaction effect of service learning and lecture to produce stronger community service intentions. Control and comparison techniques such as these, when implemented in applied, educational settings, support stronger causal inferences in research settings where more stringent control over extraneous variables is not possible or ethical.

Advanced Models and Methods

Structural equation modeling (SEM; Jöreskog & Sörbom, 1993) has become more prevalent in recent years, in part because SEM allows testing of multiple and complex models of how a set of variables are related with each other. As theories about the functional relationships among elements of service learning and elements of civic outcomes (part 2) become more complex, quantitative methods must become more complex to test those theories. As theory develops, predictions about the pattern of results become more precise and nuanced. SEM allows testing of such complex predictions and complex models of service learning components (chapter 3.4).

SEM requires a model comparison process in which multiple models with different configurations are tested and statistical fit indices and interpretations determine which complex model fits the data best. Smith (1999), for example, tested several models based on theories of political socialization to inspect the relationship between investment in early adolescent extracurricular activities and civic engagement as an adult. Smith used multiple measures to rule out alternative hypotheses, including the alternative hypothesis that political socialization is merely a function of academic proficiency. As theories of service learning become more complex and specific about the relationship among relevant variables, SEM will continue to be a preferred quantitative technique to evaluate such theories.

Theories are developing in the field of service learning and civic engagement, and the quantity of evidence is increasing. A search for the term *service learning* in Google Scholar returns over 136,000 results. As the field develops, researchers are faced with trying to make sense of research findings from a variety of contexts and fields. Meta-analysis (Cooper, Hedges, & Valentine, 2009) provides an opportunity to summarize studies from multiple institutions, samples, and contexts from research already conducted and to address whether effects of service learning vary across institutions, samples, and contexts. Meta-analyses quantitatively summarize existing research outcomes (effects) from preexisting published and unpublished studies on a specific topic. Meta-analyses can establish that the magnitude of an effect differs from zero (i.e., an effect exists) and allows for a comparison of the magnitude of effects across different conditions or types of studies. Celio, Durlak, and Dymnicki (2011) accumulated evidence from 62 studies of service learning and found that service learning students had on average one third of a standard deviation benefit in educational outcomes, including civic engagement. Warren (2012), using more selective inclusion criteria, reviewed evidence from 11 studies and found similar results. Conway, Amel, and Gerwien (2009) reviewed 55 service learning studies that addressed civic outcomes. Through moderator analyses, they found that programs using structured reflection produced greater citizenship outcomes than did programs not using structured reflection. Yorio and Ye (2012) reviewed 34 service learning studies and found that programs that focused on written reflection to deepen student understanding of social issues showed smaller effects than those focusing on discussion as a form of reflection. As studies in service learning with similar goals and outcomes increase in number, additional meta-analytic studies are useful in understanding which practices contribute to specific outcomes.

Conclusion

This chapter has advocated a model for a program of research that spans along a continuum, requiring a variety of research approaches to adequately address new research questions related to service learning and civic outcomes. Because researchers are trained in a specific set of research practices in graduate school, it will be important that service learning researchers pursue partnerships with other researchers who have complementary research skills to their own. If these partnerships happen across institutions, research projects could encompass larger samples of participants and address a variety of interesting research questions. Having cross-institution research partnerships could also help to establish comparison groups across important dimensions. Researchers might wonder, for example, whether institutional mission influences the impact of a service learning program. Research partners could implement the same service learning program at these different institutions to determine the effect of institutional mission. Researchers would need to control for a variety of preexisting differences among groups to support drawing causal inferences from the results. Collaborations across institutions can provide relevant comparison groups, varieties of student populations and institutional contexts, and also add to the generalizability of findings over time.

Service learning practitioners recognize the value of and advocate for partnerships with community agencies. Research, because of its history with laboratory-based science, can seem to be an isolating process. Service learning practitioners and researchers should find opportunities for meaningful partnerships both within and outside the academy. Participatory action research (Strand, Cutforth, Stoecker, Marullo, & Donohue, 2003) provides a useful model for greater collaboration between academic researchers and community partners. This approach is particularly relevant when civic outcomes are extended beyond students to include outcomes for community residents and leaders.

As the field of service learning research moves beyond simple models and examines more complex understandings of the impact of service learning on civic outcomes, there will be a growing need to ask more complex and nuanced questions and to pursue more complex analytical procedures to answer those questions. Service learning practitioners, students, and community partners have an important role in shaping those questions and testing theoretical assumptions of proposed models. Service learning researchers will benefit from the perspectives of these partners as well as researchers trained in both a variety and the complexity of research designs and analyses to address these complex questions. In a critique of the history of science in education, Lagemann (2002) called for greater cooperation across disciplinary boundaries. Service learning researchers should recognize that a full understanding of a construct does not end with one type of methodology or one disciplinary lens but in the adoption, use, and application of different types of methodologies across the research design continuum.

The development of more complex theories is promising for the field of service learning. Useful theories, however, are those that are only as complex as they need to be to explain the phenomenon of interest (for a discussion of parsimony and Occam's Razor, see Epstein, 1984). In order to address appropriate complexity, researchers should rely on clear and deep theoretical understanding to drive research questions and design. Complexities will naturally emerge from the implementation process as ideas meet the reality of process.

References

Astin, A. W., & Sax, L. J. (1998). How undergraduates are affected by service participation. *Journal of College Student Development, 39*, 251–263.

Astin, A. W., Vogelgesang, L. J., Ikeda, E. K., & Yee, J. A. (2000). *How service learning affects students.* Los Angeles, CA: Higher Education Research Institute, UCLA.

Baron, R. M., & Kenny, D. A. (1986). The moderator–mediator variable distinction in social psychological research: Conceptual, strategic, and statistical considerations. *Journal of Personality and Social Psychology, 51*, 1173–1182.

Black, T. R. (1999). *Doing quantitative research in the social sciences: An integrated approach to research design, measurement and statistics.* Thousand Oaks, CA: Sage.

Bringle, R. G. (2003). Enhancing theory-based research on service-learning. In S. H. Billig & J. Eyler (Eds.), *Deconstructing service-learning: Research exploring context, participation, and impacts* (pp. 3–21). Greenwich, CT: Information Age.

Bringle, R. G., Clayton, P. H., & Hatcher, J. A. (2012). Research on service learning: An introduction. In P. H. Clayton, R. G. Bringle, & J. A. Hatcher (Eds.), *Research on service learning: Conceptual frameworks and assessments* (Vol. 2A, pp. 3–25). Arlington, VA: Stylus.

Bringle, R. G., & Hahn, T. W. (2015, November). *Civic-minded graduate: Construct validation evidence.* Paper presented at the 15th meeting of the International Association for Research on Service Learning and Community Engagement, Boston, MA.

Bringle, R. G., & Hatcher, J. A. (2000). Meaningful measurement of theory-based service-learning outcomes: Making the case with quantitative research. *Michigan Journal of Community Service Learning,* [Special Issue](1), 68–75.

Bringle, R. G., Reeb, R., Brown, M. A., & Ruiz, A. (2015). *Service learning in psychology: Enhancing undergraduate education for the public good.* Washington, DC: American Psychological Association.

Brown, M. A. (2011). Learning from service: The effect of helping on helpers' social dominance orientation. *Journal of Applied Social Psychology, 41,* 850–871.

Brunswik, E. (1955). Representative design and probabilistic theory in a functional psychology. *Psychological Review, 62*(3), 193–217.

Celio, C. I., Durlak, J., & Dymnicki, A. (2011). A meta-analysis of the impact of service-learning on students. *Journal of Experiential Education, 34*(2), 164–181.

Cohen, P. S. (1980). Is positivism dead? *The Sociological Review, 28*(1), 141–176.

Conway, J. M., Amel, E. L., & Gerwien, D. P. (2009). Teaching and learning in the social context: A meta-analysis of service learning's effects on academic, personal, social, and citizenship outcomes. *Teaching of Psychology, 36,* 233–245.

Cooper, H., Hedges, L. V., & Valentine, J. C. (Eds.). (2009). *The handbook of research synthesis and meta-analysis.* New York, NY: Russell Sage Foundation.

Deans, T. (1999). Service-learning in two keys: Paulo Freire's critical pedagogy in relation to John Dewey's pragmatism. *Michigan Journal of Community Service Learning, 6,* 15–29.

Dewey, J. (1933). *How we think: A restatement of the reflective thinking to the educative process.* Boston, MA: Heath.

Engberg, M. E., & Hurtado, S. (2011). Developing pluralistic skills and dispositions in college: Examining racial/ethnic group differences. *The Journal of Higher Education, 82,* 416–443.

Epstein, R. (1984). The principle of parsimony and some applications in psychology. *The Journal of Mind and Behavior, 5*(2), 119–130.

Freire, P. (1972). *Pedagogy of the oppressed.* Transl. by Myra Bergman Ramos. New York, NY: Herder and Herder.

Gallini, S. M., & Moely, B. E. (2003). Service-learning and engagement, academic challenge, and retention. *Michigan Journal of Community Service Learning, 10*(1), 5–14.

Gergen, K. J. (1985). The social constructionist movement in modern psychology. *American Psychologist, 40,* 266.

Giles, Jr., D. E., & Eyler, J. (1994a). The impact of a college community service laboratory on students' personal, social, and cognitive outcomes. *Journal of Adolescence, 17,* 327–339.

Giles, Jr., D. E., & Eyler, J. (1994b). The theoretical roots of service-learning in John Dewey: Toward a theory of service-learning. *Michigan Journal of Community Service Learning, 1*(1), 77–85.

Hatcher, J. A., Bringle, R. G., & Muthiah, R. (2004). Designing effective reflection: What matters to service-learning? *Michigan Journal of Community Service Learning, 11*(1), 38–46.

Henson, R. K. (2001). Understanding internal consistency reliability estimates: A conceptual primer on coefficient alpha. *Measurement and Evaluation in Counseling and Development, 34*(3), 177–189.

Jöreskog, K. G., & Sörbom, D. (1993). *LISREL 8: Structural equation modeling with the SIMPLIS command language.* Skokie, IL: Scientific Software International.

Kendrick Jr, J. R. (1996). Outcomes of service-learning in an introduction to sociology course. *Michigan Journal of Community Service Learning, 3,* 72–81.

Lagemann, E. C. (2002). *An elusive science: The troubling history of education research.* Chicago, IL: University of Chicago Press.

Laird, T. F. N., Engberg, M. E., & Hurtado, S. (2005). Modeling accentuation effects: Enrolling in a diversity course and the importance of social action engagement. *The Journal of Higher Education, 76,* 448–476.

Mabry, J. B. (1998). Pedagogical variations in service-learning and student outcomes: How time, contact, and reflection matter. *Michigan Journal of Community Service Learning, 5,* 32–47.

McCarthy, A. M., & Tucker, M. L. (2002). Encouraging community service through service learning. *Journal of Management Education, 26,* 629–647.

McClelland, G. H., & Judd, C. M. (1993). Statistical difficulties of detecting interactions and moderator effects. *Psychological Bulletin, 114,* 376–390.

Moely, B. E., Mercer, S. H., Ilustre, V., Miron, D., & McFarland, M. (2002). Psychometric properties and correlates of the Civic Attitudes and Skills Questionnaire (CASQ): A measure of students' attitudes related to service-learning. *Michigan Journal of Community Service Learning, 8*(2), 15–26.

Mook, D.G. (1983). In defense of external invalidity. *American Psychologist, 38,* 379–387.

Mortensen, C. R., & Cialdini, R. B. (2010). Full-cycle social psychology for theory and application. *Social and Personality Psychology Compass, 4,* 53–63.

Newman, I., & Benz, C. R. (1998). *Qualitative-quantitative research methodology: Exploring the interactive continuum.* Carbondale, IL: Southern Illinois University Press.

Open Science Collaboration. (2015). Estimating the reproducibility of psychological science. *Science, 349*(6251).

Robinson, D. H., & Levin, J. R. (1997). Research news and comment: Reflections on statistical and substantive significance, with a slice of replication. *Educational Researcher, 26*(5), 21–26.

Rubin, D. B. (1974). Estimating causal effects of treatments in randomized and non-randomized studies. *Journal of Educational Psychology, 66,* 688–701.

Shadish, W. R., Cook, T. D., & Campbell, D. T. (2002). *Experimental and quasi-experimental designs for generalized causal inference.* Boston, MA: Houghton Mifflin

Simons, L., & Cleary, B. (2006). The influence of service learning on students' personal and social development. *College Teaching, 54,* 307–319.

Smith, E. S. (1999). The effects of investments in the social capital of youth on political and civic behavior in young adulthood: A longitudinal analysis. *Political Psychology, 20,* 553–580.

Solomon, R. L. (1949). An extension of control group design. *Psychological Bulletin, 46,* 137–150.

Steinberg, K. S., Bringle, R. G., & McGuire, L.E. (2013). Attributes of high-quality research on service learning. In P. H. Clayton, R. G. Bringle, & J. A. Hatcher (Eds.), *Research on service learning: Conceptual frameworks and assessment* (Vol. 2A, pp. 27–53). Sterling, VA: Stylus.

Steinberg, K. S., Hatcher, J. A., & Bringle, R. G. (2011). Civic-minded graduate: A north star. *Michigan Journal of Community Service Learning, 18*(1), 19–33.

Strage, A. A. (2000). Service-learning: Enhancing student learning outcomes in a college-level lecture course. *Michigan Journal of Community Service Learning, 7,* 5–13.

Strand, K. J., Cutforth, N., Stoecker, R., Marullo, S., & Donohue, P. (2003). *Community-based research and higher education: Principles and practices.* Hoboken, NJ: John Wiley & Sons.

Tashakkori, A., & Creswell, J. W. (2007). Editorial: Exploring the nature of research questions in mixed methods research. *Journal of Mixed Methods Research, 1,* 207–211.

Trochim, W. M. (2005). *Research methods: The concise knowledge base.* Cincinnati, OH: Atomic Dog.

U.S. Department of Education. (2003). *Identifying and implementing educational practices supported by rigorous evidence: A user friendly guide.* Washington, DC: U.S. Department of Education.

Van de Ven, A. H. (2007). *Engaged scholarship: A guide for organizational and social research.* New York, NY: Oxford University Press.

Vogelgesang, L. J., & Astin, A. W. (2000). Comparing the effects of community service and service-learning. *Michigan Journal of Community Service Learning, 7*(1), 25–34.

Warren, J. L. (2012). Does service-learning increase student learning? A meta-analysis. *Michigan Journal of Community Service Learning, 18*(2), 56–61.

Yorio, P. L., & Ye, F. (2012). A meta-analysis on the effects of service-learning on the social, personal, and cognitive outcomes of learning. *Academy of Management Learning and Education, 11*(1), 9–27.

Zhao, X., Lynch, J. G., & Chen, Q. (2010). Reconsidering Baron and Kenny: Myths and truths about mediation analysis. *Journal of Consumer Research, 37,* 197–206.

QUALITATIVE RESEARCH ON SERVICE LEARNING AND STUDENT CIVIC OUTCOMES

Susan R. Jones and Zak Foste

"Understanding diversity" is a sought-after outcome of service learning and civic education initiatives. In a pre- and post-survey administered to students in a service learning course, an instructor was dismayed to see that the student self-reported ratings for "understanding diversity" declined. However, in follow-up interviews conducted, the instructor determined that students were actually expressing a more complex view of what *understanding diversity* entailed. Several students indicated that prior to the course they had a good grasp on diversity, got along well with people different from themselves, and thought the university was doing too much to "jam this down our throats." After the course, students articulated an awareness of their prior short-sighted perspectives and recognized that there was a lot they did not understand after interacting with others and gaining insight into the day-to-day realities of a particular community which was dealing with racism, inequitable distribution of resources, and discriminatory public policies. This scenario provides one example of what can be gained by qualitative approaches when considering civic outcomes, particularly when depth of understanding and insight into why particular dynamics occur are sought.

An overarching consideration addressed in this chapter focuses on what is gained by using qualitative approaches to investigate civic outcomes. These outcomes include the ability to explore diverse perspectives, cultures, and world views; respect for different life experiences; intercultural competence; critical thinking; and commitment to contribute to the community and address social issues (National Task Force on Civic

Learning and Democratic Engagement, 2012). Qualitative approaches enable a more robust inquiry into the "messiness" (Hui, 2009, p. 22) of learning and outcomes related to service learning experiences, the nuances of particular phenomena, the processes that lead to specific outcomes as well as the outcomes themselves, the diversity of experiences, and the rich contexts that provide the scaffolding for civic outcomes to emerge. Stated succinctly, "the overarching purpose of qualitative inquiry is to understand action-in-context" (Demerath, 2006, p. 98) and is driven by "the primacy of meaning-making in human social life" (p. 101).

Despite the growing number of published studies addressing service learning and civic outcomes using qualitative approaches (Battistoni, 2013), there persists a lack of knowledge about what constitutes high-quality qualitative research, which can lead to an undervaluing of this approach. A "prevailing sentiment is that real scientists conduct quantitative research and that anyone can do qualitative work" (Jones, Torres, & Arminio, 2014, p. 198). The best strategy to combat this view and misunderstanding is to grasp the fundamentals involved in conducting high-quality, rigorous qualitative research. In this chapter, we present hallmarks of high-quality qualitative research and discuss the unique contribution of qualitative inquiry to deepen an understanding of student civic outcomes. We then use these hallmarks as criteria to evaluate published research on civic outcomes, highlighting three studies as exemplars. Finally, we conclude with recommendations for conducting high-quality qualitative research.

Hallmarks of Qualitative Research

Qualitative research is defined by certain elements that distinguish it from quantitative approaches (chapter 3.1). Although many scholars rely on a dichotomous portrayal of quantitative and qualitative approaches, this depiction is an oversimplification that does not acknowledge the more significant paradigmatic distinctions underlying different ways of knowing. Lather (2007) and Glesne (2011) discuss these paradigmatic distinctions in relation to the purposes of the research in each. For example, research grounded in a positivist or postpositivist tradition emphasizes prediction, whereas research framed by interpretivism highlights understanding. Each paradigm or worldview implies a perspective on the nature of reality and assumptions about how knowledge is generated. For example, positivism emphasizes reality as measurable and discoverable, and thus research is seen as objective and value neutral. By contrast, constructivism and interpretivism depend upon views of reality as socially constructed and an outgrowth of human interaction. This research approach illuminates participants' understanding and meaning making (Jones et al., 2014). Most research considered qualitative is grounded in constructivist/interpretivist, critical, or poststructural worldviews. Regardless of the approach, rigorous procedures are necessary in both quantitative and qualitative research on service learning to deepen understanding and improve practice in this "inherently integrative practice" of combining service and learning (Patton, 2012, p. 3).

Space constraints prevent a full presentation of all the defining characteristics of qualitative inquiry. Table 3.2.1 provides a snapshot of many key elements, and we provide a brief discussion of each.

Qualitative research is said to be *naturalistic* because it depends upon the scrutiny of real-life situations in particular settings, thus emphasizing social action and context. As defined by Owen (2008), *naturalistic inquiry* "is based upon the notion that context is essential for understanding human behavior" (p. 547). Elaborating on the primary goal of deep understanding, Schwandt (2001) suggested that naturalistic inquiry "emphasizes that this kind of understanding can be forthcoming only from firsthand, eyewitness accounts of 'being there'" (p. 173). Context is central in qualitative inquiry as is participants' meaning-making, which provides an *emic* or insider's point of view; therefore, qualitative designs are valued as more *emergent* than quantitative studies. This in no way means that "anything goes" or that the researcher has no plan, but instead that the researcher remains open to what is learned in the field and is responsive to what happens in the research setting. This kind of flexibility takes skill and professional judgment as the researcher balances a specific purpose of a study with the issues.

TABLE 3.2.1
Key Hallmarks of Qualitative Inquiry

Design Strategies	• Naturalistic inquiry • Emergent design flexibility • Purposeful sampling
Data Collection and Fieldwork Strategies	• Qualitative data • Personal experience and engagement • Empathic neutrality and mindfulness • Dynamic systems perspective
Analysis Strategies	• Unique case orientation • Inductive analysis and creative synthesis • Holistic perspective • Context sensitivity • Reflexivity: Perspective and voice • Use of theory

Note. Adapted from Patton's (2015) Themes of Qualitative Inquiry.

Sampling in qualitative research is always *purposeful* and dependent upon the identification of *information-rich cases*. Patton (2015) notes that the differences between quantitative and qualitative research are most distinct in the logics and strategies of sampling. The random-sampling logic of quantitative research is intended to produce large numbers of participants and results that may be generalized. By contrast, qualitative samples are purposefully selected with an emphasis on information-rich cases that hold the potential for in-depth understanding of a particular phenomenon of interest (Jones et al., 2014). Researchers grounded in random samples often question qualitative researchers about *bias* in sampling. However, as Morse (2007) pointed out, "excellent qualitative inquiry is inherently biased" because participants are "deliberately sought and selected" (p. 107). Qualitative researchers must provide criteria for sampling and a rationale for sampling decisions. This is particularly important when research is conducted in one's "backyard," where an overreliance upon convenience for sampling may be either real or perceived. What constitutes a purposeful sample is also influenced by methodological approaches (e.g., grounded theory, ethnography, narrative inquiry, case study research designs). In other words, who a researcher is looking for as participants is guided by the focus and outcome of the study. Finally and importantly, the quality of data collected is inextricably linked to who is in the sample.

Qualitative data generally come from participants' narratives, observations, photographs and artifacts, and/or documents. The data collection strategies should fit the purpose of the study, the methodological approach selected, the questions the researcher seeks to answer, and the context in which the research is situated. Qualitative data tell a story that is distinctly different than one told through statistical analyses. These stories should provide enough *rich description* that the reader is able to see how the researcher arrived at claims and be transported to the particular place and setting and develop a deeper understanding of the setting. In order to obtain good qualitative data researchers must fully immerse themselves "in the field," whether through establishing rapport with participants in interviews or by entering a community as a participant observer. As Patton (2015) summarized:

> Qualitative inquiry means going into the field—into the real world of programs, organizations, neighborhoods, street corners—and getting close enough to the people and circumstances there to capture what is happening. This makes possible description and understanding of *both* externally observable behaviors and internal states (worldviews, opinions, values, attitudes, and symbolic constructs). (p. 56)

Patton (2015) advocates for a researcher's stance of *empathic neutrality and mindfulness* to accomplish immersion in qualitative research settings. Empathic neutrality is the ability to remain open and nonjudgmental relative to what a participant communicates while also maintaining rapport, trust, and attentiveness. Qualitative inquiry also emphasizes *processes,* which are presumed to be ever-changing and dynamic. Unlike quantitative approaches that seek to control for change and extraneous variables, qualitative researchers acknowledge that their data reflect the realities of change and dynamic systems that are a part of everyday life in all contexts (Patton, 2015).

Some qualitative researchers make the mistake of thinking data analysis is simply reporting out what participants said about the service learning experience or what was observed, and then generating themes. However, data analysis is a much more complicated and structured process that involves coding, describing, interpreting, and theorizing data—all of which is connected to the focus of the study and prior research decisions. More specifically, the steps involved in analyzing data for a multisite case study and the presentation of findings should look different from those for a narrative inquiry. Although the researcher is influential in the analytic process, there should be a clear trail from the data presented to the claims and interpretations made in the findings.

Whether or not the focus of the study is on individuals, a specific case, a culture-sharing group, stories, or the essence of a particular phenomenon in a service learning setting, qualitative data analysis involves an *inductive* approach, meaning that it begins in the unique cases under study "and builds toward general patterns. Categories or dimensions of analysis emerge from open-ended observations as the inquirer comes to understand patterns that exist in the phenomenon being investigated" (Patton, 2015, p. 64). The outcomes of qualitative data analysis should provide a holistic perspective on the phenomenon of interest, which includes careful attention to the context in which the particular phenomenon is situated. A holistic perspective refers both to the importance of putting parts together into a new whole through the analytic process, which assumes context as essential, as well as understanding that all elements of the research design are interrelated. Reflexivity is essential to the qualitative research process and helps to assure the trustworthiness of one's findings. *Reflexivity* refers to an ongoing process of researcher self-scrutiny by "examining one's personal and theoretical commitments to determine how they serve as resources for generating particular data, for behaving in particular ways vis-à-vis respondents and participants, and for developing particular interpretations" from the data collected (Schwandt, 2001, p. 224). Strategies to maintain reflexivity include a research journal, member checking with participants, critically examining one's own positionality in relation to the topic and research setting, and triangulation in data analysis.

Some confusion exists relative to the role of theory in qualitative research due to the lack of a single right approach. The use of theory depends in part upon one's methodological choice (e.g., phenomenology versus grounded theory). Even so, no researcher starts with a blank slate. Theories inform how researchers approach a particular topic and the kinds of questions they seek to address. Jones and colleagues (2014) distinguish between what they refer to as a *theoretical framework*, which comes from prior scholarly literature and theories related to one's topic (in a study related to civic outcomes, this could be identity theory or social participation theory) and a *theoretical perspective*, which influences all elements of the research design, including data analysis (such as feminist theory or symbolic interactionism). The cautionary note is that most often qualitative researchers do not approach studies with an interest in confirming certain hypotheses or an intention to look for a specific response because this would be counter to the emergent, open, and particularistic emphases in qualitative research. Jackson and Mazzei (2012) convey that "thinking with theory . . . illustrates how knowledge is opened up and proliferated rather than foreclosed and simplified" (p. vii).

Unique Contributions of Qualitative Research to Civic Outcomes in Service Learning

Brandenberger (2013) urged service learning scholars to examine not only the outcomes of service learning on college student development, but also how such development occurs. He explained, "more is known about service learning outcomes than how the associated changes take place" (p. 148). Further, Brandenberger noted that "it is not sufficient to survey students at the start and end of a course or program. What first caught students' attention about a social concern, and how did the students' thinking . . . begin to change?" (p. 148) provides a more productive line of inquiry.

These are the types of questions that are best suited for qualitative research. A review of current qualitative scholarship on service learning and civic outcomes highlights this point, as a large body of research attempts to answer "How?" and "Why?" questions. Although a number of quantitative studies underscore civic gains that result from participation in service learning experiences, such as an appreciation for diversity, political engagement, charitable responsibility, perspective-taking skills, and commitment to social action (Astin & Sax, 1998; Eyler & Giles, 1999; Mayhew & Engberg, 2011), qualitative research contextualizes this knowledge by illuminating the nature of development and how influences such as personal histories, social identities, power structures, and institutional arrangements influence civic development. Whereas quantitative work may address causality, predictions, and statistical relationships, qualitative studies hold the potential to highlight both civic outcomes and the processes that promote such change and learning.

High-quality qualitative research can both deepen understanding of civic outcomes and offer new theoretical possibilities for service learning educators. A growing number of qualitative studies yield findings related to civic outcomes, including a reduction of stereotypes (Catlett & Proweller, 2011; Eyler & Giles, 1999; Teranishi, 2007), clarification of personal values and beliefs (Jones & Abes, 2004), increases in perspective-taking (Giles, 2014; Kiely, 2004, 2005), awareness of privilege (Catlett & Proweller, 2011; Jones & Abes, 2004), appreciation for diversity (Jones & Hill, 2001), and knowledge of populations served (Long, 2003; Pasricha, 2008). In the following section we introduce three studies that serve as exemplars of qualitative research on civic outcomes in service learning.

Introduction to Three Exemplars

The three studies we selected as exemplars illustrate the hallmarks of qualitative scholarship discussed at the outset of this chapter. These studies offer considerable insight into research design and analysis as well as a presentation of results that provide readers with a depth of understanding consistent with exceptional qualitative research. Table 3.2.2 provides a synopsis of each exemplar using selected hallmarks of qualitative research.

We first examine the questions posed and what these questions tell us about a qualitative approach to understanding civic outcomes. After examining the purpose and results of each study individually, we then turn our attention to study designs, specifically addressing their use of theory, sampling considerations, data collection methods, and analysis.

Jones and Abes (2004) asked, "If service-learning does promote learning about the self, what is the nature of this learning and how is it sustained or integrated into one's evolving sense of self?" (p. 150). Interviewing students two to four years after their initial service learning experiences, Jones and Abes highlighted the nuanced experiences of participants, paying particular attention to the processes that contributed to identity development. Their results offered three themes pertaining to identity development: the relationship between self and other; emerging commitments to socially responsible work; and increased open-mindedness about new ideas, people, and experiences. Through increased reflection on the self in relation to others, participants

TABLE 3.2.2

Selected Exemplars from Published Qualitative Research

Selected Exemplar	Purpose of the Study	Representative Hallmarks
Jones & Abes (2004)	To explore the enduring influences of service learning on identity development and the potential of service learning to promote self-authorship	Emergent design flexibility Purposeful sampling Qualitative data Inductive analysis Context sensitivity
Kiely (2004)	To examine students' perspective transformation during and after participation in a Nicaragua international service learning program	Qualitative data Unique case orientation Inductive analysis and synthesis Use of theory
Yeh (2010)	To study service learning experiences of low-income, first-generation college students, and their relationship to students' overall college experiences	Purposeful sampling Qualitative data Reflexivity Use of theory

became increasingly aware of economic and educational privilege. Further, service became integral to how students understood themselves. Discussing the ways in which service learning influenced the relationship between self and other, Jones and Abes (2004) explained:

> Nearly all participants spoke explicitly about how their service-learning experiences caused them to reflect on their values, beliefs, and attitudes in a way very few other activities had encouraged. Their experiences working at the community service sites enabled them to reflect on their upbringing in typically homogenous environments and what, as a result, they had come to take for granted in their own lives. (p. 154)

Jones and Abes highlight the relationship between multiple contexts, including the influence of homogenous precollege environments and more diverse community service sites. They then introduce the process that occurred, wherein students were prompted to reflect on values and beliefs that were previously taken for granted due to such precollege socialization. To further illustrate this process, Jones and Abes drew on the words of one participant, Grace, who grew up in a small town with little exposure to difference, particularly of those from lower social classes. Grace explained:

> [Prior to the service-learning course], I didn't know very much about myself, just in general. And I mean the college experience has done a lot of that, but participating in my service-learning at [the AIDS service organization] and that stuff just taught me a lot about my identity. (p. 154)

A major contribution of this work is its ability to highlight how interactions with individuals different from oneself, particularly when one accounts for homogenous precollege environments, contribute to more complex and enhanced thinking about one's place in the world.

Kiely's (2004) longitudinal case study of transformative learning through international service learning explored "how 22 undergraduate students experienced perspective transformation from participating in a well-integrated international service-learning program with an explicit social justice orientation" (p. 6). As an example of qualitative research uncovering and describing a given process, Kiely's work on perspective transformation serves as an exemplar for service learning scholars. Although previous scholarship on perspective taking and service learning reported uniformly positive experiences, Kiely (2004) sought to complicate this understanding. He explained:

> By focusing on the short-term, positive nature of individual perspective transformation, prior research has indirectly fueled a romanticized and an uncritical acceptance that the students' intent to act on perspective transformation will often lead to persistent engagement in social action. (p. 8)

Kiely's (2004) study captured a complex process, wherein students expressed an intention to act, experienced perspective transformation, but nonetheless struggled to change their lifestyles in light of transformative learning. His results suggested a number of different ways students experienced perspective transformation, including moral, political, intellectual, cultural, personal, and spiritual. Through extensive data collection he was able to complicate static understandings of perspective transformation and also conceptualize what he called "the chameleon complex" (p. 14), which describes how participants struggled to live out new commitments upon reentry into the United States. The chameleon complex challenges "conceptual models and studies that assume students' perspective transformation in service-learning will follow a linear or developmental continuum from charity to social change" (p. 14). This finding suggests that students may struggle to act on their emerging global consciousness in large part because of conflict with peers, family, and coworkers as well as dominant norms around what it means to be a U.S. citizen. Kiely highlighted this process with a quote from one of his participants, Cara, who explained:

> When I returned from Nicaragua and tried to explain to a friend what I had experienced in Nicaragua and how it had changed me she didn't want to listen, she said—"oh, you'll get over that, it's because you just returned." Well, it's been almost six months and I haven't gotten over it. I still think about the conditions down there and I still think about her attitude and other friends who are more concerned with school and social life, not social change. I just don't say anything anymore. (p. 15)

Kiely captured with this quote the difficulties inherent in acting on one's newly formed perspectives. Upon returning home to the United States, Cara encountered resistance from her friends that led to a sense of alienation. Similar to the work of Jones and Abes (2004), such rich complexity and nuance would be difficult to capture through a pre/post survey design with quantitative measures.

Yeh's (2010) study illustrates how qualitative research can pay particular attention to a specific culture-sharing group, in this case low-income, first-generation (LIFG) students in service learning. She sought to understand the impact of service learning on LIFG students' skills, knowledge, and coping mechanisms that developed and how these skills influenced persistence in college. Interviewing six LIFG students, as well as service learning staff at two universities, Yeh offered a number of findings, including the development of a critical consciousness among participants and their ability to critique social structures, both of which are imperative for participation in a diverse, democratic society. Her study provided a number of firsthand accounts from students, centering the emic perspective that is a hallmark of qualitative research. For instance, she described how a trip to the U.S.–Mexico border during an immersion trip in Mexico was instrumental for one student, Miguel. Yeh drew on Miguel's words, as Brandenberger (2013) urged, to explore the process that led to a specific outcome. Miguel explained:

> When we were in Tijuana we were taken to the border and we got to see the border from a Mexican's perspective. Being raised as an American and seeing illegal immigration in a certain light and then all of sudden switching roles and seeing it from the opposite perspective was very difficult, because it is very apparent that there is no easy answer. (p. 58)

Miguel's quote illustrates an increased interest and willingness to critique inequitable social systems. It was these "eye-opening experiences" (p. 57), those which brought students into contact with diverse others, that often served as a catalyst for growth. Alex, another of Yeh's participants, found that his experiences in South Africa helped him further make sense of his identity as an African American and in turn prompted more critical reflection around issues of power and oppression.

Yeh did not try to generalize her findings to all service learning contexts but recognized the power of her study to enrich understanding. She explained that her intent was not to apply her results to all LIFG students in service learning, but "was instead a theory-building exercise meant to generate an in-depth understanding of the service-learning experience for LIFG students" (p. 53). This is to say that her purpose was not to prove anything, but to develop rich theoretical understandings that might apply across different contexts. For instance, drawing on Miguel's experiences illustrates how an event—in this case experiencing the border from a Mexican's perspective—challenged his previous assumptions and complicated his understandings of immigration, most notably as he recognized that there is no easy answer. In turn, Miguel developed a more sophisticated understanding of inequality by recognizing the importance of and incorporating multiple perspectives.

Exemplars and Specifics of Their Research Designs

The studies conducted by Jones and Abes (2004), Kiely (2004), and Yeh (2010) serve as exemplars not only because of their ability to highlight the complexity of service learning experiences on a range of civic outcomes, but also because of the high-quality design features they employed. Given the limitations of space we do not discuss each of the three exemplars in relation to the specifics of hallmarks of high-quality qualitative research design but instead provide examples.

Use of Theory

Qualitative research is both informed by and generates theory. In her study of LIFG students, Yeh (2010) drew on multiple theoretical frameworks to inform her work. In order to understand better how service learning participation influenced student persistence, she first used Tinto's (1993) theory of persistence and retention. Because her study centered on the experiences of students whose parents never attended college, Yeh also incorporated the constructs of social and cultural capital (Bourdieu, 1986; McDonough, 1997) as a means of understanding the networks, knowledge, and skills that are often necessary in navigating higher education for LIFG students. Additionally, because all the LIFG students were of color, Yeh drew on critical perspectives of service learning and retention. Yeh used the work of Maldonado, Rhoads, and Buenavista (2005), whose theory underscores unique features of persistence for students of color, including developing particular knowledge and skills, building community ties and commitments, and challenging social norms and institutions. These central constructs formed the conceptual framework for Yeh's study informing her research design as well as the interpretation of her findings. Yeh's study, demonstrates how scholars might not only use theory but also draw on multiple theories that successively build on one another. In this case, Tinto's (1993) framework of persistence offered an important foundation, but given that it is rooted in the experiences of White, middle-class students, additional theories were necessary to assure the understanding of students from very different backgrounds such as LIFG students.

Sampling Decisions

A hallmark of qualitative scholarship is its ability to create rich, descriptive accounts of a specific phenomenon. In order to construct such accounts, researchers must give serious consideration to their sample and how they will recruit participants. This is to say that samples "reflect the primary objective of depth of understanding of a particular phenomenon" (Jones, 2002, p. 464). Providing the reader with a rationale for how and why participants were selected is important for understanding the alignment of sampling with the research questions and the research design. All three of the exemplars included here provided a detailed account of the process of sampling (i.e., how they went about finding participants, describing the participants).

Jones and Abes (2004) described the initial difficulties they encountered in following up with participants from their first point of data collection. Because only three of the six original participants responded to the follow-up study one year later, Jones and Abes contacted additional students who fit their original criteria. Jones and Abes explained their sampling rationale, "specifically, each of these 8 had completed the service-learning course 2 to 4 years prior to this study, served at either the AIDS service organization or the neighborhood food pantry, and were recommended by the course instructors" (p. 152). Rather than sampling based on convenience, Jones and Abes maintained congruence with their original research questions, the overarching purpose of the study, and sampling criteria in order to expand their sample.

Yeh (2010) offered a detailed account of her purposive sampling procedures at the following levels: "(a) the institution (college or university), (b) the service-learning office or program, and (c) the individual student participants" (p. 53). Yeh described how she arrived at her sample (e.g., identifying institutions with a variety of socioeconomic statuses and reaching out to service learning providers for information-rich cases). She also presented additional criteria she used to select her sample such as participants' social identities, high schools attended, and whether students were currently completing their service experiences. In both cases, purposeful sampling was used in order to identify participants who could offer rich and descriptive insight into the topic of interest. Rather than randomly selecting participants, or choosing students out of convenience, both studies offered a clear set of criteria for sampling that aligned with the purpose of the study.

Data Collection Methods

Although some scholars may be tempted to simply identify interviews or participant observations as their means of data collection, all three studies presented as exemplars provided a more descriptive account of their methods. Jones and Abes (2004) discussed how they conducted in-depth, semistructured interviews with each participant and piloted the process with two students before conducting the study. They also provided a copy of the protocol before the interview, allowing participants time to process the questions in advance. Such an approach underscores the ways in which qualitative inquiry is a means of coconstruction between researcher and participant.

Both the Kiely (2004) and Yeh studies (2010) drew on multiple forms of data collection. Decisions about which data collection methods to use were grounded in the methodological approach and consistent with the purpose of the study so as to yield data that were relevant to the questions under investigation. Kiely employed document analysis, participant observation in country, and semistructured interviews. Document analysis included both trip documents and written reflections through student journals. Some argue that journals have the ability to "provide a direct path into the insights of participants" and "flow directly from the participant to the page" (Hatch, 2002, p. 141). Kiely (2004) also observed students during the international service trip, paying particular attention to "participant reactions to critical incidents, the physical setting, service activities, and social interaction" (p. 9). Observing participants in their natural settings can offer unique insights that might differ from the more formal setting of the interview, which can be construed as being a social event in itself, guided by power relations and the potential need for desired self-presentation (Miczo, 2003). The use of participant observation, in conjunction with individual interviews and document analysis, offered an added layer of data that was useful in describing how students experienced perspective transformation.

In addition to LIFG students, Yeh's (2010) study also interviewed service learning staff members as an additional source of data. Their situatedness offered a different perspective on students' development of a number of skills necessary for persistence. Drawing on sources beyond the student, such as service providers, instructors, and community members, provides important contributions to studies that focus on student growth and development and is referred to as triangulation of data (Patton, 2015).

Data Analysis

In addition to the use of theory, detailed data collection methods, and sampling considerations, all three of these studies provided a detailed account of their data analysis. Such an account is important because it lends credibility to the researcher's findings by providing the reader with a sense of how given interpretations of data were established. Jones and Abes (2004) relied on a grounded theory approach (Strauss & Corbin, 1998) and utilized the constant comparison method, which they indicated was most in line with their constructivist approach. Connecting their analysis techniques to their assumptions of knowledge, they noted, "because of the constructivist nature of the study, the analytic process moved from more concrete codes to abstract themes and categories that are reflective of the meanings the participants attached to their experiences" (Jones & Abes, 2004, pp. 152–153). Additionally, consistent with a grounded theory approach, Jones and Abes explained that the process of data analysis did not follow a linear sequence but rather evolved as the study progressed, highlighting the inductive nature of qualitative research.

Kiely (2004) also used grounded theory analysis, and he relied on the constant comparison method as well as creating case profiles for each student. Case profiles reflected data collected through field notes, student journals, and papers. The initial categories developed then served to inform post-trip interviews, highlighting the back-and-forth nature between data collection and data analysis central to qualitative work. Kiely also employed trustworthiness measures, including member checks, debriefing with peers, and an audit trail. All three of the exemplars presented here provided the reader with details related to how the researchers analyzed their data, a critical consideration given that in qualitative work the researcher is indeed an instrument.

Recommendations to Assure High-Quality Qualitative Research

The three studies offer illustrations of research consistent with the hallmarks of qualitative work presented earlier. Before concluding, we offer several suggestions for assuring high-quality research on civic outcomes in service learning. These suggestions are made in light of what we see as potential pitfalls of current qualitative work that invites criticism. These critiques could be mitigated through clearer articulation of research designs, utilization of existing theory, and avoidance of claims of generalizability.

Clearly Articulating Research Design

A review of qualitative work on service learning indicates that a glaring inconsistency exists in how authors articulate their research designs. Qualitative scholars of service learning should provide a methodological roadmap. The roadmap should be rooted in the researcher's fundamental assumptions about the nature of knowledge and reality, followed by corresponding methodological considerations, sampling procedures, data collection methods, and a description of how data were analyzed and interpreted. Researchers should reveal their paradigmatic assumptions and corresponding theoretical frameworks (Jones et al., 2014), which emphasizes that high-quality qualitative research involves much more than methods. Doing so allows the reader to understand methodological approaches and why specific data collection methods were utilized. A number of examples in published qualitative work on service learning exist where direct connections between paradigmatic assumptions, methodological approaches, and corresponding methods for data collection and analysis are absent. Although space is often limited in manuscripts and it is tempting to reduce design sections in order to have more room for results, researchers must paint a clear picture of how *they* arrived at their results.

Some qualitative studies reviewed for this chapter simply stated that interviews were conducted or final course papers were analyzed. This leaves the researcher open to a number of critiques. Why, for instance, were final course papers analyzed? Might a limitation be that students write course papers with a final grade in mind and write what they sense will be rewarded with a passing grade rather than what they really think? Similarly, why were interviews utilized as opposed to focus groups or participant observations in a community setting?

Furthermore, more explicit attention should be paid to sampling. As the exemplars illustrated, sampling is conducted in a purposeful way, with the goal being information-rich cases (Patton, 2015). Qualitative work on service learning can benefit from an articulation of sampling procedures, and more importantly, the rationales for sampling decisions in order to avoid what appears to be an overreliance on convenience samples. This is not to say that convenience samples are always inappropriate, but qualitative researchers should make the case for why such a sample is appropriate and what criteria were used to make sampling decisions.

Utilizing Existing Theory

A review of current studies underscores that not all qualitative researchers are thoroughly explaining the way theory informs their work. Giles and Eyler

(2013) challenged service learning scholars to anchor their studies in theories and advance theoretical understandings of the field. Qualitative research in particular is both guided by and has the potential to produce rich, nuanced theories of particular phenomena. Drawing on preexisting theory gives the researcher a language and framework to use in thinking about a study. Wolcott (2005) described theory as a way to "help researchers of any persuasion clarify and explain to others what they are up to" (p. 181). Bringle and Hatcher (2005) contended that much of the qualitative work on service learning is "more similar to journalism than to scientific research" (p. 35). Those engaged in qualitative inquiry should not cede what counts as science, and in turn must explain decisions made in research design, including theoretical perspectives (Demerath, 2006). For instance, Kiely (2004), in his study of perspective transformation, used Mezirow's (1991) theory of transformative learning to guide his thinking. Doing so firmly anchored his study in a conceptual framework and provided the reader with a frame of reference to broadly understand the concept of perspective transformation. Similarly, Yeh (2010) drew on several theories (i.e., cultural capital, retention and persistence, and critical service learning) to form a larger conceptual framework.

Avoiding Claims of Generalization

Finally, qualitative researchers in service learning and civic outcomes should be careful about claims related to the reach of their results. Qualitative scholarship is valuable to the field of service learning, particularly in its ability to generate rich and contextualized accounts. The value of qualitative studies is evaluated using criteria to evaluate the credibility of the research (Patton, 2012). The goal of qualitative work is not to generalize results, but rather to generate theoretical understandings of a particular phenomenon that may be transferred to other settings. As Patton (2015) emphasized, "What's desirable or hoped for in science (generalizations across time and space) runs into real-world considerations about what's possible" (pp. 710–711). The strength of this approach that emphasizes knowledge of the particular is that one can read a study and consider the findings within another context. Clandinin and Connelly (2000), writing specifically about narrative approaches to qualitative work, explained that researchers should "create texts that, when well done, offer readers a place to imagine their own uses and applications" (p. 42). That is, while not generalizable to other settings, qualitative research invites the reader to consider the transferability of such experiences to their own contexts (Jones et al., 2014), which becomes "that 'vicarious experience' that comes from reading a rich case account" and "contributes to the social construction of knowledge, which, in a cumulative sense, builds general, if not necessarily generalizable, knowledge" (Patton, 2015, p. 712). We agree with Luttrell's (2010) assertion that "the attention paid to particulars should be understood as a strength, not a weakness, of qualitative research" (p. 7). Qualitative researchers should recognize the strengths and contributions of creating descriptive accounts that can enrich understandings, rather than apologize for perceived limitations (Jones et al., 2014).

Conclusion

Qualitative research holds the potential to offer unique and significant contributions to an understanding of civic outcomes in higher education. We have highlighted hallmarks of qualitative research as guideposts to investigating important questions related to civic outcomes and to do so using an efficacious research process. We are not advancing an argument that qualitative research is always better than quantitative, but instead that what can be known and understood is different (chapter 3.1). Ultimately, if educators are to be most effective in promoting civic outcomes in higher education, then the most robust understanding possible of what works, for whom, how to increase the likelihood of desirable outcomes, and to what ends is needed. This kind of understanding requires multiple research approaches to create the most complete and holistic picture of civic outcomes.

References

Astin, A. W., & Sax, L. J. (1998). How undergraduates are affected by service participation. *Journal of College Student Development, 39*, 251–263.

Battistoni, R. M. (2013). Civic learning through service learning. In P. H. Clayton, R. G. Bringle, & J. A. Hatcher (Eds.), *Research on service learning: Conceptual frameworks and assessment* (Vol. 2A, pp. 111–132). Arlington, VA: Stylus.

Bourdieu, P. (1986). The forms of capital. In J. G. Richardson (Ed.), *Handbook of theory and research for the sociology of education* (pp. 241–258). New York: Greenwood Press.

Brandenberger, J. (2013). Investigating personal development outcomes in service learning: Theory and research. In P. H. Clayton, R. G. Bringle, & J. A. Hatcher (Eds.), *Research on service learning: Conceptual frameworks and assessments* (pp. 133–156). Sterling, VA: Stylus.

Bringle, R. G., & Hatcher, J. A. (2005). Service learning as scholarship: Why theory-based research is critical to service learning. *Acta Academica Supplementum, 3,* 24–44.

Catlett, B. S., & Proweller, A. (2011). College students' negotiation of privilege in a community-based violence prevention project. *Michigan Journal of Community Service Learning, 18*(1), 33–48.

Clandinin, D. J., & Connelly, F. M. (2000). *Narrative inquiry: Experience and story in qualitative research*. San Francisco, CA: Jossey-Bass.

Demerath, P. (2006). The science of context: Modes of response for qualitative researchers in education. *International Journal of Qualitative Studies in Education, 19*(1), 97–113.

Eyler, J., & Giles, Jr., D. E. (1999). *Where's the learning in service-learning?* San Francisco, CA: Jossey-Bass.

Giles, H. C. (2014). Risky epistemology: Connecting with others and dissonance in community-based research. *Michigan Journal of Community Service Learning, 20*(2), 65–78.

Giles, D. E., Jr., & Eyler, J. (2013). The endless quest for scholarly respectability in service-learning research. *Michigan Journal of Community Service Learning, 20*(1), 53–64.

Glesne, C. (2011). *Becoming qualitative researchers: An introduction* (4th ed.). Boston, MA: Pearson.

Hatch, A. (2002). *Doing qualitative research in educational settings*. Albany, NY: State University of New York Press.

Hui, S. M-Y. (2009, November/December). Difficult dialogues about service-learning: Embrace the messiness. *About Campus, 14*(5), 22–26.

Jackson, A. Y., & Mazzei, L. A. (2012). *Thinking with theory in qualitative research*. New York, NY: Routledge.

Jones, S. R. (2002). (Re)writing the word: Methodological strategies and issues in qualitative research. *Journal of College Student Development, 43*, 461–473.

Jones, S. R., & Abes, E. S. (2004). Enduring influences of service-learning on college students' identity development. *Journal of College Student Development, 45*, 149–166.

Jones, S. R., & Hill, K. (2001). Crossing High Street: Understanding diversity through community service-learning. *Journal of College Student Development, 42*, 204–216.

Jones, S. R., Torres, V., & Arminio, J. (2014). *Negotiating the complexities of qualitative research in higher education: Fundamental elements and issues* (2nd ed.). New York, NY: Routledge.

Kiely, R. (2004). A chameleon with a complex: Searching for transformation in international service-learning. *Michigan Journal of Community Service Learning, 10*(2), 5–20.

Kiely, R. (2005). A transformative learning model for service-learning: A longitudinal case study. *Michigan Journal of Community Service Learning, 12*(1), 5–22.

Lather, P. (2007). *Getting lost: Feminist efforts toward a double(d) science*. Albany, NY: State University of New York Press.

Long, D. R. (2003). Spanish in the community: Students reflect on Hispanic cultures in the United States. *Foreign Language Annals, 36*(20), 223–232.

Luttrell, W. (2010). Introduction: The promise of qualitative research in education. In W. Luttrell (Ed.), *Qualitative educational research: Readings in reflexive methodology and transformational practice* (pp. 1–10). New York, NY: Routledge.

Maldonado, D. E. Z., Rhoads, R., & Buenavista, R. L. (2005). The student-initiated retention project: Theoretical contributions and the role of self-empowerment. *American Educational Research Journal, 42*, 605–638.

Mayhew, M., & Engberg, M. (2011). Promoting the development of civic responsibility: Infusing service-learning practices in first-year "success" courses. *Journal of College Student Development, 52*, 20–38.

McDonough, P.M. (1997). *Choosing colleges: How social class and schools structure opportunity.* Albany, NY: State University of New York Press.

Mezirow, J. (1991). *Transformative dimensions of adult learning.* San Francisco, CA: Jossey-Bass.

Miczo, N. (2003). Beyond the "fetishism of words": Considerations on the use of the interview to gather chronic illness narratives. *Qualitative Health Research, 13,* 469–490.

Morse, J. M. (2007). Sampling in grounded theory. In A. Bryant & K. Charmaz (Eds.), *The SAGE handbook of grounded theory* (pp. 229–244). Thousand Oaks, CA: Sage.

National Task Force on Civic Learning and Democratic Engagement. (2012). *A crucible moment: College learning & democracy's future.* Washington DC: Association of American Colleges & Universities.

Owen, J. A. T. (2008). Naturalistic inquiry. In L. M. Given (Ed.), *The SAGE encyclopedia of qualitative research methods* (Vol. 2, pp. 547–550). Thousand Oaks, CA: SAGE.

Pasricha, A. (2008). Service learning and pluralism: Working with immigrants. *Journal of Family and Consumer Science, 100*(2), 49–52.

Patton, M. Q. (2015). *Qualitative research and evaluation methods* (4th ed.). Thousand Oaks, CA: SAGE.

Patton, M. Q. (2012). Improving rigor in service-learning research. In J. A. Hatcher & R. G. Bringle (Eds.), *Understanding service-learning and community engagement: Crossing boundaries through research* (pp. 3–10). Greenwich, CT: Information Age Publishing.

Schwandt, T. A. (2001). *Dictionary of qualitative inquiry* (2nd ed.). Thousand Oaks, CA: SAGE.

Strauss, A., & Corbin, J. (1998). *Basics of qualitative research: Grounded theory procedures and techniques* (2nd ed.). Newbury Park, CA: SAGE.

Teranishi, C. S. (2007). Impact on experiential learning on Latino college students' identity, relationships, and connectedness to the community. *Journal of Hispanic Higher Education, 6*(1), 52–72.

Tinto, V. (1993). *Leaving college: Rethinking the causes and cures of student attrition* (2nd ed.). Chicago, IL: University of Chicago Press.

Wolcott, H.F. (2005). *The art of fieldwork* (2nd ed.). Walnut Creek, CA: AltaMira Press.

Yeh, T. L. (2010). Service-learning and persistence of low-income, first-generation college students: An exploratory study. *Michigan Journal of Community Service Learning, 16*(2), 50–65.

INSTITUTIONAL CHARACTERISTICS AND STUDENT CIVIC OUTCOMES

Emily M. Janke and Jennifer M. Domagal-Goldman

To what extent does attendance at a particular college or university influence the likelihood of future civic engagement? To what extent does the college or university matter to student civic outcomes? Answers to these questions are intended to inform decisions that are pedagogical, practical, political, and personal. Related questions may include: What practices improve student learning and development outcomes? What structures, policies, and resources make a difference? What is the public value of higher education to taxpayers? Is this college a good fit for a given student and that student's commitment to civic engagement?

Institution-level effects, as they relate to student civic outcomes, are a specific subset of student outcomes that focus on students' knowledge, skills, attitudes, and behaviors related to their interactions with their communities and with others to make a difference in these communities. Which institutional characteristics make a difference in the likelihood that students vote in elections or volunteer for a nonprofit, among other civic outcomes? For example, is there a relationship between student civic outcomes and characteristics of the organizational structure of the campus, such as size of enrollment, selectivity, demographic composition, or public/private governance? Alternatively, does a relationship exist between certain elements of the organizational context, such as types of policies and practices related to faculty scholarship and culture that may include promotion, tenure, and reappointment policies as well as faculty workloads and articulated civic outcomes for students? Are student civic outcomes connected to the presence of a central community engagement office on campus and whether such an office

261

has directors with faculty lines or student affairs appointments? Knowing what differences exist among the effects of varying institutional structures, policies, and cultures on student civic outcomes is an important first step in designing institution-wide plans to improve such outcomes. Identifying potential levers for change can surface recommendations for strategic planning and intentional decision-making and action by institutional members.

Literature Review

On the whole, very few studies examine *institutional effects*, or what are also termed *between-college effects* (Pascarella & Terenzini, 1991, 2005), on student outcomes. These include considering the institutional climate as shaped by the organizational structures, policies, and practices and faculty, staff, and student experiences and cultures. Even fewer studies focus on civic outcomes specifically (Finley, 2011). Additionally, the terminology used to describe and study the connections between certain characteristics of a higher education institution (HEI) on student civic outcomes is confusing, as terms are often used synonymously when clearer distinctions would improve conceptual clarity. For instance, scholars may use the terms *institutional* and *organizational* interchangeably when describing characteristics of an HEI. In this chapter, we use *institutional* when discussing an HEI as a single proper entity and *organizational* to address the features and functions that make up the work of an institution.

Additionally, the terms *climate, culture, context, experience, environment,* and *ethos* are also regularly used synonymously in student outcomes literature with little to no construct definition. The proliferation and conflation of terms can make it difficult to understand whether meaningful differences exist in *philosophy, phenomenology, methodology,* or *practical application*. At a minimum, introducing the various terms is likely to give pause to readers and researchers as to whether their interpretation of the ideas aligns with the intentions of the authors. This also creates challenges in understanding and synthesizing the literature as well as presenting it in a review such as this. Throughout this chapter we define these terms and articulate the importance of each in relationship to student civic outcomes.

Input-Environment-Outcomes

Conceptual understanding of institutional effects on student outcomes has been grounded for the past three decades in Astin's (1993) Input-Environment-Outcomes (I-E-O) conceptual approach depicted in Figure 3.3.1 (e.g., Barnhardt, Sheets, & Pasquesi, 2015; Bowman, 2014; Kisker,

Figure 3.3.1. Comprehensive model of influences on student learning and persistence.

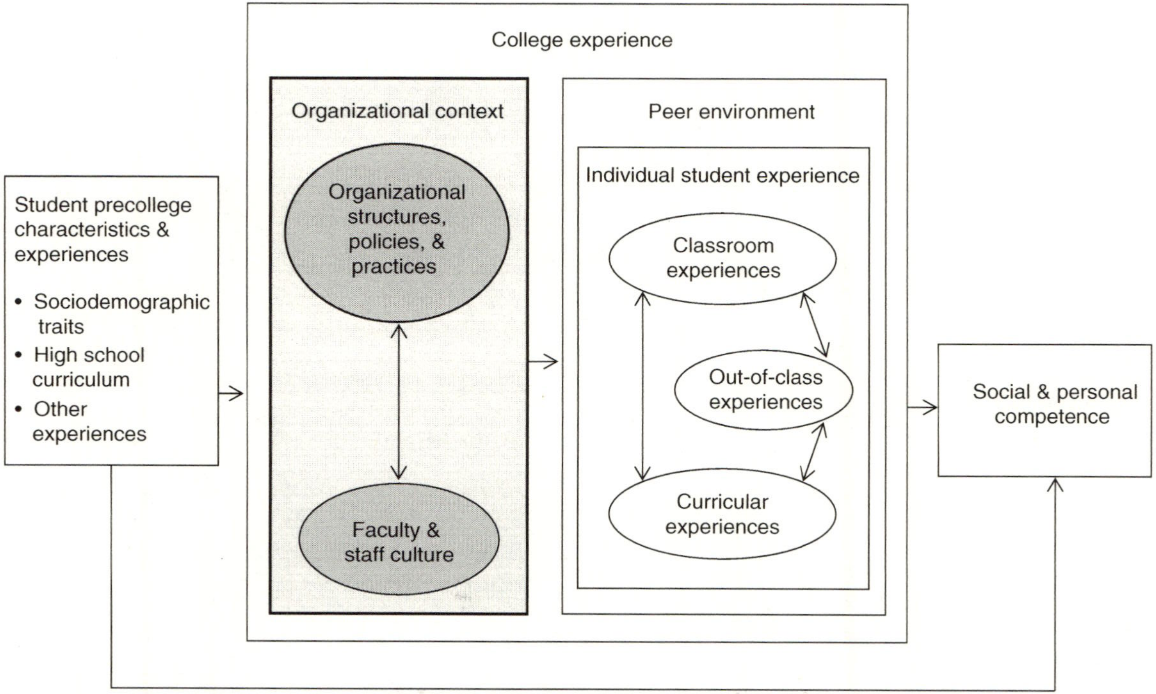

Source. Adapted from Terenzini & Reason (2005) as cited in Reason, Terenzini, & Domingo (2007).

Figure 3.3.2. Comprehensive model of institutional climate on student civic outcomes.

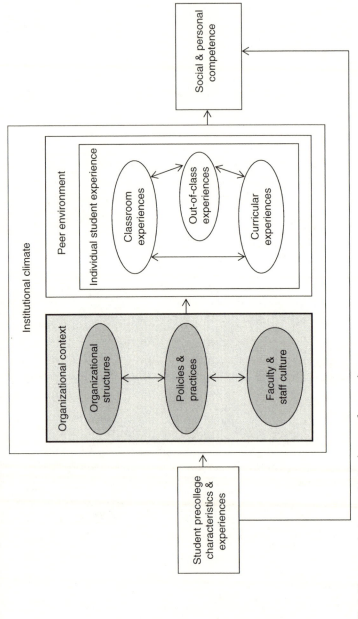

Note. Shaded box to emphasize organizational context focus on chapter.

Source. Adapted from Reason, Terenzini, and Domingo (2007).

Weintraub, & Newell, 2015; Pascarella & Terenzini, 1991, 2005; Pike, Kuh, & Gonyea, 2003; Reason, Terenzini, & Domingo, 2007; Terenzini & Reason, 2005). The I-E-O approach hypothesizes that students come to higher education with a range of demographic, personal, and academic characteristics and experiences (*input*). While enrolled in college, students interact with peers and experience various aspects of the institution, including curricular, classroom, and out-of-class experiences and conditions (*environment*). The dynamics that occur between the personal characteristics and campus characteristics result in student learning and development (*outcomes*).

The I-E-O conceptual approach introduced, among other ideas, the inclusion of institutional characteristics, along with students' curricular and cocurricular experiences, as part of their environment—or as we label it, organizational context—that influences student outcomes. Although the I-E-O framework includes many potential influences on student outcomes, this chapter focuses narrowly on the organizational context: the features and functions that shape the work of the institution.

A "Fourth Domain": Organizational Context

In several studies, Terenzini and Reason (Reason et al., 2007; Terenzini & Reason, 2005) argue for research on organizational context as an "often overlooked fourth domain" (Reason et al., 2007, p. 276) in the study of student outcomes. Based on findings from Pascarella and Terenzini's meta-analyses (1991, 2005) and subsequent research (e.g., Barnhardt et al., 2015; Terenzini & Reason, 2005), this additional domain refines and extends the environment component of Astin's I-E-O approach to suggest a more comprehensive and integrated view of students' experiences while attending an HEI. The organizational context comprises "an institution's organizational characteristics, structures, policies, and practices, and the campus's faculty and peer cultures and environments" (Reason et al., 2007, p. 276) (see Figure 3.3.1). Hence, the model suggests that students come to an HEI with a range of demographic, personal, and academic characteristics and experiences. These precollege characteristics may influence how students experience the HEI that they attend, including (a) curricular, classroom, and out-of-class experiences and conditions, which are shaped by (b) their peer environment, and (c) organizational contexts. Together, precollege characteristics and the college experience are likely to affect students' social and personal competence outcomes.

For the purpose of advancing research and practice in student civic outcomes, we offer an adapted version of Terenzini and Reason's (2005) model (see Figure 3.3.2). Because we are specifically interested in student civic outcomes, we are focused not on the broad ways in which students experience campus, but specifically on students' perceptions of their experience and the organizational structures, policies, and practices of their institutions as they relate to all things civic. For the purpose of emphasizing focus on institutional factors that may affect student civic outcomes, specifically, we have renamed "college experience" to "institutional climate." Organizational context is comprised of two distinct but related aspects: (a) organizational structures, and (b) organizational policies and practices. This decision to "pull apart" the initially single construct of organizational context is motivated by research findings that suggest distinct differences in regard to significance, or whether a connection likely exists between student civic outcomes and these constructs.

Institutional Climate

Institutional climate is the way in which students, faculty, staff, and other self-described members of the institution view and interpret institutional structures, policies, programs, practices, and cultures. It is the various meanings that members ascribe to "interrelated bundles" of experiences they have within the context of the institution (Schneider, Ehrhart, & Macey, 2013, p. 13). Hence, the focus on institutional climate places importance on meaning-making about experiences to create perceptions; experience alone is not sufficient.

Organizational culture is defined as the basic assumptions about the world and values that guide life in an organization (Schneider et al., 2013). Organizational culture and organizational climate are different constructs. Cameron (2008) clarifies the differences in her comparison of each to the other:

> Climate refers to temporary attitudes, feelings, and perceptions of individuals (Schneider, 1990). Culture is an enduring, slow to change, core characteristic of organizations; climate, because it is based on attitudes, can change quickly and dramatically. Culture refers to implicit, often indiscernible aspects of organizations; climate refers to more overt, observable attributes of organizations. Culture includes core values and consensual interpretations about how things are; climate includes individualistic perspectives that are modified frequently as situations change and new information is encountered. (p. 432)

Throughout this chapter, then, we differentiate between the terms *climate* and *culture*. We opted to use the term *climate* to describe members' perspectives and opinions of what the institution is about and what it stands for, and we use *culture* to describe the core values that are embodied within the organization and communicated and reified through faculty, staff, and student interactions and interpretations. This decision is based on institutional climate research described in the following sections, though future research will further clarify in what ways meaningful distinctions exist within a campus and across campuses.

Research on organizational, faculty, and student climate is a rich area of higher education scholarship that has been used by provosts, presidents, and other HEI leaders to understand members' experiences and perceptions of the institution. Climate studies may be administered to understand specific areas or outcomes of interest, such as openness and support for diversity (e.g., Rankin, Blumenfeld, Weber, & Frazer, 2010; Reason et al., 2007), and personal and social responsibility (e.g., Ryder, Reason, Mitchell, Gillon, & Hemer, 2015). An institution's climate related to a certain value or interest is important for understanding the aggregated experiences, attitudes, and behaviors of its members.

The Personal Social Responsibility Inventory (PSRI) is one climate tool that suggests the relevance of institutional climate on student civic outcomes. The PSRI is an institutional inventory that assesses students' self-reported behaviors and perceptions of campus climate along five dimensions of personal and social responsibility for college students, including "striving for excellence, cultivating academic integrity, contributing to a larger community, taking seriously the perspectives of others, and developing competence in ethical and moral reasoning and action" (Ryder et al., 2015, p. 5). Exploring data collected from the PSRI, Ryder and colleagues (2015) found via a multilevel modeling approach that civic-related student outcomes like openness to diversity and conflict are positively related to students' perceptions of the learning climate on campus. Although some of this may be due to self-selection into institutions, and the study is limited to the extent that it included only 15 institutions, the finding suggests the need for continued investigation into the effects of institution-level characteristics, particularly climate, on student civic outcomes.

Organizational Structures

One of the three dimensions of organizational context is structure. Organizational structures are the relatively fixed features and characteristics of an institution and include measures such as type of control (public/private), size, mission, urbanicity (i.e., urban, suburban, rural), admissions selectivity (e.g., SAT or ACT score), and racial/ethnic demographics. In their meta-analysis Pascarella and Terenzini (2005) repeatedly used the terms *modest*, *inconsistent*, and *unconvincing* to describe differences among various student outcomes, including cognitive development, academic performance, psychosocial and attitudinal change, and persistence, as they related to institutional type, size, and racial and gender composition. These conclusions were used for the studies they reviewed on civic development generally, though because between-college effects were written as summaries of large reviews, it is not always clear which studies specifically examined between college effects on student civic development.

Organizational structure variables are often confounded with other institutional characteristics that describe policies and practices (Pascarella & Terenzini, 2005). For example, when examining selective liberal arts colleges what is the influencing factor in the admissions process—the private control in terms of governance and funding, the liberal arts curriculum, or selectivity? Determining plausible and statistically significant measures of what characteristics make a difference in student outcomes is challenging. Ultimately, organizational structures, such as institution type, may be too remote from the student experience to have much, if any, relationship to student learning (Astin, 1993; Dey et al., 1997; Pascarella & Terenzini, 1991, 2005; Reason et al., 2007), despite some findings that suggest potential correlations (e.g., Lott, 2013). On the whole, organizational context is more complex and dynamic than can be described by organizational structures alone; context is shaped by organizational policies and practices, as well as by faculty and staff cultures.

Organizational Policies and Practices
Although researchers are somewhat dubious about the level of the impact of an institution's organizational structures, such as public/private, size, mission, and selectivity on student outcomes (e.g., Astin, 1993; Dey et al., 1997; Pascarella & Terenzini, 1991, 2005), they note that organizational policies, practices, and cultures (Kuh, Kinzie, Schuh, Whitt, & Associates, 2005) are likely to have relatively more, and possibly statistically significant, influences on student learning outcomes (Pascarella & Terenzini, 2005; Reason et al., 2007). To the extent that an institution's characteristics interact in some meaningful way with what students do while attending college, it is plausible, and perhaps likely, that these characteristics may subsequently influence student outcomes (Kuh et al., 2005). Some promising evidence exists for linkages between organizational policies and practices and student civic outcomes. Organizational policies are codified guidelines for how campus stakeholders are expected to interact and engage with their institution and include student recruitment, admissions, enrollment, and curriculum policies that shape students' academic pathways as well as faculty and staff recruitment, hiring, workload, and review and reward policies such as promotion and tenure.

Organizational policies that pertain to students' experiences within the institution shape students' perceptions about the values and expectations of the institution. Organizational policies may include whether service learning or community-engaged academic experiences are mandatory for completion of general education, well-integrated into disciplinary majors, or required for graduation. Other examples include whether community service is incorporated into orientation, first-year, and residential experiences and the policies that govern the extent to which students have voice and decision-making authority in institutional governance. Policies shape important ways in which an institution encourages and includes student engagement in academic, cocurricular, and extracurricular programming (Pascarella & Terenzini, 2005).

Organizational policies related to faculty and staff may also affect students to the extent that such policies shape the way in which faculty and staff interact with students. Policies may encourage or discourage faculty and staff interactions with students outside of the classroom. These policies may include providing paid time for staff to participate in alternative break trips with students or rewarding service learning and other forms of community-engaged scholarship in promotion, tenure, and reappointment policies. Our review of the student civic outcomes literature reveals very little about the effect of the presence of organizational policies on student civic outcomes within or across institutions.

Organizational practices are the ways in which organizational members act on behalf of the institution to operationalize its policies and work more generally. Examples of practices that might be relevant to student civic outcomes include how an institution's civic mission is expressed in its orientation events and campus rituals, how campus leaders talk about and include the local community in campus life, and the degree to which a campus tends to include students in important conversations and student voice in decision-making. We point out a relative dearth in this research area as much of the literature is focused on specific teaching pedagogies (e.g., service learning) and structured out-of-classroom experiences. One promising example, however, is the National Study of Learning, Voting, and Engagement at Tufts University. This study, which measures student voter turnout in midterm and presidential-year election cycles, is examining the organizational policies and practices of institutions with higher-than-predicted student voter turnout to determine what role organizational context might play on this aspect of student civic outcomes (Brower & Benenson, 2015).

Faculty and Staff Culture

Terenzini and Reason's (2005) model focuses on faculty culture to the exclusion of other professionals, such as academic affairs staff, student affairs staff, librarians, and instructional technology professionals, but the model presented here includes a broader array of higher education staff as relevant and pertinent to understanding organizational context and students' experiences. For example, professional staff may teach courses, and they may assume meaningful roles in facilitating students' service learning and cocurricular experiences with communities. Therefore, faculty and staff culture is an important component of an organization's context as their perceptions of institutional policies and practices (i.e., faculty culture) shape faculty and staff interactions with students. In this way, the faculty and staff members may be viewed by students as an embodiment of the campus's values and ethos. Faculty and staff culture as it relates to service learning, but academic work more broadly, is shaped by faculty and staff members' views and interpretations of the values conveyed by organizational policies and practices as well as those of their own academic and professional disciplines (e.g., Holland, 1999; O'Meara & Jaeger, 2006).

One illustrative example of how faculty culture is associated with student outcomes is found in the literature on students' openness to diversity, an important civic outcome. Reason, Cox, Quaye, and Terenzini (2010) examined faculty and institutional factors that "promote (student) encounters with difference" (p. 392) in first-year courses, as research shows that more frequent and higher quality encounters with diverse ideas, worldviews, and people can positively enhance students' civic and community involvement (Pascarella & Terenzini, 2005; Terenzini & Reason, 2005). Reason and colleagues (2010) found a positive and significant correlation between faculty promoting student encounters with difference and the extent to which faculty members perceived institutional emphasis on teaching, and specifically, institutional support for active teaching and assessment pedagogies. We did not find research that specifically examined the correlation between faculty and staff culture and student civic outcomes; however, research on how organizational structures, policies, and practices interact with faculty attitudes and behaviors toward civic and community engagement supports the expectation that such organizational structures may play an important role in faculty members' choosing a campus for employment as well as valuing, expressing, and practicing democratic and engaged pedagogies (Domagal-Goldman, 2010; Holland, 1999; O'Meara, 2011; O'Meara & Jaeger, 2006; Saltmarsh et al., 2009). These faculty and staff cultures are subsequently conveyed to students through in and out of class interactions.

On the whole, the body of research on the effect of institutional characteristics on student learning and development generally, and civic outcomes specifically, is relatively sparse and the findings are limited in regard to generalizability. Even in the most robust studies, institutional participants tend to come from only one or a few institutional types. This leads to a decreased ability to describe differences across institutional types, though admittedly it allows for greater understanding of particular types of institutions and their effects on student civic outcomes. Findings may ultimately be representative regardless of classification type; however, further research is required before generalizing across types. The dearth of such research is likely related to the complexity of institution-level research on student outcomes, especially if one attempts to study between institution effects (see chapter 3.6). The consequence of these limitations is that understanding of institutional effects on student civic outcomes is not conclusive; we must bring new light to bear on initial findings before drawing firm conclusions. In the following section we describe several broad research areas that warrant further inquiry and investigation.

Recommendations for Future Research

The literature review reveals the need for deeper understanding about institutional characteristics and organizational contexts and understanding how these sets of variables influence student civic learning and development. This section suggests recommended research areas and identifies important questions as well as approaches to improve research.

Building a Theory Base

Much of the research on institution-level effects on student outcomes is correlational research. The approach is used to identify whether relationships among factors are present, but it does not attempt to explain causation. A psychosocial cognitive approach, or how individuals think of and make sense of the world around them (e.g., Albert & Whetten, 1985; Scott, 2003; Weick, 1995), may be applied to the study of the interplay among institutional characteristics, faculty and staff culture, and student learning outcomes (Kezar, 2014). Psychosocial theories and findings extend beyond the more traditional focus on students' psychological beliefs to emphasize the processes through which students make meaning of their campus's climates—what campuses expect of them (Barnhardt et al., 2015; chapter 2.1). These theories posit that students' awareness and perceptions of an institution's policies and practices interact with and inform students' beliefs about an institution's climate, which then influences students' attitudes and behaviors (e.g., Kuh et al., 2005; Reason et al., 2010; Reason et al., 2007).

Suggesting the importance of student *perception* of civic context, and cognition's role as a mediating variable, Barnhardt, Sheets, and Pasquesi (2015), in a mixed-methods study of students' civic commitments and capacities for community action, found that institutional messages that advocate prosocial civic qualities may contribute, among other things, to student civic outcomes. Applying both social identity and organizational theories, the researchers suggest that, controlling for precollege characteristics, campus contexts (campus size and selectivity), and college experiences (composite measures of curricular, cocurricular, and out-of-class experiences), "students' acquisitions of commitments to and skills for contributing to the larger community are largely influenced by *the extent to which students perceive their campus as one that advocates for its students to be active and involved citizens*" (p. 622, emphasis added). That is, students who see their institution's faculty, administrators, and students advocating for civic actions, particularly in community-engaged classrooms and common spaces, are more likely to acquire the skills for and be committed to contributing civically to their communities.

In another study developed at De Anza College, early analysis of self-report survey data collected from more than 1,750 student surveys at nine community colleges suggest that institutional intentionality (civic engagement being stated in the institution's mission and goals statements) positively and significantly correlated with whether students correctly answered questions about civics, suggesting increased civic knowledge. Also supporting, indirectly, the role of faculty culture in organizational context, the study found that higher levels of full-time faculty also positively and significantly correlated to students' civic agency and civic knowledge (Kisker, Newell, & Weintraub, 2016). Student exposure to campus-based public advocacy likely influenced students' own perceptions of their civic skills and social responsibility.

Together, these studies suggest important campus practices and processes that may be mediating influences in the effective development of student civic engagement, hence supporting Pascarella and Terenzini's (2005) claim that in determining the effects of institutional climate on student learning and development, "causal mechanisms are probably more indirect than direct, mediated by other factors, such as by peer environments *and student perceptions of their institutions' priorities*" (p. 598, emphasis added).

Investigations into how institutional climates and organizational contexts are interpreted by students may be well served using sensemaking (e.g., Weick, 1993) and identity theories (e.g., Albert & Whetten, 1985; Haslam, 2004; Tajfel & Turner, 1986; Whetten, 2006). First developed by Weick (1993), applied extensively in organizational psychology, and now increasingly utilized in higher education (e.g., Eckel & Kezar, 2003; Janke, 2012; Kezar, 2014), sensemaking is a primarily retrospective "interplay of action and interpretation" (Weick, Sutcliffe, & Obstfeld, 2005, p. 409), a process through which an individual or a group of individuals, such as students attending an HEI, make sense of and ascribe meaning to their experiences and actions (Weick, 1995).

Whereas sensemaking theory examines how individuals make sense of and understand events and responses that happen in the physical world, identity theories examine how individuals define themselves as members of informal and formal groups and organizations (chapters 2.1 and 2.3). Formal affiliation with an organization, such as employment, membership, or in the case of students, enrollment, can create emotional ties because one's own *social identity* (Haslam, 2004; Tajfel & Turner, 1986) is connected to an *organization's identity,* or members' collective sense of "who we are as an organization" (Whetten, 2006, p. 219). Amid the rising attention paid to organizational identity theory (e.g., Barnhardt, Sheets, & Pasquesi, 2015; Janke, 2009, 2012; Janke, Medlin, & Holland, 2015; Kezar, 2014; Weerts & Freed, 2016; Weerts, Freed, & Morphew, 2014), greater attention to the role of *organizational image,* how others external to the institution view its identity, on student civic outcomes may be warranted, especially given increased efforts of HEI's to tell compelling stories of civic engagement (Weerts & Freed, 2016; Weerts et al., 2014) and the rise of online tracking and sharing platforms (Janke et al., 2015).

These theories may be useful in answering questions such as, how is faculty and staff culture expressed to and experienced by students? What facets of faculty and staff culture are conveyed to students and the broader public, and which ones matter as they relate to student civic outcomes? Is it the organizational culture of faculty and staff on internal governance? Is it the messages that faculty and staff send about the value of community engagement and public service as legitimate and important faculty, staff, and academic work? Which students are aware of which specific institutional programs, policies, and practices, and how does their awareness affect how they view the identity of the institution as it relates to civic and community engagement?

Refining Measures of Organizational Context

Effectively, clearly, and consistently organizational structures, policies, and practices that suggest institutional support for community engagement is becoming better defined. First, rubrics for institutionalizing service learning and community engagement (e.g., Furco, Weerts, Burton, & Kent, 2009; Holland, 2006) have been used widely in institutional self-assessments of civic engagement as well as scholarship. Second, the Carnegie Community Engagement Classification application requests evidence for how institutions track and report on specific indicators of an institution's commitment to civic and community engagement.

The Carnegie Community Engagement Classification provides a framework for a coherent and comprehensive system for summarizing evidence of an institution's civic- and community-focused structures, policies, and practices. The Carnegie Classification framework reflects the dimensions of rubrics previously mentioned (e.g., Furco et al., 2009) and requires documentation and description of the various ways in which the institution has integrated its commitment to civic and community engagement into its core features and functions.

Recent research explores "second generation" (Sandmann, 2009; Welch & Saltmarsh, 2013) infrastructures to support civic engagement activities. Describing the defining features of successful centers, Welch and Saltmarsh (2013) provide a comprehensive review of practice and structural elements of campus centers, arguing that "substantial infrastructure in the form of a community engagement office, center, or division is a key feature of a highly engaged campus" (p. 25). Examining over 100 campus applications to the Carnegie Foundation for the Community Engagement Classification, Welch and Saltmarsh identify the following "critical" (p. 27) features of institutional structures and practice: (a) institutional architecture/policy, including reporting lines, funding, strategic plan, course designation process, transcript notation; (b) center infrastructure, including space, advisory board, center vision/mission statement, database tracking system, staff; (c) center operations, including assessment mechanisms, inventories of faculty and student involvement, student/faculty/community partner recognitions; (d) programs that support faculty, staff, student, and community partner development in research, service, and teaching; and (e) in- and out-of-class civic learning experiences. Which of these organizational structures, individually or as a combination of structures, correlate to student civic outcomes?

Although not included in earlier studies as the measure of institutional structure, we suggest that future studies will find that Carnegie Community Engagement Classification can serve as a proxy for substantial institutional support for community engagement. If so, then it would be useful to study the relationship between this measure as a potential proxy of institutional community engagement in the study of student civic outcomes. Is there a significant and meaningful relationship between students' civic outcomes and whether they attend a Carnegie Community Engagement-classified HEI? This would require researchers to collect institution-level inventory of civic infrastructure and measures of student civic outcomes and then evaluate how the two interact. The Democracy Commitment's civic outcomes study is an example of a study that collects both institutional inventory of civic infrastructures as well as surveys of student perceptions (Kisker et al., 2016; Kisker et al., 2015). This type of research would advance questions about whether the presence of institutional policies, programs, and practices are significantly related to student civic outcomes using correlational research approaches.

Ultimately, understanding the relationship between institutional policies and practices and how students, faculty, staff, and community partners perceive them as part of the institution's climate requires further study. This could be accomplished intra-institutionally, such as by studying the salience of civic mission among students and their relative civic growth, or inter-institutionally, such as by exploring how different campuses with differing levels of civic context relate to an index of student civic-mindedness. This requires more theory-grounded understanding of students' awareness and interpretations of organizational structures, policies, and practices to understand why and how these features relate to the civic ethos of the institution. Theory-based research may also help to identify whether certain groupings of organizational policies and practices are likely to make a difference in student civic outcomes. For example, are there policies and practices related to faculty, student, staff, or community partner development that influence student civic outcomes? Is it more important to offer professional development and policies that incentivize civic engagement to faculty than to staff, students, and community partners?

Additionally, it is not enough to evaluate the presence of policies in student handbooks, or student enrollments in academic service learning programs or community engagement in cocurricular experiences. Scholars must also attend to the individual and social sensemaking processes that occur. This leads to other research questions, including: How does the act of tracking, recording, synthesizing, and reporting civic activities influence an institution's climate as it relates to civic engagement? What is the role of other institutional offices and units in conveying an engagement identity message? This also leads to the necessity of refining measures of institutional structures, policies, and practices as they relate to student civic outcomes.

Implications for Practice

In this era of increased accountability, tracking, measuring, and reporting, there is an improved opportunity to collect and examine institution-level data and its effects on various student, faculty, and community outcomes (Janke, 2014). We are aware of the proliferation of instruments used by campuses to assess students' levels of activity and learning outcomes—see, for example, the civic learning and engagement assessment instruments inventory compiled by the Association of American Colleges & Universities (AAC&U) and the American Association of State Colleges and Universities (AASCU)

(2015) as well as by Reason and Hemer (2015). However, this chapter focuses on research that examines how institution-level factors correlate with overall rates of civic outcomes, not how individual student experiences influence civic outcomes (as these assessments do). Many existing assessment tools hold promise for future research on tracking between college effects, but few studies exist. We suggest that one promising implication for practice is for HEIs to better map and measure student civic outcomes with a variety of quantitative and qualitative approaches and tools. Another implication for practice is for national instrument teams (e.g., NSSE, PSRI) and organizations (e.g., AAC&U and AASCU) to work collaboratively to advance understanding of what organizational contexts (i.e., structures, policies and practices) and cultures best help foster student civic outcomes (chapter 3.6).

The value of collecting information from students, faculty, and staff about their work in civic engagement is that it provides a particular view of the institution—a perspective of "who we are" (organizational identity) as it relates to an institution's civic and community engagement agenda, and indeed, organizational identity. The development of, for instance, applications for the Carnegie Community Engagement Classification (in which data are collected and synthesized) capture moments in which institutional members engage in meaning making about an institution's identity as a civically engaged campus. Elucidating ways in which members of the institution make sense of the policies, programs, and practices for civic engagement requires additional and more precise research. Such research will provide insight as to the influence of organizational contexts on student civic outcomes.

Although many civic engagement reporting and assessment measures exist (e.g., Carnegie Community Engagement Classification; NSSE; PSRI), each collects different data on institutional characteristics and students. Higher education associations and networks could leverage their ability to convene civic engagement scholars to advance the cooperation between existing research teams and tools and to further develop and refine reporting and assessment measures to advance understanding of student civic outcomes as they are influenced by various institutional characteristics. Encouraging discussions of potential overlaps, gaps, and ways to more intentionally foster data collection and analysis around civic learning outcomes would benefit the researchers, associations, and their member HEIs. Such efforts could be similar to the joint initiative of AAC&U and AASCU (2015) to develop a database of civic engagement assessments. Another example would be to leverage the Carnegie Community Engagement Classification and other tools to procure foundation or other grant funding to spur research collaborations and investigations as to the impact of organizational contexts and cultures on student civic outcomes. Finally, it is likely that our understanding of institutional effects on student civic outcomes will be enriched as mechanisms and databases for collecting institution-wide data on civic engagement increase in number, scope, and rigor. The proliferation of instruments for institutional self-assessment, if managed and used effectively, will help to inform institution-level research and advance practice.

Conclusion

This chapter focuses on the potential role that organizational characteristics of higher education institutions, including institutional climate; faculty and staff culture; and organizational structures, policies, and practices, may have on student civic outcomes. A greater understanding of which organizational characteristics contribute to student civic engagement and why can improve cross-institutional research by creating clearer parameters for selecting or grouping campuses within a study. On a practical level, knowing which institutional policies and practices contribute to student civic outcomes, beyond curricular and cocurricular student programming and opportunities, can assist academic leadership to understand how decisions made in nonacademic units can have positive student outcomes. Although most studies focus on what faculty, students, and support staff can do to support civic development, university and public relations, marketing, advancement, and alumni affairs staff may also be critical agents in the creation of an institutional climate that supports and influences civic outcomes. Building on studies that examine connections between organizational characteristics and student learning outcomes, we propose additional questions and discuss relevant organizational and psychosocial theoretical perspectives to explain the connections and interplay between organizations and the people who associate with them.

One path toward increasing scholarship and practice is to establish well-defined institutional variables that are likely to have some meaningful connection to student civic outcomes. For example, little evidence exists that suggests that grouping institutions by institutional size, selectivity, or Carnegie Classification type is likely to contribute to differences in student outcomes, civic or otherwise. Recent efforts to cluster together meaningful, organizational, civic-related characteristics provide valuable advances for future investigations about what sets of characteristics matter and why. Given the data provided by hundreds of campuses that are classified by the Carnegie Community Engagement Classification, future research can investigate what clusters of institutional variables may best serve as control variables when examining the effect of institutional climate, organizational structures, organizational policies and practices, and faculty and staff culture on student civic outcomes.

The study of institutional effects on student civic outcomes will also benefit from greater attention to and use of theories that explain why and how institutional characteristics interact with and shape student civic outcomes. Recent studies provide some indication that institutional climate may influence student as well as faculty and staff outcomes (e.g., Brower & Benenson, 2015; Lott, 2013; Rankin et al., 2010; Reason et al., 2007; Ryder et al., 2015). Theories and approaches from the fields of social psychology and organizational psychology point to the interplay between individual- and organizational-level cognition. Theoretical investigations may help administrative leaders establish strategies to cultivate civic engagement through an array of mechanisms beyond curricular and cocurricular pedagogies and programs. Identifying how aspects of organizational context (e.g., organizational structures; policies and practices; faculty and staff culture) and students' perceptions of these contexts influence student civic outcomes could and should influence a campus' approach to advancing civic engagement. Further research on institutional characteristics and contexts will advance understanding of how staff and faculty at HEI can best contribute to students' understanding of who they are as members of higher education institutions, and as members of the civic community more broadly.

References

Albert, S., & Whetten, D. A. (1985). Organizational identity. *Research in Organizational Behavior, 7*, 263–295.

Association of American Colleges & Universities & the American Association of State Colleges and Universities (AASCU). (2015). *Civic learning and engagement assessment instruments: Characteristics and dimensions inventory.* Washington, DC: Authors. Retrieved from https://www.aacu.org/civic-learning-and-engagement-assessment-instruments

Astin, A. W. (1993). *What matters in college? Four critical years revisited.* San Francisco, CA: Jossey-Bass.

Barnhardt, C. L., Sheets, J. L., & Pasquesi, K. (2015). You expect what? Students' perceptions as resources in acquiring commitments and capacities for civic engagement. *Resources in Higher Education, 56*, 622–644.

Bowman, N. A. (2014). Conceptualizing openness to diversity and challenge: Its relation to college experiences, achievement, and retention. *Innovative Higher Education, 39*(4), 277–291.

Brower, M., & Benenson, J. (2015). Practicing democracy in the classroom: Equalizing opportunities to engage with public policies and issues. *Diversity & Democracy: Civic Learning for Shared Futures, 18*(4), 8–11.

Cameron, K. (2008). A process for changing organizational culture. In T. G. Cummings (Ed.), *Handbook of organizational development* (pp. 429–445). Thousand Oaks, CA: SAGE.

Dey, E. L., Hurtado, S., Rhee, B., Inkelas, K. K., Wimsatt, L. A., & Guan, F. (1997). *Improving research on postsecondary student outcomes: A review of the strengths and limitations of national data resources.* Stanford, CA: National Center for Postsecondary Improvement.

Domagal-Goldman, J. M. (2010). *Teaching for civic capacity and engagement: How faculty members align teaching and purpose* (Doctoral dissertation). Retrieved from Proquest (816892194).

Eckel, P., & Kezar, A. (2003). *Taking the reins: Institutional transformation in higher education.* Phoenix, AZ: ACE-ORYX Press.

Finley, A. (2011). *Civic learning and democratic engagement: A review of the literature on civic engagement in post-secondary education.* Washington, DC: AAC&U.

Furco, A., Weerts, A., Burton, L., & Kent, K. (2009). *Assessment rubric for institutionalizing community engagement in higher education.* Minneapolis: University of Minnesota. Retrieved from http://www.engagement.umn.edu/sites/default/files/UMNCommunityEngagementInstitutionalizationRubric.pdf

Haslam, S. A. (2004). *Psychology in organizations: The social identity approach.* Thousand Oaks, CA: SAGE.

Holland, B. A. (1999). Factors and strategies that influence faculty involvement in public service. *Journal of Public Service and Outreach, 4*(1), 37–44.

Holland, B. A. (2006). Levels of commitment to community engagement. *Michigan Journal of Community Service Learning, 4,* 30–41.

Janke, E. M. (2009). Defining characteristics of partnership identity in faculty-community partnerships. In. B. E. Moely, S. H. Billig, & B. A. Holland (Eds.), *Creating our identities in service-learning and community engagement* (pp. 75–101). Charlotte, NC: Information Age.

Janke, E. M. (2012). Organizational partnerships in service learning: Advancing theory-based research. In P. H. Clayton, R. G. Bringle, & J. A. Hatcher (Eds.), *Research and service learning: Conceptual frameworks and assessment* (pp. 573–598). Sterling, VA: Stylus.

Janke, E. M. (2014). "Rekindle and recapture the love": Establishing system-wide indicators of progress in community engagement and economic development. *Michigan Journal of Community Service-Learning, 21*(1), 31–42.

Janke, E. M., Medlin, K., & Holland, B. A. (2015, November). *Collecting scattered institutional identities into a unified vision for community engagement and public service.* Paper presented at the International Association for Research on Service-Learning and Community Engagement Conference, Boston, MA.

Kezar, A. (2014). *How colleges change: Understanding, leading and enacting change.* New York, NY: Routledge.

Kisker, C. B., Newell, M. A., & Weintraub, D. (2016). The civic outcomes of community college. In B. L. Ronan & C. B. Kisker (Eds.), *Civic learning and democratic engagement.* No. 173 in *New directions for community colleges* (chapter 11). San Francisco, CA: Jossey-Bass.

Kisker, C. B., Weintraub, D., & Newell, M. A. (2015, November). *The community college's role in developing students' civic outcomes: Results of the national pilot.* Paper presented at the 40th annual conference of the Association for the Study of Higher Education, Denver, CO.

Kuh, G. D., Kinzie, J., Schuh, J. H., Whitt, E. J., & Associates. (2005). *Student success in college: Creating conditions that matter.* San Francisco, CA: Jossey-Bass.

Lott, II, J. L. (2013). Predictors of civic values: Understanding student-level and institutional level effects. *Journal of College Student Development, 54,* 1–16.

O'Meara, K. (2011). Faculty civic engagement: New training, assumptions, and markets needed for the engaged American scholar. In J. Saltmarsh & M. Hartley (Eds.), *"To serve a larger purpose": Engagement for democracy and the transformation of higher education* (pp. 177–198). Philadelphia, PA: Temple University Press.

O'Meara, K., & Jaeger, A. J. (2006). Preparing future faculty for community engagement: Barriers, facilitators, models, and recommendations. *Journal of Higher Education Outreach and Engagement, 11*(4), 3–25.

Pascarella, E. T., & Terenzini, P. T. (1991). *How college affects students.* San Francisco, CA: Jossey-Bass.

Pascarella, E. T., & Terenzini, P. T. (2005). *How college affects students: A third decade of research* (Vol. 2). San Francisco, CA: Jossey-Bass.

Pike, G. R., Kuh, G. D., & Gonyea, R. M. (2003). The relationship between institutional mission and students' involvement and educational outcomes. *Research in Higher Education, 44,* 241–261.

Rankin, S., Blumenfeld, W. J., Weber, G. N., & Frazer, S. J. (2010). *State of higher education for LGBT people: Campus Pride 2010 national college climate survey.* Charlotte, NC: Campus Pride.

Reason, R. D., Cox, B., Quaye, B., & Terenzini, P. (2010). Faculty and institutional factors that promote student encounters with difference in first-year courses. *The Review of Higher Education, 33,* 391–414.

Reason, R. D., & Hemer, K. (2015). *Civic learning and engagement: A review of the literature on civic learning, assessment, and instruments.* Washington, DC: AAC&U. Retrieved from http://www.aacu.org/sites/default/files/files/qc/CivicLearningLiteratureReviewRev1-26-15.pdf

Reason, R. D., Terenzini, P. T., & Domingo, R. J. (2007). Developing social and personal competence in the first year of college. *The Review of Higher Education, 30,* 271–299.

Ryder, A. J., Reason, R. D., Mitchell, J. J., Gillon, K., & Hemer, K. M. (2015, October 5). Climate for learning and students' openness to diversity and challenge: A critical role for faculty. *Journal of Diversity in Higher Education.* Advance online publication.

Saltmarsh, J., Giles, D. E., Jr., O'Meara, K., Sandmann, L., Ward, E., & Buglione, S. M. (2009). Community engagement and institutional culture in higher education: An investigation of faculty reward policies at engaged campuses. In B. E. Moely, S. H. Billig, & B. A. Holland (Eds.), *Creating our identities in ser-*

vice learning and community engagement (pp. 3–29). Charlotte, NC: Information Age.

Sandmann, L. R. (2009). Second generation: Community engagement promotion and tenure issues and challenges. In J. Strait & M. Lima (Eds.), *The future of service learning: New solutions for sustaining and improving practice* (pp. 67–89). Sterling, VA: Stylus.

Schneider, B., Ehrhart, M. G., & Macey, W. H. (2013). Organizational climate and culture. *Annual Review of Psychology, 64,* 361–88.

Scott, W. R. (2003). *Organizations: Rational, natural, and open systems* (5th ed.). Upper Saddle River, NJ: Routledge.

Tajfel, H., & Turner, J. C. (1986). The social identity theory of intergroup behavior. In S. Worchel & W. G. Austin (Eds.), *Psychology of intergroup relations* (pp. 7–24). Chicago, IL: Nelson-Hall.

Terenzini, P. T., & Reason, R. D. (2005). *Parsing the first-year of college: A conceptual framework for studying college impacts.* Paper presented at the annual conference of the Association for the Study of Higher Education, Philadelphia, PA.

Weerts, D. J., & Freed, G. F. (2016). Public engagement and organizational identity in U.S. higher education. *Recherches Sociologiques et Anthropologiques, 1,* 85–101.

Weerts, D. J., Freed, G. F., & Morphew, C. C. (2014). Organizational identity in higher education: Conceptual and empirical perspectives. In M. N. Bastedo (Ed.), *Higher education: Handbook of theory and research* (Vol. 29, pp. 229–278). New York: Springer.

Weick, K. (1993). The collapse of sensemaking in organizations: The Mann Gulch disaster. *Administrative Science Quarterly, 3,* 628–652.

Weick, K. (1995). *Sensemaking in organisations.* London: SAGE.

Weick, K. E., Sutcliffe, K. M., & Obstfeld, D. (2005). Organizing and the process of sense-making. *Organizational Science, 16*(4), 409–421.

Welch, M., & Saltmarsh, J. (2013). Current practices and infrastructures for campus centers of community engagement. *Journal of Higher Education Outreach and Engagement, 17*(4), 25–56.

Whetten, D. A. (2006). Albert and Whetten revisited: Strengthening the concept of organizational identity. *Journal of Management Inquiry, 15,* 219–234.

LONGITUDINAL RESEARCH AND STUDENT CIVIC OUTCOMES

Patrick L. Hill, Kira Pasquesi, Nicholas A. Bowman,
and Jay W. Brandenberger

Theories of lifespan development underscore how developmental periods come with differential tasks and challenges (Havighurst, 1972; Hutteman, Hennecke, Orth, Reitz, & Specht, 2014). These theoretical frameworks suggest that the adolescent and young adult years come with the primary challenge of defining the values and goals with which one will primarily self-identify (Erikson, 1959). Such work has been followed in more recent years with the suggestion that so-called emerging adulthood, a period ranging from around 18 to 30 years of age, may provide an extended opportunity to create these identity commitments, particularly with respect to roles within work, romantic relationships, and community (Arnett, 2000). One presumed reason for the development of this emerging adult period is that higher education has become more common in postindustrial societies and, thus, provides an increasingly important context in which individuals continue to develop their self-defining values and beliefs.

A primary assumption of these developmental frameworks is that the experiences and teachings endemic to the university years should carry substantial consequences throughout the adult years and into late life. Higher education theorists also posit the importance of the university years for identity formation, which includes elements of civic and occupational or professional identity (e.g., Reid, Dahlgren, Petocz, & Dahlgren, 2008; Trede, Macklin, & Bridges, 2012). These aims and hypotheses emphasize the need for well-crafted longitudinal research that accurately assesses the value of higher education for years and even decades following school. In particular, researchers must carefully contemplate both methodological and analytic considerations in order to best describe the influence of higher education on later outcomes.

Accordingly, this chapter explores the contributions of conducting longitudinal research in higher education, either assessing students multiple times during college, following up with students after graduation or, ideally, both. As an example, we will frequently discuss our recent work to explain continuity and change in prosocial, civically minded goals, such as influencing the social structure and helping others in need during the university years and into adulthood (e.g., Bowman, Brandenberger, Lapsley, Hill, & Quaranto, 2010; Hill, Burrow, Brandenberger, Lapsley, & Quaranto, 2010; Hill, Jackson, Roberts, Lapsley, & Brandenberger, 2011). This work suggests that students tend to report similar goals from freshman to senior year (Hill et al., 2010), as well as from university into adulthood (Hill et al., 2011), insofar that goal importance levels demonstrated moderate rank-order stability. That said, changes do occur relative to both other peers and to mean levels on prosocial goal importance for the sample (Hill et al., 2011), though these changes may take years to manifest. In addition, individuals differ in their patterns of change, a concept known in lifespan research as interindividual variability in intra-individual change. This chapter focuses on whether and how the university experience influences changes on civic development and related constructs, and how best to evaluate if these changes stand over years. In other words, do university experiences predict variability in interindividual differences in civic development over time?

Civic development is a consistently hypothesized outcome associated with higher education, to the point that several institutions explicitly profess a desire to develop students who are focused on benefiting societal and communal well-being. Civic engagement includes a broad range of behaviors, beliefs, and values, which are assessed with respect to outcomes such as social responsibility, social justice, civic identity, and leadership experiences (see e.g., Battistoni, 2013; all chapters from this volume). Moreover, civic development occurs as a combination of personological and contextual factors (Lerner, Wang, Champine, Warren, & Erickson, 2014). Thus, researchers must examine both how the context influences the individual as well as how individuals select and interact with the context. Research on civic development thus presents unique challenges because its assessment necessitates (a) subjective ratings for constructs related to personal beliefs; (b) more objective indices of both civic attributes (i.e., voting behavior, number of volunteer experiences) and the environmental contexts; and (c) designs and statistical techniques that readily combine these different measurement techniques.

In order to inform future higher education research, we first turn to past research on civic outcomes with adolescents and college students. We then borrow from adolescent and young adult development studies to elucidate potential issues and questions to address in future research on civic development. Specifically, the next two sections of this chapter describe and start to present solutions to the measurement, analytic, and methodological concerns that confront longitudinal research on civic outcomes in the years following higher education. Finally, we build from these sections to chart the course for future research and the types of sources available to researchers for addressing these questions.

Longitudinal Research on Civic Outcomes Among Students

Previous research on civic outcomes has tended to focus on adolescents and college students, largely because these developmental groups are dealing with identity issues (Arnett, 2000; Erikson, 1959) that entail striving to understand which values and ethics are of greatest personal importance. Although this volume focuses on higher education, we include a brief review of the literature with adolescent samples for two important reasons. First, this literature presents examples for several of the recommendations for best research practices, such as longitudinal studies that employ large-scale, archival datasets and/or sophisticated analytic approaches for examining civic development over time. Second, the overall gestalt from this literature provides support for the claim that educational systems play an important role in the development of civic outcomes, an important point for building the theoretical argument that higher education can provide a context for civic development.

Predicting Civic Outcomes in Adolescence

Although adolescents today can be described as being more self-focused than those in earlier generations (e.g., Twenge, Campbell, & Freeman, 2012; Twenge, Konrath, Foster, Campbell, & Bushman, 2008), studies have countered these claims with respect both to narcissism levels (Roberts, Edmonds, & Grijalva, 2010; Trzesniewski, Donnellan, & Robins, 2008) and greater involvement in community service (Syvertsen, Wray-Lake, Flanagan, Osgood, & Briddell, 2011). As such, it may be inappropriate to describe recent cohorts of adolescents as uniformly becoming more or less other-focused, as instead research consistently points to the need for evaluating individual variability in developmental trajectories. Research in adolescence points to at least three categories of predictor valuables for understanding civic development over time: individual characteristics of the youth, background and family characteristics, and institutional or community variables. Given our focus on educational systems as motivating mechanisms, we focus on studies examining this final group of predictors.

For instance, valuable insights in civic engagement have come from research employing the National Longitudinal Survey of Adolescent Health, which sampled thousands of youth across the United States (Gordon-Larsen, McMurray, & Popkin, 1999). One study using these data examined the role of adolescents' initial sense of connection across the domains of family, friends, and school in explaining civic outcomes approximately six years later (Duke, Skay, Pettingell, & Borowsky, 2009). Even when controlling for connections to other domains, adolescents' perceived school connectedness significantly predicted higher levels of voluntary service, political involvement, civic trust, participation in community organizations, and voting in political elections when assessed during young adulthood. School connection in this study was assessed using indicators typical to higher education research, including whether students perceived that teachers cared about them and treated them fairly, as well as if they felt safe at school and connected to their peers. Using similar items, research has demonstrated that teacher fairness and respect may be related to the development of civic commitments and positive beliefs in the American system for adolescents across ethnic backgrounds (Flanagan, Cumsille, Gill, & Gallay, 2007). As such, educational systems that promote *democratic ideals*, as defined in the previous studies, could play a role in motivating civic engagement and development.

Researchers have pointed to the value of providing a "civic context" for youth that positively models civic engagement and its benefits (Zaff, Malanchuk, & Eccles, 2008). The mere amount of civic participation alone does not appear as important for youth development as having quality experiences, including opportunities for role-taking, meaningful action, and reflection (e.g., Ferreira, Azevedo, & Menezes, 2012). One study (Lenzi et al., 2012) investigated the role of a democratic social context on civic engagement across multiple countries using a multilevel modeling approach that allowed researchers to test the contextual effects both with respect to individual students' perceptions as well as the aggregate ratings for the school. Controlling for family and neighborhood factors, student and school-level ratings of school context predicted higher civic engagement across three of five countries examined, and student ratings were a positive predictor for one of the other two countries. In sum, the adolescent literature points to the importance of democratic values within the school context. Additional research has consistently suggested that school-based extracurricular activities can play an important role, although multiple factors can moderate this influence (Feldman & Matjasko, 2005). Both of these points have been carried over into research from higher education as well.

Predicting Civic Outcomes in Adulthood

Although research on civic outcomes of college students is plentiful (chapter 1.2), fewer studies have examined the lasting effects of service learning and civic engagement into adulthood (Bowman et al., 2010). A few relevant studies have examined the influence of college experiences on postgraduation activities, including political participation (Hillygus, 2005; Nie & Hillygus, 2001), volunteering, and civic involvement (Astin, Sax, & Avalos, 1999; Bowman, Park, & Denson, 2015; Keen & Hall, 2008; Ruiz & Warchal, 2013). For example, Astin, Sax, and Avalos (1999) found that the short-term effects of undergraduate service participation in the affective and cognitive domains persisted nine years after college. A related study identified verbal SAT scores and course credits in social science as positive predictors of political participation, voting, and volunteering one year after college graduation (Nie & Hillygus, 2001), and a follow-up study identified evidence of the enduring influence of verbal skills on political participation four years after graduation (Hillygus, 2005). Moreover, within propensity score analyses that accounted for self-selection (discussed in more detail in the following sections), participation in a racial/ethnic student organization predicts several forms of civic engagement six years after graduation, including community leadership experiences, donations to nonprofit and political organizations, and volunteering commitments (Bowman et al., 2015).

Higher education researchers have addressed calls for robust evidence on civic outcomes using longitudinal assessments across multiple campuses. In particular, the Higher Education Research Institute (HERI) conducted quantitative longitudinal studies of service learning and civic engagement in postcollege years using the Cooperative Institutional Research Program surveys. For instance, Astin, Vogelgesang, Ikeda, and Yee (2000) (see also Vogelgesang & Astin, 2000) compared the effects of community service and service learning on cognitive and affective outcomes using a national sample of 22,236 students entering college in the mid-1990s. After controlling for precollege activities, values, and beliefs, they found that participating in service as part of a course had a positive effect beyond the effect of cocurricular community service on all academic outcomes (i.e., GPA, writing skills, critical thinking skills) and some affective ones (e.g., commitments to promoting racial understanding, activism, pursuing a service-related career) four years after being surveyed as first-year students.

A subsequent HERI study examined the long-term effects of service learning into the early career years using a national longitudinal sample of

8,474 students surveyed as freshmen in 1994 and again 10 years later (Astin et al., 2006). The study assessed the effects of service learning on 13 postcollege outcome measures in the areas of community/civic engagement, political engagement, and civic values/goals. The analytic approach controlled for precollege characteristics, beliefs, values, and experiences as well as institutional characteristics and college experiences. Results indicated that participation in service learning (above and beyond community service and various other indicators) predicted civic leadership, charitable giving, and political engagement. Results also suggested that the effects of service learning and community service are mediated in part by the extent to which reflection occurred within these courses.

Although this chapter focuses on quantitative research, it is also important to recognize longitudinal research on service learning and civic engagement using qualitative or mixed methods approaches. For example, Astin and colleagues (2000) drew from qualitative data in addition to the quantitative data described previously. The qualitative findings suggested that service learning facilitates increases in one's sense of personal efficacy, awareness of the world and personal values, and engagement in the classroom experience. Both the qualitative and quantitative results emphasized the power of reflection to connect service experiences with course material. Similarly, Kiely (2005) conducted a longitudinal case study examining how students experienced transformational learning during and after a service learning program in Nicaragua. Five categories of learning processes emerged from the data that described how students experienced transformative learning, including contextual border crossing, dissonance, personalizing, processing, and connecting.

Moreover, Kerrigan (2005) documented college graduates' perspectives of the effect of capstone service learning courses three years after graduation and found that graduates perceived the capstone course contributing to enhanced communication abilities, leadership skills, community involvement, understanding of diversity, and career development. Qualitative and mixed method studies such as these can provide valuable information for researchers considering which constructs to examine in the mediational tests described here. We focus next on how to employ quantitative data analysis for testing whether and why higher education influences civic outcomes.

Analytic Techniques for Assessing Longitudinal Change

In some instances, bivariate analyses can be useful for understanding the link among service learning, civic engagement, and civic outcomes. Correlations can be used to provide an overview of the relationships among not only constructs of interest but also variables that might confound the relationship among service learning, civic engagement, and civic outcomes. For instance, identifying a moderate correlation between precollege civic engagement and service learning in college would illustrate the importance of incorporating a pretest and otherwise account for self-selection to determine the impact of service learning more effectively. Moreover, experimental studies randomly assign students to different conditions, such as participating in a service learning course section versus a traditional in-class section, or they might be assigned to a service learning section that has one pedagogy intervention versus another (e.g., in-class group reflections versus private written reflections). If this were the case, then *t*-tests or one-way analyses of variance (ANOVAs) could determine the main effect of the experimental intervention, and two-way ANOVAs could be used to test whether the effect of the intervention is stronger for some groups of students than for others (e.g., men versus women).

However, these types of analyses for nonexperimental studies have notable shortcomings when attempting to establish causal effects, because they do not incorporate other variables that might account for the observed relationships. Even multiple regression analyses, which can examine unique relationships between numerous predictors and the dependent variable, generally do not provide strong conclusions about causality for nonexperimental designs (see Murnane & Willett, 2011; Shadish, Cook, & Campbell, 2002). In this section we discuss several techniques that are well-suited to making stronger claims using longitudinal data: structural equation modeling, autoregressive latent trajectory models, regression models for limited dependent variables, and propensity score matching. This list is not comprehensive, but these approaches are particularly relevant to studying longitudinal relationships between service learning and civic outcomes. These techniques can sometimes be combined with one another, such as conducting propensity score matching analyses to predict binary and ordinal civic outcomes (e.g., Bowman et al., 2015).

Structural Equation Modeling of Longitudinal Data

A typical approach to conducting analyses with measurement scales is to start by averaging the scale items together to create a mean score for the construct of interest. Although common, this approach does little to account for the possible measurement error both with respect to the items and the overall construct. Structural equation modeling (SEM) techniques were developed, in part, to help address these measurement errors by explicitly modeling them in the analyses. For instance, in the examination of prosocial goal development mentioned earlier (Hill et al., 2011), the researchers employed an SEM approach that allowed the individual goal items to load onto a broader latent construct that reflected prosocial goal-setting at any given measurement occasion. Using this method, SEM allows the researcher to account for whether items are better or worse indicators of the latent variable (i.e., if a given goal item is a better indicator of overall prosociality) as well as estimate the amount of residual error left for each item after accounting for its covariance with the other scale indicators.

When conducting longitudinal analyses, SEM approaches can prove particularly valuable because they allow researchers to make stronger assumptions regarding whether they are assessing the same constructs over multiple measurement occasions. Common longitudinal SEM approaches include *latent change models*, which are useful for studies with two measurement occasions, and *latent growth models*, which allow for more than two assessments. Lengthier reviews for each approach are available (see e.g., Duncan, Duncan, & Stryker, 2013; McArdle, 2009).

In brief, latent change and growth models serve to model mean-level change in the construct of interest and estimate whether inter-individual variability exists in these change patterns. For example, the latent growth approach taken by Hill and colleagues (2011) involved estimating a latent construct at three measurement occasions (first year, senior year, and middle adulthood) that estimated participants' levels of prosocial goal-setting at each occasion. In so doing, the model allowed for a latent construct indicating initial levels of the prosocial goal-setting as well as a latent growth parameter that measured participants' changes over time after accounting for initial levels. This approach is typically referred to as a "second-order" latent growth model because both the individual measurement occasions and the intercept and growth parameters are estimated as latent constructs; single-order models, though, are possible when the researcher is interested in using a manifest or single-item variable assessed as each measurement occasion. Additionally, the researchers were able to fix single-item loadings to be equivalent across the three assessments, which allowed for two important assumptions to be made: (a) that the prosocial goal-setting is being measured by the same items across measurement occasions, and (b) that the items are serving as equally important indicators of the latent construct across time. In other words, SEM approaches allow one to more easily "fix" the same factor structure across assessment occasions.

The value of getting to fit (and ultimately test) these modeling assumptions comes from considering measurement invariance over time using an SEM framework. These tests explore whether the items load onto the construct of interest similarly across time and whether an item differs in its factor loading (and thus relative importance) across assessment occasions. In addition, are the averages similar for the items over time, or are participants "using" the items differently over time, as evidenced by systematic differences in the item's mean that do not reflect actual change? Finally, researchers may test whether the variance of the latent factor differs across time. Although discussed here in a longitudinal context, considering whether measurement invariance holds across sampling groups (e.g., year in school, gender) also is important in order to ensure that constructs are being reported on similarly by all participants.

For higher education research, SEM frameworks provide particular benefits with respect to understanding whether change occurs over time. For instance, if a researcher is interested in whether engagement in a given course or extracurricular activity affects civic outcomes in the future, SEM approaches allow researchers to start by modeling the general trajectory for the sample on the outcome over time. Next, latent change and growth models allow for examinations of whether significant variability exists around the latent change parameter; in other words, do participants differ from one another in their change over time? This test serves as an important precondition for examining whether engagement levels affect change in civic outcomes; if all members of the sample are changing at the same rate, then there is no variability in change that the engagement measure can predict. If variability does occur, researchers then can employ latent change and growth models for understanding whether engagement influences patterns of civic change, while accounting for measurement error better than by traditional regression approaches.

Autoregressive Latent Trajectory Models

Though latent change and latent growth models provide a valuable start, more sophisticated SEM approaches for modeling change patterns over time have been developed. One of the more prominent examples is the Autoregressive Latent Trajectory (ALT) model (Bollen & Curran, 2004). ALT models serve to combine elements of the latent growth models described previously with the cross-lagged models commonly employed in longitudinal research. Specifically, the ALT model still allows researchers to estimate latent intercept and growth constructs and to examine interindividual variability in change patterns. Moreover, it adds to the model specification by allowing for cross-lag pathways between measurement occasions and accounting for the stability of the assessed constructs across these occasions.

The value of this approach is apparent when modeling longitudinal covariance in two variables of interest. For instance, researchers may be interested in examining the longitudinal relationship between volunteering and civic identity across four assessments during the college years. The latent trajectory component of the model allows researchers to test whether initial levels of volunteering and civic identity are related, as well as whether individual patterns of change on these two constructs are correlated. However, researchers may also be interested in whether volunteering precedes civic identity, or vice versa, a question that is better addressed by allowing for cross-lag paths from one construct to the other between measurement occasions (i.e., linking first-year volunteering to sophomore civic identity, and first-year civic identity to second-year volunteering) while simultaneously accounting for the other aspects of change captured by the model.

ALT models thus allow researchers to test a wide array of important questions regarding students' change in civic outcomes as well as the variables that predict these changes. However, given the complexity of the models, this approach may not prove valuable or even viable for a number of studies. For instance, these approaches typically require at least four measurement occasions in order to appropriately estimate the cross-lag parameters. In addition, given the overall number of parameters being estimated—which is even greater when researchers employ second-order rather than first-order models—ALT models typically require substantial sample sizes that may preclude their use unless researchers employ multisite or archival datasets.

Regression Models for Limited Dependent Variables

Civic outcomes are frequently not measured with continuous variables. Researchers and practitioners may be interested in dichotomous outcomes (e.g., whether or not someone voted in a federal election or took a civic leadership role) and ordinal outcomes (e.g., participating "never," "sometimes," or "frequently" in a civic experience). Other noncontinuous variable types that are less common for civic engagement are "counts" of the number of times an experience occurred (e.g., voting in an election in the past five years) or categorical outcomes (e.g., occupations with different types of orientations toward civic involvement). Predicting these outcomes using ordinary least squares (OLS) multiple regression violates key assumptions of this analysis, because assumptions pertaining to residuals often rely on the presence of an approximately normal distribution for the dependent variable (Cohen, Cohen, West, & Aiken, 2003; Garson, 2014). As a result, the findings from using OLS regression with a binary or ordinal outcome can lead to flawed inferences (e.g., Horrace & Oaxaca, 2006).

Separate analyses have been created to model each of these noncontinuous outcome types appropriately: logistic regression for binary variables, ordinal logit regression for ordinal variables, Poisson regression for count variables, and multinomial logistic regression for categorical variables (Agresti, 2013; Smithson & Merkle, 2013; Xie & Powers, 2008). Although there is not enough space to discuss each of these analyses in detail, a few general points are worth noting. First, under certain conditions, using OLS regression with these outcomes could yield nonsensical values, such as predicted probabilities above 1.0 and predicted probabilities or counts below zero. To avoid this problem, analyses that model limited and categorical dependent variables generally use a transformation of the original dependent variable, such as the log-odds or logit for logistic regression. Second, given the types of transformations that are used in these limited dependent variable analyses, OLS regression will be most likely to yield flawed results when many of the predicted values are toward the extremes (e.g., for binary outcomes, probabilities near 0.0 or 1.0). However, they will yield substantively similar results when predicted values are generally near the middle of the distribution (e.g., for binary outcomes, probabilities near 0.5).

Third, the results of limited dependent variable analyses often yield different measures of effect size (or the strength of the relationship) than do OLS regressions and *t*-tests. To some extent, this divergence occurs because the outcome is not continuous, and analyses designed to model such outcomes do not provide standardized mean differences (i.e., Cohen's *d*) or standardized regression coefficients. Limited dependent variable analyses will often produce odds ratios, which can be difficult to interpret meaningfully because an odds ratio consists of the ratio of two ratios. Other measures of effect size, such as delta-p, are available for some analyses. Finally, although these analyses avoid the problems with using OLS regression to predict non-continuous outcomes, they are sometimes based on assumptions that are different from OLS regression, and researchers must pay attention to whether the additional assumption(s) are met.

Propensity Score Matching

When conducting research on service learning and civic outcomes, students' self-selection into service learning coursework is a major concern for determining the impact of their experiences on outcomes. Specifically, students who decide to enroll in service learning courses may be more civically involved, more community-minded, have a stronger orientation toward equality and social justice, and have a more flexible schedule with sufficient time for service learning engagement, among other attributes. Therefore, in the absence of a randomly assigned control group, even analyses that attempt to control for additional variables (e.g., analyses of covariance, multiple regression) will not be able to account sufficiently for self-selection. Propensity score analyses seek to overcome this problem by explicitly modeling the process of selecting into a particular experience or "treatment" (Guo & Fraser, 2015; Holmes, 2013; Pan & Bai, 2015; Stuart, 2010). These analyses match each student who participated in the experience with one or more students who were equally likely to participate (based on a number of pretreatment variables) but did not do so. If students who participated in service learning courses have more favorable outcomes than their matched counterparts, then researchers can make stronger claims that the treatment caused improvements on the outcomes.

Propensity score analyses generally occur in at least two stages. First, a logistic regression analysis is used to predict students' participation in the treatment. Because the intent is to model participants' predispositions or propensities, only variables that occur before the treatment should be used to create the propensity score. Ideally, these variables will contribute to both participation in the treatment and students' subsequent outcomes. Given that matching occurs only on the variables used to create the propensity score, variable inclusion is much more important for providing accurate causal estimates than is deciding to use propensity score matching versus other techniques (Cook, Steiner, & Pohl, 2009; Pascarella, Salisbury, & Blaich, 2013; Steiner, Cook, Shadish, & Clark, 2010). In particular, the pretest often appears to be the most important single variable to include when creating a propensity score, and this conclusion intuitively seems to apply to service learning and civic engagement. Given the importance of including pretests and other pretreatment measures (as well as obtaining outcomes that clearly occur after the treatment), longitudinal studies are well suited for conducting propensity score analyses.

Second, participants are then matched based on having similar propensities to participate in the treatment, and the outcome(s) of these matched participants are compared to determine whether or not those in the treatment condition demonstrate improved outcomes than comparable nonparticipants. Additional analyses before predicting the outcome often examine whether the matching process was successful, because the matching approach may need to be revised if it does not successfully account for preexisting differences between students in the treatment and control conditions (Pattanayak, 2015). Many techniques are available for matching participants, but a full discussion of the various options is beyond the scope of this chapter. For better or worse, there does not appear to be a single approach that is clearly superior to others (Clark, 2015; Herzog, 2014), and new techniques are being developed and evaluated.

In short, propensity score matching can provide improvements upon other techniques (e.g., using difference scores, using the pretest as a covariate) for testing causal effects with nonexperimental data (Shadish, 2013; Stürmer et al., 2006), but this form of statistical analysis is certainly not a panacea. Specifically, it can only approximate random assignment into conditions, rather than providing a true experiment. Indeed, as with all the approaches listed here, it has inherent benefits and drawbacks, and the primary recommendation should always be to choose the analytic approach that is best suited to answer the theoretical question of interest.

Five Ms for Future Research

Understanding these analytic approaches should motivate researchers to design more sophisticated longitudinal studies. Toward this end, we present five recommendations for conducting longitudinal studies that will allow researchers to better examine whether and how higher education leads to civic outcomes, and build upon the research described previously.

Multisite Research

Several of the analytic approaches described previously work best when sampling at least several hundred students, which may prove difficult when working with a single institution. Moreover, researchers often wish to make generalizations beyond their specific campus, or they may wish to understand how their campus's program compares to alternatives at other schools. When researchers wish to make these broader comparisons, our first recommendation for researchers is to consider multisite collaborations. Although multisite studies may not address research questions specific to a given campus, such work can provide valuable insights into the higher education efforts that best promote civic outcomes over time because one can compare the duration and practices employed by different schools. An important avenue for performing these tests is through using archival datasets, such as those available from the Higher Education Research Institute at the University of California, Los Angeles (for more on employing datasets from across institutions, see chapter 3.6). In a recent example, researchers have employed data from multiple institutions across the United States in order to demonstrate which collegiate experiences appear most predictive of prosocial growth (Brandenberger & Bowman, 2015). They found that active learning practices and diversity experiences were particularly important to prosocial growth from college entry to junior year across institutions. When considering whether practices lead to consistent or different outcomes across schools, researchers should incorporate interaction terms into their statistical models that account for moderation of initial level or longitudinal change by institution, which leads to our second recommendation.

Mediators and Moderators

Higher education research often does not provide a sufficient understanding of the mechanisms underlying a given effect, such as the benefits of college experiences on civic outcomes. On this front, two questions are particularly valuable to consider, focusing on mediators and moderators. First, as noted previously, do the effects of interest differ across student characteristic, institution type, or implementation practice? Examining such moderator variables can provide valuable insights into which contexts are most likely to produce beneficial effects on civic outcomes, leading to a greater understanding ultimately of for whom, under what conditions, and why these effects occur. Second, are there mechanistic variables that help explain why higher education practices influence the outcome of interest? For instance, research suggests that taking ethnic studies courses and racial/cultural awareness workshops found lasting effects on adult well-being, in part because these workshops lead students to adopt a stronger orientation toward prosocial goals during college (Bowman, Brandenberger, Hill, & Lapsley, 2011). In statistical terms, these results suggest that the effect of diversity experiences during college on later well-being may be *mediated* through increasing prosocial goal commitment. Additional work suggests that such experiences help individuals see the "unexpected" (i.e., different perspectives or viewpoints), which in turn affects attitude change (Bowman & Brandenberger, 2012). Tests of mediation can be readily incorporated into the statistical analyses described earlier (Hayes, 2013; Preacher, 2015), and incorporating these more sophisticated routes for testing mediation also may enhance researchers' ability for making causal inferences (e.g., Muthén & Asparouhov, 2015), a critical interest for researchers going forward.

Making Causal Claims

One catalyst for adopting more sophisticated approaches is their improved ability to support causal claims. Approaches such as ALT models allow researchers greater ability to estimate the directionality of effects between two related constructs and eliminate alternate explanations, and propensity score modeling can assist researchers in situations when random assignment is not possible. This concern is particularly prominent in higher education because researchers are frequently unable to assign students to a certain course or to volunteer for a specific experience. Adopting these analytic advances provides only one path toward making stronger causal claims. Ideally, researchers should more regularly consider incorporating experimental designs into their research programs, such as randomly assigning students to different types of conditions within service learning courses (e.g., types of reflection, types of interactions with community residents, types of class discussions), which could be combined with following experimental and control group participants over time.

Measuring the Same Constructs Over Time

At first glance, this recommendation seems relatively straightforward, and this practice is common within longitudinal research on higher education (e.g., pretest, posttest designs). However, longitudinal research on civic outcomes uses different scales to approximate the same construct over time (e.g., examining "civic engagement" with nonidentical measures) or fails to assess the "outcome" variable prior to the final measurement occasion. The first issue leads to concerns regarding whether the same construct is indeed assessed using the different measures, which is further exacerbated by the fact that employing different measures fails to allow researchers to test measurement equivalence over time. The second issue is problematic for any research interested in how individuals change over time. For instance, any effort to estimate how higher education affects attitudinal or motivational changes becomes complicated without insight into the students' attitudes prior to the educational experience of interest.

Both issues require researchers to be particularly thoughtful regarding their methods and choice of measures. When possible, researchers should employ measures that are appropriate for the participants now and into the future, which may necessitate choosing scales that are not age-specific, or at least can be expected to be relatively age-invariant. In addition, researchers should identify their expected moderators, mediators, and outcomes prior to the initial assessment and assess these variables through the course of the longitudinal study. With repeated measures, researchers are better able to properly examine mediation over time (Maxwell & Cole, 2007), as well as gain better insights into the directionality (and causal nature) of the pathways tested.

Measuring Development After Graduation

Our final recommendation may be the most difficult for researchers, at least from a logistical standpoint. In order to properly test the long-term effects of higher education on civic outcomes, participants should be followed into adulthood. However, doing so requires researchers to retain contact with participants outside of the university setting, thus limiting their ability for in-person contact. Accordingly, a few methods for increasing study participation following the university years have proven valuable in our previous work. First, researchers should attempt to coordinate efforts with their university's alumni organization(s) in order to bolster enrollment, as alumni services typically retain contact information on students following graduation. Second, researchers should do as much as possible to offset any costs to participation, which may include hosting surveys online or, when paper-and-pencil surveys are necessary, providing participants with prepaid envelopes in which to return the surveys (see Dillman, 2000; Schaefer & Dillman, 1998, for more information on increasing response rates). Third, although inevitably more difficult, researchers also should reach out to those students who may have fallen short of graduation, or transferred to another institution, particularly when interested in whether the university experience influences student development regardless of graduate status. Focusing solely on a sample of graduates can lead to bias, particularly when identifying which university practices are not beneficial for student progress. Such efforts can be facilitated by posting study announcements on social media that ask potential participants to contact the study researchers should they meet certain inclusion criteria (i.e., completed previous measures, were enrolled during certain years).

Conclusion

In adhering to these five recommendations and employing the analytic models described previously, researchers can design more valuable longitudinal investigations into the benefits of higher education that will provide greater insight into how college courses, practices, and programs may influence long-term civic outcomes. Although existing research has offered some evidence of the potential for educational benefits, the field certainly can improve with respect to making better and more confident causal and mechanistic accounts of these relationships. With greater methodological and analytic foresight, future research can build from the existing foundation to better understand why, when, under what circumstances, for whom, and how higher education can promote civic engagement for decades following the university experience. Indeed, these advances can help researchers understand how university experiences influence life histories and personal activities in ways that help to explain any lasting impact that higher education holds on civic development.

References

Agresti, A. (2013). *Categorical data analysis* (3rd ed.). Hoboken, NJ: Wiley.

Arnett, J. J. (2000). Emerging adulthood: A theory of development from the late teens through the twenties. *American Psychologist, 55*, 469–480.

Astin, A. W., Sax, L. J., & Avalos, J. (1999). Long-term effects of volunteerism during the undergraduate years. *The Review of Higher Education, 22*(2), 187–202.

Astin, A. W., Vogelgesang, L. J., Ikeda, E. K., & Yee, J. A. (2000). *How service learning affects students.* Los Angeles, CA: UCLA Higher Education Research Institute.

Astin, A. W., Vogelgesang, L. J., Misa, K., Anderson, J., Denson, N., Jayakumar, U., Saenz, V., & Yamamura, E. (2006). *Understanding the effects of service-learning: A study of students and faculty.* Los Angeles, CA: UCLA Higher Education Research Institute.

Battistoni, R. M. (2013). Civic learning through service learning: Conceptual frameworks and research. In P. H. Clayton, R. G. Bringle, & J. A. Hatcher (Eds.), *Research on service learning: Conceptual frameworks and assessment* (Volume 2A, pp. 111–132). Sterling, VA: Stylus.

Bollen, K. A., & Curran, P. J. (2004). Autoregressive latent trajectory (ALT) models a synthesis of two traditions. *Sociological Methods & Research, 32,* 336–383.

Bowman, N. A., & Brandenberger, J. W. (2012). Experiencing the unexpected: Toward a model of college diversity experiences and attitude change. *The Review of Higher Education, 35*(2), 179–205.

Bowman, N. A., Brandenberger, J. W., Hill, P. L., & Lapsley, D. K. (2011). The long-term effects of college diversity experiences: Well-being and social concerns 13 years after graduation. *Journal of College Student Development, 52,* 729–239.

Bowman, N. A., Brandenberger, J., Lapsley, D., Hill, P., & Quaranto, J. (2010). Serving in college, flourishing in adulthood: Does community engagement during the college years predict adult well being? *Applied Psychology: Health and Well Being, 2*(1), 14–34.

Bowman, N. A., Park, J. J., & Denson, N. (2015). Student involvement in ethnic student organizations: Examining civic outcomes 6 years after graduation. *Research in Higher Education, 56,* 127–145.

Brandenberger, J. W., & Bowman, N. A. (2015). Prosocial growth during college: Results of a national study. *Journal of Moral Education, 44,* 328–345.

Clark, M. H. (2015). Propensity score adjustment methods. In W. Pan & H. Bai (Eds.), *Propensity score analysis: Fundamentals and developments* (pp. 115–140). New York, NY: Guilford.

Cohen, J., Cohen, P., West, S. G., & Aiken, L. S. (2003). *Applied multiple regression/ correlation analysis for the behavioral sciences* (3rd ed.). Mahwah, NJ: Erlbaum.

Cook, T. D., Steiner, P. M., & Pohl, S. (2009). How bias reduction is affected by covariate choice, unreliability, and mode of data analysis: Results from two types of within-study comparisons. *Multivariate Behavioral Research, 44,* 828–847.

Dillman, D. A. (2000). *Mail and Internet surveys: The tailored design method.* New York, NY: Wiley.

Duke, N. N., Skay, C. L., Pettingell, S. L., & Borowsky, I. W. (2009). From adolescent connections to social capital: Predictors of civic engagement in young adulthood. *Journal of Adolescent Health, 44*(2), 161–168.

Duncan, T. E., Duncan, S. C., & Stryker, L. A. (2013). *An introduction to latent variable growth curve modeling: Concepts, issues, and applications* (2nd ed.). Mahwah, NJ: Erlbaum.

Erikson, E. H. (1959). *Identity and the life cycle: Psychological issues.* New York, NY: International University Press.

Feldman, A. F., & Matjasko, J. L. (2005). The role of school-based extracurricular activities in adolescent development: A comprehensive review and future directions. *Review of Educational Research, 75*(2), 159–210.

Ferreira, P. D., Azevedo, C. N., & Menezes, I. (2012). The developmental quality of participation experiences: Beyond the rhetoric that "participation is always good!" *Journal of Adolescence, 35*, 599–610.

Flanagan, C. A., Cumsille, P., Gill, S., & Gallay, L. S. (2007). School and community climates and civic commitments: Patterns for ethnic minority and majority students. *Journal of Educational Psychology, 99*, 421–431.

Garson, G. D. (2014). *Multiple regression* (Blue Book Series, 2014 ed.). Asheboro, NC: Statistical Publishing Associates.

Gordon-Larsen, P., McMurray, R. G., & Popkin, B. M. (1999). Adolescent physical activity and inactivity vary by ethnicity: The national longitudinal study of adolescent health. *Journal of Pediatrics, 135*, 301–306.

Guo, S., & Fraser, M. W. (2015). *Propensity score analysis: Statistical methods and applications* (2nd ed.). Los Angeles, CA: SAGE.

Havighurst, R. J. (1972). *Developmental tasks and education.* New York, NY: David McKay.

Hayes, A. F. (2013). *Introduction to mediation, moderation, and conditional process analysis: A regression-based approach.* New York, NY: Guilford.

Herzog, S. (2014). The propensity score analytical framework: An overview and institutional research example. In N. A. Bowman & S. Herzog (Eds.), *Methodological advances and issues in studying college impact* (New Directions for Institutional Research, no. 161, pp. 21–40). San Francisco, CA: Jossey-Bass.

Hill, P. L., Burrow, A. L., Brandenberger, J. W., Lapsley, D. K., & Quaranto, J. C. (2010). Collegiate purpose orientations and well-being in early and middle adulthood. *Journal of Applied Developmental Psychology, 31*, 173–179.

Hill, P. L., Jackson, J. J., Roberts, B. W., Lapsley, D. K., & Brandenberger, J. W. (2011). Change you can believe in: Changes in goal setting during emerging and young adulthood predict later adult well-being. *Social Psychological and Personality Science, 2*, 123–131.

Hillygus, D. S. (2005). The missing link: Exploring the relationship between higher education and political engagement. *Political Behavior, 27*(1), 25–47.

Holmes, W. M. (2013). *Using propensity scores in quasi-experimental designs.* Los Angeles, CA: SAGE.

Horrace, W. C., & Oaxaca, R. L. (2006). Results on the bias and inconsistency of ordinary least squares for the linear probability model. *Economics Letters, 90*, 321–327.

Hutteman, R., Hennecke, M., Orth, U., Reitz, A. K., & Specht, J. (2014). Developmental tasks as a framework to study personality development in adulthood and old age. *European Journal of Personality, 28*, 267–278.

Keen, C., & Hall, K. (2008) Post-graduation service and civic outcomes for high financial need students of a multi-campus, co-curricular service-learning college program. *Journal of College and Character, 10*, 1–15.

Kerrigan, S. (2005). College graduates' perspectives on the effect of capstone service-learning courses. In M. Martinez, P. A. Pasque, N. Bowman, & T. Chambers (Eds.), *Multidisciplinary perspectives on higher education for the public good* (pp. 49–65). Ann Arbor, MI: National Forum on Higher Education for the Public Good.

Kiely, R. (2005). A transformative learning model for service-learning: A longitudinal case study. *Michigan Journal of Community Service Learning, 12*(1), 5–22.

Lenzi, M., Vieno, A., Perkins, D. D., Santinello, M., Elgar, F. J., Morgan, A., & Mazzardis, S. (2012). Family affluence, school and neighborhood contexts and adolescents' civic engagement: A cross-national study. *American Journal of Community Psychology, 50*, 197–210.

Lerner, R. M., Wang, J., Champine, R. B., Warren, D. J., & Erickson, K. (2014). Development of civic engagement: Theoretical and methodological issues. *International Journal of Developmental Science, 8*(3–4), 69–79.

Maxwell, S. E., & Cole, D. A. (2007). Bias in cross-sectional analyses of longitudinal mediation. *Psychological Methods, 12*(1), 23–44.

McArdle, J. J. (2009). Latent variable modeling of differences and changes with longitudinal data. *Annual Review of Psychology, 60*, 577–605.

Murnane, R. J., & Willett, J. B. (2011). *Methods matter: Improving causal inference in educational and social science research.* New York, NY: Oxford University Press.

Muthén, B., & Asparouhov, T. (2015). Causal effects in mediation modeling: An introduction with applications to latent variables. *Structural Equation Modeling: A Multidisciplinary Journal, 22*(1), 12–23.

Nie, N., & Hillygus, S. (2001). Education and democratic citizenship. In D. Ravitch & J. P. Viteritti (Eds.), *Making good citizens: Education and civil society* (pp. 30–57). New Haven, CT: Yale University Press.

Pan, W., & Bai, H. (2015). *Propensity score analysis: Fundamentals and developments.* New York, NY: Guilford.

Pascarella, E. T., Salisbury, M. H., & Blaich, C. (2013). Design and analysis in college impact research: Which counts more? *Journal of College Student Development, 54*, 329–335.

Pattanayak, C. W. (2015). Evaluating covariate balance. In W. Pan & H. Bai (Eds.), *Propensity score analysis: Fundamentals and developments* (pp. 89–114). New York, NY: Guilford.

Preacher, K. J. (2015). Advances in mediation analysis: A survey and synthesis of new developments. *Annual Review of Psychology, 66*, 825–852.

Reid, A., Dahlgren, L. O., Petocz, P., & Dahlgren, M. A. (2008). Identity and engagement for professional formation. *Studies in Higher Education, 33*, 729–742.

Roberts, B. W., Edmonds, G., & Grijalva, E. (2010). It is developmental me, not generation me: Developmental changes are more important than generational changes in narcissism—Commentary on Trzesniewski & Donnellan. *Perspectives on Psychological Science, 5*(1), 97–102.

Ruiz, A., & Warchal, J. (2013). Long-term impact of service-learning on alumni volunteer service activities. In P. Lin & M. Wiegand (Eds.), *Service-learning in higher education: Connecting the global to the local* (pp. 255–264). Indianapolis: University of Indianapolis Press.

Schaefer, D. R., & Dillman, D. A. (1998). Development of a standard e-mail methodology. *Public Opinion Quarterly, 62,* 378–397.

Shadish, W. R. (2013). Propensity score analysis: Promise, reality and irrational exuberance. *Journal of Experimental Criminology, 9*(2), 129–144.

Shadish, W. R., Cook, T. D., & Campbell, D. T. (2002). *Experimental and quasi-experimental designs for generalized causal inference* (2nd ed.). Boston: Houghton Mifflin.

Smithson, M., & Merkle, E. C. (2013). *Generalized linear modeling for categorical and continuous limited dependent variables.* Boca Raton, FL: CRC Press.

Steiner, P. M., Cook, T. D., Shadish, W. R., & Clark, M. H. (2010). The importance of covariate selection in controlling for selection bias in observational studies. *Psychological Methods, 15,* 250–267.

Stuart, E. A. (2010). Matching methods for causal inference: A review and a look forward. *Statistical Science, 25*(1), 1–21.

Stürmer, T., Joshi, M., Glynn, R. J., Avorn, J., Rothman, K. J., & Schneeweiss, S. (2006). A review of the application of propensity score methods yielded increasing use, advantages in specific settings, but not substantially different estimates compared with conventional multivariable methods. *Journal of Clinical Epidemiology, 59*(5), 437–447.

Syvertsen, A. K., Wray-Lake, L., Flanagan, C. A., Osgood, D. W., & Briddell, L. (2011). Thirty-year trends in US adolescents' civic engagement: A story of changing participation and educational differences. *Journal of Research on Adolescence, 21,* 586–594.

Trede, F., Macklin, R., & Bridges, D. (2012). Professional identity development: A review of the higher education literature. *Studies in Higher Education, 37,* 365–384.

Trzesniewski, K. H., Donnellan, M. B., & Robins, R. W. (2008). Is "Generation Me" really more narcissistic than previous generations? *Journal of Personality, 76,* 903–918.

Twenge, J. M., Campbell, W. K., & Freeman, E. C. (2012). Generational differences in young adults' life goals, concern for others, and civic orientation, 1966–2009. *Journal of Personality and Social Psychology, 102,* 1045–1062.

Twenge, J. M., Konrath, S., Foster, J. D., Campbell, W. K., & Bushman, B. J. (2008). Egos inflating over time: A cross-temporal meta-analysis of the Narcissistic Personality Inventory. *Journal of Personality, 76,* 875–902.

Vogelgesang, L. J., & Astin, A. W. (2000). Comparing the effects of community service and service-learning. *Michigan Journal of Community Service Learning, 7*(1), 25–34.

Xie, Y., & Powers, D. (2008). *Statistical methods for categorical data analysis* (2nd ed.). Bingley, UK: Emerald.

Zaff, J. F., Malanchuk, O., & Eccles, J. S. (2008). Predicting positive citizenship from adolescence to young adulthood: The effects of a civic context. *Applied Developmental Science, 12,* 38–53.

DOCUMENTING AND GATHERING AUTHENTIC EVIDENCE OF STUDENT CIVIC OUTCOMES

Ashley Finley and Terrel Rhodes

C ampus discussions regarding the value of civic learning, whether in relationship to new civic programming, better targeting existing civic activities, or addressing resource concerns, are greatly aided by the use of evidence from students' civic learning experiences to support assessment, decision-making, program improvement, and research. Rigorous and meaningfully gathered evidence can provide a cornerstone for developing faculty inquiry and research into students' civic learning. In this way, good assessment of students' civic learning can provide both a basis for evidence-based programmatic and curricular improvements in regard to high-impact teaching strategies like service learning (Finley, 2011) and also an empirical basis for research and scholarship of teaching and learning.

Considerations about assessment can be about many topics, but they often come down to one fundamental question: What counts as good evidence of learning and for whom? The answer to this question can often be framed in terms of dichotomies: quantitative or qualitative; direct or indirect. The answer can also come with certain value judgments about the integrity of the evidence—valid or invalid, good or bad, persuasive or irrelevant, meaningful or not meaningful. The answer can also vary dependending on who is asking or answering the question—instructors or staff, faculty in the humanities or natural sciences, practitioners or researchers. Considering how different types of evidence can be used in combination to craft a broad and coherent narrative about student learning at an institution or within a particular course or program is often the best approach to understanding the outcomes of student learning in general and students' civic learning in particular. Understanding evidence from quantitative data can be enhanced when paired with qualitative data, such as comments from student focus groups or from student reflections. Pairing different sources of data can illuminate nuances of the learning experience that often get muddied when relying on a single source of evidence. Additionally, although indirect evidence captured through student self-reported surveys or course evaluations provides insights into the ways in which students *perceive* their learning experiences, student perceptions should be balanced with direct evidence gathered from students' actual coursework in order to assess students' ability to demonstrate learning and skill acquisition.

A focus on gathering direct evidence, however, gives rise to another dichotomy—whether or not the evidence is authentic. Authentic evidence is almost always connected with direct assessment, in that student work products are used to assess students' demonstrated learning skills or knowledge. But not all products of student learning are necessarily authentic. Authentic is intended to signify a demonstration of student learning that is derived from and connected to a specific learning experience. The demonstration of learning is not, for example, an artificial prompt external to the course or programmatic work that carries little to no significance to the student. Rather, authentic evidence is course-embedded such that the demonstration of learning is relevant and meaningful to both the student and the instructor in so far as the demonstration is viewed as a component of the students' expected coursework. The concept of authentic evidence can also be the result of learning from cocurricular experiences and programs, assuming students are asked to create or apply their learning to develop a work product as the result of an intentionally designed experience and assignment (Jacoby, 2015). Whether course-based or not, the use of authentic evidence from students' civic learning experiences for assessment comes with the caveat that courses and cocurricular experiences have been intentionally designed to address identified civic outcomes. The intentional design of students' engagement to produce civic learning (chapter 1.3) should be attentive to the ways in which classroom-based activities and experiences that occur outside of class, or that are entirely cocurricular, are constructed. The manner in which students are intentionally invited to demonstrate civic learning through carefully crafted assignments is also critical for effective direct assessment.

Despite the importance and utility of authentic evidence to inform best practices and research in regard to students' civic learning, two common issues can impede their use at the institutional level. The first is the challenge of making civic outcomes explicit enough to be assessed. Even though assignments at the course level may have been constructed with civic learning outcomes in mind, the translation of those outcomes into assessable components and into a form that can hold up to the rigor and methodological standards for scholarship can be daunting for instructors, administrators, and researchers. The second challenge, assuming articulation of civic outcomes has been achieved, is collecting authentic evidence such that instructors and students can evaluate the evidence, both formatively, to see how the progression on civic outcomes develops over time, and also summatively at the end of a specified period (e.g., the completion of a cumulative capstone course or senior experience).

To address the challenge of making civic outcomes explicit enough to be addressed, we explore the approach of using multidimensional rubrics designed to be used at the institutional level for guiding the assessment of authentic evidence from students' civic learning experiences gathered across programs and departments. This approach enables the kind of broad and coherent assessment of students' progress on learning outcomes, particularly civic outcomes, that is often lacking across colleges and universities. Specifically, the Association of American Colleges & Universities' (AAC&U) Valid Assessment of Learning in Undergraduate Education (VALUE) rubrics are provided as a model for how complex civic outcomes, such as intercultural knowledge and competence, civic engagement, global learning, and ethical reasoning, can be articulated in an assessable and methodologically sound instrument (AAC&U, 2009). Examples are also provided for how these VALUE rubrics have been applied across different campuses and campus contexts.

To address the issue of collecting authentic evidence in a way that helps both instructors and students understand civic outcomes, we also highlight the significant role of electronic portfolios (ePortfolios) in providing an infrastructure and transparency for capturing student work over time. Importantly, ePortfolios are a designated place for students to catalog and critically reflect upon their learning across time. We also provide examples of how campuses have used, and modified, their approaches to gathering and assessing authentic evidence and how these modifications better support the alignment of civic outcomes with program and campus goals for student learning.

Rubrics as Tools for Assessing Authentic Evidence

Whether in writing programs or when designed for assignments within particular disciplines, the utility of rubrics is that their development typically demands levels of articulation and transparency of evaluation standards not commonly provided to students or codified by an instructor. The twenty-first century conversation about the necessity of focusing on student development of broad skills and capabilities, including civic outcomes, has importantly extended the application of rubrics from course level assessment to institutional level use. Understanding rubrics at the institutional level relative to the course level does not need to fundamentally alter the definition of a *rubric*, however as evidenced by the following:

> A rubric is a creation of the people who made it rather than a mirror reflection of some permanent and absolute reality. . . . The rubric is our best judgment about what matters most in the stage of human development we think our students are currently in. (Griffin, 2010, p. 9)

Griffin's definition applies as well to a course-level rubric developed by an instructor as it does to a program-specific rubric developed for students within a particular major or a year-long cocurricular experience. The definition also applies to an *institutional-level rubric* developed or modified by a representative group of instructors from across disciplines to address institutional outcomes that span learning from general education through the major.

The difference between course-level or program-level rubrics and institutional rubrics is the need for specific content objectives to be inserted at the course and program levels. Institutional-level rubrics should be articulated using language that is inclusive of all disciplines and provides for the progression of learning over time from matriculation to graduation. Conceived of in this way, institutional-level rubrics allow for the assessment of student learning beyond a single service learning course. These tools enable the assessment of civic outcomes across multiple civic learning experiences in college, whether these experiences occur as part of course (either inside or outside the classroom) or in the cocurriculum.

The specification of a broad yet complex learning outcome is a critical and perhaps deceptively easy task of institutional-level rubrics, particularly in regard to civic outcomes. As a starting point, rubrics should be based upon a campus's institutional learning outcomes. Outcomes at the institutional-level should reflect an institution's mission, be broadly shared across disciplines, and be simply stated to maximize understanding and communication across stakeholders, including instructors, students, and staff. The difference, however, between an institution's commitment to fostering certain intellectual and practical skills (e.g., written communication, critical thinking, information literacy) and its commitment to civic outcomes (e.g., intercultural competence, civic engagement, global learning) is that the former set of outcomes often comes with a basic understanding of its component parts. Instructors from different disciplines and institutions might quibble about the nuances of writing and critical thinking, but there is also a fundamental sense that we know what comprises these outcomes and when students are displaying them.

The civic language in campus mission statements, however, can articulate an institution's commitment to students as "citizens," "ethical leaders," "social actors," "global change agents," or even as "social entrepreneurs." Instructors and others evaluating civic experiences on campus can use this language as a starting point for beginning to design or modify an existing rubric. A campus may frame its civic mission by its placement within an international context. For example, the mission statement of Webster University—a multicampus, multinational university—promises to "transform students for global citizenship and individual excellence" (Webster University, n.d.). By contrast, an institution's civic commitment may be deeply rooted in its ties to serve the local community or faith-based traditions. An example of such an institution is the College of Charleston, which includes within its mission the promise "to meet the growing educational demands primarily of the Lowcountry" (College of Charleston, n.d.)—a regional reference to the coastal area in which the college is located. Faith-based institutions may be similarly guided by the civic elements of their religious heritage. For example, Jesuit institutions, such as Georgetown University, commonly share missions focused on the language of social justice. As indicated on Georgetown's website, "The Church's commitment to social justice and the Jesuit mission to create leaders in the service of others underscores many intellectual and spiritual pursuits at the university" (Georgetown University, n.d.). Thus, each college or university should take notice of the distinctiveness of its own civic mission as a means for further articulating assessable civic learning outcomes for students.

Clarifying the intended outcomes of students' civic experiences also means parsing whether effects target specific civic outcomes (e.g., civic-mindedness, ethical awareness, intercultural competence, global learning, social justice), certain intellectual and practical skills (e.g., critical thinking, integrative learning, civic problem-solving, creative thinking), or both. Additionally, *civic outcomes* may be defined by the exercise of certain behaviors, such as civic duties (e.g., voting behavior) or actions (e.g., writing a petition, sending a letter to the editor) (Flanagan, Syversten, & Stout, 2007); or by exhibiting certain attitudes or dispositions, such as an openness to diversity (Bowman, Park, & Denson, 2015) or intercultural competence. Using rubrics to evaluate authentic evidence from service learning courses and other civic learning experiences can clarify and catalyze important conversations among instructors and staff to describe what experiences in the community are intended to foster in regard to student learning at both the course and institutional levels.

How Structure Mirrors Function for Meaningful Assessment of Civic Learning

Any approach to research or assessment of student learning outcomes, whether civic or not, should acknowledge one sobering fact about learning—it is complex. When students are asked to demonstrate a particular skill, whether civic or intellectual in nature, they must often show multiple aptitudes at once. For example, demonstrating proficiency in written communication requires organizing ideas and mechanics *in addition to* showing an awareness of the intended audience and adeptness within a particular style or genre of writing. Similarly, a student demonstrating the disposition to appreciate others from diverse contexts and cultures suggests the abilities to take a perspective other than one's own; be empathetic; be sensitive to paralinguistic and nonverbal cues; and respect the value of diverse personal, social, and political goals.

By articulating the dimensions of a learning outcome, instructors have the ability to construct assignments designed to engage students and elicit demonstration of those key dimensions in the products students complete as part of a course or cocurricular experience. For example, instructors from multiple departments could develop assignments all connected to a common civic outcome pertaining to a common civic experience in which students are engaged, such as preparing for a public meeting to discuss environmental issues and sustainability. Certain instructors could develop assignments to (a) prepare background materials for dissemination, (b) generate interest among potential audiences, (c) introduce and frame the agenda and the speakers, (d) conduct small group discussion sessions during the event, or (e) record and synthesize the recommendations and responses from the attendees. Moreover, seeking input from community members or partners working with students can provide valuable insights for revising assignments to more fully appreciate the context of the community setting, diversity of the audience, or nuances of informal conversations during the service experience. Community members might also be invited to contribute ideas for demonstrating student learning through products and deliverables that might directly benefit community organizations or activities (e.g., websites, white papers, media publications). In brief, the multiple dimensions of learning and ways to demonstrate them become central to constructing assignments by instructors. The students' products resulting from the assignments and the individual's contribution to it could all be assessed with the institutional level rubric but also with an emphasis on the specific context and content of the multiple courses that collaborated on the event in which students participated.

Additionally, student progress in cognitive development is not linear; it often develops over time but usually only with some amount of regression or failure when confronted with new applications, contexts, or subject matter (Pauk, 2014). For example, a student who is familiar with demonstrating intercultural competence through the lens of sociology may struggle when having to do so using concepts from biology or a non-Western standpoint. The idea of regression as an important element of learning (Huston, 2009) or even ambiguity (Dewey, 1929) is particularly relevant for understanding learning within civic experiences in which interaction with diverse others and hands-on applied learning can often challenge students to confront, reexamine, and explore ideas in new and uncomfortable ways. Assessment of civic experiences should, therefore, capture the multidimensional nature of learning outcomes at progressive levels of cognitive development.

The AAC&U VALUE rubrics (AAC&U, 2009) provide a model of how institution-level rubrics can be constructed to address both complexity of learning and progression of learning over time. The VALUE rubrics were developed through interdisciplinary collaboration, primarily among instructors, across varied institutional types (Rhodes, 2010). Each of 16 development teams focused on a single learning outcome, constructing and revising each metarubric over a period of 18 months from 2007 to 2009. Collectively, development teams received feedback from approximately 100 campuses that volunteered to solicit instructor and student responses on the readability, applicability, and comprehensiveness of a rubric.

Structurally, the rows of each VALUE rubric explicate essential dimensions of a particular learning outcome that a student is expected to demonstrate. Civic engagement, for example, is articulated as a demonstration of awareness and aptitude across criteria that include "diversity of communities and cultures," "analysis of knowledge," "civic identity and commitment," "civic communication," "civic action and reflection," and "civic contexts/structures" (AAC&U, 2009). In accordance with each row, the columns of each VALUE rubric articulate students' progression in learning over time by signifying performance levels of "benchmark," "milestone," and "capstone." Descriptors at the capstone level are intended to reflect achievement at the end of a baccalaureate degree, whereas benchmark descriptors indicate the performance level of a typical student upon entry into college. Milestone descriptors help to articulate a student's progress along the path from benchmark to capstone. Additionally, "[t]he performance levels . . . do not represent year in school (freshman, sophomore . . .), nor do they correspond to grades (A, B, C, . . .)" (Rhodes, 2010, p. 2).

Because VALUE rubrics are intended to be used inclusively across stakeholders, including instructors, students, staff, and community partners (Bringle, Clayton, & Plater, 2013), they are useful resources not only for assessment and research, but also for generation of meaningful conversations that span disciplines, programs, and professions. By starting with a comprehensive articulation of what it means to be a civic-minded student, stakeholders can use the rubric to tweak language, combine criteria or entire rubrics, and ultimately adapt their own sense of what outcomes service learning and other civic experiences should foster among participating students. The nuances of these discussions may be further explored among instructors within departments and community partners who can come together as colearners to understand how civic outcomes translate within the language and practices of the disciplines as well as the community-based activities.

Finally, VALUE rubrics are also intended to be used by students as a source of reflection and self-assessment of their own learning. The accessibility of language and depth of articulation within the VALUE rubrics is intended to enable the rubrics to be easily understood by students. After being given the opportunity to explore the rubrics, students should be encouraged to apply particular rubrics to their own work as a strategy for facilitating reflection and deepening learning. In this way, rubrics can also foster conversations about the meaning of civic experiences and relevance to intended civic outcomes among students, across specific majors or fields of study.

Using Authentic Evidence to Improve Civic Learning and Civic Outcomes

Data gathered from rubrics can be used for research and improving service learning courses and other civic-oriented programs. For example, instructors at Daemon College used results from a rubric adapted from the Civic Engagement VALUE rubric to assess civic outcomes across service learning courses (Morace & Hibschweiler, 2013). As a result of their assessment and research into the efficacy of the program, instructors decided to create a common reflection prompt that would be intentionally crafted to address criteria of the rubric. In a similar way, Loyola University of Chicago used rubric data "to improve experiential learning course delivery, teaching and learning strategies, assignment development, and achievement of desired learning outcomes" (Green & Kehoe, 2013, p. 2). These examples highlight the importance of translating findings from authentic evidence into practical strategies for improving the learning experience for students. These strategies specifically relate to changing the learning environment itself through assignments, quality of students' engagement, and the depth of that engagement to better connect students with the intended civic outcome.

Rubric data derived from assessing authentic evidence can also inform modifications to the rubrics. For example, Texas A&M University, in its use of the Intercultural Knowledge and Competence VALUE rubric, received feedback from scorers regarding needed information on the actual assignment prompts in order to better apply certain dimensions of the rubric to student work samples (McLawhon, n.d.). This suggestion enabled greater transparency of the intent of the assignments to meet the criteria of the rubrics between the instructors creating the course assignments and those doing the evaluation of the products of those assignments. The result was, therefore, not only greater ability to apply the rubric tool, but also greater validity of the tool for evaluating student work. Texas A&M's experience underscores the benefit of campuses using authentic evidence from rubrics to improve the assessment process itself, in addition to improvements in the learning environment, as noted in the previous examples. Simply engaging in the assessment process can reveal critical insights into how to more consistently apply the rubric to authentic evidence, identify the parameters for acceptable or appropriate assignments, and improve the ability to interpret scores.

A focus on authentic evidence and the use of rubrics as a common assessment tool can also facilitate collaboration among campuses to improve civic work and outcomes. Mount Wachusett Community College and Fitchburg State University (Massachusetts) have partnered through the AAC&U Quality Collaborative project to provide students transferring between their institutions a common understanding and level of proficiency through the use of the Civic Engagement VALUE rubric as a common instrument. Campuses have also collaborated to create new rubrics focused on civic outcomes not in the original set of VALUE rubrics. As a result of a Teagle-funded project, Elon University and Wofford College, with guidance from the Interfaith Youth Core and AAC&U, created a pluralistic rubric (Interfaith Youth Core, n.d.). Another project funded by the Teagle Foundation brought together a consortium of six diverse institutions, all part of Imagining America, whose work culminated, in part, in the creation of a Civic Professionalism rubric (Imagining America, n.d.). This Teagle project and others, including the Rubric Assessment of Information Literacy Skills (RAILS) project on information literacy sponsored by the American Council of Research Libraries (Oakleaf, 2012), demonstrates the power of rubrics for cross- or multiple-institutional research to enhance student learning and pedagogy.

These examples suggest the myriad ways in which rubrics applied to authentic evidence can guide research and improve assessment of activities related to service learning and other civic experiences. Collectively, the examples suggest that research helps to illuminate learning at the student level and also at the level of stakeholders engaged in the research who may be instructors and staff, as well as community partners.

The next section examines the use of ePortfolios as a mechanism for capturing authentic evidence and engaging students more deeply in the learning process itself. Like rubrics, ePortfolios can also help to make the learning process within civic experiences and their relationship to civic outcomes more transparent and reflective for students.

ePortfolios for Engaged Civic Learning

Both inside and outside formal academic settings, learning occurs continuously. Minds and bodies are constantly absorbing, observing, sensing, and feeling changes in environments in the course of daily lives. In higher education, attention is focused on the curriculum and cocurriculum offered by the particular campus. There is growing recognition among educators, however, that a new, more racially and economically diverse majority of students will benefit from a more robust approach to how instructors and administrators help students connect and engage with their learning in the formal curriculum, the cocurriculum, and the communities in which they live (Penny Light, Chen, & Ittelson, 2012).

ePortfolios are a particularly responsive framework for helping students, instructors, and institutions document, assess, and understand student learning in the context of higher order skills and abilities integral to postsecondary education. ePortfolios are designed to capture and represent learning in many of its facets and manifestations, wherever and whenever it occurs. Because ePortfolios can integrate all types of technologies, modes, and temporal possibilities (e.g., audio, video, text, graphic, statistical, visual, oral, written, performed, individual, group, synchronous/asynchronous, local/global), students have the opportunity to demonstrate their learning in multiple forms. Additionally, instructors design the basic ePortfolio framework for their course, program, or institution, allowing student learning to be grounded in the knowledge and values of a specific academic context.

The biennial national survey conducted by the EduCause Center for Analysis and Research (ECAR) on ePortfolio use found that three fourths of responding institutions reported using student ePortfolios at their institution (Dahlstrom, Brooks, & Bichsel, 2014). The National Institute for Learning

Outcomes Assessment's (NILOA) most recent survey of chief academic officers also reports an ongoing expansion of ePortfolio and rubric use across U.S. campuses. "While all types of measures are being used more often, the most striking changes are the increased use of rubrics, portfolios, external performance assessment (such as internship and service learning), and employer surveys" (Kuh, Jankowski, Ikenberry, & Kinzie, 2014, p. 13).

ePortfolios are emerging in a variety of forms and contexts that illustrate the flexibility and power of what has been called integrative or "folio thinking"—thinking in terms of connections among the multiple dimensions, concepts, viewpoints and information necessary to address modern, complex problems, issues, and decisions. Following are several examples of how ePortfolios have been used to maximize student learning through displaying authentic evidence across a variety of learning outcomes, including civic outcomes.

- The use of digital storytelling at Georgetown University (pilot.cndls .georgetown.edu/digitalstories/about) reveals the interplay of technology and media with traditional text and classroom lectures as well as student interactions and communication with other audiences beyond the classroom. This learning strategy results in a student's deeper understanding of the context related to his or her own experience and encourages reflection upon one's own and others' values and backgrounds. A research project conceived as a scholarship of teaching and learning project grew out of this work. The Visible Knowledge Project, a five-year multicampus study of the impact of new technologies on teaching in history and culture field, combined open-ended interviews with students' stories and written work (Oppermann & Coventry, 2012).
- An art professor collaborated with an engineering professor at California State University, Los Angeles, to engage students in interdisciplinary problem-solving that involved multiple dimensions of learning—critical thinking, reflection, socially engaged practice, and collaboration—directly with local community organizations and community partners in order to design and produce a civic art project (see www.calstatela.edu/engagement/faculty-fellows-public-good). The project was modeled on other civic art initiatives, such as the Complaints Choirs (Birmingham, England) where community members and students sang their complaints about the cities in which they live. The municipal government implemented bicycle and bus schedule changes in response to the sung complaints (for Complaints Choir, see Lung, 2014, pp. 61–68).

- Accreditation reaffirmation through the Southern Association of Colleges and Schools's Quality Enhancement Project (QEP) provided impetus for Texas A&M University to turn a mandatory accountability requirement into an innovative research project and pedagogical assignment. Texas A&M focused their QEP on developing student ePortfolios aimed at integrating students' learning through formal courses with real-life situations that called for students to demonstrate personal and social responsibility reasoning and action, and then sharing with peers and instructors the ways in which their applied learning had direct application to life decisions. As one example of students' authentic evidence under this initiative, students demonstrated visual, written, and oral communication skills by developing and recording two-minute videos of ethical decision-making situations in their own lives. The videos were used as public service announcements, the most exemplary of which were broadcast at halftime during varsity basketball games. The videos in addition to other authentic work products from students became part of students' ePortfolios to exemplify aspects of their civic learning as well as other learning outcomes(assessmentconference.tamu.edu/resources/conf_2010_presentations/Bair_EngagingAssessment_Handouts.pdf).
- DePaul University uses ePortfolios for service learning and civic engagement outcomes as students explore community and campus-based projects and internships through their Steans Center for Community-Based Service Learning and Community Service Studies. "Discover Chicago has encouraged students to step out of their comfort zone to explore the city's geographic and cultural landscape beyond the Loop and Lincoln Park campuses" (Discover, 2015, p. 1). The VALUE Integrative Learning rubric is used with the first-year ePortfolio of in-class and community-based learning projects to examine student growth and development in connecting theory, knowledge, and practice.
- Florida State University's Career Center utilizes ePortfolios to help students integrate their knowledge derived from internship and service learning experiences. Their ePortfolio has prepared over 90,000 student and alumni users by helping them document the transferable skills developed through curricular and cocurricular experiences, relate their experiences to critical skills needed in the global economy, and market themselves to employers or graduate schools (Ford, Lumsden, & Lulgjuraj, 2009).
- Elon University piloted the assessment of students' experiences with diversity using student ePortfolios and the Intercultural Knowledge

and Competence VALUE rubric. Following this pilot, the same rubric was also used to assess student learning and growth in short-term study abroad courses. Drawing from lessons learned and conversations from earlier pilot efforts, Elon faculty and staff are currently exploring how the rubric for intercultural knowledge and competence can be applied to assess learning in other core learning experiences at the university (P. Felten, personal communication, June 22, 2016).

One of the most extensive projects to explore multicampus collaboration focused on the interplay between learning and ePortfolios has been the Catalyst to Learning (C2L) initiative funded through the Fund for Improvement of Post-Secondary Education, involving 24 diverse campuses and led by LaGuardia Community College. C2L resulted in a rich compilation of materials and examples related to a variety of service learning, personal and social responsibility, and communications outcomes as well as resources on professional development, reflective practices, and social pedagogies (i.e., the importance of multiple evaluators providing feedback and commentary on learning growth and development). "Based on campus evaluation reports, C2L findings suggest that sophisticated e-portfolio initiatives can advance student success, deepen student learning, and spur transformative institutional change" (Catalyst for Learning, n.d.).

In particular, C2L's emphasis on reflective practice (i.e., the requirement that students and instructors reflect on the learning process as well as the substantive learning itself resulting from the course or community work) emerged as an integral part of how ePortfolios help to foster student engagement in the learning process and increased the visibility of learning to students. Reflection, however, is not something most students, including students who typically are viewed as well prepared for college, are trained and practiced in doing (Rodgers, 2002). Useful models and resources within higher education have been developed for assisting students and instructors to engage in reflective practices. For example, the Describe, Examine, and Articulate Learning (DEAL) reflection model is focused on generating learning, deepening learning, and capturing authentic evidence of academic learning, civic learning, and personal growth. The DEAL model includes an explicit component that invites students to engage in critical and intentionally designed reflections throughout their civic learning experiences as a method for deepening both students' abilities to reflect and the quality of the reflections themselves, over time (Ash & Clayton, 2009). In addition, DEAL has rubrics for evaluating the level of learning using Bloom's Taxonomy and for evaluating the critical thinking represented in the product.

Implications of Using Authentic Evidence for Service Learning Research

The efficacy of using authentic evidence to assess students' academic and civic learning and personal growth through their engagement in service learning and other civic experiences is grounded in a good deal of campus-based practice and national projects that have been detailed throughout this chapter. Nevertheless, there are still many research questions to pursue. For example, what is the benefit if students engage in *multiple* service learning experiences, rather than one or even two, on their learning and development? Some colleges and universities (e.g., Tulane University, California State University-Monterey Bay) require multiple service learning experiences for graduation. Research based on indirect evidence suggests that as students' engagement in multiple high-impact experiences increases, the perceived gains in their learning also increase, a finding that is particularly relevant for underserved students who engage in such experiences (Finley & McNair, 2013). However, we know very little about the value of assessing the authentic evidence from students' multiple service learning and civic experiences on their learning and acquisition of civic outcomes. How might having more extensive evidence of this type both deepen and potentially complicate the narrative on the value of students' engagement in multiple civic experiences in college?

Additionally, much of the existing research on high-impact practices, including service learning, has been largely based on indirect evidence drawn from student responses to surveys such as the National Survey of Student Engagement (NSSE) (e.g., Kuh, 2009; Kuh, O'Donnell, & Reed, 2013). An important extension of this foundational work, therefore, will be to understand the degree to which authentic evidence drawn from students' demonstrated learning supports or deviates from previous findings based on indirect evidence. This type of research will help not only instructors and practitioners, but also those involved in assessing student learning in general to understand how findings from using rubrics to assess authentic evidence converge with or diverge from evaluations of learning outcomes based upon indirect assessments. In time, such research could guide practitioners and researchers alike to refine both rubrics and self-report surveys in such a way as to more fully and accurately encourage mixed method assessments of students' service learning experiences.

A related point of research on students' engagement in multiple service learning experiences might consider the ways in which students' development and ongoing use of an ePortfolio contributes to learning outcomes. Specifically, in what ways does having an ePortfolio integrated into service learning courses and other experiences result in deeper learning for students, whether in a single or across multiple course-based civic or service learning experiences? This question and those that precede it should also be attentive to the ways in which findings differ for different populations of students, specifically those traditionally underserved by higher education (i.e., first-generation, low-income, students of color). Service learning research should be mindful of the need to disaggregate data wherever possible to understand the nuanced effects of students' community engagement for different student populations.

Conclusion

Higher education becomes transformative when students are given the opportunity to make constructive use of their learning, rather than be passive recipients of knowledge or someone else's viewpoints (chapter 2.3). Students need to be enabled and encouraged to apply their learning to real-world situations and within real-world settings (i.e., environments outside of a controlled classroom environment) to better connect the material to their own lives, understand its contemporary relevance, and take stock of associated causes and consequences in real world settings. For this reason, service learning and civic engagement are particularly powerful modes for helping students to engage in exactly this type of application. It is also critical for helping students understand the world beyond the college's walls. Service learning and other civic experiences benefit students by encouraging them to connect with their peers, instructors, community partners, leaders, and residents. It is perhaps the lens and perspective of community members that can yield the most transformative elements for students by challenging students to understand what it means to not just be in the community, but to actually understand the diverse perspectives of others who live within the community.

But in order to capture the full promise of these experiences, assessments must include not just what students *think* they have learned, but also evidence of what knowledge, skills, and behaviors they are able to demonstrate. Moreover, the authentic evidence gathered from products based on students' service learning experiences can be accumulated over time to ensure that their demonstrated abilities grow progressively more sophisticated and complex as their abilities strengthen.

The challenge of rethinking how to approach student learning has grown even more compelling in the twenty-first century. As the world becomes increasingly complex, diversified, and globally interconnected, the demand on higher education to deliver on its promise to prepare successful generations of leaders, not only for economic prosperity but also for democratic strength and individual and social flourishing, will continue to grow. ePortfolios can play a powerful role in helping higher education deliver on transformation and preparation by providing a platform through which students can apply learning, reflect on experiences, and share that learning with external audiences. In this way, connecting ePortfolios to service learning can enhance how students are encouraged to understand who they are as individual learners, who they want to be in the world, and how those ideas and reflections interact to provide perspective on who they are as civic beings.

Just as service learning and other civic experiences are multifaceted, complex learning opportunities for student learning, the same is true for the accuracy of assessment. There will always be ways to improve service learning programs, and we rely on evidence to guide those efforts. The best that instructors and researchers can do is to ask meaningful questions about the outcomes they seek from these experiences, the appropriateness of the tools to measure those outcomes, and the intentionality with which students have been invited to reflect upon and/or demonstrate their learning. The research on service learning and the programs that foster it does not suffer from a failure to assess; it suffers most from the wrong kind of assessment and heavy reliance on self-report measures of student outcomes. Taking the time to make assessment of service learning more meaningful, inclusive of input from community partners, and guided by best practices can make the difference between simply having evidence and having evidence that can actually be used for improvement of civic learning.

References

American Association of Colleges and Universities (AAC&U). (2009). *Civic engagement VALUE rubrics*. Retrieved from https://www.aacu.org/civic-engagement-value-rubric

Ash, S. L., & Clayton, P. H. (2009). Generating, deepening, and documenting learning: The power of critical reflection for applied learning. *Journal of Applied Learning in Higher Education, 1*, 25–48.

Bowman, N. A., Park, J. J., & Denson, N. (2015). Student involvement in ethnic student organizations: Examining civic outcomes 6 years after graduation. *Research in Higher Education, 56*, 127–145.

Bringle, R. G., Clayton, P. H., & Plater, W. M. (2013). Assessing diversity, global, and civic learning: A means to change in higher education. *Democracy and Diversity, 13*(3), 4–6.

Catalyst for Learning (n.d.). *ePortfolio resources and research*. Retrieved from http://c2l.mcnrc.org/

College of Charleston. (n.d.) *Mission statement.* Retrieved from http://marcomm .cofc.edu/brandmanual/bychapter/brandfoundation/collegemission.php

Dahlstrom, E., Brooks, D. C., & Bichsel, J. (2014, September). *The current ecosystem of learning management systems in higher education: Student, faculty, and IT perspectives.* Research report. Louisville, CO: ECAR. Available from http://www .educause.edu/ecar.

Dewey, J. (1929). *The quest for certainty: A study of the relation of knowledge and action* (Gifford Lectures). London, England: Unwin Brothers.

Discover Chicago awakens students to diverse experiences. (2015). *DePaul Magazine, 1,* Article 3.

Finley, A. (2011). *Civic learning and democratic engagements: A review of the literature on civic engagement in post-secondary education.* Paper prepared for the U.S. Department of Education as part of Contract: ED-OPE-10_C-0078. Retrieved from www.civiclearning.org/SupportDocs/LiteratureReview_CivicEngagement_ Finley_Jul2011.pdf

Finley, A., & McNair, T. (2013). *Assessing underserved students' engagement in high-impact practices.* Washington, DC: Association of American Colleges & Universities.

Flanagan, C. A., Syvertsen, A. K., & Stout, M. D. (2007). Civic measurement models: Tapping adolescents' civic engagement. Washington, DC: Center for Information and Research on Civic Learning and Engagement.

Ford, C. M., Lumsden, J.A., & Lulgjuraj, B. (2009). *Reactions to curricular and co-curricular learning as documented in an ePortfolio.* Technical Report no. 48. The Center for the Study of Technology in Counseling and Career Development. Tallahassee: Florida State University.

Georgetown University. (n.d.) *Jesuit and Catholic identity.* Retrieved from www .georgetown.edu/about/jesuit-and-catholic-heritage

Green, P., & Kehoe, A. (2013). *Adapting rubrics in experiential learning courses.* Retrieved from http://www.aacu.org/sites/default/files/files/VALUE/loyolachicago.pdf

Griffin, M. (2010). What is a rubric? In T. Rhodes (Ed.), *Assessing outcomes and improving achievement: Tips and tools for using rubrics* (pp. 9–10). Washington, DC: Association of American Colleges & Universities.

Huston, T. (2009). *Teaching what you don't know.* Cambridge, MA: Harvard University Press.

Imagining America. (n.d.) *Civic professionalism.* Retrieved from http:// imaginingamerica.org/research/engaged-undergrad/

Interfaith Youth Core. (n.d.). *Pluralism and worldview engagement rubric.* Retrieved from http://www.ifyc.org/sites/default/files/u4/PluralismWorldviewEngagement Rubric2.pdf

Jacoby, B. (2015). Engaging first-year commuter students in learning. *Metropolitan Universities, 15*(2), 12–30.

Kuh, G. D. (2009). What student affairs professionals need to know about student engagement. *Journal of College Student Development, 50,* 683–706.

Kuh, G. D., Jankowski, N., Ikenberry, S. O., & Kinzie, J. (2014). *Knowing what students know and can do: The current state of student learning outcomes assessment in U.S. colleges and universities.* National Institute for Learning Outcomes Assessment. Retrieved from www.learningoutcomesassessment.org

Kuh, G. D., O'Donnell, K., & Reed, S. (2013). *Ensuring quality and taking high-impact practices to scale.* Washington, DC: Association of American Colleges & Universities.

Lung, C. F. (2014). Retooling the university: Critical thinking, creative play, collaboration and participatory public art. In A. Finley (Ed.), *Civic learning and teaching* (pp. 61–68). Washington, DC: Bringing Theory to Practice.

McLawhon, R. (n.d.). *AAC&U VALUE rubrics at Texas A&M university.* Retrieved from http://www.aacu.org/sites/default/files/files/VALUE/texasam.pdf

Morace, R., & Hibschweiler, I. (n.d.). *Daemon college and the use of VALUE rubrics.* Retrieved from http://www.aacu.org/sites/default/files/files/VALUE/daemen.pdf

Oakleaf, M. (2012). Staying on track with rubric assessment: Five institutions investigate information literacy learning. *Peer Review, 14*(1), 18–21.

Oppermann, M., & Coventry, M. (2012). *Digital storytelling multimedia archive and website.* Center for New Designs in Learning and Scholarship, Georgetown University. Retrieved from https://pilot.cndls.georgetown.edu/digitalstories/about/

Pauk, W., & Owens, R. J. Q. (2014). *How to study in college.* Boston, MA: Wadsworth Cengage Learning.

Penny Light, T., Chen, H. L., & Ittelson, J. C. (2012). *Documenting learning with ePortfolios: A guide for college instructors.* San Francisco, CA: Wiley.

Rhodes, T. (Ed.). (2010). *Assessing outcomes and improving achievement: Tips and tools for using rubrics.* Washington, DC: Association of American Colleges & Universities.

Rodgers, C. (2002). Seeing student learning: Teacher change and the role of reflection. *Harvard Educational Review, 72*(2), 230–254.

Webster University. (n.d.) *The Webster University charge.* Retrieved from www.webster.edu/globalimpact/mission-vision-values.html

USING LOCAL AND NATIONAL DATASETS TO STUDY STUDENT CIVIC OUTCOMES

Steven S. Graunke and Michele J. Hansen

A
ssessment practitioners, evaluators, and institutional researchers are often charged with determining which educational programs most effectively improve students' learning, engagement, academic performance, retention, and degree completion. Additionally, campus administrators and policymakers must make decisions about which programs to implement, continue, or expand in order to ensure attainment of institutional strategic metrics and student learning outcomes. Rigorous assessment designs can determine if service learning promotes civic learning outcomes among participants (e.g., students, instructors, community partners). Although the primary aim of assessment and program evaluation activities may not be to generalize findings beyond local settings like the focus of research investigations, it is just as critical to ensure that practitioners and scholars engaged in these activities are guided by theory, employ rigorous research designs, consider appropriate statistical analyses, use appropriate quantitative and qualitative approaches, and ensure that implications for practice are backed by sound evidence sources.

This chapter describes some approaches to investigating service learning courses as well as data sources, both national and local, which provide greater context and enhanced understanding of civic outcomes. Assessing service learning requires careful conceptualization of the processes and intended outcomes before choosing measures and evaluation designs. As such, data at multiple levels (e.g., student, instructor, course, program, institution) and information regarding which course features lead to desired civic outcomes should be considered. This chapter examines how assessment, program evaluation, and research activities can sustain and improve quality in civic engagement programs by helping policymakers understand that these programs are often mission critical in facilitating student learning, success, and persistence.

Specifically, we highlight how local and national datasets can be used to investigate the ways in which service learning changes civic-minded attitudes and increases civic outcomes both during and after college. We supplement the discussion of institution-level studies (chapter 3.3) with a discussion of data sources that can provide data on institutions as well as courses and programs. Next, we explore how the National Survey of Student Engagement (NSSE) and other national surveys can provide data on students' self-reported civic learning outcomes and how participation in high-impact practices (Kuh, 2008) affects engagement. We then discuss longitudinal studies of behaviors after college (chapter 3.4), including how workforce data from state records and alumni surveys can illuminate the employment patterns and subsequent civic behaviors of former students. We conclude with suggestions for making assessment activities sustainable and managing existing institutional data for research purposes.

Investigating Service Learning Course Processes and Outcomes

Service learning has been advocated as an intervention that positively influences student civic engagement. The attitudes, skills, knowledge levels, and complex components of the community-based setting coupled with structured reflection allows students to integrate their learning experiences between the classroom and real-world settings (Pritzker & McBride, 2006). According to Steinberg, Hatcher, and Bringle (2011), the educational and civic experiences that students participate in during their college years are often valued due to their ability to facilitate students' sense of responsibility for becoming active and engaged citizens. Although offering service learning is not the only approach to improve civic outcomes, it is recognized as one of the most effective for achieving civic learning outcomes, including civic engagement (Brownell & Swaner, 2010; Finley, 2011; Kuh, 2008; Steinberg et al., 2011). If implemented well, service learning can help students develop their capacities for public action or skills necessary for engagement in a diverse and global society (e.g., communicate effectively, work collaboratively, explore complex issues, engage with diverse peers, learn globally).

Civic engagement is increasingly seen as an integrated aspect of higher education, and this has implications for institutional assessment and research. Pike, Bringle, and Hatcher (2014) argue that institutional assessment plays an important role in improving practice in higher education. Accordingly, gathering systematic data by using local and national data sources can enhance understanding of effective programs and practices for promoting civic learning outcomes, understanding the civic commitments of instructors, and guiding the allocation of resources. These data sources can also provide insights into trends in students', faculty members', and community partners' behaviors, values, and attitudes. In addition, service learning can lead to developing a more robust evidence base about effective practices to enhance civic outcomes in higher education.

Assessment approaches document and monitor the processes and pedagogical strategies that are theoretically and empirically linked to the promotion of civic outcomes. There are course features and pedagogical factors, such as those advocated by Jacoby (2009) and Brownell and Swaner (2010), that should be carefully monitored and evaluated to ensure that intended civic outcomes are achieved (chapter 1.1). According to Jacoby (2009), enhancing civic engagement necessitates interventions that contain one or more of the following: (a) allow students to learn from others, self, and environment to develop informed perspectives on social issues; (b) recognize and appreciate human diversity and commonality; (c) work through controversy, with civility; (d) take an active role in the political process; (e) participate actively in public problem solving and community service; (f) assume leadership and membership roles in organizations; (g) develop empathy, ethics, values, and sense of social responsibility; and (h) promote social justice locally and globally. Brownell and Swaner's (2010) empirical investigation found that service learning courses are more likely to enhance student engagement, success, and learning if they (a) create opportunities for structured reflection; (b) ensure that instructors connect classroom material with the service experience; (c) require enough service hours to make the experience significant; (d) focus on the quality of the service, ensuring that students have direct contact with clients; and (e) ensure that instructors oversee activities at the service site. Accordingly, these service learning features should be monitored and assessed using national and local data sources when scholars and practitioners engage in institutional and multi-institutional research, evaluation, and assessment.

We focus on institutional research, program evaluation, and outcomes assessment because most higher education leaders and policymakers rely on these approaches to determine the extent to which the educational benefits and intended outcomes of service learning are realized. Similar to research, these approaches, if done well, are also guided by theory, involve rigorous research designs, appropriate statistical analysis techniques, and are aimed at reaching valid and reliable conclusions. Unlike research, however, the aim of institutional research, program evaluation, and outcomes assessment is not to publish generalizable findings. The primary aim is to provide key stakeholders with valid and reliable information so that they can make better and informed decisions about continuing or modifying the program (Patton, 2008).

Institutional research typically involves professionals working to support campus leaders and policymakers in effective planning, programming, and fiscal decisions covering a broad range of institutional responsibilities (Volkwein, 2011). *Program evaluation* determines the merit, worth, or value of programs. The evaluation process identifies relevant standards that apply to what is being evaluated, performs empirical investigations using techniques from the social sciences, and then integrates conclusions with the standards into an overall evaluation to improve program implementation (Scriven, 1991). Evaluation activities are typically aimed at providing information for decision-making on specific programs, are conducted within complex settings, and must take into account stakeholders' needs, priorities, resources, and timelines. We adopt the view that program evaluation is a broader concept than assessment. Suskie states that "while assessment focuses on how well student learning goals are achieved, evaluation addresses how well the major goals of a program are achieved" (2009, p. 12). As such, service learning instructors assess student learning goals (e.g., higher level cognition), but they may also assess changes in students' attitudes, behaviors, and affective states. An evaluation of a service learning program may also consider quality of community-based partnerships, the impact of activities that constitute the service, and cost effectiveness. *Assessment* can be defined as a

> continuous cycle of improvement and is comprised of a number of features: establishing clear, measurable expected outcomes of student learning; ensuring that students have sufficient opportunities to achieve those outcomes; systematically gathering, analyzing, and interpreting evidence to determine how well student learning matches expectations; and using the resulting information to understand and improve student learning. (Suskie, 2009, p. 4)

Research involves the systematic investigation, including research development, theory testing, and evaluation of how variables relate to one another, and is designed to develop or contribute to generalizable knowledge or contribute to scholarship beyond local settings.

Assessing Civic Outcomes to Enhance Institutional Effectiveness and Student Success

Higher education institutions (HEI) are facing both internal and external pressures to improve and demonstrate the worth and value of interventions to promote civic outcomes. The Association of American Colleges & Universities (AAC&U) released a national call to action in the report *A Crucible Moment: College Learning & Democracy's Future* (National Task Force, 2012). The report provides recommendations to the U.S. Department of Education and urges the higher education community "to embrace civic learning and democratic engagement as an undisputed educational priority" (p. 2). The report rejects the notion that the mission of HEIs is to focus on workforce preparation and training at the expense of knowledge basic to democracy. The report also has implications for institutional research, assessment practitioners, and evaluators as "colleges and universities are asked to examine their role in civic learning and monitor how they have an impact on students' development" (Hurtado, Ruiz, & Whang, 2012, p. 3). Another report, *Advancing Civic Learning and Engagement in Democracy: A Road Map and Call to Action* (U.S. Department of Education, 2012), also represents a call to action for ensuring student civic learning outcomes and achievement. This report states the following:

> Preparing all students—regardless of background or identity—for informed, engaged participation in civic and democratic life is not only essential, but also consistent with the aims of increasing student achievement and closing achievement gaps. It is consistent with preparing students for 21st-century careers. (p. 2)

Over the last decade there has been an increased focus on ensuring that students not only gain access to higher education but also complete their degrees. However, increased attention devoted to college completions must also consider student learning and a production of high-quality degrees (Evenbeck & Johnson, 2012). Ideally, assessment data and research will be used to inform decisions about allocating resources

> to ensure that students' learning experiences are meaningful, relevant to their lives, and deeply engaging, and that a focus on quality teaching and deep learning is recognized as the basis of a curricular model that contributes to persistence and retention. (Johnson, 2013, p. 4)

In order to determine if service learning courses are helping students attain civic outcomes, there is a need to make explicit specific assessable outcomes and incorporate direct and indirect measures of student learning and change. The outcomes should focus holistically on students' development and define the knowledge, skills, attitudes, behaviors, affects, and values that students need to develop in order to be civically engaged, cultivate civic identity and commitments, understand the diversity of cultures and perspectives, develop informed perspectives on social issues, take an active role in the political process, and participate actively in public problem solving and community service. Direct measures require students to demonstrate their knowledge and skills. They provide tangible, visible, and self-explanatory evidence of what students have and have not learned as a result of a course, program, or activity (Palomba & Banta, 1999; Suskie, 2009). Suskie (2009) argues, "no assessment of knowledge, conceptual understanding, or thinking or performance skills should consist of indirect evidence alone" (p. 19). Examples of direct measures of student learning that could be collected from students participating in service learning may include culminating projects, portfolios, reflections, written papers, oral presentations, group work, assignments, exit exams, or standardized tests. The AAC&U Civic Engagement VALUE rubric or other rubrics designed to assess civic learning outcomes may be useful for systematically measuring students' learning gains. Rubrics may be especially useful for evaluating student artifacts (e.g., writing samples, reflections, oral presentations, projects) that students include as part of a paper-based or electronic portfolio. Additionally, rather than practicing assessment as an "add on" to the existing work of instructors and students, assessment activities should routinely involve the collection of and feedback on embedded, authentic measures of learning within service learning courses. With authentic, embedded assessment tasks, students are asked to demonstrate what they know and are able to do in meaningful ways. Embedded assessment means that "those opportunities to assess student progress and performance are integrated into the instructional materials and are virtually indistinguishable from the day-to-day classroom activities" (Wilson & Sloane, 2000, p. 182). (See chapter 3.5 for further discussion on authentic evidence, rubrics, and ePortfolios.)

Indirect measures capture students' perceptions of their knowledge and skills. They can supplement direct measures of learning by providing information about how and why learning is occurring (Suskie, 2009). Students' perceptions of the extent to which service learning courses and assignments have enhanced their achievement of civic outcomes may be obtained by using any of the following methods: self-assessment, peer feedback, end-of-course evaluations, questionnaires, focus groups, or exit interviews. National surveys such as the National Survey of Student Engagement (NSSE) may be useful in assessing student learning indirectly by providing information on the amount of time and effort students report putting into educationally purposeful activities programs and the extent to which service learning participation enhances their self-reported learning and personal development outcomes (Hahn & Hatcher, 2015).

Using a combination of qualitative and quantitative assessment approaches may also help to better understand the deep and varied outcomes of service learning. Qualitative research approaches such as interviews and focus groups with students and instructors can be helpful in understanding how different service learning course features are implemented and experienced. Mixed-method evaluation designs (Creswell, 2014; Frechtling, 2002; Greene, Caracelli, & Graham, 1989) allow researchers to obtain qualitative and quantitative evidence that demonstrates how well service learning promotes academic success and learning. For example, in-depth focus groups with instructors and students may provide insights into how service learning course features such as structured reflection assignments are perceived and implemented, whereas quantitative measures such as scores on civic learning rubrics and institutional data on students' grade point averages and retention rates may help to increase understanding regarding the ways in which students' in-depth perceptions of structured reflection assignments relate to learning outcomes.

In order to make informed decisions about the effectiveness of service learning courses, investigators should consider what evaluation and research designs are most appropriate for specific research questions. The research and assessment designs, as much as practically possible, should (a) employ appropriate comparison groups and use either matching or statistical techniques that take into account differences in academic preparation, demographic characteristics, and enrollment patterns; (b) be longitudinal and consider long-term outcomes such as graduation, degree completion, sustained learning, and application of learning to academic skills/tasks at later points in time; and (c) employ pre–post designs with comparison groups to assess changes in outcomes over time, particularly gains in learning or changes in behaviors or attitudes (chapter 3.4).

A noteworthy limitation of many investigations on the effectiveness of service learning courses and programs, when posttest-only comparison group design is used, is that students may self-select into the programs (Brownell & Swaner, 2010). It is possible that the positive effects of the service learning courses are due to the fact that students who decide to enroll may have differed in substantial ways from students who decided not to participate and these differences (not the programs) may have caused the positive outcomes. Experimental designs that employ random assignment remain the gold standard in terms of being able to make causal inferences ruling out selection bias. However, the use of experimental design is extremely rare in the educational research and service learning literature with some notable exceptions (Brown, 2011a, 2011b). Random assignment to service learning courses may not be feasible due to practical, administrative, and political circumstances. Despite potential challenges, practitioners and researchers should explore possibilities for random assignment, especially when pilot programs are developed that do not involve denying academic support to large populations of students and alternatives to treatment can be offered to these students. There are also statistical approaches that have been employed to address selection bias when random assignment is not possible (chapter 3.4), such as propensity score matching (Vaughan, Parra, & Lalonde, 2014), the Heckman adjustment (e.g., Heckman, 1979), and the use of instrumental variables (Angrist, Lang, & Oreopoulos, 2009; Pike, Hansen, & Lin, 2011).

Institutional researchers, evaluators, and assessment practitioners can consider internal and external data sources when conducting investigations on civic outcomes. Some of the external sources of information may include data obtained from Integrated Postsecondary Education Data System (IPEDS), the VALUE Rubrics on Civic Engagement, national surveys such as NSSE and the Student Experience in the Research University (SERU) survey, and labor market and workforce data from national and state records. Internal data sources may include course level information from registrar records, transcripts, faculty and staff data, and other information universities collect from students (data submitted in applications, financial aid information). The next sections detail approaches to using various sources of data.

Data for Multilevel Studies

Janke and Domagal-Goldman (chapter 3.3) discuss some of the challenges associated with conceptualizing studies at the institution level. In addition to an appropriate theoretical framework and networking among colleagues at different institutions, researchers studying how institutional factors affect the attainment of civic learning outcomes need standardized, reliable data to operationalize variables. Such data can be obtained from IPEDS. Furthermore, data stored within university records might also be used to better understand differences between courses or course-taking patterns by students and how these might affect growth in civic learning. Understanding where to obtain data, what specific fields in the data mean, and how to use information in conjunction with other data sources is essential to gaining a comprehensive understanding of the effects of service learning experiences.

IPEDS

IPEDS, maintained by the National Center for Education Statistics (NCES), is an important source for information on institutions that receive federal student aid dollars under Title IV of the Higher Education Act of 1965. The IPEDS data center provides the ability to obtain institutional characteristics, enrollments, degree completions, financial aid, graduation rates, and a wide variety of other data (NCES, n.d.a.).

Data from IPEDS is useful both for understanding the effects of service learning between institutions and framing the context of an individual institution. For example, Greenwood (2015) suggested that gains in students' experiences from participating in service learning may differ among urban, suburban, and rural institutions. IPEDS can provide information about the extent to which the surrounding community is urban, which may help disaggregate the effects of institutional setting. Pragman, Flannery, and Bowyer (2012) studied the effects of service learning on empathy, moral identity, and other factors and found female students demonstrated greater gains than male students. Building off this study, a researcher might ask if students at HEIs with a larger majority of female students experience greater gains from service learning. IPEDS can supply data to both control for between-institution differences that may affect outcomes of service learning programs as well as explore which institutional differences may facilitate positive outcomes.

Researchers new to IPEDS may find the volume of available data overwhelming, become frustrated that data appear to be unavailable, or be confused by definitions. For those looking for further information on IPEDS, the NCES collaborates with the Association for Institutional Research to provide both face-to-face and online training (NCES, n.d.b). Identifying an IPEDS "keyholder" on your campus may also be helpful. Keyholders are responsible for the final submission of all IPEDS surveys at an institution and should have knowledge of data definitions and what data is available.

Course Level Data

Much like IPEDS can provide considerable information about institutions, records from the registrar's office can provide information about individual courses and enrollment patterns. Institutional policies regarding the maintenance and dissemination of course data vary among universities or even among campuses within the same system. Generally speaking, registrars are bound to consider possible implications under the Federal Education Right's and Privacy Act of 1974 20 U.S.C. §§ 99.1–99.67 (1988) before releasing individually identifiable student information. As a result, a researcher may need to obtain student or parental consent to view course records. Researchers may, however, receive educational records without prior consent if they (a) have "legitimate educational interests" for studying student records within their own institution or (b) are conducting research for an educational institution in order to improve instruction or develop valid educational measures (Federal Education Right's and Privacy Act of 1974, §§ 99.31, 1, i, A [1988]). Most assessment activities should meet these criteria, but working with the registrar will ensure compliance with university policies and federal regulations. Course data can help answer questions such as "Does class size influence the gains in civic attitudes students report from service learning courses?" or "Do students in service learning courses taught by tenure track faculty exhibit greater gains in civic-mindedness than students in courses taught by adjunct faculty?"

In order to effectively use course data, researchers should be aware of how data are managed both on the course and the student level. Each course section for which data are obtained must have a unique identifier, which must be included with both course and student level data in order to ensure accurate and efficient mergers between datasets. Each course section should have an identifier in course-level data, but it is important to include course section identifiers in student information as well. Failure to include a unique identifier may cause course and student records to be mismatched, which would lead to inaccurate analyses. Researchers should carefully check all data to ensure that each student record is connected to the correct corresponding course or section identifier in order to avoid errors.

Transcripts

Student curricular transcripts can also be useful in understanding the relationship between academic experiences and civic learning outcomes. For example, Lockeman and Pelco (2013) combined course enrollment data with preenrollment student characteristics to find that students who enrolled in a service learning course were more likely to complete a bachelor's degree than students who did not. Registrar records at an institution should be able to provide data on students' course-taking patterns, if not the entire transcript.

Although optical technology for scanning transcripts is improving, it may be unavailable to researchers. Therefore, paper transcripts or even many electronic formats still need to be coded manually in order for the data be useful for research purposes. This process can be extremely time-consuming when working with multiple transcripts, and coding errors can occur. It is important that researchers maintain rigor when coding transcript data for subsequent analysis. Much like manually coding surveys, having two data entry files may reduce the likelihood of errors by making discrepancies easier to find and correct. For most researchers, working with the university registrar, institutional researchers, or others who have access to course data may help simplify the coding process.

Data for Studying Student Engagement

Many authors (e.g., Astin, 1984; McCormick, Kinzie, & Gonyea, 2013) have proposed a connection between various positive outcomes and the time and effort students spend on educationally purposeful activities, a concept otherwise termed *student engagement*. Astin, Vogelgesang, Ikeda, and Yee (2000), for example, explicitly explored the effects of service learning using students' self-reports of volunteer activity and participation in a course-based service project. They found that service learning had a significant association with diverse outcomes such as self-efficacy, GPA, interpersonal skills, and their desire to join a more service-focused career after college.

One of the most popular methods for collecting student engagement data is through student self-report instruments. Many institutions already use national surveys such as NSSE to learn more about the engagement of their students in the learning process. NSSE is designed to collect information on the extent to which first-year and senior students report participation in activities and behaviors that are associated with student learning (National Survey of Student Engagement, 2015a). This information is most commonly used by institutions for benchmarking the engagement of their students with students at peer institutions. Pike (2013) provided evidence to suggest that NSSE data could also be valid for comparisons between any groups of 50 students or more, meaning that NSSE could also be appropriate for measuring differences between groups of students within an institution.

In 2013, an updated version of NSSE was introduced. Among other improvements, the new survey includes a reconfiguration of the traditional benchmarks into 10 new Engagement Indicators (McCormick, Gonyea, & Kinzie, 2013). A new six-item High-Impact Practices Indicator was also added, which includes an item that asks students to report how many of their courses have included a "community-based project" (National Survey of Student Engagement, 2015b). NSSE also adapted an AAC&U pilot survey to develop a 15-item optional topical module designed to collect self-report data on students' civic engagement and indirect assessment of related skills (National Survey of Student Engagement, 2014).

NSSE project administrators will have access both to Engagement Indicator scaled scores and student responses on high-impact practice and other individual items. In regard to the study of civic learning outcomes, NSSE can be used to answer questions such as "What types of behaviors are associated with participation in civic learning experiences?" Alternately, if used alongside valid and reliable direct assessment measures, NSSE could also be used to answer "What behaviors are associated with greater attainment of civic learning outcomes?" For example, in his comprehensive report on high impact practices, Kuh (2008) suggested that both first-year and senior students who reported they had done community service or volunteer work were more likely to self-report gains in personal and social skills, practical skills, and general education–related skills.

We would be remiss to conclude this discussion of NSSE and self-report data in general without first addressing some of the validity criticisms of this instrument. In a single institution study, for example, Kolek (2013) found that student self-reports of participation in service learning courses did not match registration in courses that had been identified as community-based learning courses, suggesting that self-report data for individual students may be problematic. In addition, there have been many arguments against the validity of the NSSE instrument itself (e.g., Bowman & Hill, 2011; Campbell & Cabrera, 2011; Dowd, Sawatzky, & Korn, 2011; Porter 2011). In their response to these criticisms, McCormick and McClenney (2012) emphasized Messick's (1995) unified conception of validity, in which scores are considered to be valid if there is empirical evidence that they are useful, are suitable, and convey meaningful information for the intended purpose. For McCormick and McClenney, the purpose of NSSE would be making comparisons among groups of students, rather than obtaining point estimates of a specific student's level of engagement. Many of these criticisms were levied prior to the 2013 revision of NSSE, and the most extensive review of the validity of current NSSE scores can be found as part of the NSSE psychometric portfolio (National Survey of Student Engagement, 2016). For now, we recommend that researchers become familiar with the discussion of NSSE's validity and only use the instrument for between-group comparisons.

In addition to NSSE, a consortium affiliated with the Association of American Universities uses the Student Experience in the Research University (SERU) survey. Brindt (2015) emphasized that SERU is designed with a focus on experiences outside the classroom that research-intensive universities may be better equipped to provide. Unlike NSSE, the core SERU instrument includes a civic engagement module that divides civic engagement into the subdomains of "(1) preparation for democratic citizenship, (2) community participation and community service, and (3) global awareness and knowledge" (Brindt, 2015, p. 4). SERU is still in its infancy, and research using the survey to assess service learning outcomes has yet to emerge. Nonetheless, the new module could be valuable for collecting data on specific engagement behaviors.

Whether the data are obtained from NSSE, SERU, or another existing self-report instrument, researchers must first consider the limitations of student self-report data. College students' responses on self-report surveys may be biased by social desirability (Bowman & Hill, 2011), poor understanding of items (Gonyea, 2005; Kolek 2013), inability to accurately self-assess (Bowman & Seifert, 2011), and overall impressions (Pike, 1999). Findings using self-report instruments should therefore be interpreted with appropriate caution and care. Researchers using self-report data should understand how items were derived and how data were collected before integrating the data with other information. In addition, consideration should be given to how the data will be used and the validity of arguments for and against the intended use (Messick, 1995). Porter (2011), for example, argues that students may have different interpretations of the vague quantifiers NSSE uses in its scales (e.g., *all, most, some, none*). NSSE and SERU may therefore not be appropriate for determining the specific number of service learning experiences. However, it is important to recall the findings from Pike (2013) and suggestions from McCormick and McClenney (2012) that NSSE be used for making generalized comparisons among groups. When using any survey instrument, consideration should be given to the intended and approved uses of survey responses and scale scores and combining self-report data with other types of data, if necessary.

Data for Longitudinal Designs

Many researchers exploring civic learning outcomes are naturally interested in the long-term impact of interventions during the college years on students' attitudes and behaviors after graduation. In their comprehensive review of both the long- and short-term effects of college, Pascarella and Terenzini (2005) concluded that the bulk of evidence from multiple studies suggests that those who volunteer or participate in service learning experiences during college are more likely to be involved in their communities after departure, even after controlling for precollege attitudes toward civic engagement. That said, longitudinal assessment could be extremely valuable in the assessment of specific programs and interventions, especially those designed to foster lifelong service orientations, in order to demonstrate value to internal and external stakeholders as well as improve the effectiveness of existing programs. Follow-up data collection may therefore be necessary to determine how students apply skills gained in different settings and contexts.

Labor Market and Workforce Data

One promising avenue for obtaining information on postgraduation outcomes may come from labor market and workforce data. Using state-level labor market data can provide ample opportunities to study the relationship between service learning outcome attainment and subsequent employment or compensation. If or when data become accessible, information obtained from state databases can be combined with transcript or program participation data to answer questions such as, "Are students who participate in service learning programs more likely to enter service-related occupations after graduation?" or "Is engagement in service learning associated with future earnings?"

At present, the usability of the data provided by statewide data systems varies. Not every state has a student unit record system for higher education institutions, and fewer include data from private institutions (Garcia & L'Orange, 2012). Fewer than half of all states had linked higher education and workforce data by 2010, thus making it difficult to make a connection between graduates and subsequent employment at the state level. Even when links do exist, data may not be regularly shared because of state privacy policies. For many researchers, then, the most pragmatic and reliable means of collecting data from students who have left or graduated is from student alumni surveys.

Alumni Surveys

Many disciplinary accreditation agencies now require data on graduates' success in the labor market as evidence of effectiveness. For example, the Commission on Collegiate Nursing Education requires that nursing programs show that at least 70% of graduates are employed (2013). Nursing programs may be able to obtain some information about employment of their graduates from state unit records systems, if those data are available. However, even these comprehensive data systems will not have information about alumni employed as nurses out of state. State employment data will also not be able to identify which alumni may have left the workforce voluntarily, or whether the individual is employed as a nurse or in another profession. Self-report surveys of alumni are therefore likely to be the preferred method for collecting information on graduates for at least some time.

Researchers studying civic learning outcomes would be well advised to find opportunities to collaborate on alumni surveys whenever possible. At Indiana University-Purdue University Indianapolis, for example, the Center for Service and Learning collaborated with institutional researchers to include the five-item Civic-Minded Professional Short Form (CMP-SF) on a recent survey of students who completed a bachelor's or associate degree (Hahn, 2016). Results suggested that students who completed a service learning course during college scored higher on the CMP-SF scale, controlling for gender, ethnicity, volunteer activities in high school, or participation in other high-impact practices. The CMP-SF or other instruments could be used in conjunction with existing alumni surveys to collect data on graduates' attitudes or behaviors.

Maintaining Data to Sustain Assessment Practices

Many campus offices maintain records on attendance at service projects, participation in extracurricular service activities, or students earning service-related scholarships that could be used as part of the comprehensive assessment of civic learning outcomes. However, sometimes these data are stored in unsystematic ways that may make it less useful for subsequent research. McLaughlin, Howard, Cunningham, Blythe, and Payne (2004) have identified several common obstacles that impede the collection of quality data for assessment and research.

Data Definitions

Researchers should ensure that data are coded in a manner that will be understood by all who will be using the data. For example, if an institution has a method for identifying service learning courses, be sure that this method is used consistently and appropriately across all courses and that coding standards are understood and used properly by faculty and department chairs. Otherwise, service learning courses may be mislabeled or not labeled at all, thereby increasing the likelihood that errors will occur. A data dictionary, in which the meaning of fields and codes are well documented, will also be useful for current and future researchers interpreting existing data.

Technology

Software and hardware packages used to store, manage, and analyze data can both facilitate or limit the extent to which multiple data sets can be integrated and used. For example, data on participation in a service learning course may be stored in an Excel spreadsheet that is located on the hard drive on the computer of one instructor. These data may be manually merged with existing university data but could be done much more seamlessly if integrated into a data warehouse or even added to an Access database. Before merging multiple data sources, it is important to understand the advantages and limitations of the systems being used.

Accessibility

Many internal and external data sources may be restricted only to certain users or stored in a way that they cannot be accessed. For example, institutional review board policy may prohibit the use of student identification numbers as an identifier for exempt studies. Data are also inaccessible when researchers do not know they exist or do not know they are available. Enrollment records cannot be obtained if researchers do not know to ask for them.

The same is true with publically available information maintained by governments or nonprofit organizations, such as employment data. Researchers should become knowledgeable about what data are available, what policies and procedures govern that data, and what training on proper data management and use may be needed before access is granted.

Conclusion

Assessing civic outcomes should be responsive to the expectations of diverse stakeholders around the issues of student learning, access, completion, quality, and efficiency. Ideally, assessment data and research will be used to inform decisions about allocating resources and sustaining and delivering high-quality programs, services, and pedagogical strategies to help students develop civic outcomes. Investigations should demonstrate how quality service learning programs help ensure that students have gained the critical knowledge, skills, abilities, and habits of mind necessary for being productive and engaged citizens. This is best accomplished when a campus or university system develops a comprehensive assessment strategy to understanding the civic outcomes of service learning.

References

Angrist, J., Lang, D., & Oreopoulos, P. (2009). Incentives and services for college achievement: Evidence from a randomized trial. *American Economic Journal: Applied Economics, 1*(1) 136–163.

Astin, A. W. (1984). Involvement in learning revisited: Lessons we have learned. *Journal of College Student Development, 37,* 123–134.

Astin, A. W., Vogelgesang, L. J., Ikeda, E. K., & Yee, J. A. (2000). *How service learning affects students.* Los Angeles, CA: Higher Education Research Institute. Retrieved from http://heri.ucla.edu/pdfs/hslas/hslas.pdf

Bowman, N. A., & Hill, P. L. (2011). Measuring how college affects students: Social desirability and other biases in college student self-reported gains. *New Directions for Institutional Research, 150,* 73–85.

Bowman N. A., & Seifert, T. A. (2011). Can college students accurately assess what affects their learning and development? *Journal of College Student Development, 52,* 270–290.

Brindt, S. (2015). *Research university spaces: The multiple purposes of an undergraduate education* (Research and Occasional Paper Series No. CSHE.9.16). Berkeley, CA: Center for Studies in Higher Education. Retrieved from http://www.cshe.berkeley.edu/sites/default/files/shared/publications/docs/ROPS.CSHE_.9.15.Brint_.SERUSpaces.10.25.2015%20%281%29.pdf

Brown, M. A. (2011a). The power of generosity to change views on social power. *Journal of Experimental Social Psychology, 47,* 1285–1290.

Brown, M. A. (2011b). Learning from service: The effect of helping on helpers' social dominance orientation. *Journal of Applied Social Psychology, 41,* 850–871.

Brownell, J. E., & Swaner, L. E. (2010). *Five high-impact practices: Research on learning outcomes, completion, and quality.* Washington, DC: Association of American Colleges & Universities.

Campbell, C. M., & Cabrera, A. F. (2011). How sound is NSSE? Investigating the psychometric properties of NSSE at a public, research-extensive institution. *Review of Higher Education, 35,* 77–103.

Commission on Collegiate Nursing Education. (2013). *Standards for accreditation of baccalaureate and graduate nursing programs: Amended 2013.* Washington, DC: Author. Retrieved from http://www.aacn.nche.edu/ccne-accreditation/Standards-Amended-2013.pdf

Creswell, J. W. (2014). *Research design: Qualitative, quantitative, and mixed method approaches* (4th ed.). Thousand Oaks, CA: SAGE.

Dowd, A. C., Sawatzky, M., & Korn, R. (2011). Theoretical foundations and a research agenda to validate measures of intercultural effort. *Review of Higher Education, 35,* 17–44.

Evenbeck, S., & Johnson, K. E. (2012). Students must not become victims of the completion agenda. *Liberal Education, 98*(1), 26–33.

Finley, A. (2011). *Civic learning and democratic engagements: A review of the literature on civic engagement in post-secondary education.* Paper prepared for the U.S. Department of Education as part of Contract: ED-OPE-10_C-0078. Retrieved from www.civiclearning.org/SupportDocs/LiteratureReview_CivicEngagement_Finley_Jul2011.pdf

Frechtling, J. (2002). *The 2002 user-friendly handbook for project evaluation.* Arlington, VA: National Science Foundation.

Garcia, T. I., & L'Orange, H. P. (2012, November). *Strong foundations: The state of postsecondary data systems.* Boulder, CO: State Higher Education Executive Officers Association. Retrieved from http://www.sheeo.org/sites/default/files/publications/20130107%20StrongFoundationsUpdate_Finalc.pdf

Gonyea, R. M. (2005). Self-reported data in institutional research: Review and recommendations. *New Directions for Institutional Research, 127,* 73–89.

Greene, J. C., Caracelli, V. J., & Graham, W. F. (1989). Toward a conceptual framework for mixed-method evaluation designs. *Educational Evaluation and Policy Analysis, 11,* 255–274.

Greenwood, D. A. (2015). Outcomes of an academic service-learning project at four urban community colleges. *Journal of Education and Training Studies, 3*(3), 61–71.

Hahn, T. W., & Hatcher, J. A. (2015). The relationship between enrollment in service-learning courses and deep approaches to learning: A campus study. *PRISM: A Journal of Regional Engagement, 4*(2), 55–71.

Hahn, T. W., (2016). *The relationship of participation in service learning courses with alumni civic-mindedness.* Research Brief, Center for Service and Learning. Indianapolis, IN. Retrieved from https://scholarworks.iupui.edu/handle/1805/2613

Heckman, J. J. (1979). Sample selection bias as a specification error. *Econometrica: Journal of the Econometric Society, 47*(1), 153–161.

Hurtado, S., Ruiz, A., & Whang, H. (2012, May). *Assessing civic learning outcomes.* Paper presented at the Annual Forum of the Association for Institutional Research, New Orleans, LA.

Jacoby, B. (2009). *Civic engagement in higher education: Concepts and practices.* San Francisco, CA: Jossey-Bass.

Johnson, K. E. (2013). Learning communities and the completion agenda. *Learning Communities Research and Practice, 1*(3), Article 3. Retrieved from http://washingtoncenter.evergreen.edu/lcrpjournal/vol1/iss3/3

Kolek, E. A. (2013). Can we count on counting? An analysis of the validity of community engagement survey measures. *International Journal on Service-Learning and Community Engagement, 1,* 92–108.

Kuh, G. (2008). *High-impact educational practices: What they are, who has access to them, and why they matter.* Washington, DC: Association of American Colleges & Universities.

Lockeman, K. S., & Pelco, L. E. (2013). The relationship between service-learning and degree completion. *Michigan Journal of Community Service Learning, 20*(1), 18–30.

McCormick, A. C., Gonyea, R. M., & Kinzie, J. (2013, May–June). Refreshing engagement: NSSE at 13. *Change, 45*(3), 6–15.

McCormick, A. C., Kinzie, J., & Gonyea, R. M. (2013). Student engagement: Bridging research and practice to improve the quality of undergraduate education. In M. B. Paulsen (Ed.), *Higher education: Handbook of theory and research* (vol. 28, pp. 47–92). Dordrecht, Netherlands: Springer.

McCormick, A. C., & McClenney, K. (2012). Will these trees ever bear fruit? A response to the special issue on student engagement. *The Review of Higher Education, 35,* 307–333.

McLaughlin, G. W., Howard, R. D., Cunningham, L. B., Blythe, E. W., & Payne, E. (2004). *People, processes, and managing data* (2nd ed.). Tallahassee, FL: Association for Institutional Research.

Messick, S. (1995). Validity of psychological assessment: Validation of inferences from persons' responses and performances as scientific inquiry into score meaning. *American Psychologist, 50,* 741–749.

National Center for Educational Statistics. (n.d.a.). *IPEDS data center.* Retrieved from http://nces.ed.gov/ipeds/datacenter/

National Center for Education Statistics. (n.d.b). *Training and outreach.* Retrieved from https://nces.ed.gov/ipeds/outreach/

National Survey of Student Engagement. (2014). *Topical module: Civic engagement.* Retrieved from http://nsse.indiana.edu/pdf /modules/2015/NSSE%202015%20Civic%20Engagement%20Module.pdf

National Survey of Student Engagement. (2015a). *About NSSE*. Retrieved from http://nsse.indiana.edu/html/about.cfm

National Survey of Student Engagement. (2015b). *National Survey of Student Engagement: The college student report*. Retrieved from http://nsse.indiana.edu/pdf/survey_instruments/2015/NSSE%202015%20-%20US%20English.pdf

National Survey of Student Engagement. (2016). *NSSE's commitment to data quality.* Retrieved from nsse.indiana.edu/html/data_quality.cfm

National Task Force on Civic Learning and Democratic Engagement. (2012). *A crucible moment: College learning & democracy's future.* Washington DC: Association of American Colleges & Universities.

Palomba, C. A., & Banta, T. W. (1999). *Assessment essentials: Planning, implementing, and improving assessment in higher education.* San Francisco, CA: Jossey-Bass.

Pascarella, E. T., & Terenzini, P. T. (2005). *How college affects students: A third decade of research* (Vol. 2). San Francisco, CA: Jossey-Bass.

Patton, M. Q. (2008). *Utilization-focused evaluation* (4th ed.). Thousand Oaks, CA: SAGE.

Pike, G. R. (1999). The constant error of the halo in educational outcomes research. *Research in Higher Education, 40,* 61–86.

Pike, G. R. (2013). NSSE benchmarks and institutional outcomes: A note on the importance of considering the intended uses of a measure in validity studies. *Research in Higher Education, 54,* 149–170.

Pike, G. R., Bringle, R. G., & Hatcher, J. A. (2014). Assessing civic engagement at Indiana University-Purdue University Indianapolis. *New Directions for Institutional Research, 2014*(162), 87–97.

Pike, G. R., Hansen, M. J., & Lin, C. H. (2011). Using instrumental variables to account for selection effects in research on first-year programs. *Research in Higher Education, 52*(2), 194–214.

Porter, S. R. (2011). Do college student surveys have any validity? *The Review of Higher Education, 35*(1), 45–76.

Pragman, C. H., Flannery, B. L., & Bowyer, S. D. (2012). Teaching social responsibility through service learning: A study of antecedents leading to change. *International Journal of Society Systems Science, 4,* 257–277.

Pritzker, S., & McBride, A. M. (2006). Service-learning and civic outcomes: From suggestive research to program models. In K. Casey, G. Davidson, S. Billig, & N. Springer (Eds.), *Advancing knowledge in service-learning: Research to transform the field* (pp. 17–43). Greenwich, CT: Information Age Publishing.

Scriven, M. (1991). *Evaluation thesaurus* (4th ed.). Newbury Park, CA: SAGE.

Steinberg, K. S., Hatcher, J. A., & Bringle, R. G. (2011). A north star: Civic-minded graduate. *Michigan Journal of Community Service Learning, 18*(1), 19–33.

Suskie, L. (2009). *Assessing student learning: A common sense guide* (2nd ed.). San Francisco, CA: Jossey-Bass.

U.S. Department of Education, Office of the Under Secretary and Office of Postsecondary Education. (2012). *Advancing civic learning and engagement in democracy:*

A road map and call to action. Retrieved from https://www.ed.gov/sites/default/files/road-map-call-to-action.pdf

Vaughan, A., Parra, J., & Lalonde, T. (2014). First-generation college student achievement and the first-year seminar: A quasi-experimental design. *Journal of the First-Year Experience & Students in Transition, 26*(2), 51–67.

Volkwein, J. F. (2011). *Gaining ground: The role of institutional research in assessing student outcomes and demonstrating institutional effectiveness* (Occasional paper no. 11). Champaign, IL: National Institute for Learning Outcomes Assessment. Retrieved from http://www.learningoutcomesassessment.org /documents/Volkwein.pdf

Wilson, M., & Sloane, K. (2000). From principles to practice: An embedded assessment system. *Applied Measurement in Education, 13*(2), 181–208.

Marcia B. Baxter Magolda is an independent scholar and distinguished professor emerita at the Miami University of Ohio (USA). She received her PhD in higher education from The Ohio State University. Her scholarship addresses the evolution of learning and development in college and young adult life and pedagogy to promote self-authorship. Her longitudinal study of young adult development is in its 30th year; she is also a coprincipal investigator for the longitudinal Wabash National Study. Her books include *Assessing Meaning Making and Self-Authorship*: *Theory, Research, and Application* (coauthored with P. King; Jossey-Bass, 2012), *Authoring Your Life: Developing an Internal Voice to Meet Life's Challenges* (Stylus, 2009), *Development and Assessment of Self-Authorship: Exploring the Concept Across Cultures* (coedited with E. Creamer & P. Meszaros; Stylus, 2010) and *Learning Partnerships: Theory and Models of Practice to Educate for Self-Authorship* (coedited with P. King; Stylus, 2004). She has received the Association for the Study of Higher Education Research Achievement Award and the American College Personnel Association's Lifetime Achievement and Contribution to Knowledge Awards.

Claire Berezowitz is pursuing a joint PhD at the University of Wisconsin–Madison in the School of Human Ecology's civil society and community research program and the School of Education's educational psychology program. She studies the development of civic dispositions and the relationship between civic engagement and well-being among diverse college students, youth, and families engaged in both formal and informal community-based learning opportunities. She utilizes community-based participatory research and evaluation methods in order to study child and family well-being from an ecological perspective, particularly through the transformation of school and community food systems. As a 2016 recipient of the Association of American Colleges & Universities' K. Patricia Cross Award, she was recognized for demonstrating exemplary promise as a future leader of higher education and for her commitment to both academic and civic engagement.

Lisa M. Boes is dean of academic services at Brandeis University and adjunct lecturer on education at Harvard University's Graduate School of Education. Previously, she served as Allston Burr Resident Dean of Pforzheimer House at Harvard College. At Brandeis, an institution with an explicit social justice mission, she leads a cohesive network of peers, staff, and faculty who provide academic advising and support services for undergraduate students in all facets of their college experiences. She received her EdD in learning and teaching from the Graduate School of Education at Harvard University.

Nicholas A. Bowman is an associate professor in the Department of Educational Policy and Leadership Studies and the director of the Center for Research on Undergraduate Education at the University of Iowa. His research interests include college diversity experiences, religion and worldview in higher education, assessment of student outcomes and experiences, college admissions and rankings, and student retention and graduation. His work has appeared in *Review of Educational Research, Educational Researcher, American Educational Research Journal, Personality and Social Psychology Bulletin, Social Psychological and Personality Science,* and other top journals. He received the Promising Scholar/Early Career Award from the Association for the Study of Higher Education in 2012. He earned a PhD in psychology and education from the University of Michigan.

Jay W. Brandenberger is the director of research at the Center for Social Concerns and concurrent associate professor of psychology at the University of Notre Dame. He received his PhD in developmental and educational psychology from the University of Pittsburgh and has taught at Notre Dame since 1992. His research interests include social cognition, moral and ethical learning, and engaged scholarship in higher education. He has collaborated on national research initiatives examining means to enhance social responsibility, leadership, and moral development.

Robert G. Bringle is currently chancellor's professor emeritus of psychology and philanthropic studies and senior scholar in the Center for Service and Learning at Indiana University-Purdue University Indianapolis (IUPUI). From 2012 to 2015, he was the Kulynych/Cline Visiting Distinguished Professor of Psychology at Appalachian State University. He was the founding executive of the IUPUI Center for Service and Learning from 1994 to 2012. He was awarded the Thomas Ehrlich Faculty Award for Service Learning, the IUPUI Chancellor's Award for Excellence in Teaching, and the Legacy of Service Award from Indiana Campus Compact. In 2004, he was recognized at the fourth annual

International Association for Research on Service-Learning & Community Engagement for his outstanding contributions to the service learning research field. The University of the Free State, South Africa, awarded him an honorary doctorate for his scholarly work on civic engagement and service learning.

Patti H. Clayton is an independent consultant (PHC Ventures, www .curricularengagement.com) with over 15 years of experience as a practitioner-scholar and educational developer in community-campus engagement and experiential education. She serves as a senior scholar with the Center for Service and Learning at Indiana University-Purdue University Indianapolis and with the Institute for Community and Economic Engagement at the University of North Carolina at Greensboro. She facilitates institution-wide visioning and planning processes for community-campus engagement and supports campuses in applying for and leveraging the Carnegie Community Engagement Classification. She codeveloped the DEAL model for critical reflection and the SOFAR partnership model and coproduced student and instructor versions of the tutorial *Learning through Critical Reflection*. She was coeditor with Bringle and Hatcher of the two-volume set *Research on Service Learning: Conceptual Frameworks and Assessment* (Stylus, 2012). She received her PhD in ecology from the University of North Carolina at Chapel Hill.

Jennifer M. Domagal-Goldman directs the American Association of State Colleges and Universities' American Democracy Project, a national network of public higher education institutions committed to preparing informed, engaged citizens for our democracy. She earned her doctorate in higher education from the Pennsylvania State University. Her dissertation focused on how faculty learn to incorporate civic learning and engagement in their undergraduate teaching within their academic discipline. She holds an ex-officio position on the *eJournal of Public Affairs'* editorial board and is a member of the Citizen Alum advisory board of Citizen Alum.

Victoria Faust currently organizes a statewide health equity alliance in Wisconsin focused on community-empowered health promotion and is completing her PhD at the University of Wisconsin–Madison. In previous positions, she managed national and community service programming for young adults. Her research and evaluation work focuses on civic engagement, well-being, multilevel empowerment, and systems change across problem domains. At the University of Wisconsin, she has taught courses on organizational and community learning, community leadership, and community-based research and evaluation.

Ashley Finley is associate vice president of academic affairs and dean of the Dominican Experience at Dominican University of California. She is also national evaluator for the Bringing Theory to Practice project, a national project dedicated to understanding the intersection of students' engaged learning, civic development, and well-being. Her recent publications include the edited volume *Civic Learning and Teaching* and also *Assessing Underserved Students' Engagement in High-Impact Practices* (American Association of Colleges and Universities, 2013) with Tia McNair, in addition to several other book chapters and monographs. Prior to joining Dominican University of California, she was senior director of assessment and research at the Association of American Colleges & Universities, where she remains a senior scholar. Her work at Dominican and with colleges and universities nationally focuses on engaging faculty and staff in developing student-centered, sustainable practices that enable the advancement of student success and learning with an emphasis on equity and evidence-based standards for improvement.

Constance Flanagan is the Vaughan Bascom Professor of Human Ecology and associate dean of the School of Human Ecology at the University of Wisconsin–Madison. Her scholarship focuses on factors that foster identification with and action for the common good in young people. Her book *Teenage Citizens: The Political Theories of the Young* (Harvard University Press, 2013) won the 2014 Best Authored Book Award from the Society for Research on Adolescence. Other awards include the 2015 Blanche F. Ittleson Award from the American Orthopsychiatric Association for research linking civic engagement, social justice, and youth well-being; the 2012 Research Prize from the Tisch College of Citizenship and Public Service at Tufts University; and an honorary doctorate in Humanities and Social Sciences from Örebro University in Sweden. She serves on many national and international advisory boards such as CIRCLE (www.civicyouth.org).

Zak Foste is a doctoral candidate in the Higher Education and Student Affairs program at The Ohio State University, where he currently teaches undergraduate service learning courses. His primary research interests include Whiteness in higher education, college student identity development, and qualitative research methodologies. He earned his MS in student affairs in higher education from Miami University.

Steven S. Graunke is the director of institutional research and assessment at Indiana University-Purdue University Indianapolis. He has conducted over 25 workshops and presentations at local and national conferences on topics including survey research methods, student success and retention, and assessment. He has served as a reviewer for the *Journal of College Student Development Research in Brief,* the *National Symposium on Student Retention,* and in several capacities for the Indiana Association for Institutional Research. He was named a Fellow in Institutional Research from the Association for Institutional Research and the National Center for Education Statistics, which included participation in the National Data Policy Institute in 2011. He is currently a doctoral student in the higher education and student affairs program at Indiana University.

Thomas W. Hahn is the director of research and program evaluation at the Center for Service and Learning at Indiana University-Purdue University Indianapolis (IUPUI) where he is responsible for conducting research and program evaluation on student participation in curricular and cocurricular activities involving community engagement. His research interests include understanding the influence of participation in service learning courses and service-based scholarships on students' learning and development and civic outcomes. He also oversees the planning and implementation of the annual IUPUI Research Academy.

Michele J. Hansen is the executive director of Institutional Research and Decision Support at Indiana University-Purdue University Indianapolis, where she is responsible for institutional research, planning, and evaluation in the areas of student success, learning, enrollment management, and institutional effectiveness. She has more than 15 years of experience in institutional research and assessment in higher education. Her primary research interests are in the areas of learning outcomes assessment and program evaluation methods, understanding the effectiveness of interventions to enhance retention and academic success of undergraduate and graduate students, applying social psychology theories to higher education, survey research methods, and incremental and fundamental change implementation. She received her doctoral degree in social psychology from Loyola University Chicago.

Julie A. Hatcher is executive director of the Center for Service and Learning and associate professor of philanthropic studies in the Lilly Family School of Philanthropy at Indiana University-Purdue University Indianapolis (IUPUI). Hatcher serves as coeditor of the IUPUI Series on Service Learning Research (Stylus, 2011, 2013). Her research focuses on the role of higher education in civil society, civic learning outcomes in higher education, philanthropic studies as a new field of study, and the philanthropic motivations of professionals. She serves on the national advisory board for the Carnegie Foundation's Community Engagement elective classification. She participated on the development team of the Association of American Colleges and Universities VALUE Rubric for civic engagement as well as a new Civic Knowledge Rubric sponsored by the Massachusetts Board of Higher Education. She was the 2008 recipient of the International Association for Research on Service Learning and Community Engagement Dissertation of the Year award. She earned her PhD in philanthropic studies with a minor in higher education at Indiana University.

Kevin M. Hemer is a doctoral student in the School of Education at Iowa State University. He works in the Research Institute for Studies in Education at Iowa State with the Personal and Social Responsibility Inventory and the Global Perspective Inventory. His research examines the public role of higher education in a democratic society employing a human developmental perspective and focusing on undergraduate student outcomes, civic learning, and campus climates. He received an MS in higher education from Florida State University, where he worked for the Center for Leadership and Social Change in the community engagement programs. He also spent a year working with Florida Campus Compact and The University of Tampa as an AmeriCorps VISTA.

Patrick L. Hill is an assistant professor in the Department of Psychology at Carleton University in Ottawa, Ontario, Canada. His research interests include understanding how individuals find a purpose in life, the health benefits associated with having a sense of purpose, and personality development across the lifespan. His work also considers the role of collegiate experiences on the exploration and commitment to life goals. He received his PhD in psychology from the University of Notre Dame.

Emily M. Janke is the founding director of the Institute for Community and Economic Engagement and an associate professor in the Peace and Conflict Studies Department at the University of North Carolina at Greensboro. She has served as chair of the University of North Carolina system-wide initiative to create annual metrics for community and economic engagement, as a member of the national advisory review board for the Carnegie Foundation's Community Engagement elective classification, and on the board of the International Association for Research on Service-Learning Community Engagement. She codesigned and licensed The Community Engagement Collaboratory to advance research on and the practice of institutional and regional change strategies to enhance community engagement activities and outcomes.

Steven G. Jones is director for the Center for Faculty Development and associate professor of political science at Georgia College and State University. He is a coeditor, with Robert Bringle and Julie Hatcher, of *International*

Service Learning: Conceptual Frameworks and Research (Stylus, 2010). He edited *Introduction to Service Learning Toolkit: Readings and Resources for Faculty (Second Edition)* (Campus Compact, 2003) and is a coauthor of two other Campus Compact monographs, *The Community's College: Indicators of Engagement at Two-Year Institutions* (Stylus, 2004) and *The Promise of Partnerships: Tapping into the Campus as a Community Asset* (Campus Compact, 2005). His most recent publication is a book chapter in *International Volunteer Tourism: Critical Reflections on Good Works in Central America* (Palgrave Macmillan, 2013). He received a PhD in political science from the University of Utah in 1995 and was an associate professor of political science at the University of Charleston from 1995 to 2002, where he also served as the director of the Robert C. Byrd Institute for Government Studies.

Susan R. Jones is professor and program director in the higher education and student affairs program in the educational studies department at The Ohio State University and previously served as associate professor and director of the college student personnel program at the University of Maryland–College Park. Her research interests include psychosocial perspectives on identity, intersectionality and multiple social identities, service learning, and qualitative research methodologies. She is the coauthor with Elisa S. Abes of *Identity Development of College Students* (Wiley & Sons, 2013), and *Negotiating the Complexities of Qualitative Research: Fundamental Elements and Issues* (Routledge, 2nd ed., 2014), with Vasti Torres and Jan Arminio. Jones is one of the coeditors of *Student Services: A Handbook for the Profession* (Jossey-Bass, 5th ed., 2011; 6th ed., in press).

Janice McMillan joined the University of Cape Town (UCT) in 1994, first in the Department of Adult Education, and since 2000 has been part of the Centre for Higher Education Development. From 1999 to 2001, she was the UCT representative on a national service learning research and development project funded by the Ford Foundation. She was also service learning coordinator of Stanford University's program in Cape Town (2010–2014) where she led a required seminar on service, citizenship, and social justice. Currently, she is senior lecturer and director of the UCT Global Citizenship program, which she cofounded in 2010. She obtained her PhD in sociology in 2008 from UCT, analyzing service learning as a form of boundary work in higher education. Her teaching and research interests focus on service learning, global citizenship, critical pedagogy and reflective practice, and the identity and role of educators in higher education.

Tania D. Mitchell is an assistant professor of higher education in the College of Education and Human Development at the University of Minnesota.

Her teaching and research focuses on service learning as a critical pedagogy to explore civic identity, social justice, student learning and development, race and racism, and community practice. She is a recipient of the Early Career Research Award from the International Association for Research on Service-Learning and Community Engagement and the American Fellowship from the American Association of University Women. Her scholarship has been published in numerous books and journals, and she is coeditor of *Civic Engagement and Community Service at Research Universities: Engaging Undergraduates for Social Justice, Social Change, and Responsible Citizenship* (Palgrave Macmillan, 2016).

Kira Pasquesi is a doctoral candidate in the Higher Education and Student Affairs program at the University of Iowa. Her current research examines how colleges and universities use language to represent diversity and inclusion in community engagement. She previously served as a community engagement professional at Colorado College where she facilitated collaborations among students, faculty, and community partners to examine social issues and catalyze collective action.

Alisa Pykett is a PhD student at the University of Wisconsin–Madison in the School of Human Ecology's civil society and community research program. She studies critical civic development and the pedagogies, processes, and organizations that foster it.

Robert D. Reason is professor of higher education and student affairs in the School of Education at Iowa State University. He studies how college and university policies, the campus climate, and students' experiences in college interact to influence student outcomes. Recently, he has been working with the Research Institute for Studies in Education (RISE) at Iowa State to administer the Personal and Social Responsibility Inventory and the Global Perspective Inventory. He is currently an associate editor of the *Journal of College Student Development* and an ACPA Senior Scholar. His publications include *Developing Social Justice Allies: New Directions for Student Services, 110* (Wiley Periodicals, Inc., 2005, with Ellen Broido, Nancy Evans, & Tracy Davis) and *College Students in the United States: Characteristics, Experiences, and Outcomes* (Jossey-Bass, 2012, with Kristen Renn).

Terrel Rhodes is vice president of the Office of Quality, Curriculum, and Assessment and executive director of VALUE at the Association of American Colleges & Universities (AAC&U), where he focuses on the quality of undergraduate education, access, general education, ePortfolios, and assessment of student learning. He was a faculty member for 25 years. He leads the faculty-driven assessment project on student learning titled Valid Assessment of Learning in Undergraduate Education (VALUE). VALUE faculty teams developed rubrics for the full range of essential learning outcomes that can be used with authentic student work to demonstrate quality student learning. He also led the Quality Collaboratives initiative, working in 9 states with 20 2- and 4-year partner campuses testing the usefulness of the Degree Qualifications Profile, a transfer framework focused on student learning mastery rather than seat time or credit accumulation. For the past 7 years, he has led AAC&U's e-portfolio initiatives to enhance student learning, including the annual E-Portfolio Forum.

Dan Richard is an associate professor of psychology and director of the Office of Faculty Enhancement at the University of North Florida (UNF). He leads research activities assessing student learning outcomes related to UNF's Quality Enhancement Plan on community-based transformational learning. His research interests include the long-term impacts of service learning and community engagement on lifelong civic engagement. He teaches a community-based learning seminar, "Is Revenge Sweet?", that explores the psychological issues of lasting resentment faced by ex-offenders who are transitioning from prison back to the community.

Colleen Rost-Banik is a doctoral student at the University of Minnesota. With master's degrees in sociology and world religions, she approaches her work from an interdisciplinary lens. She has worked in higher education at a variety of institutions in Maine, Rhode Island, and Hawaii. Her work has ranged from teaching undergraduate and graduate level courses, academic advising, and student life advising to coordinating service learning and providing extracurricular multicultural education opportunities. Her current research explores how undergraduate students learn about and practice social justice, particularly as it relates to race, class, gender, and citizenship.

Stephanie T. Stokamer is the director of the Center for Civic Engagement and an assistant professor at Pacific University. She has a doctorate in educational leadership from Portland State University. Her scholarship is focused on service learning and civic engagement, particularly with respect to pedagogical practices and faculty development. She is the 2011 recipient of the International Association for Research on Service Learning and Community Engagement Dissertation of the Year award for her work, *Pedagogical Catalysts of Civic Competence: The Development of a Critical Epistemological Model for Community-Based Learning* (2011). She is a coauthor of *Community*

Partner Guide to Campus Collaborations: Strategies for Enhancing Your Community as a Co-Educator (Stylus, 2015) and has published chapters in *Learning through Serving: A Student Guidebook for Service-Learning and Civic Engagement Across Academic Disciplines and Cultural Communities*, (Stylus, 2015 2nd edition), *Democratic Dilemmas of Teaching Service-Learning: Curricular Strategies for Success* (Stylus, 2011), and *Crossing Boundaries: Tension and Transformation in International Service-Learning* (Stylus, 2014). She is an AmeriCorps*VISTA alum and former national service fellow for the Corporation for National and Community Service.

and instruments, develop future research agendas, and consider implications of theory-based research for enhanced practice.

Both volumes open with common chapter focused on defining the criteria for quality research.

Volume 2A presents research related to *students*, comprising chapters that focus on cognitive processes, academic learning, civic learning, personal development, and intercultural competence. Its concluding *faculty* section presents chapters on faculty development, faculty motivation, and faculty learning.

Volume 2B addresses *community* development, and the role of nonprofit organizations in service learning. It focusses on *institutions*, examining the institutionalization of service learning, engaged departments, and institutional leadership. The final section on *partnerships* in service learning includes chapters on conceptualizing and measuring the quality of partnerships, inter-organizational partnerships, and student partnerships.

Sty/us

22883 Quicksilver Drive
Sterling, VA 20166-2102

Subscribe to our e-mail alerts: www.Styluspub.com

Also available from Stylus

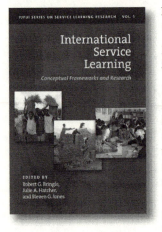

International Service Learning
Conceptual Frameworks and Research

Edited by Robert G. Bringle, Julie A. Hatcher, and Steven G. Jones

Focused on conducting research on international service learning (ISL), which includes developing and evaluating hypotheses about ISL outcomes and measuring its impact on students, faculty, and communities, this book argues that rigorous research is essential to improving the quality of ISL's implementation and delivery, and providing the evidence that will lead to wider support and adoption by the academy, funders, and partners. It is intended for both practitioners and scholars, providing guidance and commentary on good practice. The volume provides a pioneering analysis of and understanding of why and under what conditions ISL is an effective pedagogy.

Individual chapters discuss conceptual frameworks, research design issues, and measurement strategies related to student learning outcomes; the importance of ISL course and program design; the need for faculty development activities to familiarize faculty with the component pedagogical strategies; the need for resources and collaboration across campus units to develop institutional capacity for ISL; and the role that community constituencies should assume as co-creators of the curriculum, co-educators in the delivery of the curriculum, and co-investigators in the evaluation of and study of ISL. The contributors demonstrate sensitivity to ethical implications of ISL, to issues of power and privilege, to the integrity of partnerships, to reflection, reciprocity, and community benefits

Research on Service Learning
Conceptual Frameworks and Assessments
Edited by Patti H. Clayton, Robert G. Bringle, and Julie A. Hatcher

Volume 2A: Students and Faculty
Volume 2B: Communities, Institutions and Partnerships

The purpose of this work is to improve service learning research and practice through strengthening its theoretical base. Contributing authors include both well-known and emerging service learning and community engagement scholars, as well as scholars from other fields. The authors bring theoretical perspectives from a wide variety of disciplines to bear as they critically review past research, describe assessment methods

(Continues on previous page)